DEGREES OF EQUALITY

ANTISLAVERY, ABOLITION, AND THE ATLANTIC WORLD

R. J. M. Blackett and Edward Rugemer, Series Editors
James Brewer Stewart, Editor Emeritus

DEGREES OF EQUALITY

Abolitionist Colleges and the Politics of Race

JOHN FREDERICK BELL

Louisiana State University Press

Baton Rouge

Published by Louisiana State University Press
lsupress.org

DESIGNER: Michelle A. Neustrom
TYPEFACE: Adobe Garamond Pro

COVER IMAGE: Helen Ferris (Bisbee) and her 1855 Preparatory Department class.
Courtesy Oberlin College Archives.

Portions of chapters 1 and 2 were previously published as "Confronting Colorism:
Interracial Abolition and the Consequences of Complexion," *Journal of the Early Republic* 39:2
(Summer 2019): 239–65. Copyright © University of Pennsylvania Press.
All material used here with permission.

LIBRARY OF CONGRESS CATALOGING-IN-PUBLICATION DATA

Names: Bell, John Frederick, author.
Title: Degrees of equality : abolitionist colleges and the politics of race / John Frederick Bell.
Description: Baton Rouge : Louisiana State University Press, [2022] | Series: Antislavery,
    Abolition, and the Atlantic World / R. J. M. Blackett and Edward Rugemer, series editors |
    Includes bibliographical references and index.
Identifiers: LCCN 2021053983 (print) | LCCN 2021053984 (ebook) | ISBN 978-0-8071-7194-3
    (cloth) | ISBN 978-0-8071-7783-9 (PDF) | ISBN 978-0-8071-7784-6 (epub)
Subjects: LCSH: College integration—United States—History. | Oberlin College—History. |
    New York Central College—History. | Berea College—History. | African American college
    students—Social conditions—Case studies. | Discrimination in higher education—United
    States—Case studies. | African Americans—Education—History—19th century. | Education,
    Higher—Moral and ethical aspects—United States—History—19th century. | Education,
    Higher—Political aspects—United States—History—19th century.
Classification: LCC LC212.72 .B45 2022 (print) | LCC LC212.72 (ebook) |
    DDC 378.1/982996073—dc23/eng/20220217
LC record available at https://lccn.loc.gov/2021053983
LC ebook record available at https://lccn.loc.gov/2021053984

For Leah

CONTENTS

PREFACE ix

Introduction 1

1. Oberlin College and the Trial of Interracial Education, 1835–1853 15

2. The Rise and Fall of New York Central College, 1848–1860 50

3. Oberlin's Black Alumnae and the New Birth of Freedom, 1852–1867 . . . 80

4. Berea College and the Boundaries of Equality, 1866–1880 111

5. The Unraveling of Interracial Oberlin, 1874–1892 139

6. Berea's Race Problem, 1889–1895 171

Epilogue 200

ACKNOWLEDGMENTS 215

NOTES 219

BIBLIOGRAPHY 261

INDEX 289

PREFACE

Charles and Gideon Langston arrived to find they were the only people of color there. In the fall of 1835, every other student at the Oberlin Collegiate Institute, almost three hundred men and women in total, was white.[1] So were the entire faculty and staff. The Langston brothers were not the first African Americans to enroll at an American college or secondary school, but they would be the first of many to study at Oberlin. Before the Civil War, the Ohio college educated more Black students than all other institutions of higher education combined.[2] Oberlin's experiment in racial coeducation inspired New York Central, Berea, and other abolitionist colleges to be founded on the same principles. Access to these institutions came irrespective of race, yet once they were on campus, did African Americans and other people of color receive the same measure of respect? Exactly what more interracial colleges owed students of color beyond an equal opportunity to learn would be debated long after the Langstons left Oberlin. Indeed, the debate continues to this day. The histories of Berea, New York Central, and Oberlin show that colleges can be agents of racial justice. Their stories also demonstrate that without collective will and regular reflection, institutions can reproduce the racism they profess to reject.[3]

Those with the privilege of writing history have a duty to represent past lives and perspectives fairly. It seems to me this obligation is most incumbent on historians writing about people whose life experiences differ markedly from their own. A primary goal of this book is to recover the ideas, voices, and actions of some of the first collegians of color, whose contributions to the history of American higher education and nineteenth-century social reform have largely been overlooked. I have tried to do my part to do them justice here. But while I recover their stories, I do so knowing that my understanding of their circumstances is limited. To me, the capitalization of "Black" and not "white" acknowledges this reality. By not capitalizing "white," I also intend to signal the ways in which whiteness has long been the frame of American history writing and the racial default of American academe.

When they pioneered the large-scale admittance of people of color and committed themselves to both academic and human freedom, abolitionist colleges challenged the structures of power that undergirded American universities. Their experiments posed critical questions about whose interests higher education serves, who belongs at college, and to whom colleges belong. The mixed success of their efforts at promoting racial equality should by turns inspire and admonish anyone working in their wake to make universities equitable spaces for everyone.

DEGREES OF EQUALITY

INTRODUCTION

In their mid-nineteenth century heyday, abolitionist colleges like Oberlin came as close as any American community to approaching the ideal of a multiracial democracy. That outcome was far from apparent, however, when the Langston brothers arrived on campus in the fall of 1835. Oberlin had only decided to start admitting African Americans earlier that year. School leaders took up the issue after prospective donors conditioned their gifts to the institution on its adopting color-blind admissions. At the time, almost all colleges and universities in the United States were restricted to white men. The handful that admitted men of color—schools like Amherst, Bowdoin, and Middlebury—did so in token numbers and not as a matter of official policy.[1] Oberlin was going out on a limb, and the Langstons would be the ones most exposed. Being the first Black students at a desegregated institution took courage. Like so many of the civil rights heroes who came after them, the two brothers pursued their education at great personal risk. Public hostility to interracial schooling was as vigorous in the pre–Civil War period as it was in the *Brown v. Board of Education* era. Historian Kabria Baumgartner finds that between 1834 and 1843, at least ten northern schools that educated African Americans were physically attacked, including six in Ohio.[2] The Langstons' safety at Oberlin was by no means assured, let alone their success. But if they wanted advanced education, they had few other choices.

In the summer of 1835, a committee of the National Convention of Free People of Colour reported that just six colleges or high schools nationwide "admit[ted] colored students upon an equal footing."[3] Recent attempts at expanding secondary and higher education for African Americans had met stiff and violent resistance. In 1831, abolitionists had tried to found a college in New Haven that would provide African Americans with both classical and vocational instruction. Overwhelming local opposition scuttled the project.[4] One year later, the townspeople of Canterbury, Connecticut, withdrew their daughters from a girls' school after its proprietor, Prudence Crandall, admitted a Black student. Converting her academy into a "High School for Young Colored Ladies and Little Misses" raised tensions further. Town officials successfully lobbied the legislature to prohibit the education of "colored persons who are not inhabitants of this state" unless local authorities assented. Crandall persisted in teaching African Americans and was jailed. Meanwhile, a mob smashed the school's windows, poisoned its well, and threatened its students.[5] An interracial secondary school in New Hampshire suffered similar reprisals. Noyes Academy was only open for five months in 1835 before townspeople used oxen and chains to drag the school building into a nearby swamp.[6] A few Black refugees from Noyes and Canterbury found their way to Oneida County in upstate New York's "Burned-Over District."[7] In this hotbed of religious activism, abolitionists operated the Young Ladies' Domestic Seminary and a small men's college, the Oneida Institute. Together, these predominantly white institutions educated around twenty Black students before closing in 1840 and 1843, respectively.[8]

Schools that taught African Americans struggled to gain traction in the Early Republic because education was considered a stepping stone to citizenship.[9] In the 1820s and 1830s, more and more whites supported legal and extralegal efforts to limit, if not eliminate, Black participation in civil society. A free Black citizenry, possessed of equal rights, undermined justifications for enslavement and supposedly threatened the economic and political status of whites in the free states.[10] Defending white supremacy was not just the work of mobs. Civic institutions were also involved in the project of making the United States a white republic, colleges and universities included. Historian Craig Steven Wilder describes how American higher education had been providing "intellectual cover" for white supremacy since before the Revolution.[11] Both in the North and South, colleges produced research aimed at discrediting Black people's intelligence and propping up slavery, the profits from which formed the basis of many of their endowments.[12] When whites did promote African Americans' education, it was often with an eye toward preparing them for deportation to Africa.[13] The movement for Black removal, a project known as colonization, was fashionable among "enlightened" whites and represented a powerful political interest.[14]

College campuses were often centers of colonizationist ideology.[15] The summer before the Langstons arrived at Oberlin, the subject of slavery arose at a town lyceum. Almost everyone voiced support for gradual emancipation and colonization.[16] Several months later, when the college board of trustees deliberated over whether to "receive applicants irrespective of color," several members deemed it an "impropriety . . . [for] blacks to be in the same school with the whites."[17] Racial coeducation violated social custom and, in turn, the social order. The combination of the races learning together and living together suggested they were both intellectually and socially equal. In the nineteenth-century United States, "social equality," according to historian Hannah Rosen, referred to "forms of association between white and black people that did not convey a hierarchical meaning for race and that did not serve to mark racial difference."[18] Such relationships were offensive to the vast majority of white Americans because they emptied race of its traditional function of policing social relations. If race's mediating role was removed, what meaning, if any, did it retain?

Even those at Oberlin who supported abolition voiced concern over interracial education. Reverend John Keep, the trustee who had cast the deciding vote in favor, was still apprehensive about the idea of "[congregating] such a mass of negroes at Oberlin as to darken the whole atmosphere." The specter of sinful, unrefined African Americans defiling the virtuous white reformers haunted him, however preposterous the image was. Keep sought assurances that "the prime object" of admitting Black students was a respectable one, to train them "in a better manner for the ministry."[19] Many moderate white abolitionists were as conflicted as Keep when it came to just how equal African Americans were or could be. They believed that Black people were fully human and possessed a moral nature. These attributes made African Americans deserving of freedom and access to the gospel like everyone else. White moderates were not, however, as ready as white radicals like William Lloyd Garrison to imagine a future "raceless equality" in which color held no significance.[20] They believed slavery had debased Black people morally, intellectually, and socially. How readily the Black race could overcome its "degradation" and whether white people could ever overcome their anti-Black prejudice was a matter of debate between abolitionists and colonizationists.[21] Keep and other white evangelical reformers took seriously the Bible's teaching that for anyone who became a believer, the "old things are passed away." The converted became "a new creature."[22] In their abolitionist reading, that meant Black people were not destined to remain the downtrodden, degenerate race whites considered them to be. They could be elevated from deficiency to respectability with the right instruction. Through a regimen of education and religious devotion, individual African Americans could attain refinement, gain whites' respect, and help "uplift" other members of their race.[23]

Black abolitionists subscribed to the idea of self-improvement as a means for African Americans to cope with the trauma of slavery and racism and combat white prejudice. They engaged in "the politics of respectability" advisedly, however, and did not suffer the condescension of white reformers gladly.[24] Instead, Black activists put forward their own vision of race and reform, one not based in racial essentialism but rather in racial egalitarianism. It was premised on the understanding that all races, by virtue of their common humanity, were of the same worth and dignity. They cited a verse from Robert Burns: "A man's a man for a' that."[25] No one needed to earn equality; it was innate to the human species, of which all people were duly a part. The Bible taught that all nations descended from a common origin, that everyone was made in the divine image and likeness, and that God was no respecter of persons, having created all people "of one blood."[26] Furthermore, because Jesus had died for the sins of the world, his sacrifice made believers "all one in Christ" and "members of that one body."[27] Caste distinctions denied these sacred truths. Egalitarians argued that if white Americans learned to see other races as brethren, the dream of American democracy might finally be fulfilled. Instead of being riven by tribalism, the nation would be united by ties of love, friendship, and mutuality.[28]

Talk of human unity raised questions about interracialism—marriage, intercourse, or procreation between members of different races.[29] As historian Amber Moulton explains, only the most radical abolitionists committed to actively "advancing interracialism." The majority of reformers considered it either distasteful or distracting from the larger struggle for emancipation and equal rights.[30] Nevertheless, because the membership of the antislavery movement was composed of Black and white men and women, abolitionists were frequently attacked for promoting "amalgamation," what would later be termed "miscegenation." Some of the antislavery donors Oberlin courted had seen their homes and businesses ransacked in 1834 after their New York church hosted an interracial event.[31] In 1838, following the burning of the headquarters of the Pennsylvania Anti-Slavery Society, an antiabolitionist newspaper asserted that arson was just deserts for "a Temple of Amalgamation."[32] Abolitionists were quick to point out that the real hub of interracialism was the South, where white masters raping enslaved women was commonplace.[33] The Langston brothers were the sons of a Virginia plantation owner and a Black woman whom he had freed.[34] It was interracial relationships in the North that whites considered the real threat, however. Uniting white and free Black partners undercut the image of America as a white nation and struck at the heart of white male hegemony, especially if these pairings were of Black men and white women.

The comingling of the races subverted the idea of racial purity on which white womanhood, in particular, was based.[35] The inclusion of women at Oberlin magnified anxieties about interracial intimacy. It was the first college in the nation to make higher learning available to both sexes in one institution. In the summer term of 1834, 38 of Oberlin's 101 students were women.[36] School leaders hoped that this program of "joint education" would, among other things, foster a familial atmosphere on campus.[37] Admitting African Americans to this circle connoted that they were, or could be, whites' kindred, that they could be received as rightful members of the family. The trustees did not see Black admissions in such inclusive terms, but to some campus women, the upshot was the same. They would have to consort with Black women, who were considered unvirtuous by nature, and with Black men, who were believed to prey on white women's virtue. Faced with those options, a number of female students said they would sooner "'wade Lake Erie'" back home than remain.[38] Twenty-three of the thirty-eight women who were enrolled in the summer of 1834 had left by the time the Langston brothers arrived a year later.[39] Of the fifteen who returned, eight had previously signed a petition against "the practicability of admitting persons of color."[40]

Abolitionist dollars helped Oberlin recruit new, reform-minded faculty, who helped revitalize enrollment. In the fall of 1835, Oberlin matriculated four times as many students as it had lost since the spring of that year. Many newcomers hailed from New York's Burned-Over District, which made them predisposed to support reform causes. Theodore Weld, a renowned white abolitionist, visited campus that fall. After his rousing series of lectures, the campus was purportedly "abolitionized in every thought and feeling and purpose."[41] What did that transformation mean for the Langstons? According to one white alumnus, the "great hesitation and reluctance" some felt toward racial coeducation quickly subsided.[42] In January 1836, John Keep wrote the abolitionist Gerrit Smith that the "two, from Virginia of color . . . are as well received & treated as others." Oberlin had experienced a miraculous transformation, he said. It was now a place "where prejudice is so far conquered that colored people are admitted, to the full enjoyment of all & the same privileges with others."[43]

It was true that the Langstons' routine was no different than their white classmates'. They kept the same busy schedule of classes and prayer meetings, and seating was not segregated in either setting. They ate at the same tables as everyone else in the dining hall and sat in the same pews in church. Oberlin had a manual-labor curriculum in place—essentially, a mandatory work-study program. Charles and Gideon were assigned sections of the college green to clear just like their white male counterparts. Every week, they dropped off their linens for washing by female classmates, who became some of the only white women in antebellum America doing Black men's laundry.[44] The Langston brothers enjoyed equal access to these features of campus life, but were they seen as equal members of the community? After a semester of studying, eating, and working with African Americans, how did white peers and professors view Black equality? Oberlin intended racial coeducation as a means of uplifting African Americans, but to what extent did it become a form of social engineering for whites to unlearn racism?

Proximity has been said to reduce prejudice. In 1954, the same year the Supreme Court handed down its landmark ruling in *Brown v. Board of Education*, social psychologist Gordon Allport published an influential book called *The Nature of Prejudice*. In it, he outlined a theory of integration known as the contact hypothesis. Allport contended that regular intergroup interactions can reduce bias, but only if certain factors are in place. For contact to be constructive, institutional authorities must strongly support the groups' association. The groups should be allowed to mingle freely and collaborate on projects that reflect shared values. Any differences in status between them must be minimized. None should be ranked above others. The emphasis must remain on everyone's equal personhood.[45] Almost seventy years after its publication, Allport's framework remains foundational to the study of social integration.[46] As the historical sociologist Christi Smith notes, Oberlin put the principles of contact theory into practice over a century before Allport articulated them.[47] So did its sister schools, New York Central College and Kentucky's Berea College. They were founded to be for the Northeast and the Upper South what Oberlin became to the Midwest, a college where higher learning and racial justice went hand in hand. As such, these three institutions became laboratories for testing when and whether contact curbs intolerance.[48] Examining their experiments confirms what numerous insightful studies of American education have shown, namely that schools and colleges are critical sites for understanding how conceptions of race, justice, and national belonging coevolved in the nineteenth and early twentieth centuries.[49]

This book is the first comparative study of Berea, New York Central, and Oberlin. Gender is crucial to my analysis as it intersects with Blackness, but my focus is on the ways interracial education prompted reconsiderations of racial norms and prejudices.[50] What follows is not an institutional history of abolitionist colleges but rather a social and cultural history of their experiments in interracial education.[51] Not only did these institutions face similar challenges; they also evolved in tandem, trading students, faculty, and benefactors. New York Central, Oberlin's radical cousin to the east, was founded in 1848 near the Burned-Over District. Before financial pressures prompted its closure in 1858, it hosted some of the era's most avant-garde activists and became the first American college to hire white women and Black men as professors. Berea began as a schoolhouse in the foothills of the Cumberland Mountains in eastern Kentucky. It had collegiate aspirations from the start, but its antislavery founders were chased out of the state shortly before the Civil War. Berea resumed operations in 1866 and was hailed as a model of Reconstruction-era education reform. It was the first college in the South to coeducate men and women, not to mention African Americans and whites. From the 1870s through the early 1890s, the ratio of Black to white students averaged five to four, a figure that remains largely unmatched in American higher education.[52]

Abolitionist colleges were unique among American universities at the time for extending opportunity to all. The term "abolitionist colleges" was coined by the historian Richard Hofstadter. He used it to designate antebellum colleges, which "contributed much to the moral agitation over slavery" by permitting the free exchange of ideas on campus.[53] While free speech was indeed vital to spreading abolitionist principles, the free association of the races on campus was more revolutionary. I use "abolitionist colleges" to refer to those that were not only sympathetic to Black freedom but also welcomed significant numbers of Black men and Black women as students.[54] Other predominantly white colleges and universities did not come close to enrolling as many African Americans until well into the twentieth century.[55] By 1900, over fifty had studied at New York Central, over a thousand at Oberlin, and over twelve hundred at Berea.[56]

It was Black students' presence on campus that truly "abolitionized" these colleges. Apart from their manual-labor programs, the schools' curricula did not differ substantially from men's colleges and women's seminaries of the period. Sunday sermons might touch on current events, and guest speakers regularly addressed the struggle for Black freedom and equal rights. But while a visiting lecturer like Theodore Weld extolled the principles of liberty and equality, students of color *embodied* them. Every day they demonstrated their unconditional belonging at their alma mater. Far from passive observers or helpless victims of reform dynamics, they were agents of change. When they earned degrees and certificates, they defied stereotypes of Black people's incapacity for higher learning. When they joined student organizations, assumed leadership roles, and put on campus events, they disproved period arguments about their race's unfitness for citizenship.[57] When they formed friendships across the color line, they prompted whites to examine their prejudices. Racism did not vanish entirely, to be sure. Nevertheless, for a time, the collective efforts of African Americans and white allies helped make racial animus more the exception than the norm on campus.

It did not last. Come 1900, hope had turned to despair. By then, New York Central had long since folded, and while Berea and Oberlin had survived, their experiments in racial coeducation were on the rocks. Color lines had emerged on both campuses in the 1880s. Some whites had begun openly discriminating against Black peers, arguing social distance befit racial difference. Simply tolerating African Americans' presence was kindness enough, they said. Veteran faculty and alums were stunned to see separation displacing solidarity on campus.[58] Black graduates watched with particular alarm as white interests increasingly took precedence at their alma maters. Almost everyone assumed Berea and Oberlin were exceptions to the growing "race problem" that saw Jim Crow angling to replace slavery as a force for subjugating African Americans.[59] Why were abolitionist colleges not inoculated from this virulent new strain of racism? Why had the vanguard retreated from reform?

Distinguishing between degrees of equality helps account for the tragic failure of these interracial experiments.[60] Then as now, there was an important difference between African Americans being equally admitted as students and being equally accepted as people. From the beginning of impartial admissions,

FIG. O.I. Helen Ferris (Bisbee) and her 1855 Preparatory Department class.
Courtesy Oberlin College Archives.

interpretations of racial equality varied on campus, particularly at Berea and Oberlin, whose politics were less radical than New York Central's. At all three institutions, however, there was a disconnect between equal rights for all races and complete social equality between them. An 1855 class picture from Oberlin (Fig. O.I) illustrates the difference. Admittedly, the image is remarkable for its time. Almost nowhere else in antebellum America would an interracial group of men and women be photographed together in such a convivial scene. The picture shows classmates affectionately resting their arms on each other's shoulders, their expressions as cheerful as long-exposure photography allowed. Yet in only one instance do students of different races appear to touch. The white woman seated at the center rests her right hand awkwardly on the folded hands of a Black classmate. The stiffness of the pose speaks to the way race continued to hold sway at abolitionist colleges, even in times of harmony. Apprehension or aversion to the most intimate forms of interracial contact exposed the persistence of race as a framework for governing relations on campus. Black and white students might dine or study together, but as a rule they did not room

9

together. There were very few interracial courtships, and those that did occur panicked college officials. The handful of Black men and women who were appointed to teaching positions were subject to special scrutiny as African Americans exercising authority traditionally reserved for white men. Most left their positions prematurely, frustrated by their circumstances or forced out.

Gaps between egalitarianism and residual racism invited more pernicious forms of bigotry to eventually corrupt campus life. Scholars typically describe how Jim Crow infiltrated these institutions by the end of the nineteenth century, but the seeds of segregation were also sown before then on campus.[61] Often in emphasizing the ways abolitionist colleges were exceptional or influential, historians have overlooked those practices of race that racial coeducation did not, on its own, undo. Prior studies have described the uniqueness of these schools within the landscape of higher education and highlighted their contributions to the national struggle for racial justice.[62] *Degrees of Equality* focuses primarily on the student experience. This vantage point reveals that while interracial accord was, for a time, an astonishing reality in some corners of campus, it was never a guarantee. Even the early victories for equality were more contingent than they have been made to seem. By and large, white members of these communities were more comfortable reforming specific racial injustices than reimagining race itself.

Abolitionist college leaders condemned slavery, but most found it expedient to avoid discussing race whenever possible. Sociologists today argue a "colormute" or color-blind approach can perpetuate discrimination by preserving whiteness as the racial standard.[63] Indeed, the history of these institutions shows that when push came to shove, administrators were more likely to uphold racial conventions than risk reprisal for subverting them. At the same time, by not segregating their campuses as some suggested, they allowed goodwill to grow organically.[64] Students were expected to respect each other's equal right to learn, but it was up to them to decide whether or not to affiliate across racial lines. That choice depended in large part on Black and white classmates having a shared goal. As the psychologist Allport would later write: "While it may help to place members of different ethnic groups side by side on a job, the gain is greater if these members regard themselves as part of a *team*."[65] Joining together in the fight for abolition and equal rights created that esprit de corps.

Obviously, the cause of racial liberation held special significance to the oppressed, but the struggle had religious implications that transcended color.

Bondage and disenfranchisement violated individual liberty, a cornerstone of evangelicalism. Without autonomy, a person was unable to fully obey God's will.[66] By extension, until America rid itself of slavery and caste, it would never become the redeemer nation evangelicals believed it was called to be. The longer these evils continued, however, the stronger the bonds that formed between young Christians intent on conquering them. Black and white collegians might disagree over whether racial equality was an eventuality to work toward, an actuality to defend, or some combination of the two. Yet as long as their political goals remained aspirational, both sides could come together in the common cause of human freedom. When they greeted each other as friends on campus, they did so anticipating a future when Black and white Americans everywhere would do the same.

It was when the battle seemed won that the dynamic started to change. Scholars debate the extent to which white abolitionists and Republicans shrunk from their commitments to African Americans after emancipation and enfranchisement.[67] The 1860s and early 1870s witnessed the ratification of the Thirteenth, Fourteenth, and Fifteenth Amendments and the passage of accompanying civil rights legislation. The same evangelical impulses that had motivated white Christians to fight slavery drove many to participate in schooling newly freed African Americans.[68] But once legal and educational barriers to Black advancement finally began to fall, many white humanitarians concluded they had done their part. African Americans could see to their own elevation now that their basic rights and freedoms were protected. As Black people proved their mettle, white people would presumably become more accepting, and social equality would grow.[69] In the meantime, white evangelicals felt free to turn their benevolent attentions to other groups and causes. Their retreat from solidarity aligned with the strain of postbellum liberalism that understood fairness in terms of laissez-faire. All individuals had the right to make their way in the world without interference. With obstacles to opportunity removed, the only thing standing in the way of anyone flourishing was a lack of initiative. The same liberties that had allowed the white race to thrive would theoretically permit other races to do the same. As the distance from the Civil War and Radical Reconstruction grew, white reformers continued advocating equality before the law as the best remedy for racism, oblivious to the rising threat of Jim Crow.[70]

The pace at which whites at abolitionist colleges withdrew from the cause of Black equality could vary. Age was a crucial factor. Faculty from the antislavery generation were more likely than professors and students who came of age afterward to sympathize with African Americans.[71] Younger whites could interpret freedom of association on campus to mean the right to snub or even scorn Black peers. Among the forces fueling racism after Reconstruction were emergent theories of social evolutionism. Beginning in the 1870s, social scientists influenced by Darwinism and other biological theories of evolution began developing scales for ranking the progress of the world's peoples. They hypothesized that races evolved like organisms, moving up a hierarchy of sophistication. Sociologists disagreed as to whether competition or culture drove that process, but the stages of advancement from primitive to civilized were believed to be the same across nations. Moreover, each race was supposedly evolving on its own timetable.[72] That made promoting mutuality between them at a place like Berea or Oberlin premature. From an evolutionary standpoint, tolerance was as much as one race owed another. If coexistence sufficed, camaraderie was unnecessary. Once it entered the popular consciousness and merged with prevailing notions about the strength of Anglo-Saxon character, this line of thinking made whites reluctant to affiliate with members of a race they perceived as less "advanced" than their own. More and more on abolitionist campuses, they kept their distance.

African Americans did not sit idly by while their alma maters slid into de facto segregation. Black students and alums spoke out. They acted as the consciences of their colleges, holding them to account when they gave ground on racial justice, just as they always had. Like other nineteenth-century African American activists, they knew that ending prejudice would require a demonstrable, unequivocal, and steadfast commitment to human equality from whites.[73] Every time new varieties of racism emerged, they marshaled arguments to rebut them. Over and over, they pressed their institutions to embrace egalitarianism as the lodestar of their missions. Black collegians insisted that decency and goodwill prevail on campus, anticipating Martin Luther King Jr.'s vision of a "beloved community" governed by fellow feeling.[74] African Americans suffered most when their schools fell short of this ideal, but they did not abandon their quests for equal dignity and respect. When they left college, they used their educations to continue advocating for Black empowerment as teachers and professors, ministers and missionaries, writers and artists.

Their children and grandchildren carried on this legacy of activism. Among them was Langston Hughes, the bard of the Harlem Renaissance. In 1951, he wrote a poem from the perspective of a college student who is the only African American in his literature class. "Theme for English B" ends with the speaker addressing the instructor:

> You are white—
> yet a part of me, as I am a part of you.
> That's American.
> Sometimes perhaps you don't want to be a part of me.
> Nor do I often want to be a part of you.
> But we are, that's true!
> As I learn from you,
> I guess you learn from me—
> although you're older—and white—
> and somewhat more free.[75]

Had he lived to read it, Hughes's maternal grandfather might have appreciated these verses more than most. After all, Charles Langston had lived them.

The chapters of *Degrees of Equality* proceed chronologically from the launch of racial coeducation at Oberlin in the mid-1830s to Berea's retrenchment in the mid-1890s. Each chapter focuses on a critical period in one of the three colleges' histories, but since these schools developed in dialogue with one another, I highlight their personal and institutional connections throughout the narrative. Chapter 1 begins by analyzing the rationale behind Oberlin's decision to admit African Americans. It goes on to demonstrate how the first generation of Black students interpreted educational equality as a recognition of their equal humanity. Taking every opportunity to spread that message, they secured new allies while contending with old prejudices. Chapter 2 investigates the rise and fall of New York Central College. This community's outspoken enthusiasm for reform outpaced the college's ability to raise an endowment sufficient to maintain its ideals. Attempts at moderating the school's image by dismissing a Black professor and suppressing free speech only succeeded in alienating students and faculty. Mired in debt and dissent, Central College closed on the eve of the Civil War. Chapter 3 follows the careers of four Black women who studied at

Oberlin between 1852 and 1865. It shows how experiences of gendered racism during and after college informed their activism. As the dream of abolition finally became a reality, these African American alumnae demanded that egalitarianism assume pride of place in the reform imagination. Racial uplift was not simply a matter of ensuring equal rights, they contended, but of restoring the equal dignity that slavery and racism had robbed of Black people.

Chapters 4, 5, and 6 chronicle abolitionist colleges during and after Reconstruction. Chapter 4 recounts how solidarity and intimacy grew between Black and white students at Berea but clashed with the paternalism of its Oberlin-trained faculty and staff. The administration's policing of interracial dating led to the estrangement of the student body along color lines by the late 1870s. Chapter 5 details how faith in liberalism and cultural evolutionism blinded some white Oberlinites to the staying power of prejudice while emboldening others to spurn Black classmates. Even after incidents of blatant discrimination in the early 1880s, African Americans struggled to persuade whites of the realities of racism on campus. Chapter 6 returns to Berea, which experienced its own racial reckoning in 1889. Unlike at Oberlin, the college recommitted to equality in response, but the revival was short-lived. A new administration antagonized African American alums by forcing out a Black instructor and reimagining Berea as a college primarily for the "mountain whites" of Appalachia. As at Oberlin, the rhetoric of individual merit and racial pedigree was used to justify these moves. Despite African Americans' vigorous protests, their stake in the college was increasingly disregarded as Berea's rebranding began to pay dividends. The epilogue describes how race relations at Oberlin and Berea further deteriorated into the early twentieth century. It ponders how these histories might inform the work of diversity and inclusion in American higher education today.

1

OBERLIN COLLEGE AND THE TRIAL
OF INTERRACIAL EDUCATION
1835–1853

After admitting its first Black students in 1835, Oberlin began receiving letters from white prospective students inquiring about the particulars of racial coeducation. Most had never interacted with African Americans as equals, if at all. They wondered whether they could make the adjustment. "I have ever lived among whites exclusively," wrote one in 1843, "and to be now associated with Blacks would be disagreeable, admitting it to be right."[1] By 1851, these inquiries had evidently become so frequent that the college bulletin, the *Oberlin Evangelist,* printed an exchange between a young man with the initials S.B. and Professor Henry Cowles, the *Evangelist*'s editor. "I wish to know if the colored students associate with the whites on all occasions," S.B. asked, "if they recite in the same class and dine at the same table." Rumor had it that at Oberlin "[white] students are obliged . . . to mingle with the colored population farther than is right with the difference nature has made between the two classes."[2]

Cowles responded that African Americans enjoyed equal access to all areas of campus, including the dining hall, chapel, and recitation rooms. But only "when both are agreed to do so" did two men or two women of different races walk, eat, study, or worship together. Freedom of association prevailed on campus—among members of the same sex, anyway—but Cowles added that the college also put "principles of impartial equity" into practice. These precepts were specifically aimed at disabusing notions like S.B.'s that "'nature' has made any such difference between the colored and the white 'classes.'" Oberlin preached that regardless of their skin tone, all people shared a "common origin and a common nature." Their "intrinsic merits" were what mattered. As Cowles stressed: "Our doctrine is that the mind and heart, not color, make the man, and the woman too."[3] The young man would have to decide for himself whether he could tolerate an atmosphere so contrary to his upbringing.

Professor Cowles had only ever known Oberlin as an interracial institution. He and his wife Alice had arrived in 1835, Oberlin's annus mirabilis.[4] That year, antislavery philanthropists rescued the college from potential ruin. In exchange for their support, Oberlin trustees adopted a color-blind admissions standard and a guarantee of free speech for students and faculty, namely on the issue of abolition. The board was not intentionally endorsing immediate emancipation and Black citizenship with these actions. They either couched Black admissions in the language of individual liberty or asserted it was an act of charity, avoiding the transgressive implications of complete racial equality. Still, by agreeing to welcome African Americans and radical reformers to campus, they heralded a new movement in American higher education for human freedom and equality.

The presence of people of color at a once all-white institution transformed Oberlin into the model abolitionist college. It was the trustees' decision to embark on this fateful course when others advised turning back. But it would fall to students—Black and white, male and female—to chart the new territory. They would be the ones to try to realize the abolitionist college ideal. Together they would put reform ideals into everyday practice, sharing in experiences of learning and labor and devoting themselves to common causes like abolition. The spirit of reform became contagious on campus. Ohio governor Jacob Dolson Cox, class of 1851, recalled that regardless of whether a young person came "seeking the means of an education cheaply, or was drawn hither by half-formed sympathy on his own or his parents' part with the spirit of the place . . . the first year was enough to insure catching the zeal that was endemic."[5] Sometimes students outpaced school leaders in their embrace of egalitarianism. Always the college community outraged the wider public. As one Black alumnus, Congressman John Mercer Langston (Fig. 1.1) explained, Oberlin became "the object of intense general hatred" in the antebellum period "because of its fair[,] humane treatment of colored people."[6] The congressman recalled that prior to coming to Oberlin, "[I] had never before had a young white friend who was willing to treat me as his friend."[7] But he also recollected outsiders threatening him for socializing with white women on campus, while his white classmates were accused of supporting interracial sex, the third rail of American culture.[8]

FIG. 1.1. John Mercer Langston.
Courtesy Oberlin College Archives.

A few white students dispelled these insinuations by denigrating their Black classmates. "Tell anybody that asks that we don't have to kiss the Niggars [*sic*] nor to speak to them without we are a mind to," a white student wrote home in 1852.[9] "Tell Bill Blair that there is no danger of my turning abolitionist here," wrote another in 1860. "I am not Pro Slavery," he went on, "but still I believe in letting them stay where they are and not having them among us. . . . For all the stuck up Folks the Darkeys take the Bag of the Bush."[10] Clearly some whites arrived resistant to the college's values and remained so. They were unsettled by the confidence of Black classmates, who interpreted equal admissions as an endorsement of their full human equality. By the early 1840s, a critical mass of Black students had developed on campus. They would grow in strength over the next decade. African Americans never accounted for more than 5 percent of Oberlin's antebellum student body, but their influence belied their modest numbers. Black students embodied the principles of freedom and equality, and they became the most vocal exponents of their alma mater's values. African Americans drew on their religious and rhetorical training to defend their rights, assert their dignity, and challenge any limits on their belonging.[11]

As antebellum Black enrollment peaked in the early 1850s, gaps persisted between the college's unconditional admissions policy and whites' conditional acceptance of their classmates. Oberlin had not begun as an antislavery enterprise, and almost twenty years after its "abolitionizing," the college was still growing into its ideals. African Americans encountered a mix of condescension, compassion, and occasional contempt on campus. Unlike their white counterparts, Black students needed no lessons in racial equality. They knew their worth. What they learned at Oberlin was how to demand whites' respect. When paternalism qualified their membership in the campus community, they pushed back. When prejudice kept them from enjoying their full share of respect, they spoke out. In word and deed, African Americans insisted on being seen as peers, pure and simple.

Oberlin's Founding Ideals, 1833–34

In 1833, two Congregational ministers, John Jay Shipherd and Philo Stewart, founded a utopian community in northeastern Ohio. The region known as the Western Reserve had been inhabited by the Wyandotte and Ottawa tribes until a series of treaties with the US government forced them to vacate those lands at the turn of the nineteenth century.[12] White settlers from New England and New York migrated to the Reserve and established towns and villages patterned on the ones they came from. Education and religion were important to these communities but especially to Oberlin, named for Jean-Frédéric Oberlin, an Alsatian minister and educator whose writings Shipherd and Stewart admired. The two men were steeped in the evangelicalism of the Second Great Awakening, a revival movement that inspired the converted to work for the salvation of the world. They and the other colonists they recruited from the Northeast to join them believed their community's pious example had the potential to "redeem" the American frontier and that the sanctification of the West would spark the spiritual rebirth of the nation, culminating in no less than the return of Christ.[13] Reform of the self would bring about the reform of society.[14] Colonists signed the Oberlin Covenant pledging to live abstemiously, dress and eat plainly, and act charitably. Echoing the words of the apostle Paul, signatories swore "to show that we, as the body of Christ, are members one of another."[15]

Abolitionism was not part of their covenant, but education was central. The college was to be the centerpiece of this evangelical scheme. It would train students to become foot soldiers in the war against sin, whether as ministers, missionaries, or teachers. The urgency of the world's reformation demanded that both men and women be equipped to the task of spreading the gospel.

The colonists vowed to "educate all our children thoroughly, and train them up in body, intellect and heart, for the service of the Lord." To that end, they established the Oberlin Collegiate Institute as a school for both sexes.[16] At a time when no other American college admitted women, they represented about one-third of Oberlin's student body.[17] Five departments made up the collegiate institute: the preparatory, female, collegiate, and theological departments and the teacher education program. The preparatory department, a regular feature at early colleges, equipped students to matriculate into one of the school's higher-level programs. It offered a secondary curriculum comparable to what a boy or girl might receive at an academy: geography; arithmetic; sacred and ancient history; English, Greek, and Latin grammar (the last only for men, as it was considered prerequisite for professionals).[18]

Only Oberlin's female department was expressly gendered. Its mission was to "furnish instruction in the useful branches taught in the best Female Seminaries" such as Catharine Beecher's school at Hartford, Connecticut, or Emma Willard's at Troy, New York.[19] These institutions taught women literature, natural sciences, theology, and philosophy. Oberlin intended a similar curriculum for its female students, but with the important difference that women would study some of these subjects with men. Coeducational academies were commonplace in the Northeast in the early nineteenth century, but higher-level seminaries and colleges were segregated by sex.[20] Of the coeducational colleges that opened after Oberlin, almost all were off-limits to African Americans before the Civil War.[21] Some white western colleges opened as coeducational academies but dropped their female departments upon receiving collegiate charters.[22] Oberlin, however, was committed to affording women "all the instructive privileges which hitherto have unreasonably distinguished the leading sex from theirs."[23] Qualified students in the female department could take classes "in the Teacher's, Collegiate, and Theological Departments as shall best suit their sex, and prospective employment."[24] Although women were not forbidden from pursuing the bachelor's degree, it was assumed that they would not.

When Oberlin's male leadership wrote of women's sex and careers, they had evangelical ends in mind.[25] The "elevation of female character" was high on the school's priority list, second only to the education of ministers and school teachers according to the 1834 report.[26] Women were considered predisposed to piety, and school leaders felt their presence would soften the unruly character of college men and teach them not to objectify the opposite sex. Learning practical subjects together with men would better equip female graduates to impart their moral influence to their children and husbands. Alice Cowles, who became principal of the female department after her husband Henry's appointment, explained that "a very high degree of mental improvement, skill . . . and the various graces of the heart are all indispensable" to women's vocations.[27] Any coursework that could improve women's service as teachers, mothers, and homemakers was incorporated into their curriculum, including classes cross-listed with the collegiate and theological departments. The 1835 catalog confirmed that "young ladies . . . attend recitations with young gentlemen in all the departments."[28] It was not until 1837, however, that any women formally applied to pursue the bachelor's degree and not until 1847 that any women sought admission to the theological course.[29]

Oberlin also boasted a manual-labor curriculum, which promised to offset tuition and board through a program of work-study. Like coeducation, manual-labor education was unusual, even controversial, for the time. Critics deemed it a distraction from academic pursuits, but proponents contended it was essential to fortify the body as well as the mind. Rural and frontier institutions claimed that combining learning and labor would better prepare their students for pioneer life. Manual-labor curricula were also in keeping with the democratic idealism of the Jacksonian age. Not only did its cost savings make a once privileged path available to more Americans, but it was also thought that common work regimens would build camaraderie across class lines. For some, belief in the nobility of labor and the anathema of caste carried antislavery implications as well. A number of abolitionists started their careers as advocates of manual-labor education. The Burned-Over District's Oneida Institute became an early nexus of the two movements. Arguably the first abolitionist college, the upstate New York school forswore racial (though not gender) proscription in 1834 when the abolitionist Beriah Green was appointed president. Before it closed in 1844, Oneida would educate at least one Native American and fourteen African Americans, including William G. Allen, Alexander Crummell, and Henry Highland Garnet. Among its white alumni was Theodore Dwight Weld, who would play a pivotal role in "abolitionizing" Oberlin.[30]

Together, Oberlin's coeducational and manual-labor offerings attracted students from across the North, but primarily from the vicinity. Many of the forty-four students enrolled in 1833–34 hailed from nearby towns. Others came from elsewhere in Ohio, and some were from New York and New England. Oberlin Hall, the college's main building, housed twenty young men in its third-story attic, another twenty women downstairs, and the Shipherds, who lived with their children in the basement. This cozy arrangement quickly proved inadequate. Between the winter and summer terms of 1834, the student body climbed to 102, prompting a housing shortage. Students began boarding with families in the village or on nearby farms. Toward the end of the year, Oberlin broke ground on a new, larger residence hall intended primarily for women. Yet insufficient funding slowed construction.[31] By November 1834, the collegiate enterprise was at a crossroads.

Enrollment surged as Oberlin's reputation grew, but the college's finances were far less favorable. Building expenses and administrative costs from the manual-labor program strapped the institute of cash, and donations from the critical northeastern fundraising field were not forthcoming. Academically, only the preparatory department was functioning as intended. Without a president, key faculty, or adequate funds, the institute was falling short of its collegiate aspirations. Caught between auspicious goals and inauspicious prospects, the school's leadership was divided over its future. Should Oberlin downsize into an academy or redouble its efforts to become a college? Cofounder John Shipherd exhorted his community to think big, believing that "God would grant the means if his people would ask, & labour for the object in faith."[32] The trustees dispatched him forthwith on a fundraising mission. Fatefully, he chose Cincinnati as his first destination.

The Lane Seminary Rebellion, 1834

Cincinnati was home to Lane Seminary, a theological school for Congregationalists and Presbyterians. Perched on a hill overlooking the city center and the Ohio River beyond, the seminary attracted students from both North and South. Lane's founders envisioned the school as a place where young men would prepare for missionary service in the Ohio and Mississippi Valleys. They appointed the respected New England moral reformer and colonizationist Lyman Beecher president in 1832. Beecher simultaneously assumed a professorship in theology endowed by Arthur Tappan, a wealthy New York merchant and philanthropist. Trouble arose not long after Beecher arrived. One-fifth of the incoming class hailed from the Oneida Institute. Their hero was not Lyman Beecher but his adversary, Charles Grandison Finney, the outspoken revivalist and pastor of New York City's Chatham Street Chapel.[33]

Finney's mode of evangelicalism relied on confrontational "new measures" to encourage conversion, methods that Beecher had criticized.[34] These included holding intentionally protracted church services, identifying the unconverted by name, and permitting women to pray aloud in mixed company. At the core of Finney's theology was a belief that individuals must strive to commit themselves perfectly to God's will. Christians should weigh the morality of all actions and institutions, great or small, to determine whether they were in keeping with benevolent design or beholden to selfish interests. The goal of this perfectionist ethic was to avoid "expediency" in moral decision-making and maximize virtue in every context. Intense scrutiny could lead to miraculous transformation, both of individuals and communities. The pursuit of perfection extended from the self to society. Having experienced sanctification, the converted endeavored to purify the world. Women, who were the primary sponsors of Finney's revivals, and young people founded innumerable benevolent organizations and auxiliaries aimed at promoting social reform.[35]

Inspired by Finney's ideas if not converted by Finney himself, the Oneida alumni pursued ordination at Lane with the hope of morally transforming the nation, beginning with the frontier. Led by the charismatic Theodore Weld, who was already an accomplished reform lecturer, they took the seminary by storm. Oneidans brought with them their fierce commitments to temperance, manual labor, and especially abolitionism. In February 1834, they staged a campus-wide debate at Lane on abolitionism and the morality of the colonization movement, which advocated deporting African Americans to Africa. Patterned on a Finney-style revival, the affair was thoroughly scripted. A parade of student witnesses, coached by Weld, recounted the horrors of slavery and the sincerity of African Americans' aspirations for freedom. The most effective testimony came from James Bradley, the seminary's lone Black student. Having once been enslaved, he offered himself as living proof of the falsehood of white arguments about Black indolence and irresponsibility. Bradley reasoned that between caring for their masters' families and their own, enslaved people were laden with more duties than most free people: "It would be strange if they could not provide for themselves when disencumbered from this load."[36]

Arguments like his helped persuade born-and-raised southerners at Lane of the necessity of immediate emancipation. Eighteen days of proceedings ended with the "conversion" of almost the entire student body to abolitionism.[37]

Lane's administration begrudgingly permitted the debates, but they refused to condone the activities of the campus antislavery society that formed afterward. Student activists set about establishing schools, Bible classes, and lyceums for Cincinnati's free Black community. Some accepted invitations to dine or stay the night in Black homes. In return, a few Lane students hosted a group of African American women for a visit to campus. Another student was spotted walking in town "with a colored female to the seminary or its vicinity, and returning in like manner." The faculty could tolerate students' charity work, but they could not countenance the young men putting into practice "the doctrine of social intercourse." Students vigorously defended their actions, asserting that "any reference to color, in social intercourse, was an odious and sinful prejudice."[38] The faculty, however, deemed interracial associations a direct threat to the reputation of the institution, particularly given its location: "The vicinity of a large city & on the borders of a slave holding state, calls for some peculiar cautionary measures."[39] White rioters had attempted to oust the city's Black residents in 1829 and would do so again in 1836.[40]

In response to negative press coverage and in President Beecher's absence, Lane's trustees decided to crack down. The board disbanded all extracurricular organizations, forbid any public discussion of nonacademic topics, and targeted Theodore Weld and other leaders of the antislavery society for expulsion. They also fired John Morgan, a professor sympathetic to the students' activities. Only one trustee, a Finneyite reverend named Asa Mahan, dared speak out in support of the students. In October, forty students took the unusual step of requesting dismissal from Lane. Between those who withdrew and those who did not return for the fall term, 95 of the previous year's 103 students had left by the end of 1834.[41] About a dozen of these so-called Lane Rebels decamped to the outskirts of town and established their own ad hoc seminary in an area known as Cumminsville.[42]

James Bradley does not appear to have lived with the other "rebels" at Cumminsville, but he stayed in contact with his former classmates. He was among the signatories of a public statement composed by the rebels in November 1834. Published independently and reprinted in the *Liberator*, the document recounted the history of the conflict and enumerated the students' grievances with Lane. Bradley received special mention for his contributions to the cause. After a lifetime of slavery "he now leaves [Lane] unwilling to surrender, again, inalienable rights" and loath to renounce the antislavery society "of which he is a beloved member, and officer, and which he assisted in organizing, for the redemption of his poor perishing brethren."[43] Several of the Rebels continued ministering to Cincinnati's Black community after leaving Lane.[44]

Lane's biggest donor, Arthur Tappan, admired their tenacity. He gave them $1,000 and promised $5,000 more if they continued their studies at Liberty Hall. But the Rebels craved more formal instruction. Oberlin's John Shipherd learned of their predicament when he arrived in December 1834. He began negotiating for their transfer to Oberlin, where he promised a new theological department would be created. Tappan's backing gave the students leverage. In light of their travails at Lane, they requested a guarantee of free speech on campus. They also asked that their mentors be appointed to vacant positions on Oberlin's faculty: Asa Mahan as president of the college and professor of moral philosophy, John Morgan as professor of mathematics, and were he to consent to come, Charles Finney as professor of theology.[45] Mahan and Morgan were enthusiastic, but they added their own caveat, almost certainly with the approval of the Rebels: that henceforth, all applicants to Oberlin "be received . . . irrespective of color," just as Bradley was at Lane.[46]

Shipherd accepted this final term as eagerly as the others. He had no qualms about racial coeducation. Some months earlier, in fact, he had told a donor that color blindness was Oberlin's official admissions standard.[47] That, however, was a private communication, and one made without the knowledge or approval of the trustees or the community. Mahan and Morgan wanted an official, public guarantee of Black admissions. Shipherd was convinced that the prospect of "some thousands" from "benevolent & able men" like Arthur Tappan and his brother Lewis would give the board enough incentive to endorse the measure.[48] He dashed off a letter requesting approval for each provision of the deal. Where the first points were greeted with enthusiasm, the last was met with dread.

"A Matter of Great Interest," 1835

Word of the admissions proposal hit Oberlin like a bombshell. According to one trustee, "On this information reaching Oberlin—a general panic & dispair [sic] seized the Officers[,] Students, & Colonists." Shipherd's cofounder declared "Mad!!" for even entertaining the idea of interracial education.[49] Oberlin was not founded as an abolitionist colony. African Americans comprised some portion of the body of Christ, Oberlinites agreed, but the prospect of the two races being "members one of another" the way the covenant described was inconceivable to most. The day before the trustees were to deliberate, students circulated a survey among themselves gauging attitudes on the "practicability" of Black admissions "under existing circumstances." Fifty-eight students participated. Opponents of the measure outnumbered supporters thirty-two to twenty-six. While a slight majority of men voted in favor, the vast majority of women were opposed.[50] They felt they had more to lose than gain by associating with African Americans. The mere suggestion of contact with Black men threatened to sully their reputations back home.

A chief concern of integration's opponents was "amalgamation," the period term for interracialism.[51] Interestingly, the word amalgamation was also used at the time to describe the comingling of the sexes. Lyman Beecher, for instance, condemned coeducation at Oberlin, saying, "This amalgamation of sexes won't do. If you live in a Powder House, you blow up once in a while."[52] Anxieties about sexual impropriety helped fuel opponents' antagonism toward gender coeducation. The Oberlin catalog of 1835 stated emphatically that women's "rooms are entirely separate from those of the other sex, and no calls or visits in their respective apartments are at all permitted."[53] To add African Americans to this coed environment would be downright incendiary. One of the college's fundraising agents wrote Shipherd that absent a provision to "keep the blacks entirely separate so as to veto the notion of amalgamation . . . every interest of the enterprise . . . will be blown *sky high*." That students of different sexes and races might be admitted "on precisely the same standing" and "mingle in recitation, board, and study" appalled him. "If the time ever comes for this, it has not now come," he wrote Shipherd, adding that he would not even enroll his own children "in such a Seminary."[54]

Shipherd was absent for the trustees' initial deliberations on January 1, 1835. Confident in the board's approval, he had gone to New York with Mahan to confer with Finney and potential donors. Were Finney to accept the theology professorship, Arthur Tappan pledged to contribute $10,000 to the school up front and more in the future. His brother Lewis and other wealthy New York donors formed the Oberlin Professorship Association, which pledged permanent endowment of eight faculty positions also contingent on Finney's move.

Finney agreed to take the job provided that, among other things, "the internal management of the institute [be left] entirely to the Faculty, inclusive of the reception of students." According to Shipherd, Finney favored "educating at Oberlin colored persons who are worthy" and said "he would not join any institution where they were excluded."[55] Finney's emphasis on merit was consistent with his theology, which was deeply informed by Lockean liberalism. A trained attorney, Finney approached faith in terms of contractual responsibility and moral agency. Since all people were "members of the government of God," the earthly distinctions between them should not be allowed to interfere with their ability to receive and obey divine law. Individual liberty was, in effect, the freedom to obey God. To Finney, the right to righteousness implied the chance to learn as well as to worship, since both were necessary to grow in faith.[56] However, while he believed in educational equality as a recognition of spiritual equality, later events would reveal Finney's reluctance to endorse the social equality of the races.

Oberlin's trustees were less convinced than Finney or Shipherd of the wisdom of interracial education. Although they supported the new appointments, they decided they needed more convincing on Black admissions. Members of the Oberlin community felt the same. Prior to the board's New Year's Day meeting, thirty-two townsmen and male students, including a few who had voted against racial coeducation in the earlier straw poll, petitioned the board for transparency in their deliberations. For all their misgivings about race mixing, they wrote: "We feel for our Black brethren. . . . We want to know what is duty—and God assisting us we will lay aside every prejudice and do as we shall be led to believe God would have us do."[57] Shipherd took it upon himself to address their concerns and those of the trustees in two dispatches from New York. Written in his respective capacities as cofounder of the college and pastor of the Oberlin church, these complementary letters offered an ideological basis for Oberlin's desegregation. Shipherd wrote with the boldness of a visionary and the biases of his times. His framework informed the board's eventual motion, which opened the Oberlin community to African Americans but qualified their belonging in unsubtle ways. In time, these racist presumptions would become the object of Black students' resistance.

Shipherd's first epistle was to the trustees. Admissions reform was not meant as an act of radicalism, he reassured them. The intention was not to "hang out an abolition flag or fill up with filthy stupid negroes." Intrinsic merit, assessed by white arbiters, would be the standard: "We should receive *only* those to whom no objection could be made except by prejudice against a dark skin." Shipherd reasoned that literate, pious students should not be denied an education at Oberlin merely because "God had given them a darker hue." White opposition to associating with people of color was akin to the Pharisees refusing to dine with tax collectors and sinners, he said, implying that Blackness itself was somehow immoral. Shipherd went on to claim interracial contact was not as deplorable as it was made to seem. As evidence, he cited the recent visit of a Black collegian from another institution to Oberlin. Most likely he referred to John Sykes Fayette, who became the first African American graduate of Western Reserve College (now Case Western Reserve University) in 1836. Shipherd recounted that when Fayette "ate at the Ob[erli]n table no one seemed troubled."[58] James Bradley's tenure at Lane Seminary was further proof that Black admissions was feasible. "The difficulties there did not grow out of the reception of colored students," Shipherd noted. "Br[other] Bradley" was received "without objection" and "was much respected & beloved."[59] Lane had lost God's favor by denying other freedoms, but even it had been broad-minded enough to admit a token Black student.

A key difference between Lane and Oberlin, however, was the presence of women, a factor that amplified fears of race mixing. Shipherd acknowledged the potential "shipwreck of Amalgamation" and cited the debacle at the Foreign Mission School in Cornwall, Connecticut, a decade earlier. Founded in 1817, the so-called "heathen school" welcomed Native American and South Asian students to prepare for missionary careers alongside whites. In 1824 and again in 1826, Cherokee students scandalized the local community by marrying white women. Shipherd did not mention how the controversy hastened the Foreign Mission School's demise.[60] Instead, he pointed to the exemplary character of the Native students throughout the ordeal. Their integrity proved that prejudice against them was unfounded. Where interracial sex was concerned, Shipherd was no more fearful of the prospect than he was the danger of "fornication among our white sexes." In both cases, he said, "We risk that sin among them to gain important ends."[61] Coeducating the races, like coeducating the sexes, served a higher purpose: training the rising generation in righteousness. Means that some considered unseemly justified ends that most deemed godly.

Shipherd's pastoral letter cast Black admissions as a test of faith. By subscribing to the terms of the Oberlin Covenant, colonists had set themselves apart from a fallen world and enlisted in a holy mission. Now, said Shipherd, quoting scripture, it was time for them to "'perform the doing of it.'"[62] Fulfilling their calling meant accepting the "peculiarity" that comes with undoing social norms. "Overturnings and inventions" would be necessary to bring about the kingdom of God. Shipherd told his flock: "Fear not, brethren, to lead in doing right." Duty to Christ should always trump expedience. Addressing their "recent expressions of unwillingness to have youth of color educated in our Institute," Shipherd acknowledged that many disliked the prospect of integration for the same reason they opposed immediate abolition. Both measures suggested African Americans deserved equal citizenship, yet Oberlinites felt them unqualified. Shipherd saw the matter in reverse. How better to prepare the Black race for liberty, he asked, than to admit "those of promising talent and piety" to Oberlin, "elevate and educate them as fast as possible," and send them forth to uplift "their untaught, injured, perishing brethren"?[63] Duty and practicality were closer than they appeared, if whites could only see past their prejudices.

Shipherd appealed to ethics as well as scripture to make his case. Not only was education essential for Black uplift, he wrote; it was also necessary reparation for slavery. "The extremity of their wrongs at the white man's hand" demanded extraordinary restitution. Segregated solutions were half measures. African Americans deserved access to the best institutions. "They will be elevated much more rapidly if taught with whites, hitherto far more favored, than if educated separately." The desegregation of American colleges was inevitable, in his view, and taking the lead would secure valuable donations from New York. Financial incentives aside, Shipherd said a righteous community like Oberlin should not "wait to do justice and show mercy till all others have." Would fulfilling the Bible's injunctions be acknowledging innate racial equality? Shipherd did not address the point directly. Quoting scripture, his letter variously referred to African Americans as "little ones," "our neighbors," and "of blood with us . . . our fellows."[64] Whether Black admissions was ultimately an act of charity, amity, or consanguinity, Shipherd did not say. But he did remind his flock of the capriciousness of color and caste: "Suppose, beloved, your color were to become black, what would you claim . . . to be your due as a neighbor?"[65] If they were too close-minded to see his point, Shipherd vowed to leave Oberlin entirely. He told the trustees the same.

At the next meeting of the board in February, Shipherd's first letter was read, and a vigorous discussion ensued. Black admissions eventually passed by a vote of five to four. The trustees approved of the terms of Finney's appointment and ceded admissions authority to the faculty, effectively sanctioning Black admissions. John Keep, incoming president of the board and a prominent abolitionist minister in Cleveland, cast the deciding vote. Although he endorsed the measure, Keep told Finney he feared Oberlin would be slandered as a den of racial and sexual deviance.[66] A reputation like that, however baseless, could spell the college's demise. The board's apprehension shone through in a supplemental resolution passed at the February meeting. Intended to clarify the intentions behind Black admissions, the motion was anything but straightforward:

> Whereas there does exist in our country an excitement in respect to our colored population, and fears are entertained that on the one hand, they will be left unprovided for, as to the means of a proper education, and on the other that they will in unsuitable numbers be introduced into our Schools, and thus in effect forced into the Society of whites, & the state of public opinion is such as to regain from the Board some definite expression on the subject, therefore

> *Resolved* That the Education of the people of color is a matter of great interest and should be encouraged in every proper way and manner & sustained in this Institution.[67]

The excision of "in every proper way and manner" reflected the board's unease. Their statement suggested only a small number of African Americans would ever be welcome as equals in "the Society of whites." Phrases like "unsuitable numbers" and "our Schools"—both possessive and plural—showed that wholesale integration was far from their desire. By distinguishing "the Education of the people of color" from the communion of the races, the resolution captured the vital distinction in their minds between Black uplift and Black equality. One thing was clear from their trustees' statement: they would not be the ones reforming white hearts and minds. Instead, Black students would be left to take up the charge, gaining white allies as they went. In the ensuing decades, campus activists would work to narrow the gap between equal admission and equal acceptance.

Oberlin "Abolitionized," 1835–36

Oberlin's tentative embrace of abolition coincided with a critical phase in the wider antislavery movement. In the spring of 1835, the American Anti-Slavery Society launched a great postal campaign to spread the cause of immediate emancipation to the nation. Abolitionists flooded the US mail with literature, directing over a million pamphlets to public officials and civic leaders across the North and South. The campaign stoked enthusiasm and inspired the formation of many new antislavery societies. At the same time, it also elicited violent responses from proslavery elements, who considered abolition synonymous with sedition. The postmaster of Charleston, South Carolina, declined to deliver the mailings, which were burned by a mob along with effigies of prominent abolitionists. Free African Americans were assaulted elsewhere in the South, while vigilantes attacked antislavery meetings in the North.[68]

Fearing the notoriety that came with the cause, Oberlin downplayed any abolitionist influence when it publicized recent developments on campus. Omitting mention of Black admissions, college notices instead highlighted Finney and the other professors' appointments and the outpouring of private donations and endowments that accompanied them.[69] These were touted as proof that the colony was becoming the next cauldron of millennial fervor, a successor to upstate New York's Burned-Over District. Young people from that region began flocking to Oberlin, in fact; the number of New Yorkers nearly matched the number of Ohioians within the 1835–36 student body.[70] They had grown up amid the excitement of revivalism and social reform. To them, Finney would have been a household name. In all likelihood their families had attended his revivals or heard one of his itinerants preach. The chance to study in an evangelical environment under his influence led them to enroll in record numbers. The student body nearly tripled between the autumns of 1834 and 1835, with 225 new students matriculating. Two new dormitories were hurriedly built that summer to accommodate them, and ground was broken on three more.[71]

The first to arrive were the Lane Rebels. James Bradley did not join them initially; he would enroll in one of Oberlin's affiliated secondary schools the next year.[72] When his Cincinnati classmates appeared on campus in June 1835, they wasted no time in forming the Oberlin Anti-Slavery Society (OASS). Shipherd was elected president of the group, whose membership included colonists, faculty, and students. The terms of the OASS constitution closely resembled those of Lane's antislavery society. Members committed themselves to "the emancipation of the free colored man from the oppression of public sentiment and civil disabilities; Because color, condition of birth, poverty, calamity and complicated woe deserve no punishment." The lengthy list of signatories included both men and women, and Oberlinites continued to add their names over the course of the year. About half of the incoming male students and one-sixth of the incoming female students signed, compared with more than three-quarters of returning men and one-half of returning women (including, incidentally, at least six who had earlier voted against desegregation).[73] The newcomers' more limited embrace of the OASS confirms that other factors besides abolition were behind Oberlin's enrollment boom.

Antislavery enthusiasm grew over the school year, however, thanks in large part to a visit from Theodore Weld. Rather than continue his studies at Oberlin with his Lane brethren, Weld had decided to pursue activism full time as a lecturer for the American Anti-slavery Society. In November 1835, he delivered a rousing series of talks on campus. His aim was not only to win converts to abolition but also to train students to become antislavery agents themselves. Halfway through his stay, Weld wrote Lewis Tappan to describe the scene at his lectures: "You may judge some of the interest felt at Oberlin on the subject of abolition when I tell you that from five to six hundred males and females attend every night, and sit shivering on the rough boards . . . without any thing to lean back against, and this too until nine o'clock."[74] His charisma held their attention. One of those present, future Oberlin president James Fairchild, would later rave of Weld: "It is doubtful whether any community was every more profoundly moved by the eloquence of a single man. . . . Oberlin was abolitionized in every thought and feeling and purpose."[75] The next month, female students founded the Young Ladies' Anti-Slavery Society and Oberlin townswomen the Female Anti-Slavery Society.[76] Over the winter break, around twenty male students went out on the lecture circuit. Their receptiveness to Weld's message revealed the extent of Oberlin's political transformation since the previous winter.

That school leaders allowed Weld's efforts to interrupt the strict routines of campus life signaled their support for free speech and reform. As a longtime faculty member later explained, "It was not the teaching nor practice at Oberlin to omit any opportunity or action against slavery, social, or political, or religious."[77] Human bondage represented the grossest violation of liberty and Christianity, Oberlin's most cherished values. As such, school leaders took a pragmatic approach to abolitionist activism. Even as the antislavery movement fractured around 1840 over tactics and principles, the community largely avoided the infighting between radicals and moderates. Historian J. Brent Morris argues that Oberlin was "devoted to emancipation by any means necessary, even if that was through unconventional methods or by an abandonment of strict ideological consistency."[78] In 1836, faculty allowed a short-lived student campaign to forgo all products of slave labor, including cotton linens.[79] In 1844, a "Liberty School" for the formerly enslaved was established in town, staffed in part by students of the college.[80] In 1846, Stephen and Abbey Kelley Foster spoke on campus. The Garrisonian pair were outspoken critics of organized religion, the Union, and the Constitution, all of which they considered proslavery. Less radical in their politics, Oberlin faculty disagreed with the Fosters but welcomed them to campus for a polite debate with Professors Mahan and Morgan. The next year, Oberlin hosted Garrison himself. The *Liberator* editor had fiercely criticized Finney and the college for not embracing his positions, but the firebrand and his entourage were nevertheless invited to present their arguments. Joining Garrison on the stage that day was Frederick Douglass, making the first of his numerous appearances on campus.[81]

For all their open-mindedness, white Oberlinites charted a moderate course even before the abolitionist schism. Stumping for emancipation in 1836, Oberlin-affiliated agents played down the issue of social and political equality for African Americans. James Thome, a Lane Rebel turned Oberlin theology student, wrote Weld about a hostile encounter on the Ohio circuit. He told his mentor how he had rebutted a hostile crowd in Akron by making an effort "to disclaim certain things which are confounded with abolitionism; such as social intercourse, amalgamation, etc." Thome had gone on to explain that abolitionism "did not claim for the slave the right of voting, immediately, or eligibility for office . . . that we did not wish them turned loose, having the possession of unlicensed liberty."[82] These qualifications resembled the ambiguities of the OASS constitution, which pledged to elevate African Americans "to an intellectual, moral, and political equality with the whites" in due time but declared that freed people should neither be "turned loose upon the nation" nor "instantly invested with all political rights" upon emancipation.[83] Whatever their personal views, Thome and other Oberlin agents avoided the most controversial aspects of abolition when speaking off campus.[84]

An incident involving Thome's sister revealed that racial mores were disputed on campus as well. Mary Thome belonged to the Young Ladies' Literary Society, a women's literary society established for "the intellectual and moral improvement" of its members and "the promotion of literature and religion."[85] Literary societies flourished in the Early Republic as spaces where educated women could apply classroom learning to contemporary issues and develop public voices necessary for articulating what historian Mary Kelley has called "the values and vocabularies of civil society."[86] Members of the Ladies' Literary Society regularly put on skits for each other addressing moral issues—in this case, slavery. On the heels of Weld's abolition revival, while her brother stumped across Ohio, Mary Thome decided to dramatize the plight of an enslaved mother. Covering her face, neck, and hands with burnt cork, she purportedly "succeeded in making herself look exactly like a black slave."[87]

Thome's blackface performance shocked some of the matrons in attendance, not only for its outrageousness but also for its amalgamationist overtones. The Thomes were the children of a Kentucky slaveholder, a fact that lent credence to James's testimonials against the institution. Yet his sister's act went a step further. Matrons like Alice Cowles, whose husband Henry joined the faculty that fall, judged Mary's performance in "bad taste." It was objectionable, she said, "for young ladies to appear in any coloring, except what nature had given them." By donning blackface, Mary Thome exercised white people's perverse privilege to put on another racial identity without assuming its related burdens.[88] Her intentions aside, the act reinforced white hegemony. However tactless, taking on the persona of an enslaved woman also represented a radical attempt at interracial identification. The fact that she did not try to imitate a Black woman's "manner and mode of speaking" might have meant she wanted her white audience to recognize their kinship with oppressed women across the color line. While some of those present appreciated her intention "to make a more vivid impression of the condition of the slave," others could not countenance her subversion of racial categories.[89]

If Thome's routine underscored the plasticity of race, to some it also endorsed the logic of interracialism. Alice Cowles hinted at this broader concern when she expressed her "anxiety" that Thome's act "would give our enemies occasion to speak reproachfully."[90] Charles Finney echoed those fears in a contentious exchange with Lewis Tappan in the spring of 1836. Tappan not only sponsored Finney's appointment at Oberlin but was also a trustee and major contributor to Chatham Street Chapel, the evangelist's New York City church. Finney initially split his time between New York and Oberlin. In the preacher's absence, a Black man was appointed to the church's board and the sanctuary's segregated seating area was abolished. When Finney returned in March, he infuriated Tappan by reversing these decisions.[91] The philanthropist suspended his vital contributions to the Oberlin Professorship Association in protest, but Finney held firm.[92] A reputation for race mixing "would do infinite mischief to our cause," he wrote Tappan. "If no distinction is to be made between white & colored people, what is this but amalgamation[?]" Finney recognized that slavery represented a "direct and outrageous violation of fundamental right," and he conceded that distinctions of color derived from "a silly and often a wicked prejudice." But his racial philosophy also privileged individual choice. Whites should be free to decide whether or not to fraternize with African Americans. To Finney, it was a matter of "constitutional taste" rather than moral duty.[93]

Critical Mass, 1836–50

Oberlin made almost no attempt to recruit African American students after 1835. Black enrollment grew steadily but never amounted to more than 4.6 percent of Oberlin's student body before the Civil War—a small fraction but three times larger than African Americans' share of Ohio's population at the time.[94] By 1861, Oberlin had matriculated an estimated 245 African Americans.[95] Only Black colleges and secondary schools could boast larger enrollments of African Americans by the time of the war, and most of those were not fully operational until the 1850s. John Mifflin Brown, who matriculated at Oberlin in 1841, remarked that nowhere else could a person of color get an education "as cheap as he can at Oberlin, and at the same time, be respected as a man."[96] To be sure, African Americans at colleges and seminaries like Eleutherian, New York Central, Oneida, or the Young Ladies' Domestic Seminary were also proud of their alma maters. Yet Oberlin exceeded these schools in influence, in part because it bested them in enrollment. In the antebellum period, as many African Americans studied at Oberlin as at all other interracial colleges put together.

The first were Charles and Gideon Langston, lately of southern Ohio but raised on a Virginia plantation. Its owner, their father, had established a bequest for their education, which they used to enroll in Oberlin's preparatory department. The everyday routine at Oberlin meant they spent most of the day with whites of both sexes. In the classroom, men and women sat on opposite sides of a wide aisle, but otherwise seats were not assigned.[97] "No one was required to sit next [to] a colored student," according to one early alumnus, but every student had to "consent to being in the same class with him."[98] Seating at chapel services was also racially integrated.[99] Worshipping with the Langstons and witnessing their baptisms in March 1836 may have influenced whites' opinions on segregated seating at Finney's church in New York.[100] Weld reported to Tappan that "not one of the students with whom I have conversed (and I have talked with all the principal ones) agrees with brother Finney about Negro seats, and they tell me that they don't know one of the members of the seminary who does."[101] Not only did these students pray alongside the Langstons, they also ate with them. Like partaking in the Lord's Supper, dining together symbolized the oneness of all Oberlinites in Christ. Sharing a meal was considered one of the greatest expressions of social equality short of physical contact. Bench seating placed students of different races immediately adjacent.[102] According to the sensationalist exposé, *A History of Oberlin; or, New Lights of the West,* some whites were eager to pay "homage" to African Americans, competing to eat beside them.[103]

Amalgamation was a central theme of that exposé, which was published in 1837 and salaciously subtitled *Oberlin Unmasked*. The author was Delazon Smith, a disgruntled dropout of the college who would go on to become a US senator from Oregon. Smith expressed special disgust for the "reception and treatment of the Negro species in Oberlin," the way they "commingle[d] intimately with their white brethren sisters." Scurrilously he alleged that campus parties concluded with Black men accompanying white women back to their rooms. He also recounted how one of his classmates, Henry Fairchild, took a Black woman named Ann, Shipherd's housekeeper, for a carriage ride in the fall of 1836. Smith branded Fairchild a "practical amalgamator" for driving her to his family's home, where she stayed the weekend to recover from an illness.[104] That she not only rode with Henry but attended his parents' church and sat in his family's pew was the stuff of scandal. The local paper picked up the story and published an outrageous account that included Henry murmuring suggestive passages in her ear from the Song of Solomon. Reprinted in the Cleveland press, the story showed how any whiff of interracial intimacy could become cause for uproar.[105] Rumors like these gave ammunition to antiabolition elements in the Ohio state legislature, who took aim at Oberlin's charter and tried repeatedly to rescind it into the 1840s.[106]

Besides pretend threats of intermarriage, legislators attacked the college for its very real involvement in the Underground Railroad. Black students at Oberlin and one of its affiliated secondary schools played key roles in trafficking fugitive slaves to freedom. *Oberlin Unmasked* described how "a negro, late a member of Sheffield Institute," assisted a conductor in liberating fourteen people from a Kentucky plantation in the summer of 1836.[107] There were only three Black students at Sheffield; the student in question was either one of the Langston brothers, both of whom transferred to the auxiliary school, or James Bradley, who was assigned there on his arrival from Cincinnati. Five years later, another ex-slave turned student led a decoy operation that helped half a dozen fugitives evade capture. Sabram Cox had been a close associate of the white printer Elijah Lovejoy, whose murder by an Illinois mob made him an abolitionist martyr.[108] Afterward, Cox relocated to Oberlin and continued his acts of resistance. In 1841, he and six other African Americans disguised themselves as escaped slaves and were mistakenly apprehended by slave catchers, buying the real runaways time to escape.[109] The other members of Cox's troop likely included a mix of townspeople and students. There were four African American families in Oberlin by the time of the 1840 census. Since 1835, a total of twenty Black students, five women and fifteen men, had enrolled in the preparatory, female, or collegiate departments.[110] At least one of them, William P. Newman, had been a fugitive from slavery. Oberlin would welcome several others over the next two decades, including Mary and Emily Edmonson and Anthony Burns.

Oberlin's Black enrollment continued to grow over the next two decades, reaching a critical mass in 1841. As many African Americans were enrolled that year as in all prior years combined. Whereas the first few Black students had tended to leave after one or two years, now they were remaining at Oberlin for longer durations. In July, an ad hoc Black student committee was formed, arguably the first Black student organization in American history. The committee was composed of Charles Langston, John Mifflin Brown, and George Vashon. Langston had taken a few years' hiatus after Sheffield. When he reenrolled in Oberlin's preparatory department, he met Brown, an aspiring preacher from

Philadelphia. Vashon, though only seventeen, was more advanced in his studies. He had just become the first African American to complete year one of Oberlin's college course. He had grown up in an activist family in Pittsburgh, attended primary school with the future Black nationalist Martin Delany, and helped organize a youth antislavery society. Now, he, Brown, and Langston put their heads together to draft a resolution to the college's donors on behalf of Oberlin's Black students.

British support had recently rescued Oberlin from the devastating effects of the Panic of 1837. As American donors defaulted on pledges and creditors came calling, the trustees commissioned an overseas fundraising mission. They left in March 1839 armed with numerous letters, appeals, and petitions, most notably a circular composed by Theodore Weld and his wife Angelina Grimké Weld. It was signed by the most prominent American abolitionists, Black and white, including Samuel Cornish, William Lloyd Garrison, Gerrit Smith, James McCune Smith, and Arthur and Lewis Tappan, the last of whom endorsed the school despite their grievances with Finney. According to the circular, Oberlin had been established "merely as a Preparatory School" and the Lane rebellion and Oberlin's concomitant embrace of abolitionism were to thank for the college's ascent. Aside from the Oneida Institute, the Welds wrote, Oberlin was "the only Institution in the United States in which the black and colored Student . . . is fully and joyfully regarded as 'A man and a brother.'"[111] Once feared a liability, racial coeducation had become the college's chief asset. Oberlin's agents returned in December 1840 with $30,000 in gold, the equivalent of four years' worth of college operating expenses.[112]

The Black student committee composed an "Expression" thanking those donors who had "exerted themselves on behalf of our race" by aiding Oberlin. The authors understood accurately that a great many patrons had made contributions "upon the ground that colored persons are here admitted to equal privileges with whites." By acknowledging the circumstances of British donations, Black students asserted their own indispensability to Oberlin's livelihood.[113] After all, only they could truly determine whether Oberlin was "conducted upon such principles" as it propounded. Black students deemed their faculty and trustees "worthy of our confidence . . . and that of the British Public." They shamed the American public for failing to display as great a concern for racial equality. And they praised Oberlin for providing Black students a "most efficient means" of elevating themselves. However, while they appreciated the institution's concern for African Americans, they said they had "reason to believe" not all their classmates were as supportive of their presence. To a British audience who had read only of Oberlin's racial tolerance, the committee clarified that this so-called abolitionist community was not immune to prejudice. As they explained, "There are a few persons even here, who would rejoice to see us excluded from its privileges, on account of our complexion."[114] Whatever white leaders and boosters might say, six years of interracial education had not cured Oberlin of racism. The committee might have concluded their resolution with another word of thanks or praise, but instead they closed by reiterating their disgust for any who "would make color instead of character the ground of our reception to Literary and Theological Institutions."[115] What began as a gesture of gratitude became an articulation of moral authority.

Coursework at Oberlin had helped prepare Black students to compose their "Expression" as well as subsequent addresses and appeals. Although Vashon pursued a more advanced course of study than Langston and Brown, all three received rhetorical training. The catalog for 1840–41 indicated that compositions, "extempore discussions," and declamations were "weekly" features of the collegiate and preparatory curricula, as were Cicero's orations.[116] When Vashon entered the second year of the college course that fall, he studied Richard Whatley's *Elements of Logic* and *Elements of Rhetoric,* the era's essential primers in expository writing. His instructor was James Thome, who had joined the faculty as professor of rhetoric after his stint as an American Anti-Slavery Society lecturer. Vashon also gained rhetorical experience as a member of a literary society. At the time, any man pursuing a bachelor's degree was eligible to join either the Union Literary Society (later Phi Delta) or the Young Men's Lyceum (later Phi Kappa Pi). Of the fifteen Black men enrolled in the college course before 1852, four joined the Union and three the Lyceum.[117]

If the 1841 "Expression" reflected a coalescence of Black consciousness on campus, that same spirit of self-determination was on display the next summer. In August 1842, African American students and townspeople organized a daylong celebration to commemorate the ninth anniversary of British West Indian emancipation. Across the antebellum North, African Americans marked the First of August as an abolitionist alternative to the Fourth of July. Black activists put on public ceremonies to push back against white racism and demonstrate that they were deserving of full citizenship.[118] Although they contended with less prejudice at Oberlin than African Americans did elsewhere in the

North, Black Oberlinites also used the First of August to express their equality. They were not, as the trustees' 1835 resolution had suggested, intruders in "the Society of whites" but instead refined and worthy members of the community. By all accounts, whites were moved by the celebrations. They applauded the "great propriety" of the proceedings, "executed with excellent judgment" and in a manner "highly creditable to all."[119] For many, the highlight was a program of speeches presided over by Sabram Cox, whose costumed caper had tricked local slavecatchers. Black student speakers George Vashon and William P. Newman held their own alongside Professors Thome and John Morgan. Whites watched African American presenters with "earnest attention and moistened eye," according to the *Oberlin Evangelist*.[120] Here again was a chance for Black students to put their rhetorical training into practice. Professor Amasa Walker remarked: "The speakers showed themselves to be men of talent. . . . I was astonished[,] confounded."[121] His surprise reflected another dynamic at work that day, white paternalism.

Rushing to stand in solidarity against racism, Oberlin whites could overcompensate by patronizing African Americans. As Walker confessed: "The fact is, that our prejudice against them is so strong, that we do not do them justice, notwithstanding our wishes to do it."[122] One moment from the celebration epitomized that paradox. Before Cox could introduce the speakers, Asa Mahan, Lane trustee turned Oberlin president, rose unsolicited. Oblivious, it seems, to the irony of his words, he "stated that justice to the colored people (as this was their day) demanded that he should bear testimony for them." Mahan attested to African Americans' upstanding character and deportment, but as the *Oberlin Evangelist* noted, the president "need not have said [what he did] if he had waited till after the exhibitions" and let the performances speak for themselves.[123] At the end of the program, Cox rejoined Mahan's interjection when he made a motion of the African Americans present to "return thanks for the prayerful attention of the audience." It was "received with a smile . . . by the colored people" and carried.[124] Black onlookers may have chuckled at Cox's comeuppance of Mahan. Whereas the president took the liberty of speaking for Oberlin's African Americans, they voted to thank him and the other white listeners. Cox had displayed greater decorum. Moreover, his motion suggested that whites should neither assume African Americans' appreciation nor presume African Americans' need for approval. Acceptance was, after all, elective on each party's part.

In the ensuing years, Black Oberlinites continued using First of August celebrations to rebut racism. "Throughout the whole, the true principle of equality, the essential brotherhood of man, prevailed," the *Evangelist* wrote of the 1843 ceremony.[125] The star that year was William Howard Day, who would go on to assume Cox's role as emcee. "Many hearts were melted into deeper sympathy with them in their struggles," the paper reported of the African American speakers at the 1844 festivities.[126] This admiration contrasted the racism of some whites toward Black peers. A white student notorious for his "disgraceful conduct toward the coloured people" was expelled in 1843 after calling one of his peers a "black nigger."[127] Soon after, a newcomer told a Black classmate who greeted him as "brother" never to refer to him by anything but his given name.[128] These exchanges illustrated the limits of some white students' tolerance. Yet Black students like Day refused anything less than complete respect. Day's pride was again on display in 1849, when he became the first African American to address the Ohio General Assembly. He told legislators: "We ask for equal privileges, not because we would consider it a condescension on your part to grant them—but because we are MEN, and therefore entitled to all the privileges of other men in the same circumstances."[129] Day, Charles and John Langston, and John Mifflin Brown were then leading a campaign against Ohio's discriminatory Black Laws, most of which were repealed as a result of their efforts.[130] The classrooms and daises of Oberlin had prepared them to make their appeals.

African Americans also recruited white allies to preach racial equality. In 1846, Day and his First of August co-organizers chose their classmate, future Congressman James Monroe, to close the program. In a speech entitled "Human Brotherhood," Monroe urged unity across racial divisions. "Mountains shall not separate us. Oceans shall not shut in our sympathies," he declared. "We have come together to shake hands with the whole human family."[131] Also tapped was Lucy Stone, a white student who taught at Oberlin's Liberty School and later achieved renown as a women's rights activist. As a rule, women were forbidden from sharing the stage with men at campus events.[132] Stone and others practiced debate and oratory in secret at the home of one of her Liberty School students.[133] First of August organizers gave Stone her public debut.[134] Her speech anticipated the "new bond of common interests, and common hopes" that emancipation would forge between Black and white Americans.[135] The presence of Stone and two other women on stage symbolized another union: the making of common cause between advocates of women's rights and abolition. Partly over the issue of women's participation in reform, moderate abolitionists had split from Garrison's American Anti-Slavery Society in 1840. Black activists at Oberlin and elsewhere remained supportive of Garrison, however. Day's committee acknowledged African Americans' and women's parallel oppression by redubbing the 1846 First of August a "Celebration by the Disfranchised Americans of Oberlin, Ohio."[136] Appearing on the next year's program was Stone's friend Antoinette Brown, who would go on to become the first American woman ordained a minister by a major denomination.

Black women performed their own movement in this symphony of reform. For the first decade of racial coeducation at Oberlin, they were few in number. Thirteen matriculated, compared with thirty-four Black men. Only one Black woman participated in any of the early First of August celebrations, and she was not a student. But as their enrollment grew in the late 1840s, African American women also began advocating for the interests of their race. Two standouts were Sarah Margru Kinson and Lucy Stanton. Kinson was born in present-day Sierra Leone in 1832. Sold into slavery, she wound up on the *Amistad*, the ship whose captives were famously tried for mutiny in 1839. After the Africans' acquittal by the Supreme Court in 1841, the Black-led Union Missionary Society helped fund their return home. Five years later, the society merged with white abolitionist missionary organizations to become the American Missionary Association (AMA).

Dominated by white Oberlin alums from the start, the nondenominational AMA wed abolitionism with evangelism. Its goal was not only converting the unchurched but also uplifting oppressed peoples at home and abroad, especially through education. Kinson was one of the first students the AMA sponsored. She enrolled at Oberlin with the hope that she might return to West Africa as a teacher and missionary. As a student in the preparatory department, she learned English, survived illness, and overcame loneliness to complete its course of study in 1849. Kinson's teachers maintained that the young African's remarkable success in the classroom roundly disproved stereotypes of Black deficiency.[137] Her peers were equally impressed. A white student described her as being "black as black can be, and she is dignified, respected, and loved."[138] Seventy years later, Antoinette Brown still remembered the pathos with which Kinson advocated the cause of her people.[139]

Lucy Stanton was Kinson's roommate for at least one year. A white classmate described Stanton as "a mulatto of refined manners and beautiful dress."[140]

She grew up free in Cleveland but faced discrimination from an early age. Because Black children were barred from the city's public schools, her stepfather founded a separate institution for their education. Training there prepared Stanton to enroll at Oberlin in 1846. She pursued the literary degree, the female equivalent of a bachelor of arts. Women in the "ladies' course" studied many of the same subjects as men, including Whatley's *Logic* and *Rhetoric*.[141] A sharp mind and gentle manners quickly earned her an invitation to join the Ladies' Literary Society, where she read essays and discussed issues with Stone, Brown, and other outspoken women.[142] As far as can be determined, Stanton was the first African American admitted to the Ladies' Literary Society and remained the sole Black woman among its roughly fifty members until she graduated in August 1850.[143] Shortly before commencement, she was elected president of the society. Her nomination prompted "great outcry" at first, with some fearing it would make their alma mater "more notorious and hated than ever."[144] Nevertheless, Stanton prevailed. Among her duties was presiding over the anniversary exercises, a year-end exhibition of members' compositions. The sight of a Black woman chairing an academic proceeding "with dignity and honor" was only surpassed by the spectacle of Stanton's commencement address a week later.[145]

Graduates of the ladies' course had only recently been permitted to deliver orations at commencement. That Lucy Stanton was the first Black woman to complete a four-year course of advanced study made her presence on the graduation stage all the more exciting. "Expectation was raised, and expectation was more than gratified" by Stanton's address, "A Plea for the Oppressed," which the *Oberlin Evangelist* heaped with praise. "Her charming voice, modest demeanor, appropriate pronunciation and graceful cadences, riveted attention," the paper effused. Its commendations resembled overeager praise of the First of August orators eight years before. Also as in 1842, a white speaker interjected to corroborate a Black voice. After Stanton concluded her speech, John Keep spontaneously arose. The trustee whose vote had tipped the balance in favor of Black admissions reminded the crowd of the fear and doubt that had accompanied the board's fateful decision. "It was then predicted that this would ruin the institution," Keep recollected, hastening to add: "The piece to which you just listened shall decide upon the credibility of the prophecy." Clapping was taboo at commencement, but the crowd erupted in applause after his remarks.[146]

Were their cheers for Keep or for Stanton? Certainly he deserved credit for opening Oberlin's doors to African Americans, but she and her peers had more than made good on the opportunity afforded them. Beginning with George Vashon in 1844, six Black men had earned bachelor's degrees by 1850. Over the next decade, five more would complete the college course and nine Black women the literary course, with dozens of others enrolling for shorter periods (as was common for white students as well).[147] The *Evangelist*'s assessment of Vashon could have gone for other Black students: "[He] evinced that genius, talent, and learning are not withheld by our common Father, from those whom the prejudice against color would fain doom to unthinking degradation."[148] Only African Americans' achievements could vindicate Oberlin's experiment by proving their race was worth the risk, that they were indeed worthy of equality. At the time of Stanton's address, the country was in the grips of a national crisis, with debates raging in Congress over the future of slavery in the West and the rendition of fugitive slaves in the North. Stanton's display of learning and refinement that August showed she was more than deserving of the rights of citizenship. The coalescent Fugitive Slave Act placed the interests of enslavers above African Americans' civil liberties. Even Stanton, born free, would have been ineligible to testify at trial if falsely accused of being a runaway.

Amid these ongoing threats to Black freedom, African Americans also faced challenges within abolitionist circles. White reformers' paternalism remained an obstacle, especially as Black activists sought greater leadership in the movement. Not long after his first visit to Oberlin, Frederick Douglass broke with William Lloyd Garrison by starting his own newspaper and embracing the political abolitionism of his mentor's rivals. At Oberlin and elsewhere, white support for abolitionism remained strong but could still be tinged with condescension.[149] Compare Stanton's "A Plea for the Oppressed" with "Our Duty to the Oppressed," an essay by her white classmate Mary Sheldon. Speaking before a women's antislavery gathering the same year, the white woman assailed her race's crimes against African Americans. Slavery had "degraded and imbruted" its victims, Sheldon said. It was whites' responsibility to uplift them through education. But if African Americans wanted whites to respond out of anything more than "naked duty," the oppressed would have to show appreciation. Any "jealousies and suspicions on the part of those whom we would elevate" would "close the sympathies" of white "benefactors," she said, whereas "a thankful spirit would invite the continuance of favors."[150] Stanton, on the other hand, put the onus squarely on whites. Reminding her listeners that "humanity is a unit," she implored them to act out of identification, not obligation. Common personhood entitled African Americans to the blessings of liberty and brotherly love perforce. Addressing her female listeners, Stanton appealed to motherhood and sisterhood, gender roles that spanned racial categories: "Mother, sister, by thy own deep sorrow of heart, by the sympathy of thy woman's nature, plead for the downtrodden of thy own, of every land."[151] Women had an instinct for compassion, she maintained, and they should extend that concern to all members of the human family.

Framing the work of reform in familial terms begged questions about race and difference, dilemmas that white leaders and watchers of Oberlin had been pondering for fifteen years. If the basis for racial justice was the kinship of humankind, was racial equality a goal to be realized or a fact to be honored? As long as the material condition of African American life remained unequal, whites would still be tempted to ascribe inequality to inherent Black degradation, however backward that reasoning was. In 1835 Keep and the other trustees considered Black equality an eventuality. But to the Black student activists who arrived thereafter, it was a reality—the starting point of any discussion of social change, not the endpoint. The only thing deficient was whites' understanding, which Stanton and her peers worked hard to correct. Prejudice against dark skin was misplaced, they argued. Beneath color differences lay a consanguine human race. By 1851, white leaders like Henry Cowles, editor of the *Oberlin Evangelist*, were echoing that sentiment. As the professor informed the prospective white student S.B. in 1851, Oberlin could not be proud of itself until it had eradicated "the notion that 'nature' has made any such difference between the colored and the white 'classes' [such] that it would be wrong for either to associate with the other as beings of common origin."[152] That truth represented a foundation for a new, pluralistic vision of American race relations. It also renewed concerns, both external and internal, that Oberlin was promoting racial amalgamation. Misgivings mounted as African American enrollment grew.

The Progress and Problem of Equality, 1850–53

Oberlin's Black enrollment continued to rise into the 1850s. The 1852–53 school year was the high-water mark; forty-seven African Americans (sixteen men and thirty-one women) studied in the preparatory, ladies', or collegiate department that year. They accounted for over 4 percent of Oberlin's one thousand students, the largest proportion to date. Two-thirds of eligible Black men who were enrolled that school year eventually joined literary societies. The rate of Black men's membership had risen 20 percent over the previous fifteen years. While Black men's rate of membership still lagged behind white men's (93 percent), Black women's equaled white women's. Six percent of Black and white women enrolled during the 1852–53 school year eventually joined the Ladies' Literary Society.[153]

Rising Black enrollment renewed interest in hiring Black faculty. A decade earlier, Professor James Thome had expressed hope for such an appointment, believing it would "exert a very happy and extensive influence."[154] The man he had in mind for the job was George Vashon, then a freshman at the college, but Vashon was not hired when he graduated in 1844. The idea appears to have laid dormant until 1852, when the trustees received a petition from "a portion of the community" asking that a Black professor be appointed to the faculty.[155] The particulars of the petition do not survive. Perhaps some believed that African American students deserved to see a member of their race represented among Oberlin's teaching staff. Employing a Black instructor would affirm African Americans' full belonging in society. "Why should Oberlin not set such an example?" one abolitionist wrote.[156]

The events of the day kept the cause of Black freedom close to mind. *Uncle Tom's Cabin* had been serialized in an antislavery newspaper in 1851, and the wildly popular story would soon appear in book form. Harriet Beecher Stowe's novel captured the moral crisis that the infamous Fugitive Slave Act had spawned. Not only did the law call into question the legitimacy of African American freedom itself; it also pitted individual conscience against federal law by requiring northerners assist in the remand of escaped slaves. Getting between a Christian and his or her faith was a textbook violation of Charles Finney's theology, which held that a person's paramount compact was with God. Historian J. Brent Morris argues that this teaching united white and Black Oberlinites in "a real sense of shared oppression, though clearly differing in degree."[157] In 1851, eighty-five students, almost all of them white, organized the Young Men's Anti-Slavery Society. The organization was dedicated to African American freedom and education. Members appointed John Mercer Langston chairman and educational agent to Ohio's Black community. The society also brought Free Soil politicians to campus, including Salmon Chase and John Parker Hale, US senators from Ohio and New Hampshire, respectively.[158]

Whites' interest in racial solidarity was mixed with apprehension, however. Around the time she nominated Lucy Stanton for the presidency of their literary society, Sallie Holley asked permission to attend a First of August celebration in Sandusky. Oberlin matrons agreed provided that she turn down "any invitation to stay in a coloured man's house." Holley replied: "I certainly feel it my duty to accept any such invitation as a testimony to my principles, and, really, to those professed by this Institution."[159] Although she appeared unbowed by the potential harm to her reputation or her school's, others did not interpret Oberlin's impartial standard so broadly as to include white women socializing with Black men. When, for instance, a Black student threatened to drown himself in the town well after being refused by a white love interest, Lucy Stone advised him to slit his throat rather than "spoil the water for the whole college."[160] Even Stone, an outspoken advocate of Black and women's rights, judged interracial romance too extreme to entertain seriously. Some of these same concerns may have motivated a counterpetition submitted to the trustees. Signed by a "smaller number of the [Oberlin] community," it opposed the call to appoint a Black faculty member, though it is unclear from the trustee minutes on what grounds.[161] Out-and-out racism is certainly a possibility. Another is that its sponsors feared hiring an African American would make Oberlin an even greater target for outside ridicule. Granting a Black man a professorship at a coed college, whatever his qualifications, meant investing him with authority over white women. Even some reform-minded white Oberlinites might balk at that proposition. The college's foes would certainly see it as further evidence of Oberlin's amalgamation plot.

John Mercer Langston became well acquainted with the public's antipathy toward his alma mater anytime he left campus. Stumping for an antislavery candidate for Congress, he confronted a heckler at a rally near Sheffield. The man condemned "'nigger social equality'" and needled Langston for "[learning] to walk with white women" at Oberlin. "Nothing daunted by the accusation implied in these words," Langston advanced to the edge of the stage and told the man in no uncertain terms: "If you have in your family, any good-looking, intelligent, refined sisters, you would do your family a special service by introducing me to them at once."[162] The retort astounded the audience and silenced his detractor. Oberlin had indeed accustomed Langston to viewing white women (and men) as his peers if he did not already, and he counted white classmates of both sexes as friends. Still, while he might make light of popular stereotypes of Oberlin as a den of amalgamation, he knew that interracial romance remained a Rubicon. At a state Black convention in 1849, Langston voiced his frustration with whites' misplaced fears of Black men: "If you ask[ed] a white man whether you may associate with his daughter, or whether you may marry her, he will tell you no! I want to separate myself from such a government."[163] Langston would go on to marry Caroline Wall, another biracial child of the South unafraid to speak out against prejudice in the North.

For all the fear and loathing it occasioned, according to an 1895 history of the college, there were only two instances of intermarriage between former students. That source claims that in both cases, women of color married white men.[164] It does not indicate the two couples' names, but other sources confirm that one was Georgiana Mitchem and Joseph Adams. Mitchem, a fair-skinned southern woman with "an 'invisible admixture of African blood,'" enrolled in the preparatory department in 1852. In 1855 she became the first woman of color to enter the college course and a short time later, the second to be elected president of a literary society. In that time, she met a white preparatory student whom she soon married. The couple left Oberlin before Mitchem could complete her degree. They settled in the Ohio River town of Martinsville and became teachers at a local white school. She passed as white for six months until rumors of her ancestry filtered south. "At once the magnanimous people, indignant that their children should have been so long and so well instructed by a negro woman, and that they should have invited her to their tables and their parlors, promptly dismissed them both from the school."[165] Their positions rescinded, Mitchem and her husband left Ohio for Illinois soon after.[166]

Recalling the incident in an editorial some years later, alumnus Henry Fairchild, now principal of the preparatory department, characterized the affair as the exception that proved the rule where interracialism was concerned. Oberlin's policy of granting African Americans "equal privileges with whites" did not "produce the predicted consequences" of amalgamation, he said. Students of different races might "recite in the same classes, sit upon the same seats, and eat at the same tables," but these gestures did not imply the complete collapsing of racial distinctions. In keeping with Oberlin's values, students enjoyed the freedom to associate with their peers across the color line, and many availed themselves. Yet students observed caution where the most intimate gestures were concerned. Fairchild, like other white reformers, interpreted their apprehension as the natural limit of egalitarianism rather than as a socially conditioned response.[167] Of Mitchem and Adams's marriage, he concluded: "This is the beginning and the end of amalgamation in this Institution, and such has been its

FIG. 1.2. Fanny M. Jackson (Coppin).
Courtesy Oberlin College Archives.

punishment."[168] Langston's comments, on the other hand, indicated that not everyone at Oberlin accepted interracialism as transgressive. Where both the Black alumnus and the white professor agreed was on the danger intermarriage posed to the school's reputation and its livelihood.

The trustees tabled the 1852 petition and counterpetition regarding the appointment of a Black professor.[169] At their next meeting in 1853, they issued this brief response: "that in the choice of Professors and teachers of all grades we are governed by intrinsic merit irrespective of color."[170] It was the same impartial standard that Professor Cowles had outlined in 1851 when replying to the prospective student. Talk of "intrinsic merit" refuted racist ideas of inherent difference. At the same time, however, by removing race entirely from the conversation, color blindness papered over persistent forms of discrimination. A reset approach to racism suggested white hearts and minds could automatically be erased of their biases and that decision makers were immune to outside pressures. The issue of Black tutors in the preparatory department indicated otherwise.

Every semester, as a cost saving measure, the administration hired juniors, seniors, or theology students as instructors in Oberlin's secondary school, as many as thirty or forty in total.[171] In the decade after the trustee's 1853 statement on race and hiring, twelve African Americans met the qualifications for a tutor position, yet none was hired.[172] A person's "intrinsic merits" were supposed to be what mattered at Oberlin. The passing over of so many qualified Black collegians for tutorships indicated how race still held sway. There was "an old custom of giving classes only to white students," explained Frances "Fanny" Jackson (Fig. 1.2), who was appointed Oberlin's first Black tutor in 1863.[173] While Oberlin had broken down barriers since 1835, boundaries remained. Jackson's cohort would rise up to challenge them.

2

THE RISE AND FALL OF NEW YORK CENTRAL COLLEGE 1848–1860

In the winter of 1853, fifty-six New York Central College students signed a petition to the trustees. The document opened by expressing admiration for their alma mater, now in its fourth year of operation: "We love it for the principles upon which it is founded because we believe them to be right."[1] First among those ideals was a commitment to educating "both sexes and all classes."[2] One in three students enrolled there in 1853 was female; one in twenty was Black. These proportions resembled Oberlin's enrollment for 1853, but by other measures, Central College exceeded its sister institution in reform zeal. It offered no separate "ladies' degree" program, nor were its literary societies segregated by sex. Women made up half of the Central College faculty in 1853. Although they were designated "teachers" rather than "professors," other women faculty had previously held the higher rank.[3] Oberlin would not formally appoint a woman to a professorship until 1878. An African American, Charles Reason, was appointed to the Central College faculty in 1849, and another, William Allen, replaced him after Reason left in 1850.

The college's advancements in reform were a point of pride for its students, but the petitioners also recognized the liabilities of being in the vanguard. For one thing, Central College's board of trustees hemorrhaged members from the start. Some one hundred different members cycled through the board's twenty-four seats between 1848 and 1858.[4] The school also went without a president for two and a half years after the first stepped down in 1850, only a year into his term. Potential successors appeared wary to take the helm of such a radical enterprise. From the student petitioners' perspective, the vacant presidency was a liability: "To cause [the college] to receive the patronage its principles merit, it must have a President."[5] For want of donor support, Central College could not afford a library or scientific apparatus sufficient to sustain advanced study. Students asked the trustees to sell scholarships to raise an endowment. Oberlin had recently launched such a fund drive, and Central College students knew their school would also need "a firm basis" in order to thrive.[6] They believed their alma mater stood "first in the world" in its principles. But without proper leadership, facilities, and finances, students feared Central College "[would] never rise to any degree of merited eminence."[7]

Those resources never materialized. Plaintive appeals to the abolitionist public had little effect. Although they shared the school's politics, reform-minded donors appeared skeptical of Central College's chances. Administrators' attempts at moderating the college's image only succeeded in offending faculty and students. A national financial panic in 1857 exacerbated matters. By 1858, the school had suspended operations. Its wealthiest benefactor, Gerrit Smith, agreed to purchase the buildings and maintain the property until the trustees could raise sufficient funds to reopen. In the fall of 1860, Central College briefly revived, only to collapse again by December. Its failure was unremarkable for its time. Impulsive spending, insufficient revenues, and inconsistent local and denominational support spelled the downfall of 20 percent of colleges founded between 1800 and the Civil War.[8] What set this "failed" college apart, however, were its victories on other counts.[9] To the extent that its social advances contributed to its economic deficiencies, Central College was a victim of its own success like the Oneida Institute before it.[10] New York Central's travails illustrate a persistent reality of campus politics: while activists champion change, institutions privilege continuity. The principle of preservation can outweigh the preservation of principle.

Central College made full equality the foundation of its educational experiment. Since 1835, Oberlin had demonstrated the practicality of racial and gender coeducation. But absent precedent for these reforms, incrementalism prevailed on that campus where social questions were concerned. Beyond Oberlin's steadfast guarantee of equal access, the idea of interracial fellowship progressed in fits and starts there—too slow for its champions, too fast for its opponents. Concern for the plight of the enslaved elicited some white Oberlinites' compassion for Black peers, and at times, their sympathy drew closer to empathy as classmates made common cause. At Central College, camaraderie across the color line coalesced in comparatively short order, thanks to the more egalitarian ideology that fired its crucible. Where Oberlin spoke mostly of racial uplift, Central College talked about human equality. They forged their radical values amid a national crisis over fugitive slaves. And the college preached—though it did not always practice—a message of free speech and expression that drew outspoken students and reform luminaries alike. Once unleashed, revolutionary zeal would prove difficult to contain. Central College became the supernova to Oberlin's star, burning bright but flaming out fast. For all its incandescence, however, the experiences of some Black students and faculty revealed how the campus was still beholden to racial caste.

The Seed and the Soil, 1847–49

The Second Great Awakening motivated some born-again Protestants to renounce their churches as unredeemed. Inspired by the biblical injunction "come out from among them, and be ye separate," they funded schismatic churches that maintained rigorous standards for individual purity and social responsibility.[11] Among the worldly behaviors scorned by "come-outer" sects was slaveholding. Debates over slavery fractured multiple denominations in the 1840s, including the Baptist General Missionary Convention. In 1846, a group of abolitionist Baptists split off into a rival organization, the American Baptist Free Mission Society (ABFMS). Concentrated in upstate New York, this come-outer sect never represented more than 6 percent of Baptists in the North. But what they lacked in numbers, they made up for in ambition. The new sect set out to create antislavery alternatives to all of the General Convention's outreach projects, including Bible and tract societies and a newspaper. Its domestic and foreign missions served the border states, Haiti, and fugitive Black communities in Canada. For their piece de resistance, the ABFMS devised a "Free Seminary" whose purpose would be to "provide for the literary, scientific, moral and physical education of both sexes, and of all classes of youth."[12] "Free" in this case referred not only to human freedom but also to the freedom of thought.

The idea of starting a college came about in response to an incident at Madison University (now Colgate), a leading Baptist institution of higher learning in upstate New York. A student named George Ritchie was expelled in 1846 for writing an essay opposing a recent state referendum banning Black suffrage.[13] Reformers interpreted his removal as an attack on free speech. Like the Lane Rebels before them, abolitionist Baptists condemned repression on campus.

"Believing this restraint to be not only useless but unjust, and pernicious in its tendency," they envisioned an environment where students would "be left free to discuss among themselves any one or all of these great moral questions."[14] The school would be nonsectarian, although the ABFMS would sponsor the institution and supply its first trustees. It would operate on a manual-labor curriculum similar to Oberlin's. The ABFMS hoped that a work-study model would discourage the sort of elitism they identified as the root of Madison University's proslavery stance. To further break down barriers to access, the new college would admit students irrespective of both race and sex.[15]

Impartial admissions policies reflected the ABFMS theology, which was outspoken in its commitment to human equality. Free Mission Baptist leaders defended "the rightfulness of the African's claim to intellectual and moral equality with the European."[16] ABFMS missionaries preached the biblical teaching that God "hath made of one blood all the nations of men."[17] They championed racial consanguinity in stronger terms than did the American Missionary Association, the antislavery mission with which Oberlin was allied. Like all the Free Mission Society's enterprises, this new college would affirm "the doctrine of the unity, common origin, equality, and brotherhood of the human race."[18] Future students would applaud their school for not submitting to the common prejudices of colonizationists, who made "a mockery of reform, by adopting the most impious of heresies, that children of the same Divine Parent cannot, or should not, dwell together."[19] The new college aimed to disabuse this notion in principle and in practice.

The ABFMS was also supportive of female education. College organizers believed women had a special role to play in society as mothers and teachers of civic virtue. "The destinies of this great nation are in the hands of Woman," they preached. "She has it in her power to send into its halls of Legislation, its courts of Justice and the pulpits of our land, men who will maintain our civil and religious liberties."[20] The sentiment was consistent with attitudes about gender roles propounded at Oberlin and elsewhere among evangelical reformers. But Central College founders went further, vowing to "contribute to the settlement of the equality of the sexes."[21] With gender as with race, intellectual equality was not social equality.[22] But by using the word, school leaders invited more egalitarian possibilities on gender, consistent with their broad-minded views on racial kinship. The first woman to receive a bachelor's degree from New York Central would cherish her alma mater for the freedom it afforded her sex: "There are none here to whisper, '*that* is beyond *thy* sphere, thou couldst never scale those dizzy heights'; but, on the contrary, here are kind voices cheering me onward."[23]

McGrawville, a village near Cortland, New York, made the short list of host sites for the new college. Midway between Binghamton and Syracuse, the village was centrally located but far enough from other colleges to avoid competition. Townspeople saw commercial advantages in bringing the school to McGrawville. They hoped the new institution would increase property values and expand the market for goods and services.[24] The ABFMS was more progressive in its politics than local Baptist churches, where antislavery sentiment was more individual than collective.[25] Cortland County was not part of the Burned-Over District as it is usually defined, although there was a period of religious awakening among Baptists there in the 1820s. Proximity to the hotbed of upstate reform helped locals keep tabs on reform trends.[26] A McGrawville physician was an outspoken supporter of the Free Mission Society and probably the one responsible for nominating the village. The ABFMS announced that pledge totals would ultimately decide which municipality would be awarded the campus. A town meeting at McGrawville Baptist Church in November 1847 appointed agents to solicit subscriptions.[27]

McGrawville raised $12,000 in subscriptions, the most of any contender, but the town's bid came with conditions. They stipulated that local pledges go toward administration and salary costs, not fixed assets. Between a women's boarding hall, a college farm of 167 acres, and a stately Greek Revival college building (which housed classrooms and the men's dormitory) (Fig. 2.1), capital costs totaled roughly $50,000. It was a huge sum considering the Free Mission Society's annual operating budget never exceeded $26,000 and averaged less than half as much.[28] With their caveat, McGrawville residents indicated they could not be counted on to support the entire venture on their own. They further stipulated that any fundraising campaign should take place outside the boundaries of the Cortland County. Sympathetic brethren from further afield would have to do their part if the college were to thrive.[29] To preempt any misunderstanding about tuition fees, an especially vital source of income under the circumstances, the college changed its name from Free Central College to New York Central College.[30] The cornerstone was laid in McGrawville on July 4, 1848. Cyrus Grosvenor, a white ABFMS minister and confirmed advocate of equal school rights, was appointed president.[31]

FIG. 2.1. New York Central College, McGrawville, NY.
Courtesy McGraw Historical Society.

While other academies in the area practiced gender coeducation, racial coeducation was a novelty.[32] Cortland County claimed few Black residents. According to the 1850 census, African Americans made up 1.5 percent of New York state's population but less than one half of 1 percent of the population of Cortlandville, which included Cortland and McGrawville. Of Cortlandville's four thousand citizens, only twenty-three were people of color, excluding Black students or faculty at the college.[33] Samuel Ringgold Ward, the abolitionist reverend and former fugitive from slavery, was one of them. The white philanthropist Gerrit Smith described Ward as "black as ink" and the most "eloquent and logical debater" he had ever heard. From 1846 to 1851, Ward served as pastor of a predominantly white Congregational church in Cortland.[34] The local chapter of the Sons of Temperance invited him to join its ranks, defying the state policy barring nonwhite members. When the state division ordered his expulsion, the Cortland chapter forfeited its charter instead.[35] The incident suggested that in small numbers at least, African Americans could find welcome in the community.

Ward was one of the featured speakers when the college held its first convocation exercises on September 4, 1849. Incoming students also heard from

FIG. 2.2. Charles Lewis Reason.
Courtesy New York Public Library.

Charles Reason (Fig. 2.2), whose appointment as professor of belles-lettres and French made him the first Black professor in American history. Frederick Douglass praised Central College for hiring Reason and thereby "[placing] its heel upon the venomous viper of American prejudice against color."[36] Reason's appointment affirmed African American matriculates would be welcomed as equals, both intellectually and socially. His presence on the faculty averred African Americans' full belonging in society and their moral and intellectual equality with whites. Douglass wrote: "It is easy to see that a college established on such a foundation, is far more entitled to support, than any which may offer education to the colored man on terms which must exclude him from the society of white persons, and stamp him as being of a different, if not a degraded class."[37] The appointment of two women to the faculty conveyed a similar message. Eliza Haven and Sophia Lathrop, professors of French and English respectively, were among the first female college faculty in the United States. Haven doubled as matron of the women's dormitory, and Lathrop's name appears on the female labor list, suggesting that neither was paid the same as Reason, who did not do chores for the college.[38] Nevertheless, their inclusion among the school's faculty was groundbreaking.

The Fugitive College: 1849–52

Central College's first school years coincided with a national crisis over slavery's expansion in the West and the remand of fugitive slaves in the North. Both issues, but especially the latter, pitted individual conscience against federal law to an unprecedented degree. The Fugitive Slave Law, passed in September 1850, made it a federal crime to assist someone fleeing slavery and mandated ordinary citizens assist in renditions. The law also brought southern standards of jurisprudence north by denying formerly enslaved people jury trials or the right to testify in their own defense. By trampling the moral agency of individuals and infringing on civil liberties, these provisions outraged antislavery moderates and abolitionist radicals alike.[39] Prior to the law's passage, prominent Central College supporters, including Frederick Douglass, Samuel J. May, and Gerrit Smith, participated in a "Fugitive Slave Law Convention" in Cazenovia, thirty miles north of McGrawville. Black and white reformers gathered in a peach orchard to celebrate freedom and protest the ignoble statute pending before Congress. In addition to speeches, the program featured protest songs by Emily and Mary Edmonson, sisters who had recently escaped slavery and would enroll at McGrawville for a time before transferring to Oberlin. Also present was Theodosia Gilbert, fiancée of Central College fundraising agent William Chaplin. Besides securing support for the college, Chaplin moonlighted as a conductor for the Underground Railroad. He had helped the Edmonson sisters to freedom but was arrested in Washington, DC, for assisting others to escape.[40]

Just as the Cazenovia convention drew like-minded abolitionists from across the region, Central College became a beacon to young people who shared its reform ideals. Over the institution's lifespan, a majority of the Black and white students in the collegiate and preparatory departments hailed from beyond Cortland County and environs. However, whereas most of the whites were from upstate New York, Black students came from much further away, including Baltimore, New York City, and Washington, DC. The school's national draw underscored the scarcity of opportunities for equal education. A former fugitive was among the first matriculates of color. Sold into slavery in present-day Benin, Mahommah Gardo Baquaqua managed to escape to Haiti, where he was recruited by ABFMS missionaries to study at McGrawville. Several other former fugitives would enroll in the coming years. Central College also educated a few Native American students, at least one of whom, Mary Edmonia Lewis, also had Black ancestry. Over the college's ten-year history, students of color averaged 5.5 percent of the student body, a figure Oberlin would not match until after the Civil War.[41]

The college's egalitarian ethos made it an ally of other abolitionist communities, notably the village of Byberry, Pennsylvania. Located outside Philadelphia, Byberry was an interracial Quaker community and Underground Railroad depot. Its residents included leading African American members of the Pennsylvania Anti-Slavery Society, such as James Forten, Harriet Forten Purvis, and Robert Purvis, who had cofounded the American Anti-Slavery Society with Garrison. The Fortens and Purvises each sent sons to study at Central College rather than see them educated in local segregated schools. Among their classmates at McGrawville was Tacie Townsend, a white woman from Byberry who became the student body's unofficial poet laureate. Years later, she married the elder Robert Purvis after his first wife Harriet died. There is no evidence to suggest this interracial marriage caused controversy in Byberry. Robert Purvis later defended Frederick Douglass when he upset the Black community by choosing a white woman as his second wife.[42]

Women represented around one-third of the student body at New York Central on average, comparable to their proportion at Oberlin. Yet the ratio of Black women to Black men was much lower, roughly one to four compared to one to one.[43] Accounting for the paucity of Black women at Central College is difficult. Perhaps some chose Oberlin instead, particularly if they valued a distinctively "female" curriculum. Although Central College employed a matron to oversee women's deportment, unlike its sister school, it offered no separate ladies' degree or even a separate literary society.[44] Founders held that "the mind of woman is capable of as high cultivation as that of Man."[45] All students, regardless of sex, studied the same curriculum in the preparatory and college departments. As at Oberlin, a significant majority of male and female students enrolled in the preparatory department. Given that there were other options available for secondary schooling in Cortland County, white women likely chose Central College for its politics, its low cost, or some combination thereof. By matriculating, they demonstrated their willingness, if not their interest, to affiliate with Black peers.

Camaraderie between races and sexes coalesced rapidly on campus. Combined with the radical egalitarianism of the ABFMS, the cataclysms of the times fostered fellowship within the community. In March of 1850, pro- and antislavery forces were clashing in Congress over California's admission to the Union and the future balance of power between free and slave states. A speech of New York's junior senator, William Seward, who lived not far from McGrawville in Auburn, was among the most dramatic moments in the debate. To those who defended the extension of slavery westward with constitutional arguments, Seward thundered that there was a "higher law than the Constitution" governing the nation. The will of God took precedence where abominations like slavery were concerned. Supplanting positive law with divine law suggested the nation had entered what theologians call a *kairos* moment, one in which human history is abruptly torn from its moorings in sin and a new epoch of righteousness appears at hand.[46] Three days after Seward's speech, the Cortland County newspaper reported a kairos-like event had transpired at Central College.

What began as a guest lecture transformed into a miraculous display of interracial amity imbued with millennial significance. The leader of a nearby Cayuga tribe had been invited to campus to deliver a speech on temperance. The Cayuga were the original inhabitants of the Finger Lakes region, where McGrawville was located, and were formerly part of the Haudenosaunee, known to Europeans as the Iroquois Confederacy. Members of another Haudenosaunee tribe, the Onondaga, were also on hand visiting Baptist Scanado, Central College's lone Native student. After the Cayuga chief's lecture, dinner was served in the boarding hall. "'Caste' was cast out,'" the local paper reported, as Black, white, and Native participants sat down together for a meal of baked beans and Graham bread. A matron sang songs in French and Latin and led some of the young women in a song called "Be Kind to Each Other." The Onondagans responded with a tune of their own, presumably in their language. Mahommah Baquaqua, the recently arrived West African, chanted some Qur'anic verses he had learned in childhood. "By way of carrying out the idea," the college's president, Cyrus Grosvenor, concluded with a few words of Hebrew.[47] The "idea" Grosvenor had in mind appears to have been Pentecost. In that famous moment of kairos from the book of Acts, the Holy Spirit descended on the apostles in the form of flames, enabling them to speak in new languages. Reenacting that scene in the spring of 1850 consecrated the Central College campus as a place where dreams and visions of a new world could take root.

Some displays of racial accord were sillier than they were saintly. At one point, students put on a "Great Pumpkin Pie Jubilee" to celebrate a funny poem a classmate had written about his fondness for the dessert. The topic was actually somewhat salacious since pumpkins were associated with sexual desire in early American culture.[48] A. C. Hills's *Pumpkin Pie Offering* indicated he was as keen on the dessert as on a woman who baked it, regardless of her appearance: "Tho' brown her complexion, and hazel her eye, / . . . Provided she know how to temper a pie." His poem went on to name-check several of his male peers. In addition to one of the Purvises, Hills mentioned Jacob Gilliard, a Black student from Baltimore. The poet praised his classmate's skill "with a well-sharpened razor," conceivably as a barber. Once again, Hills made reference to color: "He does it up brown we will never deny." While the phrase connotes a job well done, given Gilliard's race, it could have been a double entendre.[49]

Gilliard may have been in on the joke because the next day he was appointed chairman of the jubilee celebration, during which college women presented a pie and some doggerel of their own to Hills and the other college men. Toasting their efforts, Gilliard saluted Tacie Townsend, in particular: "The Ladies of Byberry: Can any other *Town* send such a grateful tribute to the mighty *Hills*?" Another Black student, John F. Cook, submitted: "May our Steward and Stewardess forever be wise, / In making the students more good pumpkin pies." Whimsical as the celebration was, it showed how students at this inter-racial, coeducational institution felt free to engage in the same sort of shenanigans that were common at men's and women's colleges. At the same time, if Hills's sophomoric verses did in fact refer to race, they invoked a reality of Central College life that set it apart from other institutions of higher learning. For all the hijinks sparked by the *Pumpkin Pie Offering*, Hills's female classmates hoped he would apply his poetic talents to the cause of the enslaved:

> O, may'st thou ever fearless stand,
> And lift thy warning voice on high,
> For those who pass regardless by
> The bondman's tears, the bondman's sigh,
> Thou champion of the pumpkin pie.[50]

Somber events occasioned comradeship, too, none more so than the smallpox outbreak that struck in May 1850. Six students—one Black and five white, two men and four women—took ill. Classes were suspended, and half the students returned home. The others remained quarantined on campus, where they continued their chores and tended to the sick. "This may sound like gloom times," a student wrote her brother, but the ordeal had made her "more and more attached" to her peers, to the point she "could scarcely be *induced* to leave."[51] The upper floor of the main building was converted to a hospital for two ailing students, a white woman who recovered, and the Black man, Erskine Spring, who did not. The matron and several of Spring's female classmates "gave up their whole time in endeavors to alleviate his anguish." On his deathbed, Spring was said to have "had all the attention and kindness that could have been shown to him, had he been surrounded by his relations," who lived over one-hundred miles distant.[52] White women became the Black man's surrogate mother and sisters.[53] The morning after Spring's passing, church bells pealed as a procession accompanied his body to a grave freshly dug on the hillside west of campus. Tacie Townsend memorialized the occasion in verse: "His sun had set in manhood's prime, 'twas meet he should be borne / By his comrades, to his place of rest, thus in the early morn."[54] President Grosvenor's eulogy contrasted the excitement of prior assemblies to the solemnity of their present gathering. The "uncertainty of time" rendered earthly joys ephemeral, he said. But in an age to come, neither death nor worldly distinctions would separate the human family.[55]

In the coming years, other departed students would be buried alongside Spring. Anna Pierce, a white woman from Byberry, succumbed to meningitis in the spring of 1851, as did Robert Purvis's son Joseph.[56] Townsend composed an elegy for her Byberry neighbor praising his character and intellect. She mourned the loss of a friend whose abilities testified to the fact: "That 'tis mind that makes the true man, / God-like mind, and Mind alone."[57] The autumn following Purvis's death, a white student from Ohio also passed away and was buried in the college cemetery. An outbreak of mumps and measles in 1852 was probably responsible for the death of a white student from Vermont, who was likewise interred there.[58] Peers took up a collection for the fencing and improvement of the burial ground, a site of silent but permanent social equality on campus.[59] As one student would later write: "All of the human race are children of one Father—heirs of a common heritage, and must eventually share a common resting-place."[60]

The smallpox epidemic of May 1850 cleared up in time for commencement to go forward that July. Students were apparently allowed to select the keynote speaker, and they chose one of the most prominent antislavery and women's rights advocates in the country, Lucretia Mott. She and her husband James were members of Greater Philadelphia's abolitionist community, cofounders of the Pennsylvania Anti-Slavery Society, and frequent visitors to Byberry. In fact, Harriet Forten Purvis accompanied Mott on her journey to McGrawville. Mott's Quaker modesty famously contrasted with her radical opinions. She arrived on campus expecting to find an open forum for her ideas, but her incendiary speech proved an early test of the college's commitment to liberty of conscience. Mott parted ways with the ABFMS in her belief that religious orthodoxy furthered social problems and that individual conscience should supersede church authority. Despite having "come out" from the mainline Baptist convention over the issue of slavery, Free Mission Baptists still considered the church central to the work of social reform and embraced denominationalism in a way that other come-outer sects did not.[61] They incurred particular criticism for refusing communion to non-Baptists.[62]

Mott had no compunction about disputing their orthodoxy or anyone else's. "She hewed into modern theology with great severity," the local paper reported, "denying the divinity of Christ;—exalting reason above revelation, and dwelling upon the imperfections of the clergy with great freedom."[63] To a friend, Mott described how she "shocked the orthodoxy of the Trustees" with her comments. "They are Anti Slavery Baptists—but I had supposed sufficiently liberal to bear opposing views to their own."[64] Students admired her poise before the "formidable array" of clergy and college officials, whose authority they seldom saw questioned.[65] By insisting on the truth of her own witness, Mott defied the institutional basis of church-sponsored reform. Radical abolitionists like John Brown, Frederick Douglass, and Gerrit Smith shared a belief that the indwelling of the Holy Spirit should inspire social activism. Recognizing the kingdom of God within themselves was the foundation of their efforts to overturn worldly hierarchies, collapse social distinctions of race and gender, and bring heaven to earth.[66] That these heterodox sentiments came from a woman added to some listeners' dismay. McGrawville's Methodist minister, unaccustomed to "[measuring] lances with a lady," saw fit to rise and rebuke her "infidel sentiments." The local paper applauded him for putting "this talented, well meaning, but misguided, veteran scorner" in her place.[67]

Apart from her student supporters, who gave her a vote of thanks, Central College's Black professor was the only person who came to Mott's defense.

Charles Reason argued that Mott's supporters in the community had patiently listened to opposing views "from day to day." It was only fair that an alternative perspective received a fair hearing as well.[68] This Black man's support for a white woman's speech mimicked solidarities between white women and African Americans at Oberlin in response to that administration's paternalism. Despite its celebrated liberality, Central College remained an institution preoccupied with keeping order. Reason's subsequent clashes with Cyrus Grosvenor over the president's "unbearably willful and domineering" leadership epitomized this classic conflict between freedom and authority on campus.[69] A measure of equilibrium was restored when both men, unable to resolve their differences, resigned their positions in the fall along with several other faculty. Reason's departure was a great disappointment to the students, who greatly admired him.[70] The college secured William Allen as his replacement. The new professor was an alumnus of the Oneida Institute and a Black abolitionist famous for his eloquence.[71]

Appointing Allen to replace Reason signaled that despite dissension among its ranks, the college leadership remained committed to promoting racial equality. Students continued pursuing their abolitionist activism as well. In the fall, they submitted a commendation of William Chaplin to the *Liberator*. Their tribute praised the jailed Underground Railroad conductor for his "Philanthropy, Humanity, and Heroism." The times demanded such displays of daring, they said. Not only was "a thorough, permanent and radical reform in the unjust laws of our country" in order, but it was the duty of "each one . . . to purify public sentiment from those wicked and cruel prejudices, which recognize distinctions of caste."[72] As the Fugitive Slave Law crisis continued, students stayed abreast of the latest developments by continuing to welcome prominent reformers to campus, including Frederick Douglass, Horace Greeley, and Wendell Phillips.[73] Lucy Stone and Antoinette Brown visited in 1852. Brown was the first woman to study theology at Oberlin and had recently declined a matron position at Central College, apparently because she suspected the school would not, in the end, grant her "real practical equality—a privilege of speaking, lecturing, &c" like the male faculty received.[74] Still, she and Stone were permitted to preach and lecture, respectively, during their visit. Both wore bloomers, the long skirt and pantaloons uniform of women's rights advocates. According to an alumnus, every girl on campus was wearing bloomers within a week of their departure.[75] Future women's rights and health reformer Lydia Sayer enrolled at Central College after a ladies' seminary forbade her to wear the garment.[76]

Gerrit Smith also arrived on campus for the first time in 1852. By then, Smith was already a longtime patron of abolitionist education. He had subsidized a short-lived manual-labor school for African Americans in 1834 and sent his daughter to study at the integrated Young Ladies' Domestic Seminary in Oneida County.[77] In 1839, he donated twenty thousand acres of Shawnee heritage lands in Virginia to Oberlin (who hired a down-and-out John Brown to survey it).[78] Smith was thoroughly charmed by Central College's reform-minded atmosphere and would go on to become the institution's most steadfast benefactor. He despaired that a year after Cyrus Grosvenor's departure, the college still lacked a president. At least two candidates, an Oberlin professor and a Baptist minister, had declined the post, which would remain vacant until 1853.[79] When the minister demurred, he cited his wife's "incurable aversion . . . to the intermingling of the sexes in the same school."[80] Central College had, in fact, begun to incur public backlash for coeducating the sexes and races.

The school's charter came up for debate in the New York state assembly in 1851. A senator objected that "no distinction between the colors" was made at the institution and that "the two sexes were seated together."[81] The ensuing floor debate would "have disgraced a very assemblage of pagans," according to Professor William Allen. [82] The college was incorporated nonetheless, but the debate put the school in the crosshairs, where it would remain.[83] An Albany newspaper disparaged the McGrawville school as a "conglomerate of insanities" for teaching a white woman "the moral, intellectual, and social equality of her Ethiopian brother" and a white man "that he is in no respect superior to the negress who is his daily companion." Editors were appalled that the legislature would sanction the "unnatural equalization and commingling" of the races by chartering this "black and white college . . . where amalgamation is reduced to practice."[84] Racial and gender coeducation made Central College as vulnerable to these accusations as Oberlin, arguably more so given its outspoken egalitarianism.

When these slanders reached McGrawville, the community claimed to be unfazed. Trustees told detractors: "Our confidence in the truth of our principles is such, that we rather invite than repel examination."[85] School leaders and boosters viewed the institution as an antidote to the injustices of the era exemplified by the Fugitive Slave Law. "Men educated under the conservative influences of our pro-slavery and anti-reform institutions . . . are not adapted to achieve any great victory in favor of social or political reformation," a commencement speaker argued in 1852. If America was to regain its moral footing and freedom prevail, "we must have a class of men and women educated for the specific work of reformers," students schooled in "the inviolability of human rights [and] the equality of the brotherhood of man."[86] A white student speaker at the same ceremony agreed. John C. Porter's oration, entitled simply "Radicalism," decried moderation and incrementalism in social reform. Radicalism, he said, "never asks, Is the world prepared for the reception of so great a principle?" Instead, its exponents considered only their "immediate duty" and then "perform[ed] it," for "truth never comes too soon." Porter called on his audience not to be swayed by expediency but instead to "gaze with the clear serenity of moral rectitude" and set their faces toward heavenly ideals.[87]

However strong its faith, Central College struggled financially. Three years into its operations, the institution, by its own admission, still awaited "the confidence and support of the great mass of Northern Reformers." Disbursements exceeded expenditures, and the college's debts totaled $20,000. Trustees blamed budget shortfalls on lingering "suspicions of sectarianism" occasioned by dustups over Mott and another visitor's heterodox preaching.[88] But there were larger forces at work. In an age of fugitivity, Central College billed itself a refuge for renegade individuals and ideologies. But it was also an institution dedicated ipso facto to its own continuity. Containing two contrary impulses, revolution and conservation, under one roof was bound to produce conflict. Would-be donors hedged their bets, only to watch the situation grow more volatile in 1853.

"The Logical Results" of Social Equality: 1853–56

Central College regularly advertised its offerings in the abolitionist press. A February 1853 notice in *Frederick Douglass' Paper* avowed that contrary to the "cast[e]-bound world," the institution celebrated "the universal brotherhood of mankind."[89] Since 1849, twenty-six students of color had studied at McGrawville. The Byberry contingent had waned, deterred perhaps by pandemics that had taken the lives of two of its youth. But they were replaced by Black students from even further climes, recruited through Free Mission Society networks in Canada, the Caribbean, and West Africa. Also matriculating were

Joseph Hayden and John F. Cook Jr., members of two of the leading African American families of Boston and Washington, DC, respectively. In early 1853, there were a total of ten students of color enrolled, the most to date, representing nearly 5 percent of the student body.[90]

Within a year, that figure had dropped to four, the fewest to date. In that time, the college community was shaken to its core over Professor Allen's engagement to a white student, Mary King. Interracial marriage was legal in New York. Allen considered it "one of the logical results of the very principles on which the college was founded."[91] After all, the Black professor argued: "God has made us of one blood, and thereby to intermingle."[92] Three-quarters white, he was living proof that the union of the races could produce people of character and ability. Still, his eventual engagement put the reform college to the test. The fugitive slave crisis had arisen from beyond McGrawville to galvanize interracial communion on campus. But the Allen-King controversy arose from within, forcing the college to decide what price it was willing to pay to live out its principles. Although the community had prided itself on "[casting] out caste" on campus, endorsing interracial marriage meant defying the ultimate racial taboo.[93]

School leaders and boosters had always known Allen "meant to have a white wife," and they feared the consequences of such a marriage.[94] He courted a white woman in the fall of 1852, and after that relationship ended, he turned his attention to Mary King. They were engaged in January 1853. King's stepmother and brothers strongly objected to the match. Her father, an abolitionist minister, was initially supportive, but as public outcry mounted, he withdrew his blessing. A mob confronted Allen and King while they were visiting the home of John C. Porter, who had delivered the address on "Radicalism" the previous summer. Four to five hundred men surrounded Porter's house, and a "committee" of community leaders warned those inside that Allen would be killed and Porter tarred and feathered unless King left her fiancé and returned home. Having no choice, they submitted. The couple was kept apart for two months, during which time Allen resigned his professorship. Shortly thereafter, he and King secretly rendezvoused in New York City, where they wed and sailed for England.[95]

The professor and the trustees recalled the terms of their parting differently. When Allen resigned, the secretary of the board wrote an open letter to Frederick Douglass lamenting the professor's ordeal and attesting that Allen and the administration had parted ways "with the best of feelings on both sides."

In his version, "public prejudice and hate" were responsible for driving this "superior teacher" away.[96] Allen remembered his resignation differently. "They [appeared] anxious that I should resign," he wrote in his memoir, "though, of course, they did not express so much to me in words."[97] While it was a mutual decision, in Allen's recollection the institution's interests clearly took precedence. He explained their decision process this way: "The college had already received a terrible shock by reason of the cry of 'amalgamation' which had been raised by the mob. And though the trustees were willing, at heart, to face the storm of prejudice, worldly wisdom . . . dictated that they should not incur the odium which they could not avoid bringing upon the college, if they persisted in retaining me longer as one of their professors. The trustees thought it would be better to be cautious, and save the college for the good it might do in the future."[98] Allen supposedly became the college's agent to Europe, but for all intents and purposes, he was dismissed. Retaining him would have made McGrawville a target for mob violence. But by relieving Allen, the trustees effectively upheld racial caste.

Abolitionists despaired of the scandal at Central College and bemoaned how Allen and King's marriage exposed "how few [people] . . . believe in the great doctrine of equal rights . . . [or] admit that God is the Common father of us all."[99] Some critics placed the blame on school leaders rather than on the circumstances. They chastised its overseers for reneging on their college's promise of full equality by not standing by Allen. One commentator compared the trustees to a character from *Uncle Tom's Cabin*, Miss Ophelia, the Yankee transplant whose abolitionism thinly veils her racism. Like her, Central College leaders "[meant] honestly to be reckoned philanthropists," but "many of the departments, after all, don't feel so in their hearts."[100] Scholar Karen Woods Weierman maintains that when all was said and done, the African American professor's departure demonstrated the staying power of racism: "At the end of the day, New York Central College was glad to see Allen go, and the narrative of Black inferiority triumphed."[101] While the school would live on to fight prejudices that excluded African Americans from education and respectability, it would not challenge society's deepest assumptions about hereditary racial difference.

This synopsis is accurate in the main, but it discounts the small but significant victory that Allen and King's engagement represented. Although their engagement and elopement transpired rapidly, the two had discussed the potential repercussions of their marriage for months prior, even separating for a time to consider the matter dispassionately. Only after lengthy deliberation did King assent. Allen called hers an act of "moral heroism," one that exposed his wife to "the anathemas of the community" and made her "an almost total outcast, not only from the society in which she formerly moved, but from society in general."[102] Were it not for her education in social equality at Central College, she might never have summoned the strength to defy her family and follow her heart across the color line. "I have endeavoured to solve, honorably, conscientiously and judiciously, the greatest problem of human life," she wrote, not race per se but fear for the unknown. Accepting Allen's proposal of marriage, King told him: "God and the holy angels have assisted me in thus solving."[103] Even if her alma mater did not always practice what it preached, her time at McGrawville had taught her to live out her ideals. Among those taken by the couple's bravery was the novelist Louisa May Alcott, whose uncle, the abolitionist Samuel J. May, briefly chaired Central College's board. At the height of the Civil War, Alcott published a short story inspired by Allen and King's romance.[104]

The other overlooked party in the scandal are the students who remained at Central College. White enrollment did not diminish in the wake of the Allen and King's marriage. The student body grew 16 percent the next school year to 434, and whites accounted for the entirety of the increase.[105] Allen's ouster may have reassured some prospective students that the college was not as radical as had been rumored. Others, it seems, saw the college's notoriety as a selling point. "The world will frown upon me, because I am a student of this unpopular institution," wrote freshman Angeline Stickney. "If this is fanaticism, I will glory in the name."[106] Stickney embraced her alma mater especially for the educational opportunity it extended her as a woman. Under other circumstances, her Black peers might have expressed similar sentiments. Yet the Allen-King controversy seems to have strained their relationship with the school. Some may well have felt betrayed by the administration's treatment of Allen. Others may have feared that threats to the professor would be redirected toward them in Allen's absence. It is also possible that the uproar created a rift between Black and white peers, and that African Americans began to feel less welcome on campus. Whatever the case, only one of the ten Black students enrolled in 1852–53 returned the next fall.

A report by the white teacher of Central College's elementary class—the institution's most integrated—spoke to the contingencies of interracial fellowship in McGrawville in the wake of Allen-King scandal. Writing to the trustees in July 1853, Kezia King (no relation to Mary King) claimed the school's "experiment" in racial coeducation had still "not been fully tested." True, she said, integration promised to place a Black student "where his maker placed him—on the broad and elevated platform of human rights, the basis of which is equality and the common brotherhood of the human family so ruthlessly torn down and trampled upon by Slavery." Yet from the teacher's observations, even when Black students equaled or outnumbered white classmates and matched them intellectually, African Americans still had whites' "ignorance to contend with on the one hand, and prejudice, the legitimate offspring of ignorance, on the other."[107] Mahommah Baquaqua, the West African who delighted school audiences with recitations from the Quran, confirmed his teacher's impressions of racism in the community.

Baquaqua's autobiography is the only surviving account of Central College life authored by a Black student. His narrative shows that not all white students at McGrawville were committed to reform, particularly not those in the lower grades. Despite the fanfare that accompanied Baquaqua's arrival on campus, his classmates harassed him mercilessly. Foreign, uneducated, older, and especially dark-skinned, Baquaqua became a target.[108] "Some of the young gentleman [*sic*] there . . . played considerable many practical jokes upon me, and tried to make me some mischief with the principals," Baquaqua recalled. They scattered his papers, shuffled his books, and stuffed wood shavings in his chimney to make it smoke. His only recourse was to report them to teachers, which became tiresome. "I did not like to be continually complaining of them, so I endured a great deal of their vexatious tricks in silence." He sensed his features made him less sympathetic to his peers. Pondering "why they plagued me so," he could only surmise that his tormenters "did not like my color, and that they thought I was a good subject upon which to expend their frolicksome humor." Kezia King affirmed that Baquaqua's background and color doubly disadvantaged him. A poem she wrote for him to recite (and which he included in his autobiography) begins:

> You can't expect one of my race,
> With wooly hair and sable face,
> And scarce a ray of knowledge
> To interest his friends at college.

Light-skinned, well-educated Black men like Professors Reason and Allen might earn the esteem, even love, of white students. But Baquaqua's travails showed that not all people of color at Central College could expect ready acceptance.[109]

Allen and King's marriage made Baquaqua's situation in McGrawville even more precarious. The summer after the professor resigned, rumors circulated around Cortland County that the African student intended to marry a white girl, a fellow member of a nearby Baptist church. The young woman's mother forbade Baquaqua from visiting her household. When whispers of their imminent elopement persisted, he was warned to stop attending his own church for fear that violence might ensue. Public pressure forced Baquaqua, like Allen, into exile. "I have a great trouble with these wickit [*sic*] people," he told a correspondent in the fall of 1853. A few months later he left Central College for the ABFMS mission in Canada.[110] The next academic year, all but one of the Black students were new to McGrawville. "[This] school has not secured for it that degree of popularity with the colored people that was anticipated by its founder," the trustees' report observed in 1854.[111]

The effects of the professor's ordeal on Black enrollment were significant but temporary. As the cloud of controversy over McGrawville lifted, the total number of Black students returned to earlier levels and remained steady. In 1854, eight matriculated and three returned, bringing the Black percentage of the student body to 4 percent.[112] Five Black men enrolled in the college course that year, where only one had previously. Renewed matriculation may have simply reflected a lack of advanced educational opportunities for African Americans elsewhere in the Northeast. Another newcomer to McGrawville was George Vashon, who was hired to take William Allen's place. If the college was wary of endorsing the complete social equality of the races, it was still willing to defend their intellectual equality by hiring another African American to fill a vacancy. Since becoming the Oberlin's first Black graduate in 1844, Vashon had also become the first African American admitted to the New York state bar. He struggled to secure clients as a Black attorney, however. Needing to support himself and his deceased sisters' children, he turned from law to education. At Oberlin, he had been a mentor to the young John Mercer Langston, who remembered him as "a person of rare scholarly character, attainment and name . . . and a teacher of unusual ability."[113] Vashon would go on to teach

John Bunyan Reeve, New York Central's first Black graduate and Howard University's first theology professor.

Reeve and two other African Americans were among the few dozen students selected from the collegiate and preparatory departments to speak at the public exhibitions marking the conclusion of the 1854–55 school year.[114] It was a banner year for Central College academically. Total enrollment was virtually unchanged, and the collegiate department boasted its largest ever classes. The first bachelor's degrees were awarded at that year's commencement. Before Gerrit Smith gave the closing address, five graduates delivered speeches and received degrees. All were white men apart from Angeline Stickney, the white woman who had reveled in her alma mater's progressive politics. A year earlier, the trustees had predicted: "Should all who believe in the superiority of the principles of this school unite their means and influence . . . all our wants would be met."[115] Yet by 1855, the college reported debts of $16,000, with mortgage and capital costs yet to be paid off. Subscriptions pledged to meet the balance totaled only $10,000.[116] Agents reported that the general public remained reticent to give, still skeptical, it seemed, of the abolitionist college.[117]

Anemic fundraising led to penny-pinching on campus, notably in the form of pay cuts for faculty.[118] Three of the nine professors in the fall of 1855 were newly minted graduates of the college, who were presumably willing to work for less. One of them was John C. Porter, whose sheltering of his friends Allen and King had cost him any chance at local school teaching.[119] The modest qualifications of new faculty may have contributed to the outflow of students from the collegiate department. Enrollment there fell 40 percent between 1854–55 and 1855–56. The number of women coming from beyond Cortland County and environs also plummeted in that span and continued declining, suggesting the preparatory program was losing its broad appeal or faced competition. Total enrollment at Central College dropped 8 percent between 1854–55 and 1855–56. The next year, it declined another 11 percent, as the preparatory department witnessed an exodus of men hailing from far beyond Cortland County.[120] Apparently, fewer and fewer white students felt Central College was worth the trip. The decline set up another political showdown on campus. Realist administrators squared off against the reform-minded students and faculty who remained. Just as they had in 1853, concerns for the college's future would collide with defenses of its values in 1857.

Going for Broke: 1857–58

On March 6, 1857, the US Supreme Court handed down its notorious ruling in *Dred Scott v. Sandford*. Chief Justice Roger B. Taney's decision deemed African Americans "altogether unfit to associate with the white race." Because they were "beings of an inferior order," they possessed "no rights which the white man was bound to respect."[121] The very same day as the court's decision, the *Liberator* published a sequence of letters concerning New York Central College, the first from the school's new president, Leonard Calkins. In contrast to Taney's claim that Black people had no natural rights, Calkins declared that "color has nothing to do in making a true man." His institution would continue admitting any Black student "on terms of perfect equality with the white student," since both belonged to "the brotherhood of the human family." These sentiments earned the school endorsements from prominent radicals like Gerrit Smith and the Transcendentalist minister Theodore Parker, whose testimonials ran below Calkins's article. Parker, who had recently visited campus, wrote admiringly of the faculty's "self-denial" where salaries were concerned. "I do not know where more good may be done with a little money," he concluded, indicating both the promise of the institution and the extent of its hardship.[122]

A final appeal from Azariah Smith, one of the alumni professors, reiterated the school's predicament. Central College was the sort of cause *Liberator* readers should embrace, Smith wrote, an institution where "all, without invidious distinction, have been welcomed, and have enjoyed equal facilities." Despite the school's abolitionist credentials, however, Smith lamented that too many reformers were still "waiting to seek excuses for not thus aiding" the school. The qualities radicals most admired about the college were precisely what made it difficult to raise money among anyone else. "We cannot, unaided by you who sympathise with us, build up this Institution so that it shall accomplish all the good it ought to," Smith explained. If abolitionists would not support Central College's "high mission," who would?[123] School leaders would do their best to keep administrative costs balanced with revenues, but as long as the mortgage remained unpaid, the institution could not survive, at least not in its current iteration. Increasingly, pressure to moderate the college's image accompanied the need to cut costs.

These overlapping concerns ensnared George Vashon most of all. Although the professor was by then one of the longest serving members of the faculty

THE RISE & FALL OF NEW YORK CENTRAL COLLEGE, 1848–1860

and was admired by students as "'the best-read man in the college,'" he was told his job was in jeopardy.[124] More and more, the administration's criterion for employing faculty was who could work for the least pay. Vashon received only half of his $400 salary for the 1856–57 school year. The younger professors could scrimp more easily, perhaps, but Vashon had his sister's three children to support. President Calkins advised him that his future on the faculty would depend on his finding work for his dependents. It was an especially exasperating suggestion considering Calkins had just informed one of Vashon's nieces that he could no longer afford her housekeeping. The steward of the boarding hall likewise could not find the money to keep his other niece on.[125] Vashon told Gerrit Smith he had come to Central College "with the hope of freeing myself from pecuniary difficulties." Now he feared he would have to leave Mc-Grawville for the same reason.[126]

While finances were the stated reason, the professor suspected racism also made him vulnerable. He learned there was a growing feeling among the trustees "that it is the duty of the College to dispense with colored teachers in order that it may become an object of popular favor."[127] Vashon doubted that school leaders would ever discriminate "avowedly," but he suspected it would be in their interest "if they did not employ another colored teacher in the position." The Dred Scott decision had devalued Black people's humanity, officially endorsing white supremacy. As long as "the spirit of caste prevailed to any extent in this country," the presence of a Black man on the faculty could dissuade the public from supporting the institution, no matter how popular the professor was with the students.[128] Radicals might celebrate Vashon's appointment, but goodwill did not pay the bills. At the end of the school year, Vashon wrote the trustees for clarification on his "anomalous position." Despite the specter of racism, he repeated his desire to be retained as a professor: "I love N.Y. Central College and am deeply interested in its welfare."[129] The trustees' reply, if they made one, does not survive. Vashon and the children left in November 1857, returning to Pittsburgh, where he became principal of the city's Black schools.[130] Later he would become Howard University's first Black professor.[131]

Four other instructors had also departed by the end of 1857. Azariah Smith and his brother Metcalf were among the four faculty—three of them Central College alumni—who resigned in protest that summer. Their departures came in response to what they considered a violation of the college's principles by President Calkins.[132] As usual, several collegians delivered speeches at graduation. Trustee Samuel J. May praised the student addresses, claiming there would not be "anything better given forth at Harvard" and singling out the speeches "colored brethren" as "among the best."[133] Missing from the dais, however, was Lewis Spaulding, a white student whose name appeared in the program. At the last minute, it seems, President Calkins forbade him from delivering his address. The speech he wrote was an homage to Transcendentalism in the mode of Ralph Waldo Emerson. In it, Spaulding criticized the church for inserting itself between humanity and God. People should instead cultivate the divine within, he said, and express godliness in their actions.[134] The president denied rejecting the essay on religious grounds; he may have merely interpreted Spaulding's speech as insolent since it rejected vested authority.[135] Still, the president's meddling rekindled debates about sectarianism and free speech on campus that had been smoldering since Lucretia Mott's visit in 1850. The *Liberator* published the address with a headnote from Spaulding. He accused Calkins of betraying the college's reform values, principles that the president himself had reiterated in the *Liberator* only a few months earlier. Like critics of the Allen-King affair, the new graduate rebuked the administration for its hypocrisy in executing the institution's ideals.

Spaulding was among the twenty-seven students—almost the entirety of the collegiate department—who signed a public testimonial to their departed professors in October 1857. Their statement expressed regret at their teachers' departure and attested to the men's devotion "to carry out the fundamental principles of this institution." Besides extending their appreciation, they conveyed their concern for the health of the college's ideals. Signers voiced their "earnest desire . . . that New York Central College may succeed in meeting the demands of a progressive age, by showing itself the truthful exponent of the noble and humane principles upon which it was founded."[136] Yet the Spaulding fiasco and Vashon's departure put the future of those ideals in doubt. Professor Metcalf Smith and his younger brother Judson, a student, departed McGrawville for Jefferson County, Indiana. There they continued their educational activism as members of the faculty of Eleutherian College, another Free Mission Baptist institution "open to all without regard to sect, sex, or color."[137] At least 18 of Eleutherian's 109 students were African American.[138] The Indiana school was only a little better off financially than its New York counterpart, however. In the winter of 1856, its president wrote Gerrit Smith of "the great difficulty we find in raising funds" and solicited his aid.[139]

Central College's 1858 commencement exercises would be the college's last. John Bunyan Reeve received his degree at the ceremony, making him the first and only Black recipient of a bachelor of arts from Central College.[140] Four of the institution's five remaining African Americans were also among the student orators and poets. Left off the program was the young Mary Edmonia Lewis, the last remaining woman of color.[141] That summer, she and three other Black classmates departed McGrawville for Oberlin.[142] It had become clear to them that New York Central would not reopen in the fall. The school's latest report to the New York Board of Regents indicated its debts had increased 9 percent over the previous year, while pledges had fallen 40 percent.[143] The Panic of 1857 had set off a worldwide economic crisis, which made the already difficult work of raising subscriptions impossible. With bankruptcy looming, the trustees persuaded Gerrit Smith to buy the college property. The college's wealthiest booster purchased the main edifice and some surrounding land for less than a third of what they had cost ten years prior.[144] Smith pledged to maintain the vacant campus. If the trustees could raise enough money, he would mortgage it back to them. Even after Smith's purchase and the forgiveness of other debts, however, the college still owed creditors nearly $5,000.[145] For the time being, Central College closed.

Twilight Years: 1859–60

Gerrit Smith did not promise the New York Central College trustees exclusive rights to the McGrawville campus. Early in 1859, he corresponded with a separate group of village residents about buying the property for use as an academy, but negotiations stalled. Privately, Smith favored a third option: creating an entirely new college with his friend James McCune Smith at the helm and Charles Reason and George Vashon forming the core of the faculty. He and McCune Smith, a preeminent Black physician and public intellectual, had apparently tossed around the idea as early as 1857, perhaps in response to Vashon's troubles. Now McCune Smith conferred with Reason in New York City about the hypothetical school, which the doctor dubbed "Gerrit Smith College." "I would rejoice to see you woven into the coming years by just such an institution," McCune Smith told his philanthropist friend, "and would rather see you found and foster it during your life . . . than have you leave it to others to establish when you are no more." The new school would extend the values of social equality and social activism that radical abolitionists held dear. Gerrit Smith trusted McCune Smith and the others to carry forward these ideals more than he did the Central College trustees. If the original trustees were ever to pay the debts and reopen the school, Smith expected them to begin making mortgage payments after the first year of operations.[146] But he offered his friends the school gratis and promised to underwrite a new president's salary for five years.[147]

McCune Smith had two conditions for assenting to his friend's offer. First, the college's student body and its leadership should be integrated. McCune Smith recalled he had once advocated the founding a predominantly Black trade school. During the National Colored Conventions of 1853 to 1855, he, Frederick Douglass, Charles Langston, and Charles Reason had advocated the founding of a coeducational, industrial institute specifically, although not exclusively, for African Americans.[148] The manual-labor school they envisioned would have been controlled by African Americans instead of white benefactors. In the five years since, McCune Smith had come to realize that African American associations could not yet afford to support Black higher education by themselves. Pittsburgh's Avery College, a minority serving institution founded in 1849 as the Allegheny Institute, had a Black president and trustees, McCune Smith among them, but it depended on white patronage. The physician supported the school because it encouraged economic mobility, but he still held out hope for the future of social equality in the United States, whereas others associated with Avery increasingly espoused Black nationalism and emigration.[149] If Gerrit Smith College was to succeed as a force for racial justice, attracting white and Black students alike, McCune Smith felt "it would be preferable to have the Instructors as well as the Trustees partly black men, partly white men." He predicted "a purely 'black college' in the present day would meet with cordial support from neither black men nor white men," given the political winds.[150]

The second condition was financial. Gerrit Smith College would need an endowment to protect its principles, the sort of financial cover Central College never had. Fifty thousand dollars was McCune Smith's estimation, enough to pay the salaries of the instructors for the near term and maintain the college's ideals. The doctor pledged to raise $10,000 if the school's namesake could promise the remaining $40,000. "It is a large sum for you to give to this cause," McCune Smith recognized, but a necessary one. "If worth undertaking at all in your part, this matter is worthy of being placed by you on a safe and successful basis."[151] Land rich but cash poor, Smith told his friend he could not afford to donate any more than the college property and the president's salary. "I cannot see my way clear in regard to McGrawville, unless the College be endowed," the doctor replied in March 1859.[152] Gerrit Smith College would remain a pipe dream.

In the months that followed, Gerrit Smith suffered a nervous breakdown after John Brown's raid at Harper's Ferry, a foiled insurrection aimed at ending slavery. Smith had helped to finance the disastrous uprising. After his release from the New York State Lunatic Asylum, he significantly curtailed his activism.[153] Central College, an institution almost renamed in his honor, became just another asset on his balance sheet. By April 1860, the trustees had managed to raise enough money to settle its debts and staff the school.[154] A circular printed in July promised that Cyrus Grosvenor would return as president and that the school would dispense with "the restrictions, usually deemed expedient, regarding sex, or other adventitious circumstances."[155] Unlike earlier New York Central promotions, however, the circular made no mention of color. A white woman from Cortland County wrote a note to her brother on the back of one surviving copy. It reads in part: "You must send some of those sutherners [sic] here as I don't think there will be any collord [sic] ones here now at least I hope not for I am going there myself."[156] Black students may not have been proscribed, but judging from this one piece of evidence, white students were not eager to study with them. In the end, it seems no African Americans matriculated. Although enrollment records from this period do not survive, of the Black residents listed on the 1860 census for McGrawville, none lived at the college.[157]

Returning faculty were appalled at the institution's reversal on racial justice. The reinstated President Grosvenor lamented the betrayal of Central College's "great and sacred political principles" by new trustees, whom he claimed were intent on "forever excluding all colored persons from its advantages."[158] Warning signs had appeared after the Republican National Convention in May 1860, when "it was seen that the principles of the school were in advance of the principles of the party." Grosvenor criticized the new, moderate trustees for not embracing abolition and racial equality as the institution once had. They responded by calling his fitness to lead the college into question.[159] Financial mismanagement accompanied this administrative infighting. Neither inspired public confidence in the restored college. All of its fundraising agents were dismissed in November 1860 amid allegations of embezzlement.[160] Their replacements struggled to secure subscriptions to pay faculty salaries and make necessary improvements. Even "the citizens who do not oppose the College are wearied out with perpetual calls for money," faculty reported to Gerrit Smith.[161] The school fell into disrepair, and instructors resigned, leaving Grosvenor to assume all teaching responsibilities. Matters worsened as winter set in. The school filed a legal complaint in December against its former treasurer and agent, who was accused of stealing furniture and stoves.[162] With no place to sit and no way to keep warm, all but a few students left. The college shuttered for good.[163]

The abortive revival of 1860 showed the foresight of James McCune Smith and his preconditions for establishing Gerrit Smith College. A radical, integrated institution stood little chance of prospering absent the safeguards he outlined. When Gerrit Smith mortgaged the campus back to the Central College trustees, he hoped that the newest iteration of the school might preserve its "original reform character."[164] But after Lincoln's election and in the lead-up to southern secession, northern sentiment shifted strongly against abolitionists, who were viewed as the cause of the growing sectional crisis. Free African Americans also became the targets of mob violence.[165] In this political climate, the countercultural values on which Central College was founded would have needed even larger endowments to sustain them. Instead, in 1864, local investors turned the college into an academy, which in turn was converted into McGrawville's public high school in 1868. New York Central College lived on in histories of Black education thanks to scholars like Carter G. Woodson, but the school's collapse consigned it to relative obscurity.[166] Even in McGrawville (eventually renamed McGraw), public memory of the institution warped. In 1944, a local newspaper column reported on the state of the college graveyard. The article claimed that all those buried in the cemetery were Black. Moreover, it described the institution as having served "young Negro men and women" exclusively. Related news clippings from the time show that the community shared these misunderstandings.[167]

The college's long absence had effaced its history of racial coeducation. Its failures as an institution eclipsed its successes as an experiment. Central College's ideals were crafted by its founders but realized by its students and faculty—Black and white, male and female. It was they who were responsible for bringing principles of freedom and equality to life, sometimes in ways that unsettled school leaders, as in the cases of Lucretia Mott and Lewis Spaulding's addresses or William Allen and Mary King's marriage. Campus celebrations, memorials, and exhibitions demonstrated the potential of Americans of different races and sexes to enact democratic visions in community. The college's principles quickly became its calling card but also its cross to bear. Being all things to all people made for regular excitement and near permanent volatility on campus. Innovation and institutionalism operated in tension on campus, with each trying to prevent the other from achieving its most radical or conservative ends. Not only did instability repel donors, it jeopardized the well-being of Black students and faculty. African Americans stood most to gain by New York Central's survival. They suffered most from its demise.

3

OBERLIN'S BLACK ALUMNAE
AND THE NEW BIRTH
OF FREEDOM
1852–1867

When Frederick Douglass moved his family to Rochester in 1848, he enrolled his nine-year-old daughter Rosetta in Seward Seminary, a private academy for girls. Seward's principal was willing to admit Rosetta, but the school's trustees protested. As a compromise, Rosetta was placed in a separate classroom apart from her peers. Douglass was enraged when he learned of his daughter's segregation. The principal tried justifying her actions by polling Rosetta's classmates, expecting they would resent a Black girl joining their classroom. When, to her surprise, they eagerly welcomed Rosetta, the principal polled their parents. Only one objected, but that was enough for the principal to keep Rosetta out of the classroom. Douglass withdrew his daughter and for the next seven years lobbied to integrate Rochester's public schools. Rosetta, meanwhile, studied with private tutors and enrolled in Oberlin's preparatory department in 1854.[1]

Young Black women like Rosetta Douglass faced tremendous obstacles in acquiring advanced education. In an era when most colleges excluded both African Americans and women, Oberlin was the premiere exception. Between 1833 and 1865, its student body included 140 women of color. Black female enrollment surpassed Black male enrollment in 1850. Two years later, they outnumbered them nearly two to one. By the end of the Civil War, fifty-six Black women had studied for bachelor's or literary ("ladies'") degrees, with three earning the former and twelve the latter.[2] Higher learning was a path to empowerment for African American females, doubly disenfranchised by virtue of their race and gender.[3] The adversity they faced along the way sometimes proved its own education.

Black feminist Patricia Hill Collins coined the phrase "outsider within" to describe the wisdom African American women glean from institutional experiences of gendered racism.[4] Regular confrontations with intersecting forms of discrimination lends special insight into the structures of racial and gender disenfranchisement. That was certainly the case for the four Black Oberlin alumnae profiled in this chapter, women for whom the personal was always political and the political personal.[5] The educations and early careers of Fanny Jackson (Coppin), Mary Edmonia Lewis (Fig. 3.1), Blanche Harris (Brooks) (Fig. 3.2), and Sara Stanley (Woodard) coincided with a pivotal moment in American history: the cataclysmic shift from slavery to emancipation and eventually to Black citizenship. These four women did more than simply witness that transformation. They marshaled the knowledge they learned as outsiders within to

FIG. 3.1. Mary Edmonia Lewis.
Courtesy National Portrait Gallery, Smithsonian Institution.

FIG. 3.2. Blanche Virginia Harris.
Courtesy Oberlin College Archives.

help shape debates about the pace and scope of reform. Their everyday activ-ism, what period reformers called "practical abolitionism," exposed the contin-ued workings of racism, both beyond and within the antislavery movement. Through editorials, letters, and artwork, they informed white abolitionists of the obstacles to racial equality postemancipation and proposed means of erad-icating prejudice.

Jackson, Harris, Lewis, and Stanley studied at Oberlin between 1852 and 1865. Their school careers partly overlapped, but there is no evidence any two of them were well-acquainted. They grew up in different regions of the coun-try and under different circumstances. They followed different paths while at Oberlin as well, enrolling in its academic programs for varying lengths of time. Stanley and Lewis left before finishing their courses of study (which was not uncommon), while Harris completed the literary course in 1860 and Jackson the bachelor's degree in 1865. After leaving Oberlin, Lewis pursued sculpting, while the other three became teachers, two in the South and one in the North.

For all these differences, they came of age at a dynamic moment in American abolitionism. At every level of the movement, African Americans took the lead, exercising their autonomy as political actors and directing the course of the campaign for Black freedom.[6]

Some of the foremost African American male activists of the 1850s and 1860s were Oberlin alumni, figures like William Howard Day and John Mercer Langston. John Anthony Copeland and Lewis Sheridan Leary fought in John Brown's Provisional Army at Harper's Ferry. Neither was an Oberlin alumnus, but both were Oberlin residents. A year prior, Copeland was among those indicted for participating in the celebrated Oberlin-Wellington Rescue, when an interracial posse of abolitionists liberated the fugitive John Price from his captors. The 1858 episode amplified Oberlin's reputation as the country's leading antislavery community. John Langston's older brother Charles, one of Oberlin's first two Black students, along with their brother Gideon, was also among the participants who were subsequently tried. The incendiary speech Charles delivered at his sentencing was widely printed in the northern press. Langston called on African Americans to defend their God-given equality in light of the Dred Scott decision's judgment to the contrary. Addressing the Fugitive Slave Law, the statute under which he had been charged, Langston declared resistance to be a matter of "self-protection" for Black citizens. Vagaries of the law made rendition a threat to anyone with dark skin. But the Oberlin alumnus also made his case in terms that transcended race. "We have a common humanity," he told his white listeners.[7] It was human nature to defend one's freedom and human decency to defend others.' Moved by Langston's eloquence, the judge greatly reduced his sentence and fine.

Langston and other Black male abolitionists often couched their appeals in the language of "manhood," arguing racism kept them from fulfilling the essential duties of their gender.[8] Harris, Jackson, Lewis, and Stanley could make similar arguments about their womanhood. Yet knowing the special mixture of prejudice arrayed against them as women of color, they, like Langston, invoked universal standards of human rights. Theories of polygenesis, the idea that the races were in fact separate species, were on the rise among American ethnologists in the 1850s and 1860s, as were white nationalist visions of America's future as a purely Anglo-Saxon nation. Defying a scientific racism predicated on the idea of inevitable racial conflict and a Manifest Destiny that made no room for any but whites, these Black women activists insisted on the races' consanguinity as children of God. Shared humanity should be the foundation of a postemancipation, pluralistic United States, they argued.[9] As emancipation dawned, each alumna demanded that the recognition of full and fundamental equality precede the fight for equal rights. Defeating prejudice would be a tall order, taller even than ending slavery. Black women knew better than anyone else that the odds were long. But from lifetimes of belonging to the most maligned subset of Americans, they also knew the cost of inaction. When the Civil War ushered in an era of revolutionary possibility, they seized the moment and pushed for change.

School Days: 1852–63

Harris, Jackson, Lewis, and Stanley were already better educated than most Black women of their time when they entered Oberlin. Each arrived with enough prior schooling to receive advanced standing within the preparatory department or enter the ladies' course directly. Sara Stanley came to college from New Bern, North Carolina, where her parents ran a school for free Black children. She and her childhood friend Ann Hazle (Fig. 3.3) enrolled in Oberlin's ladies' course in 1852. Neither joined the Oberlin Female Moral Reform Society, a women's circle devoted to promoting sexual virtue among men and women. Its participants included a disproportionate number of African Americans, including Sarah Margru and Mary Edmonson. Historian Carol Lasser finds that in 1852, Black women were twice as likely as white women to join the Society; she argues membership afforded them the opportunity to assert racial and gender equality.[10] Agitating for social purity also refuted defamations of Black women as licentious, a slander that perversely originated in the rape of enslaved women.[11] As Black female southerners, Stanley and Hazle may have deemed the topic too fraught to discuss week after week.

The North Carolina pair must have adhered strictly to the campus code of conduct because they managed to escape the dragnet of the Ladies' Board of Managers, the disciplinary body that policed college women's behavior. Lasser shows that in the early 1850s, despite representing only 5 percent of the female population, Black women made up 42 percent of those called before the Ladies' Board.[12] Most of the cases they adjudicated concerned individuals, but a year before Stanley and Hazle's arrival, the board investigated a scuffle between Black and white students on a town sidewalk. Two Black women, Josephine

FIG. 3.3. Young Female Graduates of the Class of 1855.
Ann Hazle is pictured second row, *center.*
Courtesy Oberlin College Archives.

Darnes and Penelope Lloyd, had encountered three white women coming the other way. Two of them were townspeople, but the other, Caroline Heldman, was a current student. After "neither part would give the walk," a fracas sent Heldman into the muddy street. She "retaliated by applying several vile epithets to the colored ladies." Lloyd and a Black classmate, Caroline Wall, composed a send-up of the incident and delivered it before their writing class, which included Heldman. The Ladies' Board made Heldman apologize but also required Lloyd and Wall "acknowledge the impropriety of their conduct" in parodying the incident.[13] The episode showed the administration's insistence on mutual respect but also displayed how a culture of modesty could make it difficult for Black female students to pursue both respectability and equality. When push came to shove, getting justice for their race could mean violating the polite expectations of their gender.

Sara Stanley may not have been as vocal as others about racial issues while at Oberlin, but she was certainly outspoken afterward. Family troubles forced her to leave college early. The harassment of North Carolina's free Black community drove her family to migrate to Delaware, Ohio, where Sara rejoined them. Although she was not able to complete the ladies' degree like her friend Ann Hazle, Stanley left Oberlin prepared to become both a teacher and an activist.[14] One of her greatest strengths was as a writer. In an 1856 petition she authored on behalf of the Delaware Ladies' Antislavery Society, Stanley demolished popular notions of Black inferiority. "Let American religion teach adoration to the demon Slavery. . . . Let scientific research produce elaborate expositions of the inferiority and mental idiosyncrasy of the colored race"; she dared, "one truth, the only essential truth, is incontrovertible:—The Omnipotent, Omniscient God's glorious autograph—the seal of angels—is written on our brows." In recognition of her eloquence, Stanley was made an honorary member of a Black fraternal organization, the National Young Men's Literary Association, in 1862. She worked as a teacher in Cleveland until 1864, when she joined the American Missionary Association.[15]

Blanche Harris also grew up in a household that deeply valued education. Michigan was one of the few states that permitted African Americans to attend its primary schools. Once Harris completed her studies in 1855, her parents moved the family to Oberlin so that she and her siblings could further their education.[16] She became the first of her siblings to make good on her parents' dream and complete one of Oberlin's courses of study. Along the way she and three other Black classmates joined the Aeolian Literary Society. African Americans exceeded whites in their rates of literary society membership on the eve of the Civil War. One hundred percent of the eligible Black men and women enrolled in 1860 eventually joined a literary society compared with 65 percent of white men and only 21 percent of white women.[17] Harris's generation took full advantage of opportunities to demonstrate their abilities and empower themselves. Among her fellow Aeolians was Mary Jane Patterson, who became the first Black woman in America to earn a bachelor's degree in 1862.

Following in Harris's and Patterson's footsteps was Fanny Jackson, who arrived on campus in 1860. Born into bondage in Washington, DC, Jackson was the child of an enslaved woman and a white politician. She grew up an orphan until an aunt purchased her freedom at age thirteen. The two resettled in Newport, Rhode Island. Jackson found work as a maid in one of the city's elite households. Being in service placed her, as she put it, "in contact with people of refinement and education."[18] Jackson learned to play piano and sew but spent most of her free time studying. After primary school, she entered the Rhode

Island State Normal School. Once she finished its teacher education program, she set her sights on Oberlin. She enrolled in the ladies' course in 1860, but her real prize was a bachelor's degree. After completing the prerequisite classes, she qualified for admittance in 1861.

Jackson arrived at Oberlin a year after Mary Edmonia Lewis, another orphan. Apart from that, the two had little in common. Lewis was seven years younger, the daughter of a Black man and Chippewa woman. She had spent her adolescence among her late mother's tribe. That experience educated Lewis in Native ways but left her relatively unschooled in white social norms. Her "quickness and brusqueness of voice and motion" were ascribed by one white abolitionist to "want of drill in the conventional rules of society."[19] Many would interpret her ignorance of social graces as insolence. With the support of her brother, a California gold miner, Lewis entered New York Central College in 1856. She remembered how her teachers there admonished her for being uncouth: "[I] was declared to be wild,—they could do nothing with me."[20] Lewis struggled in arithmetic and especially grammar.[21] Teachers attributed her difficulties to her Indian heritage rather than her lack of preparation. They encouraged her to stick with "the book of Nature" over classical study.[22] Central College was unequipped to nourish her artistic talents. When the institution folded, Lewis and other Black students left for Oberlin. Its fine arts offerings, however limited, may have made transferring palatable to Lewis. She studied for a year in the preparatory department before matriculating into the ladies' course.

Compared to Stanley's or Harris's time on campus, Jackson's and Lewis's college careers are far better documented. The two became the subject of significant public interest for their actions as Black women at Oberlin in the middle years of the Civil War. For Jackson, distinction meant fame; for Lewis it meant infamy. Jackson's refined manners and scholastic ability helped white students more readily see her as one of them and inspired white faculty to appoint her Oberlin's first ever Black instructor. For want of these qualities, Lewis was more easily characterized as a racial other, even a menace.

Both women boarded in the homes of college leaders. Mary Lewis was assigned to the home of John Keep, the college trustee who had cast the deciding vote in favor of Black admissions in 1835. Whatever early reservations he once harbored about "a mass of negroes at Oberlin . . . [darkening] the whole atmosphere" appear to have dissipated as the community's Black population grew.[23] Keep's vote had opened the door to their settlement, and they hailed him as a "venerable friend and advocate . . . for the cause of the oppressed."[24] Into his retirement, he promoted Oberlin's endeavor "to break down the cruel prejudice against colour" and receive Black students "on an equal footing with their white brethren."[25] He and his wife kept close watch and ward over Lewis, who was only fifteen when she arrived and therefore on probation by the Ladies' Board. The Keeps had a reputation for housing only "ladies against whom no tongue of slander could be used."[26] Lewis was given her own room; whether by her request or by custom is unclear. Students of different races did not generally room together, even off campus. The other dozen boarders in the Keeps' home were white. One account claims that Lewis and her housemates were "friends" who enjoyed each other's company and confidence.[27] Another indicates some of the boarders were "in the habit of 'running on' [her] considerably."[28] Likely she was the target of at least some teasing, if only for her accent and eccentricity.

For most of her Oberlin career, Jackson boarded in the home of Professor Henry Peck, a zealous abolitionist, editor of the *Lorain County News,* and future US minister to Haiti. The Pecks had invited Jackson to recuperate at their home after she got sick from the food at the Ladies' Hall her first year. A few days' convalescence turned into a few years' residence. Jackson remembered being "treated with the most disinterested kindness" by the Pecks and the other boarders. She appreciated how she was made to feel "an honored member of the family circle."[29] Jackson made friends fast and was invited to join the Ladies' Literary Society.[30] Still, the polite atmosphere of the Peck home and the larger campus could make it difficult to share her struggles as a woman of color. Pursuing a bachelor's degree in the 1860s remained a daunting path for any Oberlin woman, especially if she was Black. As Jackson recollected, nearly twenty-five years after the first four women were permitted to pursue bachelor's degrees at Oberlin, "the faculty did not forbid a woman to take the gentleman's course, but they did not advise it."[31] When she entered the college course in 1861, she invariably stood out as one of only a handful of African Americans among the department's two hundred students and one of only three Black women. The other two were Mary Jane Patterson and Frances Josephine Norris. Like Jackson, both were light skinned. Patterson was a free woman of color from North Carolina who grew up in Oberlin and graduated from the college course in 1862. Norris, the daughter of a Georgia enslaver, would graduate with Jackson in 1865, although she may have completed her coursework a year earlier.[32]

Despite the college's claims to impartiality, color-blind rhetoric could make whites oblivious to the continued significance of race at Oberlin. College officials had long insisted that "mind and heart, not color, make the man, and the woman, too."[33] Oberlin's goal was "to break down the barrier of caste" and "elevate [African Americans] to a common platform of intellectual, social, and religious life" with whites.[34] To achieve this end, they instructed that every student be "judged according to his character and scholarship and not according to any extrinsic circumstances."[35] Although Jackson praised Oberlin's liberal creed, she also indicated that its color-blind standard did not completely erase the significance of color on campus. In the classroom she still felt the burden of race acutely: "I never rose to recite in my classes at Oberlin but I felt that I had the honor of the whole African race upon my shoulders. I felt that, should I fail, it would be ascribed to the fact that I was colored."[36]

Jackson illustrated the dilemma in her memoir when she recalled an exchange with a white housemate. Once during a study session at the Pecks', one of her housemates suddenly stopped to ask Jackson if she had ever been enslaved. "I said yes; and she burst into tears." The question exposed an uncomfortable truth: despite their ostensible equality, a member of their circle had suffered in ways the others had not. Still, Jackson appears to have appreciated the acknowledgment: "Not another word was spoken by us. But those tears seemed to wipe out a little of what was wrong."[37] The exchange recognized the obstacles Jackson had faced in getting to Oberlin, barriers unknown to her white housemates. She wanted to be accepted for who she was—for her color and her past, not in spite of them. Her memoir shows how she treasured friendships that transcended race without discounting it. Reminiscing about her college years, she thanked several white students who eased her adversity with their kindness: "I can never forget the courtesies [of those] who seemed determined that I should carry away from Oberlin nothing but most pleasant memories." Of the classmates she included by name in her memoir, all nine were white, five men and four women.[38]

Although Jackson valued her friendships with whites, she also appreciated opportunities to spend time with other African Americans. Fondly she remembered the open-door policy of John Mercer Langston, who lived across the street from the Pecks. Since graduating from the theological course in 1852, Langston had become the first African American admitted to the Ohio bar and, in 1857, the first Black man in America to hold elected office. Besides serving as Oberlin's town clerk, he also held appointments on the town council and board of education and remained active in the affairs of his and his wife Caroline's alma mater.[39] The Langstons were known for providing "a warm welcome to colored students."[40] At least one subsequent Black boarder at the Pecks, future Wilberforce president William Sanders Scarborough, also frequented the Langstons' parlor.[41] Having a Black social space afforded Oberlin students of color a place of refuge and solace set apart from the primarily white environment in which they lived. Seven-tenths of a mile away at the Keeps' house, Mary Lewis did not enjoy the same convenient access to the Langston home. Still, she knew to seek out the attorney when trouble arose. In February 1862, Langston defended Lewis against charges of poisoning two of her white housemates. Whereas Jackson's experience at the Pecks demonstrated the possibilities for interracial camaraderie, Lewis's ordeal reiterated the difficulties women of color still faced in receiving the respect and trust of their peers.

Since Lewis had no other place to call home, she passed the long winter break at the Keeps and attended remedial classes ahead of the next term. One day in late January 1862, two male students invited two of her housemates on a sleigh ride to the town of Birmingham, Ohio, where one girl's family lived. The night before, all the young women of the house stayed up late chatting. The two girls admitted to feeling somewhat sick, though not enough to warrant canceling their trip. The next morning, Lewis invited the pair to her room for a hot drink to fortify them against the cold. Reportedly the three "had once had a difference," so Lewis's gesture seemed conciliatory.[42] She prepared three glasses of warm spiced wine, apparently drawing on a secret stash, since school rules prohibited alcohol. Her guests drank up, but Lewis decided the concoction was too cold for her taste.[43] When the young men arrived, everyone gathered in the yard to see them off. Part way into the nine-mile trip, the girls became seriously ill. On reaching Birmingham, they took to bed, but not before accusing Mary Lewis of having poisoned them. Local physicians confirmed the diagnosis. Based on the symptoms only (no physical evidence was recovered), they identified the toxic agent as cantharides, or "Spanish Fly," an aphrodisiac known to inflame the kidneys. Lewis maintained her innocence. Anticipating a trial, her attorney Langston traveled to Birmingham accompanied by a surgeon. The doctor visited the girls and declared that absent any physical proof, it was impossible to determine conclusively that they had been poisoned. Locals remained convinced of Lewis's guilt, however, and very nearly took out their aggression on Langston. On his way out of town, the Oberlin lawyer narrowly avoided being shot by one of the girls' fathers.[44]

Interestingly, it was not the girls' parents who "caused the arrest of the suspected girl" but the father of one of the young men.[45] His family hailed from Berlin, Ohio, more than sixty miles from Oberlin. Apparently, his father went to great lengths to see Lewis charged and without delay. If he was eager to place his son above suspicion for drugging the girls, he had the perfect scapegoat in Lewis, and not merely because she had served the girls wine. Her identity as a Black-Native woman made her especially vulnerable to charges of dealing in the dark arts. Women of color had been charged with meddling in potions with wicked intent since the colonial period.[46] Departing the Keeps' house one evening, Lewis was waylaid by assailants, who took her to a nearby field, delivered a brutal beating, and left her for dead on the frozen ground. Given the sexual implications of Spanish Fly, Lewis's abduction and assault resembled a lynching: a Black person punished for purportedly violating white women's bodies. The attack was nearly fatal. For several days thereafter, Lewis lay as bedridden as her accusers. Langston's recognizance saved her from having to recuperate in jail after her arrest. Classmates had to carry her into the courtroom when the trial commenced.[47]

"No case ever tried in Oberlin or originating in that community, had produced such popular feeling as this," Langston later wrote. As many townspeople thought Lewis guilty as innocent. Some were "prejudiced against the accused on account of her color," yet "the major part of the colored people themselves" also thought Lewis to blame. Langston attributed African Americans' opposition to Lewis's "easy and rather unusual social relations to the whites." She lived "after the style and manner of a person of ample income," thanks presumably to her brother's wealth.[48] Some may have felt she took too many liberties or got above herself with her high-spiritedness or her fancy clothes. Black Oberlinites' readiness to "pronounce her guilty in advance" suggests they did not like her. Perhaps they did not know her at all if she kept to herself or socialized only with whites. Lewis's Native heritage would have also made it easier to cast her as an outsider to the African American community. Some Black Oberlinites discouraged Langston from defending the young woman: "An aged lady among them expressing their feeling in a general way, told him that he had better not attempt such a thing."[49] Even some of the most prejudiced whites respected Langston.[50] The stature that came with his law practice and his public service made his representing Lewis synonymous with the larger Black community's support for the young woman. It seems some hesitated to stand with someone accused of such a crime.

School leaders approached the scandal with caution. An official inquiry into the poisoning incident would have reflected poorly on the Keeps. More than likely the administration did not wish to embarrass one of Oberlin's most venerable families by probing how alcohol—let alone aphrodisiacs—could have been kept under their roof. When Henry Peck and the staff of the *Lorain County News* finally addressed the controversy in an editorial, they took pains to note that "the young lady, who furnished the wine . . . has always borne the highest character." Lewis's conduct had heretofore been "exemplary," they said, perhaps in a nod to the Keeps' care. Still, intemperance was a serious offense, one that could not go overlooked. But it paled in comparison to sexual immorality, which was vigorously guarded against at the coeducational college. The Spanish Fly element of the case was too shocking for the paper to even mention. "The facts in the case are of such sort that it would be improper for us to pass any judgment upon it," the editorial demurred.[51]

Besides protecting the Keeps from embarrassment, Peck and his staff seemed determined to defend Oberlin's color-blind standard. They noted that Lewis "had been assailed . . . by ruffians who almost took her life, and up to the present time she has hardly been able to leave her bed." And they acknowledged that despite her otherwise commendable behavior, her "color subjects her to prejudice." Nevertheless, they had "hitherto refrained from speaking of the matter," believing that "the ends of justice would be best promoted by our silence." It was not Lewis's assault that finally spurred them to action but rather accusations from Burlington "that the people of Oberlin are not willing to have the case brought to a trial." The *County News* was writing to correct the record. Their editorial reported that Oberlin's mayor had promptly attended to the charges against Lewis. Moreover, "the people of Oberlin will not only not stand in the way of a fair trial, but will forward it by all means within their power." Justice would be served, but on whose behalf? All "candid and just people" would accord Lewis "the common rights of law," yet the paper made no mention of a separate investigation into her assault.[52] Indeed, neither the town nor the college would make one. Reciprocity was rarely a woman of color's privilege.

A few weeks later, the *County News* reported: "Tedious examination of witnesses in the alleged poisoning case . . . results last week in the discharge of Mary

Lewis."[53] At trial, the two girls, their boyfriends, the doctors, and a few others had appeared as witnesses. Lewis herself had not taken the stand. As expected, the Burlington physicians attributed the young women's sickness to poisoning by cantharides.[54] But after the surgeon testified that proof of Spanish Fly required specimens and not merely symptoms to diagnose, Langston moved that the case be dismissed. No physical evidence of the poisoning had been preserved by the other doctors, he pointed out, which rendered their analysis inadmissible. A spirited debate between the attorneys concluded with the court sustaining the defense's motion.[55] The judge dismissed the charges and set the young woman free. Classmates carried her out of the courtroom, this time in triumph.[56]

The trial did wonders for Langston's reputation. The gambit put the lawyer's acumen on full view. As he remembered, "The expressions of admiration, compliment, and praise, bestowed . . . were numerous, cordial and flattering." Langston's performance occurred amid a national debate as to whether soon-to-be free African Americans were "susceptible of higher cultivation" and thus deserving of emancipation and citizenship.[57] Langston's brilliant legal display was a testament to Black intellect. According to the attorney, even "a white gentleman coming from the South . . . exalted his appreciation of him." Langston also recalled a "change which came over the colored people through the results of the case." The same older woman who had warned him against defending Lewis hosted a congratulatory dinner for him, "distinguished as well for the number and character of her guests as the richness and abundance of the repast."[58] It is unclear from Langston's account if Lewis was invited. His achievement was as much the cause for celebration as her exoneration.

Langston later claimed Mary Lewis's character had been "fully vindicated" by the judge's ruling, and historians have since argued her acquittal confirmed the Oberlin community's commitment to racial justice much like the rescue of John Price in 1858.[59] No doubt Lewis received as fair a trial for such a charge as any Black woman of that era could have hoped for. Still, the failure of local authorities to investigate her assault illustrated the incompleteness of Oberlin's progress toward equality, as did Lewis's ostracism in the wake of the poisoning scandal. Once tarnished by such allegations, her respectability proved impossible to restore. Lewis remained under the Keeps' care and had their sympathy, but her social life seems to have suffered. "Look out for Spanish Flies!" white classmates joked behind her back. One referred to Lewis as a "wench," an epithet that connoted the social and moral inferiority of women of color.[60] As friends failed her, art became Lewis's refuge.

On the night of January 2, 1863, newspapers bearing the text of the Emancipation Proclamation arrived in Oberlin. A crowd of Black and white students and townspeople spontaneously assembled to celebrate the day of freedom so long awaited and so long delayed. Almost twenty-eight years earlier, the college community had pledged itself to slavery's abolition with the formation of the Oberlin Anti-Slavery Society. Now some of those same individuals gathered on campus with dozens more. Their dream had at last become a reality. John Keep, who presided over the impromptu celebration, called on John Langston to read the document. Many of Langston's listeners were, like him, the children of enslaved people; some had even been enslaved themselves. He read the Proclamation twice, as if to rebuke the institution on behalf of its victims living and dead. Later that evening, amid the crash of fireworks and the thunder of cannon salutes, a crowd of African Americans paraded triumphantly to Langston's home, where the usually loquacious lawyer could manage only a few words on the day's significance.[61]

Pariah status may have kept Lewis from fully enjoying that remarkable evening. In February, she was accused of stealing art supplies and a picture frame. Once again, a lack of evidence shielded her from prosecution but not retribution.[62] That Lewis, scarcely eighteen years old, had been at the center of two town scandals was grounds enough for her expulsion from the Ladies' Department. The spring 1863 term would have been her final semester, but its principal, acting on her own authority, refused Lewis's registration. "I don't care if she can't graduate for it will humble her some," a white classmate sneered, echoing earlier impressions of Lewis as arrogant.[63] Effectively expelled, Lewis lingered around town for a time before leaving for Boston, where John Keep had helped arrange for her training as a sculptor.[64] In an act of artistic redefinition, she started going by her middle name, Edmonia. Once she became an established artist, the local paper quipped: "If Miss Mary E. is none other than Miss Edmonia, she is indeed enjoying a checkered career."[65]

Lewis was suffering in her final year at Oberlin, but Fanny Jackson was thriving. For all her self-consciousness as an African American woman in the bachelor's degree program, she excelled at her studies. To her, higher learning was a "delightful contest," one for which she was both well suited and well prepared.[66] Besides the benefit of a year's preparation in the ladies' course, she also had the support of her housemates when it came time to tackling difficult subjects like advanced Greek. Jackson refined her skills as a writer over her four years. In 1863, her ode to the 54th Massachusetts Infantry, the nation's first African American regiment, was published in a leading Black magazine and reprinted in Peck's *Lorain County News*. Jackson's poem praised Black troops' valor while denouncing their former exclusion from the Union army: "When their offers were spurned and their voices unheeded, / And grim Prejudice vaunted their aid was not needed."[67] Classmates recognized her literary talents when they elected her Class Poet in 1865. Hers was the largest graduating class in Oberlin's history, making her selection especially impressive.[68] Jackson's abilities helped elevate her to an unprecedented level of responsibility. In 1863, she was the first African American chosen as an instructor in the preparatory department, making her one of the first Black teachers of white students in American history.[69]

Faculty like Edward Henry Fairchild, Jackson's supervisor as principal of the preparatory department, defended the intellectual equality of African Americans in the press.[70] Yet Oberlin hesitated to appoint African American tutors even after Jackson broke the color barrier. None of the other five Black students studying in the college course with her in 1863 was selected. Eight years later, the situation was unchanged. In a letter to a national reform newspaper in 1871, a critic writing under the name Don Carlos assailed the college for not hiring any Black tutors since Jackson. He sarcastically observed that at Oberlin, having "a black skin totally incapacitated [someone] for teaching the pale-faced Christian."[71] An African American who had studied at Oberlin wrote into the *New National Era* under the moniker "One Who Has Suffered" to corroborate Don Carlos's analysis. "What the writer says about the faculty not permitting colored students to teach in the preparatory department is, alas, too true. The faculty has always urged that it was 'inexpedient' for colored students to teach."[72] James Fairchild, Henry's brother, who by that time had succeeded Charles Finney as Oberlin's president, denied that race or expedience was a factor in tutor appointments. The hiring process was highly selective, he explained. Typically, Black students did not have high enough grades to be among the 20 percent of eligible students chosen or their "success [as a teacher] was doubtful" for some other reason.[73] Dozens more Black collegians studied at Oberlin through the turn of the twentieth century, but only one, Anna Julia Cooper, class of 1884, is known to have been appointed a tutor.[74] An 1895 history of Oberlin showed how far the situation had deteriorated by that point.

Without a hint of irony, the white author marveled at how African Americans there enjoyed access to "teachers of pure Caucasian blood to bestow upon [them] all reasonable assistance."[75] The idea of Black instructors doing the same for whites was clearly beyond his ken. Presumptions of whiteness help account for the long delay in Oberlin College appointing a Black man to any teaching position. The college hired Wade Ellis as assistant professor of mathematics in 1948, ninety-five years after the trustees' ruling on race and hiring.

A combination of factors account for Jackson's unprecedented selection. Appearance and deportment mattered significantly in the faculty's assessment of her fitness for teaching. In 1864, when Henry Fairchild wrote Mary Jane Patterson a letter of reference for a teaching position, he described her as a "a light quadroon, a superior scholar, a good singer, a faithful Christian, and a genteel lady."[76] No doubt the principal and the other faculty judged Jackson by similar criteria when they appointed her at Oberlin. According to James Fairchild, tutors were "selected with reference to Christian character, scholarship, aptness to teach, and general personal influence and power." But the single most important criterion was "the prospect of their success."[77] For Jackson, thriving in the classroom would mean preempting objections from white students and parents. Her aptitude and character had to be unimpeachable. Age gave her additional credibility in the classroom (she was three years older than Patterson). Finally, normal school training made her better prepared than other undergraduates, white or Black, to assume teaching responsibilities. She had already proven her talents as a volunteer instructor in Oberlin's night school for newly freed African Americans.[78]

Although the appointment of a Black teacher was overdue, the timing was ominous. The ecstasy of the Emancipation Proclamation in January 1863 had given way to draft riots and attacks on African Americans in New York that summer. Jackson recalled the "very bitter feeling . . . exhibited against the colored people of the country, because they were held responsible for the fratricidal war then going on." Under the circumstances, she appreciated the faculty's "moral courage" in selecting her. Still, she remembered administrators' saying: "If the pupils rebelled against my teaching, they did not intend to force it."[79] A Black woman appeared less threatening than a Black man teaching white students, especially young white women, yet gender bias could compound racial prejudice. One white student was purportedly "flaming with indignation" after arriving at his first recitation and learning "his teacher was a *woman,* and a BLACK woman." He vowed to leave Oberlin in protest, but one of the matrons "persuaded him to a little delay," believing the young man would change his mind after a few lessons.[80] By her own account, Jackson's passion and preparation helped her counteract any misgivings. "Fortunately for my training at the normal school, and my own dear love of teaching, tho[ugh] there was a little surprise on the faces of some when they came into the class, and saw the teacher, there were no signs of rebellion."[81] In fact, thanks to her prowess, her classes became some of the most popular in the department. The same bigoted white student purportedly came to "[prefer] Miss Jackson to any other teacher."[82] Enrollment swelled to eighty, at which point Principal Fairchild had to divide her class in two. Visitors to her classroom were frequent, and her achievements were covered widely in the reform press.[83]

Critiques of Color Prejudice: 1864–67

Experiences at Oberlin and in other reform settings gave Jackson, Lewis, Stanley, and Harris a window into the white racial imagination. The conflicts they encountered in these avowedly abolitionist settings exposed the limits of whites' egalitarianism and, in turn, the bedrock prejudices on which race and gender were constructed in the mid-nineteenth century. In response, they crafted appeals for equality aimed at overcoming a fundamental obstacle to racial justice: whites' incapacity to see Black people as natural equals. Many reform-minded whites believed it was their duty as Christians to act with charity and forbearance toward African Americans. But these four women exhorted would-be allies to take an even greater leap of faith. Black alumnae tried to teach white reformers to see African Americans as God did, as coequal members of the human family. If whites were to be emancipated from prejudice, they would have to lift up their hearts and recognize the races' kinship in the body of Christ.

Jackson was the first to issue a call to repentance. Her manifesto came one year into her tutorship in response to allegations of discrimination at Oberlin. In the spring of 1864, the *Commonwealth,* an abolitionist newspaper from Boston, reported that white students in Oberlin's preparatory department had mounted a campaign to deny their Black classmate, Richard Greener, a speaking part at the annual literary exhibition. Students in each department nominated their peers to participate. Given Greener's ample academic ability (he would go on to become Harvard's first Black graduate), the paper attributed his snubbing to the resentment of his white peers. Principal Fairchild acknowledged Greener's worthiness of the honor but refused to order a new vote. "So much for Oberlin!" editors of the *Commonwealth* grumbled. "When we think of the prejudice that meets the black man everywhere, and add this instance, at such a Seminary, we must feel there is a need of more discipline yet for the American people."[84] While racism may have motivated Greener's opponents, painting all of Oberlin's "educated white young men" as prejudiced overstated the case. As historian Linda Perkins notes, older white students in the collegiate department elected an African American classmate to a speaking role at the same event.[85]

With John Langston's support, Fanny Jackson published a response to the *Commonwealth*'s story in the *National Anti-Slavery Standard*, the weekly paper of Garrison's American Anti-Slavery Society. "Prejudice at Oberlin is preached against, prayed against, sung against, and lived against," Jackson wrote. The faculty judged every student "with uniform respect and kindness." Professors set an example of "high toned and upright character," especially Henry Fairchild. Jackson defended the principal's treatment of Black students, noting from her own experience that he "is always pleased when he has the opportunity to accord them any unusual honor." To be sure, prejudice existed "in some of the students." Oberlin was "not the pool of Bethesda for the sin of prejudice," she wrote, alluding to the place of divine healing in ancient Jerusalem.[86] But overall, the campus "[came] nearer to it than any other place in the United States." In a preface to Jackson's article, Langston endorsed her testimonial as "a fair and truthful statement," one that did "justice to the good people of Oberlin."[87]

Langston and Jackson defended their alma mater, but her rebuttal revealed that the *Commonwealth*'s call for "more discipline" from whites did, in fact, resonate with her. Jackson conceded that the acceptance she found at Oberlin as a woman of color was not a foregone conclusion. On the contrary, she characterized antiracism chiefly as work, the hard labor of pure love. Bigotry was an insidious creature of "human nature." The staying power of prejudice made it difficult to suppress. Her instructorship revealed firsthand how successive cohorts of young white students brought the "mean and vile sentiment" with them to campus. From her teaching experience she knew well that "the moment [whites] enter the purer atmosphere of Oberlin they do not immediately divest themselves of it." Oberlin would not be "entirely free from prejudice" until the

Day of Judgment, when "America washes her robes of her national sin." In the meantime, Oberlinites were called to begin the work of redemption, laboring in anticipation of the world's ultimate renewal when Christ returned.[88]

Keeping prejudice at bay required conscious effort, and Jackson reminded readers of Christians' obligation to resist racism in thought, word, and deed if they would be "Christ-like." In her view, "true Christian refinement of character" entailed cultivating selflessness, not "[attaining] a high state of civilization." For someone who had against all odds dedicated herself to higher learning, this was a statement of remarkable humility. Jackson believed "there is an upper as well as a lower stratum of humanity." But what determined a person's ranking was not one's achievements but one's capacity for compassion. At its root, the spirit of wisdom was a spirit of understanding. Jackson claimed whites achieved this moral standard when they "regard a colored man as a man, and do not consider that they are conferring a favor upon him by so doing." Oberlin faculty showed themselves African Americans' "true friends" because "their sympathy is not a milk-and-water article, such as it degrades one to receive." The word "empathy" had yet to enter the English language at the time of Jackson's writing.[89] But from her experiences seeking solace after being "slighted" or receiving "a sly thrust," she could attest to the depth and sincerity of the faculty's concern: "It is genuine, it soothes, it revives."[90]

In this fight against prejudice, Jackson never asked special treatment for her people, but she did claim racial bias would require special education to unlearn and special effort to withstand. "Human nature in Oberlin is about the same as human nature in New York," she observed, "until it has taken a collegiate course, and not unfrequently [sic] it requires a theological [course] to purify it entirely." It was not surprising, then, that white preparatory students—"the less cultivated"—would discriminate against a Black classmate while their collegian counterparts would not. Empathy was a critical sensibility that took time as well as care to develop. Its more sophisticated practitioners among Oberlin's faculty recognized that compassion could be multivalent. In some places, she described the kindness of her teachers as "uniform" and "disinterested," suggesting objectivity. Elsewhere she praised Principal Fairchild, who, "while . . . strictly just to both parties, has always shown the most thoughtful kindness in regard to the colored students."[91] To her, this was no contradiction. The most agile mind was an open one, and vice versa. Discerning souls knew which moments obliged an even hand and which a generous heart.

Less than two weeks after Jackson's essay was published, Sara Stanley began issuing similar calls for compassion to her white colleagues at the American Missionary Association. The eloquent Cleveland activist and educator had joined the AMA earlier that year, becoming one of its first Black teachers. Like Jackson and Mary Jane Patterson, Stanley's light skin tone may have helped her get the job. "I am a colored woman," she wrote in her application, "having a slight admixture of negro blood in my veins." Stanley expressed her strong desire to apply her teaching skills to raising the newly freed people of the South "from the pale of humanity, into the family of man." She couched her application in the paternalistic idiom of the missionary organization, noting her desire to effect "the moral and intellectual salvation of these ignorant and degraded people." However, she characterized the formerly enslaved chiefly as "heirs of the kingdom of Heaven," beloved by God no less than her or the white leaders of the AMA.[92] Like so many African Americans who became freed people's teachers, Stanley felt specially called to aid her race: "By the ties of love and consanguinity, they are socially and politically, 'my people.'"[93] The AMA assigned her to the Union-held city of Norfolk, Virginia. She arrived in April 1864.

Stanley's pupils proved more considerate than some of her colleagues. The teaching staff of the Bute Street School was racially mixed. They reported to the same school, housed in the church of Oberlin alumnus John Mifflin Brown, coauthor of the 1841 "Expression of the Sentiments of the Colored Students." AMA teachers also lived in the same boarding houses. Stanley believed maintaining a united front among Black and white missionaries was essential. If their enterprise was to prosper, "there should be a Christian unity and sociality among the laborers." She admired the example of "kindness, forbearance, and love" set by the Norfolk mission's white superintendent, William Woodbury. His manner starkly contrasted the tone of his temporary replacement, William Coan, who assumed leadership of the mission when Woodbury returned home to New England for the summer. Stanley and her compatriot Edmonia Highgate wrote Woodbury in protest over Coan's "negro-hating principles and malign prejudices," sentiments they could not abide. "When great principles are involved[,] I deem silence criminal," Stanley seethed. Coan was guilty of "advocating the inferiority of 'negroes' and the necessity of social distinctions" among the teachers, she claimed. In so doing, he revived the spirit of racial caste that undergirded slavery, jeopardizing the entire mission. "I fully and heartily concur with my gifted friend," Highgate added in a postscript.[94]

Coan had objected vociferously when Highgate hosted a white AMA teacher from a different mission. Coan and another white staffer took offense to women of different races sharing a room, if only for a night. They also used the occasion to gripe about the other forms of social equality practiced at the mission house. Stanley did not dispute anyone's right to "select his own circle of acquaintances" under other circumstances. However, she insisted that "here in the missionary field, it is different." The AMA held itself to a higher standard; it had to if it was to present a new model of racial equality for the South and the nation to emulate. Stanley made clear she was not advocating intermarriage. A Democratic smear campaign against Lincoln had recently stoked fears of that prospect, coining the racist term "miscegenation" (a neologism meaning "the mixing of kinds") to describe the supposed endgame of his administration's emancipation policy.[95] Although Stanley herself would marry a white man in 1868, she knew that the topic of interracial marriage was to be avoided, even among abolitionists. What she asked instead was that the AMA's discipleship be undertaken "as one family" of Christians, in reflection of their common creation by God "of *one* blood." Their ministry would gainsay Jesus's teachings if it did not rest on the "fundamental and elementary constituent" of the Gospel: "the brotherhood of man."[96] "The deep underlying principle" of their work had to be the recognition of "the Son of God in the person of a negro." Without such displays of empathy, teachers could never hope to gain the trust of the freed people, who "[knew] intuitively who is faithful to their interests." Stanley explained that as a woman of color, she could "perceive more clearly than others the deleterious effects of [Coan's] influence." She begged Woodbury to return quickly before any more damage could be done.[97]

Coan was eventually transferred to another mission, but Stanley continued encountering prejudice among other white staff. That fall, the new matron of the mission house balked at its racial integration and demanded the Black teachers living there relocate. This time, Stanley wrote directly to AMA general secretary George Whipple, former Lane Rebel and Oberlin graduate. Her letter avowed that there was nothing "defective" about the character of the mission's Black teachers to justify their ouster. She and the others deserved to be "treated with the deference due any other lady," respect Stanley was accorded when mistaken for white. "Oh the profound wisdom of this prejudice against color!" she groaned. "When one half shade difference is to determine whether an individual is to be respected or despised." What was needed was a "pure and catholic spirit of love," one that did not scrutinize skin color or insist that "the great desire of all hearts should be to be near a Saxon complexion." Adopting this ethos would incur God's favor, she claimed. The hard-hearted alternative represented no less than a "demon," hell-bent on squandering this moment of promise.[98]

Stanley could not dismiss racism as the rot of a few bad apples. The stakes of the AMA's work were too high to make exceptions. Stanley stated her case for egalitarianism in terms of individual merit. Because "the character of nations, communities, societies depend on the character of individuals composing them," she reasoned, "there can be Truth, Honesty Equity, in the whole, only as these qualities inhere in individuals." Just as every Christian bore the name of Christ, all those engaged in "the cause of human elevation" must hold themselves to a higher standard of humanitarianism and be held to it. This tension between personal prerogative and collective responsibility would only magnify in the coming years as laissez-faire individualism gained favor among reformers. For her part, Stanley refused to accept a white woman's supposed right to disrespect her as a Black woman. "I have no desire to change my place of residence in compliance with the wishes of any teacher," she told Whipple, "willing however to accede to any arrangement that your better judgment may determine."[99] Effectively, she dared the AMA to evict her. They did not.

Blanche Harris encountered similar prejudices several months later at her second AMA posting in Natchez, Mississippi. After completing the ladies' course, she became one of the AMA's first missionary teachers in Norfolk. Harris arrived late in 1863, several months before Stanley. Her experience there was far more positive than Stanley's, perhaps because all of the other teachers Harris worked with were Black. She was appointed principal of a school of over two hundred freed children and adults. Edmonia Highgate was among the school's three teachers, and William Woodbury was a source of support to her like he was to Stanley. "I feel that God is in our midst," Harris wrote hopefully of their labors.[100] When serious illness forced her resignation in April 1864, she was crestfallen. Harris returned to Oberlin to recuperate. In time, she reapplied for a posting and was assigned to Mississippi in October 1865. Natchez would prove as trying to her psyche as Norfolk had been to her health.

Harris's duties at her new posting closely resembled the work she had been doing in Virginia, but the atmosphere in Mississippi was decidedly different. She kept a busy schedule teaching children in the mornings and adults in the afternoon and evenings and helping coordinate weekly sewing circles and singing classes. And she worked closely with two other Black teachers, one of whom was her younger sister Frances. Unlike at Harris's previous posting, however, she did not live in the mission house, nor did she receive much support from the mission's leader, Oberlin alumnus Palmer Litts.[101] "I cannot go to the Superintendent as I did at Norfolk for sympathy," she explained in a letter to George Whipple. Instead, she and the others were "left to the mercy of the Colored people or themselves." Before the war, Natchez was home to Mississippi's largest free Black population.[102] Because their middling backgrounds resembled those of the AMA's African American teachers, Black locals were especially concerned about the educators' treatment. "The distinction between the two classes of teachers (white and colored) is so marked that it is the topic of conversation among the better class of colored people," Harris noted. She did not offer specifics about her experience, determined, it seems, to avoid any impression that she was ungrateful or sullen. "Mr. Whipple, pray for me that when my trials are heaviest that I may have more grace," she wrote, demonstrating her humility while inviting his concern. From her prior service in Norfolk, Harris had established a reputation as an enthusiastic educator. She knew she could awaken Whipple to the injustices at Natchez with a letter that was not "full of cheerfulness" per usual.[103]

When Whipple responded soliciting more "facts" about her situation, Harris felt at liberty to detail the state of affairs at Natchez. She began by clarifying her feelings about residing outside the mission house. Harris and the others "preferred" staying in the Black community, believing "our influence would be greater, if we were to board with our own people." Nevertheless, they resented how mission leaders had extended this opportunity in bad faith. Whites' feelings toward Black teachers became apparent when Harris took sick with dengue fever. Arrangements were made to move her into the mission house. But she was informed she would not be rooming with the other teachers, nor dining at the "first table." She would sleep and eat with the servants. Harris "might come in the sitting room sometimes," but otherwise she was confined to her room. The steward of the mission house claimed it was merely a precaution against mob reprisal.[104] Regardless, to Harris and her Black supporters, it was an insult they would not tolerate: "I consulted with some of the old citizens (colored) [and] they did not think it would be right." Instead, Black civic leaders put up the funds for Harris and her sister's room and board elsewhere. Their school's enrollment nearly doubled, another indication of the trust they had built within the community. But Superintendent Litts and the other mission officials were threatened by the Black women's success. White leaders "seemed determined to have us go in the country or any place but Natchez," Harris explained. "And the colored people seemed equally determined to have us remain, and they would support us."[105]

Politely but firmly, Harris made the case that whites' pride threatened to undo the entire AMA mission at Natchez. Superintendent Litts, she said, had "lost the confidence of the greater and richer portion of the colored people here" by announcing Black teachers would be barred from teaching at a new school the AMA was building. His words all but guaranteed that African Americans with means would not contribute to the project. The steward did not help matters when he remarked that the Black teachers "could not compare with the white ladies," women of equal if not lesser education. A minister sympathetic to the Black teachers responded to Litts with sarcasm. Had Harris and the others somehow "lost [their] knowledge coming down here" to Natchez, he asked the steward? Sharing this comeback with Whipple was as far as Harris would go in criticizing any AMA official. She left the general secretary to form his own conclusions. "Should we resign you will know the case," Harris told him matter-of-factly. As before, she closed with pathos. She and her fellow teachers were sometimes "discouraged" by their circumstances, but they kept faith in God's protection "when all others forsake." She would not impugn whites' motives, at least not directly. But as for her and her sisters, their purpose was clear: "We wish to do right."[106] That they demanded to be done right in return went without saying. Harris left Natchez a few months later. Fed up, it seems, with the AMA, she took a job working for a Quaker association in North Carolina.[107]

Whereas Harris, Stanley, and Jackson bore witness to injustice with words, Edmonia Lewis made her testimony in stone. Sculpting satisfied her creative desire to "make the forms of things"—not just the physical world, but the world's ways.[108] After her ordeal at Oberlin, Lewis claimed that were it not for the chance to pursue an artistic career, she would have sworn off society altogether and "[returned] to wild life again."[109] Art afforded possibilities that American life, as of yet, did not. As an artist and activist, Lewis pushed the limits of representation beyond appearances. Her work anticipated racial formation theory in her attention to the way social structures construct and replicate race.[110] "I have not one drop of what they call white blood in my veins," she boasted, rejecting white supremacy.[111] "Some praise me because I am a colored girl," but she scorned any condescension.[112] Lewis wanted to be judged firstly as an artist. She drew notice for her early works depicting white abolitionists and reformers, including John Brown, Diocletian Lewis, and Robert Gould Shaw. In the words of one contemporary critic, the "genius" of her oeuvre proved that regardless of her racial identity, she bore "the image of Him who made all nations under the sun."[113]

Besides revealing her considerable talents, Lewis's sculpture gave form to a vision of interracial empathy that transcended her personal history and anticipated America's liberation from prejudice. Like her fellow Black alumnae, Lewis recognized the need to reorient white minds so that they might recognize the suffering of others. To open their eyes to the plight of the oppressed, she enlisted the trope of the imperiled white female, a symbol whose resonance she had learned firsthand from her near lynching. Unlike her portrayals of African and Native American men, Lewis's depictions of women of color often abandoned verisimilitude by representing these women with white physiognomies, an effect compounded when her clay models were translated into white marble. While she never shared her rationale for doing so, her pieces addressed the racism at work in society and disrupted the racial gaze of her audience. As art historians have argued, white viewers expecting to draw parallels between the sculptor and her subjects were instead confronted by versions of themselves.[114]

After joining an artist's colony in Rome, Lewis crafted two works to commemorate the Emancipation Proclamation. *The Freedwoman and Her Child* (1866) has since been lost, but it is recognized as "the first by an African American sculptor to depict this subject."[115] The sculpture portrayed an emancipated slave woman blessing God upon "first hearing of her Liberty." Broken shackles dangled from her wrist, and her son, "ignorant of the cause of her agitation," clung to her waist.[116] Her posture—kneeling with "clasped hands and uplifted eyes"—evoked the familiar antislavery medallion of the bondswoman on bended knee pleading "Am I not a woman and a sister?"[117] The female figure in *Forever Free* (1867, originally titled *The Morning of Liberty*) (Fig. 3.4) is likely based on *The Freedwoman and Her Child*, but the piece differs from its predecessor in several respects. An adult couple replaces the mother and child of Lewis's prior work. A petite woman kneels in prayer beside a muscular man, who crushes a ball and chain beneath his foot and raises a shattered manacle in triumph. Half-life-sized, they face forward and gaze outward with similar expressions, yet their features differ. His curly hair and broad nose read as African. Her flowing hair and thin lips read as Caucasian. Despite their contrasting physiognomies, his right hand, resting on her shoulder, connects them. Their union atop a compact base suggested a shared future, both for newly freed people and for Black and white America.

By inverting and juxtaposing racial markers, Lewis exposed the capriciousness of color prejudice. These aesthetic moves reflected the insights she gleaned from her college experience. Oberlin taught her not to presume whites' acceptance. Since they did not readily see her as one of them, she invited whites to see themselves in figures like her. But for the whims of fate, she implied, their situations might be reversed. Other abolitionists used the photographs of freed slaves to achieve the same effect, circulating images of emancipated children who were so light skinned as to appear "white." Like Lewis, these reformers

FIG. 3.4. Edmonia Lewis, *Forever Free* (1867).
Courtesy Howard University Gallery of Art, Washington, DC, Licensed by Art Resource, NY.

sought to cultivate compassion among white northerners toward the newly emancipated. They hoped whites would recognize that chance and circumstance were all that separated them from slavery and, thus, learn to empathize with the plight of the enslaved.[118]

No writings from Lewis survive to provide insight into her artistic choices, but from her promotion of the work, she clearly was determined that *Forever Free* should assume a place a prominence in abolitionist circles. She instantly raised its profile by dedicating the statue to William Lloyd Garrison, whom Lewis credited for having "given his whole life for my father's people."[119] From Rome she sent a photograph of her study for *Forever Free* to the New England Freedmen's Aid Society, a benevolent organization for the newly emancipated. Confident in her piece's positive reception, Lewis borrowed $800 to have the sculpture completed in marble. She then took the liberty of shipping the completed statue and accompanying bills to an unwitting abolitionist attorney in Boston, who paid a $200 customs duty to save the sculpture from auction. Lewis was certain that the other costs could quickly be raised by subscription, but the fundraising effort took almost two years.[120]

Among reformers, reactions to Lewis's latest work were mixed. The Freedmen's Aid Society reported receiving the photograph in their newsletter and published a review extolling Lewis's "decided improvement in modelling the human figure." Still, they noted that "the type is less original and characteristic than in the 'Freedwoman,' which she sketched in the Spring."[121] Art historian Charmaine Nelson interprets this review to mean "that Lewis's first black female in Freedwoman was somehow 'more' black than the one in her second attempt." If, as Nelson writes, *Forever Free* presented "a more interracial, *white Negro* visualization of the black body," it was a depiction that disconcerted some white viewers.[122] The Freedmen's Aid Society review concluded: "Her next step will be to combine the merits of [*The Freedwoman and Her Child* and *Forever Free*] and give us a really valuable group."[123] Lydia Maria Child, one of Lewis's first white boosters, privately deemed *Forever Free* a "a poor thing." Child did not indicate whether her criticisms extended beyond the anatomical ("the limbs were like sausages") to the racial. She had a history of differentiating the spiritual and physical attributes of Black people from white and would later criticize Lewis's rendering of the biblical character Hagar for looking too European.[124] Child recalled how her friend, the Boston intellectual and educator Elizabeth Palmer Peabody, "rebuked me for what she called my 'critical mood'" of *Forever Free*.[125] The reviews Peabody published showed she understood the work to be less about veracity than empathy. Elsewhere Peabody wrote that this "rare work" succeeded by "uniting grace and sentiment," figure and feeling. Lewis's characters were "speaking forms," imploring compassion.[126] The scene was clothed "with so much sacredness that it perhaps made a cold critical analysis impossible," Peabody wrote. "It went to my heart, as it came from hers."[127]

In moments like these, *Forever Free* elicited the emotional identification from whites that had eluded Lewis in life. Through art, she attempted to transcend the racial divide that kept her from happiness at Oberlin. Religious education there had taught her that in the kingdom of heaven, the least would become the greatest and the greatest the least. Perhaps with *Forever Free,* she offered a foretaste of that millennial moment. As her masterpiece envisioned the last becoming first, it invited the first to become last.

"As Fast as the American People Would Let Me"

Fanny Jackson left Oberlin a minor celebrity in 1865. An article on Oberlin's commencement in the *Anglo-African* magazine devoted a special subheading to "MISS FANNY M. JACKSON" and remarked: "This lady is undoubtedly possessed of talents of a high order, and she will yet make her mark in the world."[128] A number of eastern papers subsequently carried news of Jackson's graduation, mistakenly hailing her as Oberlin College's first female graduate of color.[129] Immediately after she received her degree, she left for Philadelphia. The Institute for Colored Youth had set aside the principalship of its ladies' department especially for her. Jackson's new life in Philadelphia offered a rude reminder that her alma mater's racial mores were not representative of northern society. Dashing for a streetcar in a downpour, she was swiftly turned away by its conductor, who told her she would have to wait in the rain "until one came in which colored people could ride." Jackson made her first homecoming to Oberlin the next summer. When President Finney approached her and asked, as was his habit, how the alumna was "growing in grace," she had her answer prepared: "I told him that I was growing as fast as the American people would let me."[130]

Life at Oberlin educated Jackson and her fellow alumnae in the possibilities of racial justice as well as the obstacles to African American equality, hindrances they would encounter anew in their early careers. Being women of color made them at once the most likely to face discrimination and the most prepared to speak out against it. In stirring appeals for change, these outspoken alumnae cut racism to the quick, attacking the prejudices that kept even sympathetic whites from treating African Americans as brethren. At different times and in varied forms, the four communicated a fundamental message: race was a skin-deep measure as flawed as the humans who created it. God formed all people of the same substance, impressing them with the divine image and likeness. Because Black and white shared this heavenly parentage, freedom was their common birthright and dignity their equal due. America's tortured racial history had been false to these truths, but with the defeat of the Confederacy and the abolition of slavery, a new millennium of peace and justice appeared within reach. Oberlin and the AMA, interracial entities long committed to Black freedom, seemed well positioned to herald its advent. Yet for all their bona fides, they came to this work with a history of condescending to African Americans and conditioning Black belonging on ideals of whiteness. These four women challenged whites to make egalitarianism the precondition for their activism. Racial reform, they contended, would have to encompass both public and private spheres were the nation to truly have its new birth. They exhorted their counterparts to join them in enacting a new standard of equality unqualified by custom or context.

The Reconstruction period would witness the passage of federal laws and constitutional amendments extending citizenship, male suffrage, civil rights, and equal protection under the law. Education was often a frontline in this war for equal citizenship. Three hundred alums of Oberlin traveled to the South to teach during and after the war. Of those, one-third were Black—an astonishing statistic given that African Americans represented only one-thirteenth of the student body. Data from the Freedmen's Teachers Project shows Black alums also exceeded their white counterparts in tenure of service. African Americans' teaching careers in southern schools from 1861 onward averaged 10.43 years compared to 4.27 years for whites. Black women's service was the most steadfast. In the aggregate, they taught one year longer than Black men, 6.5 years longer than white women, and 7 years longer than white men.[131] Clearly whites' investment was more ephemeral. As historian Ronald Butchart has argued, white teachers of freed people were less concerned with collapsing racial hierarchy than they were with inculcating Christian values.[132] Black teachers, conversely, were in it for the long haul. Their goal was empowering their people, and they sustained their commitments accordingly. These differences in missionary zeal carried serious implications for the movement for African American advancement in the postbellum decades.

The disconnect between Black and white visions of reform was nothing new at Oberlin or within the abolitionist movement. As historians have shown, the egalitarianism of Black activists regularly contended with the paternalism of their white counterparts, yet they came together in their hatred of slavery.[133] Jackson, Harris, Lewis, and Stanley learned to navigate these competing currents as students at Oberlin before or during the Civil War. Now that the war had ended, however, they recognized that the dynamic had changed. Emancipation was a dream come true for Black and white reformers, but it removed their common enemy in slavery. Racism remained, and education was necessary to uproot it. As Don Carlos observed to the *New National Era* in 1871: "One thing is certain, if our educators do not plant themselves on advanced foreground on the great questions of man's duties to man, the mass of the people will remain in the dark alley of ignorance and bigotry."[134] For racism to suffer the same fate as slavery, whites would have to invest even more of themselves in the cause. Prejudice would have to be "lived against" the way Jackson and her fellow alumnae prescribed.

4

BEREA COLLEGE AND THE BOUNDARIES OF EQUALITY 1866–1880

Sergeant Angus Burleigh got word that someone at the chaplain's office wanted to see him. It was the spring of 1866, and his regiment, the 12th US Colored Troops, was about to be mustered out of service. Burleigh had escaped slavery in 1864 at age sixteen and secured his freedom by joining the US Colored Troops. His regiment garrisoned Camp Nelson, a Union depot near Lexington, Kentucky, that doubled as a refugee camp for African Americans displaced by the war. Burleigh had been summoned by the white abolitionist who ministered to this makeshift community. "'I am Mr. Fee,'" the reverend told him. "'John G. Fee. I live in Madison County in this state. You are expecting to be discharged soon; what have you planned upon doing?'" Before the war, Fee had founded a school in the hill country of eastern Kentucky. It had been closed since then but was now reopening to Black and white youth, both male and female. He told Burleigh: "We are making arrangements so that everyone will have an opportunity to work his way. You can be useful here in Kentucky."[1] Burleigh accepted Fee's offer on the spot. He would study at Berea College for nine years; in 1875, he became one of the first Black Kentuckians to earn a college degree.

During Burleigh's tenure at Berea, his alma mater transformed from backwoods schoolhouse to abolitionist college, second only to Oberlin in the esteem of reformers and far exceeding its sister school in Black enrollment. The institution's ascent coincided with Radical Reconstruction, that astounding but fleeting period when the South stood a chance at becoming a multiracial democracy. Emancipation and equality before the law swept the old racial order away, setting up innumerable local contests over the new boundaries between civil rights, social custom, and personal taste.[2] Fee's college was at the forefront of that revolution in Kentucky, especially since African Americans there did not enjoy the same protections as other Black southerners. The Freedmen's Bureau operated within the state until 1869, but otherwise white supremacy thrived and Ku Klux Klan violence was rampant. As a border state, Kentucky was exempt from military occupation and the provisions of the Reconstruction Acts, which protected Black voting rights and disenfranchised ex-Confederates. Two former Confederate officers were among the series of Democrats who held the state's governorship continuously from 1859 to 1895.[3] Although African Americans made up one-sixth of the Kentucky's population, none was elected a state legislator until 1936 and none to statewide office until 2015.[4]

Were it not for Berea, Burleigh would not have had any other options for education had he remained in Kentucky. The state only made provisions for African Americans' common schooling in 1874, and by law, funding for Black schools came exclusively from Black tax dollars. Until 1879, Berea was the only college or university in the state open to African Americans, and before 1904, nearly 98 percent of the college's Black students hailed from Kentucky. Most of Berea's white students did, too, at least before the mid-1890s.[5] While its student body was more local than New York Central's or Oberlin's, Berea's significance as an institution extended well beyond Kentucky's borders. It was a paragon of the "anticaste movement" in nineteenth-century American higher education. Promoted by the Oberlin-educated boosters and leaders of the American Missionary Association, anticaste ideology championed racial coeducation as the best means of dismantling prejudice in a postemancipation society. Reformers viewed integrated college campuses as incubators of a fair-minded, multiracial leadership class for the South.[6] Since southern institutions of higher learning almost all excluded African Americans, anticaste philanthropists helped found numerous private colleges and universities during Reconstruction. These institutions are known today as historically Black colleges and universities, but they have been open to whites from the start.[7] Howard University's first five students were white, for instance. Furthermore, they were women.[8] Berea and other anticaste colleges were the first in the South to coeducate the sexes. Most whites who matriculated at these institutions enrolled in professional programs such as law or medicine because they were not available elsewhere in the vicinity or were cheaper than other local options. Historians have found little evidence of social contact between races on these campuses in their first decades.[9]

Even where the South's anticaste colleges were concerned, Berea was unusual. It was the only such institution to successfully enroll large numbers of Black and white men and women in its primary, secondary, and collegiate programs. For more than twenty-five years, the two races were closer to being evenly represented there than at any other American college before or since. Between 1866 and 1893, African Americans made up one-half to two-thirds of the student body.[10] This racial composition endowed Berea with more revolutionary potential than any other abolitionist school. One white alumnus went so far as to deem his alma mater "America's only thoroughgoing experiment along the lines of inter-racial scholastic equality." Unlike at Oberlin, he said, African Americans at Berea had the power "to demand a certain line of treatment by force of numbers" and "take the lead in establishing the school atmosphere to which students of the white race must adjust themselves." White students who matriculated during Reconstruction had to be open to becoming "partners with the colored majority" if they were going to take any pleasure in studying at Berea, let alone derive any benefit.[11]

Reverend Fee extolled the equivalence of the races in keeping with their common creation by God. Berea's founder cherished the verses from the book of Acts that taught that the Almighty was "no respecter of persons," having "made of one blood all nations of men."[12] To him, that meant race was only skin-deep and that Black equality was an actuality, not an aspiration. Fee was uncompromising on this point. Any qualification based on color could not be accommodated. If race mixing offended some people's sensibilities, they offended Christ's first. Everyone at Berea knew Fee had suffered violence for preaching this gospel of impartial love before the war. His past sacrifices made his message that much more compelling to Berea students, who took his words to heart. In the late 1860s and early 1870s, groups of Black and white youth reached across the color line, collapsing social distinctions between them and realizing Fee's dream of racial egalitarianism.

John Fee was Berea's chief architect, its lead spokesman, and president of its board of trustees, but his racial vision competed with another on campus. From Berea's inception before the war, the scholastic colony was staffed by white Oberlin graduates and American Missionary Association agents, who were often one and the same. Fee himself was commissioned an antislavery missionary by the AMA in 1848.[13] It was in the pages of the *American Missionary* magazine that he first articulated his idea for an anticaste manual-labor college. "We ought to have a good school here in central Kentucky," he wrote in 1855, "which should be to Kentucky what Oberlin is to Ohio, anti-slavery, anti-caste, anti-rum, anti-secret societies, anti-sin."[14] Three years later, when Berea began as a primary school, four of its teachers were AMA-sponsored Oberlin alums.[15] Once Berea reopened after the war, the association began advertising the school to northern reformers, forwarding donations to its endowment, and holding large contributions in trust. The AMA also resumed supplying Berea with Oberlin-trained faculty and administrators, many of whom it salaried. In sum, the college quickly came to depend on the missionary organization.[16] New York Central's failure had shown what might befall Berea for want of such a patron.

Ostensibly, Fee and the AMA were committed to the same anticaste ideal, but they understood it differently. The white leaders and missionaries who staffed the association strongly supported the legal, political, and educational rights of African Americans. They defended Black citizenship and advocated for their access to all civic institutions. But opposing racial proscription was not the same as questioning the significance of race entirely. As at Oberlin, where so many of them had trained, there were misgivings within the AMA ranks regarding the social equality of the races, particularly the issue of interracial romance. Intimacy across the color line unsettled white missionaries and superintendents. Some harbored biases against Blackness; others feared that deviating radically from social norms risked retribution.[17] Just as Black Oberlin alumnae denounced the racism they encountered as AMA teachers and insisted that the association embrace African Americans' full equality, Fee, Burleigh, and other like-minded students rebuked the prejudice they observed among AMA appointees at Berea.

These competing philosophies came into open conflict on campus. During the 1871–72 school year, administrators intervened to police race relations on campus by discouraging relationships between students of different races and sexes. African Americans and their white allies protested these incursions as a violation of Berea's credo of the unity of humankind. When the faculty could not quell dissent, the board of trustees intervened to delineate the boundaries of social equality. Their ruling endorsed racial equality per se but disavowed interracialism. The decision carried significance well beyond Berea or Kentucky. It was the first time an affiliate of the AMA, the largest educational organization in the Reconstruction South, formally articulated the implications of racial difference. As Black Bereans later observed, the ruling set the stage for an estrangement of the races at their alma mater. The reinforcement of racial and gender barriers foreclosed possibilities for fellowship. From that moment on, the brightest hope for racial reconciliation in the South began to dim.

Berea's Early Years, 1853–66

Berea was a colony before it was a college. Cassius Clay, wealthy landowner and swashbuckling politician, helped establish the antislavery community on the ancestral lands of the Shawnee and Eastern Band Cherokee. Clay was a slave-holder turned Republican, but no abolitionist. He supported gradual emancipation and colonization as a means of uplifting his poor white neighbors, who struggled to compete against enslaved labor and were dominated by the white planter elite. Clay organized a settlement around his free labor principles in Madison County, located between the Kentucky Bluegrass and the state's eastern mountains. In 1853, he and the colonists invited John G. Fee to become the spiritual leader of the community. With his support for immediate emancipation and Black equality, Fee's beliefs were far more radical than Clay's, but for a time the two managed to find common ground. When the new minister arrived in 1854, he dubbed his new home Berea after the faith community in the book of Acts that "received the word with all readiness of mind."[18]

Like Clay, Fee was a son of the Upland South. Born in 1816, he grew up in Bracken County, Kentucky, near the Ohio River. His slaveholding father disowned him after he embraced abolitionism while a student at Lane Seminary in the early 1840s. Dissenting beliefs persisted on that campus even after the Rebels left in 1834. Fee soon returned to Kentucky and became an itinerant preacher. Attacking the sinfulness of slavery subjected him to regular ridicule and violence but also secured him sponsorship from the AMA. The association sponsored four Oberlin alums as ministers or teachers in the area as well. The success of the community's one-room school stoked Fee's interest in starting an anticaste college. In 1856, he wrote Gerrit Smith of his hope that this institution would provide "an education to all colors, classes, cheap and thorough."[19] Fee and his comrades drafted founding articles for the college and identified land for the campus. The charter was adopted in July 1859. It specified good moral character as the only requirement for admission, leaving the door open for Black and female admissions. But before plans could take root, the surrounding population rose up against Berea. They got word that Fee had praised

John Brown in a speech to a northern audience. While the reverend had taken pains to distinguish the Brown's convictions from his methods, any kind words toward him were fighting words to enslavers. Rumors swirled that Bereans were planning a Harpers Ferry–style campaign from their mountain outpost.[20]

By this time, Fee had fallen out with Clay after alleging his Republican patron was a closet advocate of the higher law doctrine. Clay rebuffed the notion that God's law superseded civil law and disavowed his former ally Fee. When a mob threatened the Berea community in December 1859, its erstwhile protector did not come to its defense. Ninety-four residents were forced from their homes and the state altogether. Between the exile and the Civil War, the college project was delayed by five and a half years. The trustees retained the option on the land, however, and Fee managed to raise the funds to purchase it. In April 1865, he and two of his closest antebellum collaborators, his cousin John Hanson and Oberlin graduate John A. R. Rogers, regrouped in Berea and made plans to resume. The "Berea Literary Institute," began operations in January 1866. The first Black students enrolled shortly thereafter.[21]

For the first three months of 1866, eighty-five students, mostly adolescents, attended Berea's school. Twenty-seven were white. They left the school in late February when the first Black students were "admitted to equal privileges."[22] Fee had personally recruited most of these African Americans from nearby families or from among the refugees at Camp Nelson. Years later, he opined that a "paper declaration that they might or could come" to Berea would not have enticed Black students to enter. Individual appeals were necessary. "Often when prejudice is strong and general sentiment is against that which is right in itself . . . decision and action require personal encouragement and help."[23] Generally speaking, even the most integrated colleges in the North—Oberlin and New York Central included—did not recruit the Black students they admitted, relying instead on word of mouth within abolitionist networks. Berea's southern location and the postemancipation moment account in part for Fee's hands-on approach. After all, under slavery, education had been off limits to African Americans. But Fee's personalized recruitment strategy also spoke to his belief in the importance of individual relationships for racial reconciliation. His vision of integration extended beyond the campus to the community. Drawing on his wife Matilda's inheritance, Fee acquired 130 acres of land around the college, divided it into allotments, and sold it to Black and white families, taking care that their homesteads were interspersed.[24]

African Americans enthusiastically embraced the opportunity to study at Berea. Costs were kept low, and a manual-labor system helped students defer expenses. Eighteen Black students initially matriculated in the lower class. Angus Burleigh arrived from Camp Nelson in April 1866 and entered the upper class. "There was a holding of breath and look of surprise around the room when I went [in]," Burleigh recalled, but he reported no overt animosity from his classmates.[25] Over the next several years, Burleigh became "friendly chums" with Fee's son Burritt as they worked to complete the college course. Burleigh fondly recalled how the two of them "wrestled and romped and slept in Father Fee's old study" many a night.[26] Their friendship embodied Fee's preaching that God was no respecter of persons. Fee became Burleigh's legal guardian, the third Black child Berea's founder had adopted since emancipation.[27] In all, ninety-six African Americans enrolled in 1866, five more than whites.[28] At least a dozen of the African Americans who made Berea home were veterans.[29] Like Burleigh, they saw it as a place to enact the ideals for which they had served.

"To Make Our Principles Understood": 1866–71

As African Americans flocked to Berea's classrooms, the college became a target for public abuse. "I do not think a majority of the people here appreciate our character or principles," Fee wrote Gerrit Smith, who became one of the college's largest individual donors.[30] Berea's anticaste politics confounded and offended its white neighbors. Ku Klux Klan harassment grew frequent. On more than one occasion, Klansmen rode through campus at night firing guns and threatening students. Some took to carrying knives and pistols on campus in self-defense.[31] Nevertheless, Fee sanguinely concluded to Smith: "God has been on our side."[32] Promotional materials reaffirmed the college's belief that access to education should be as impartial as Christ's love. Just as Jesus "condescended to men of low estate" and preached humility, institutions ought to practice tolerance and welcome students regardless of race. "[Whether] the larger part of its students will in the future be from the colored race, or as now in nearly equal numbers from the white and colored inhabitants," the college could not predict. The future of their enterprise would "be directed by the providences of God."[33] The hostility they met from locals was offset by support they received from outside groups. The Freedmen's Bureau bought fifty four-year scholarships, which were distributed to formerly enslaved Black students between 1870 and 1874. Executors of the estate of Charles Avery, an abolitionist minister and wealthy manufacturer, essentially created Berea's endowment when they gave $10,000 on the condition that the college continue to serve African Americans.[34] Prior to his death in 1858, Avery had made a large bequest to Oberlin, $6,000 of which was earmarked as a scholarship fund for Black students.[35]

While college leaders did not maintain a quota for Black or white enrollment, they did make an effort to advertise the benefits of integration to whites. "In exercising kindness and courtesy toward a proscribed class," one pamphlet explained, white matriculates were "ennobled and attained greater gentleness and firmness of character."[36] Fee reiterated this theme in an open letter to the citizens of Lexington. White students stood to gain spiritually from racial integration, he claimed. Their courtesy toward Black classmates exemplified "that which is not merely chivalric, but is higher—Christ-like." In blessing they would find blessing, Fee said.[37] Did pronouncements like these invite white students to patronize Black classmates? Fee knew it was a possibility if whites significantly outnumbered African Americans on campus. Keeping the races balanced would ensure "that the colored pupil [would not] feel that any courtesy to him is a mere matter of condescension to him as a feeble minority." Racial uplift was often characterized as a Black endeavor with white supervision, but Fee believed it had to be an interracial partnership. He echoed Oberlin's African American alumnae when he told the AMA that the only way to "successfully elevate the colored race" was to place them on a level plane with whites and have both parties put their equality into everyday practice. "Practical" was Fee's watchword. In the span of just a few lines of an 1867 letter to the AMA, he advocated "practical recognition of the brotherhood of mankind," "practical moral & social equality," and African Americans' "true manhood . . . honestly[,] practically & freely recognized."[38] To him, equality was meaningless unless it was performed.

One of the first major public demonstrations of Berea's ideals took place in the summer of 1868, when the college held its commencement exercises. Oberlin's new president, James Harris Fairchild, was on hand and described his impressions in a letter published in *American Missionary* magazine. Fairchild was awestruck at the collective enthusiasm he witnessed for racial coeducation, "the interest and enthusiasm of those connected with the school . . . and the hold which it manifestly has upon the surrounding country." Twelve hundred people, white and Black, assembled in the college grove to hear the student speakers, twelve Black and fourteen white. Despite Fairchild's "long experience" with light-skinned African Americans, he had trouble identifying some Berea students as Black, "[failing] in three instances." Like so many people of color in the Upper South at the time, these students could have easily passed as white. Between biracial students and the racially mixed crowd, Fairchild sensed "the moral power and efficiency of the movement" awakening at Berea to deliver the South from its slaveholding past. He likened the "spirit and tone of the place" to "the early days of Oberlin," where a similar zeal for interracial amity had prevailed among abolitionist students like himself. If Oberlin had proven the viability of open admissions in the North, then Berea "[looked] like a successful solution of the problem of 'impartial education' in the South."[39] Fairchild's letter was reprinted on the first page of a pamphlet that commended the college to donors as "An Important Aid to Permanent Reconstruction in the South."[40]

Around the same time, Fee and the trustees recruited James Fairchild's brother to become Berea's first president. Henry Fairchild was the Oberlin alumnus and longtime preparatory department principal who had appointed Fanny Jackson to her teaching post. Like his brother James, he was judicious and discreet by nature. The diplomacy of his 1869 inaugural address was characteristic of his temperament: "We shall use all appropriate endeavors to make our principles understood, and to avoid shocking the sensibilities or even prejudices of our neighbors, with whom we desire to be . . . on terms of the most friendly intercourse." Fairchild recognized that Berea was going against Kentucky's grain in advocating integrated education. He did not share Fee's gospel certainty in the mission's success, acknowledging the possibility that "our efforts in this direction will fail; that the prejudices of race will be found too powerful to be overcome." Nevertheless, the new president agreed that principle must be placed before popular opinion. Not only did African Americans "have, and ought to have, the same civil and political rights as white men," but segregated schooling was contrary to "the whole system of universal education" necessary for a democratic society.[41] This was the anticaste philosophy of higher education neatly stated. But would race itself be reconstructed as part of this reform? What social significance, if any, would it retain?

From his time at Oberlin, Fairchild anticipated the smear that impartial admissions would lead to intermarriage. To anyone who suspected as much, he replied that it was, in fact, "slavery and ignorance [that] had resulted in almost unlimited amalgamation" long before Berea came on the scene. His brother's observations of students' skin color bore out the point. Like most white abolitionists, Henry Fairchild considered interracialism a product of slavery's perverse power structure. It almost always originated in white men's sexual assaults on Black women, to him the worst of the South's manifold sins.[42] How could slavery's opposites, liberty and learning, yield the same heinous result? "Our answer is, freedom and education do not tend to evil," he said. The presence of young women on campus amplified concerns, but Fairchild's career at Oberlin had taught him "the safety and expediency of this arrangement." He was confident that "propriety and decorum" would prevail, and he put great faith in students' discretion. As long as they were "allowed such a measure of social intercourse as their natures demand," Fairchild said, "they will acquiesce in such regulations." To that end, a new code of conduct, reminiscent of Oberlin's, was implemented that fall. It formalized the role of "lady principal," whose job it was to oversee the "general conduct [and] company" of young women (those living on and off campus) and regulate their socializing with men.[43] To help her in her duties, the lady principal relied on the Ladies' Board of Care, a group of matrons who monitored women's behavior much like the Ladies' Board of Managers at Oberlin.

Fee shared Fairchild's view that gender coeducation would foster a community of mutual respect and support. He deemed the "social intercourse of educated, cultivated, enterprising, Christian society . . . a valuable part of an education, inspiriting . . . young men and young ladies with hope, with self-respect, and noble resolve."[44] Under the proper supervision, young women and men would benefit equally from coeducation, just as both races would be mutually uplifted by integration. Neither he nor Fairchild acknowledged the possibility of consensual relationships between young men and women of different races. Fairchild had only observed one such instance while at Oberlin: the marriage of Georgiana Mitchem. He had dismissed her and her husband's expulsion from their Ohio teaching positions as just deserts. For his part, Fee had once accepted interracialism ("better that we have black faces than black hearts"), but he had not raised the issue publicly since before the war.[45] In 1866, the Kentucky legislature banned marriages between a white person and anyone more than one-eighth Black.[46] Whether Berea would conform to that standard or would permit interracial dating remained a hypothetical question until 1872, a year of reckoning for the fledgling college.

The Social Equality Controversy, 1872

By the 1871–72 school year, Berea's enrollment stood at 263 students, about two-thirds of whom were Black. The ratio of men to women was three to two. With the consent of the faculty and trustees, Fairchild had reorganized the curriculum after Oberlin, creating separate collegiate, ladies' (later "literary"), preparatory, and normal (teacher training) courses of study, as well as a grammar and intermediate school, in 1869.[47] The college department launched that year but made up only 10 percent of Berea's enrollment through the 1890s.[48] The first college class consisted of five white students. Fee's son and two others had been at Berea since 1866, another young man since 1867. The fifth, a young woman, was the daughter of the college's treasurer.[49] Subsequent undergraduates also tended to have matriculated from Berea's preparatory ranks, meaning they were well-acquainted with the school's ideals. By the fall of 1871, Berea had sixteen undergraduates total, including seven African Americans and the sons of Fee, Fairchild, and Rogers. Half of the ten students in the ladies' course were Black.[50] As at Oberlin or New York Central, African Americans were better represented at the primary and preparatory levels than in the advanced courses of study. Historian Elisabeth Peck notes that compared to whites, Black Bereans had limited opportunities for prior schooling, were more often called away from their studies to work, and "were more needed as teachers, especially after 1874," when Kentucky finally made provisions for Black education.[51]

Students either lived on campus or boarded with local families. Between 1869 and 1874, the years for which some residential information is available, Black and white men in the college department opted to live in the men's dormitory in roughly equal numbers.[52] Fee wrote Gerrit Smith in 1873 that "the impartial demonstration [had] been complete" in Howard Hall. The building was paid for by the Freedmen's Bureau and named for its commissioner, General Oliver O. Howard, who was also an active member of the AMA.[53] According to the 1871–72 catalog, Black student John T. Robinson may have roomed with his white classmate John D. Roberts in Howard Hall, Room 37. If he did, it is the only recorded instance in abolitionist college history of Black and white students sharing a dorm room, quite possibly the only instance in nineteenth-century American higher education.[54] Robinson fondly remembered the camaraderie of that time: "When we left Berea I could name at least fifteen young men, white and colored, who were chums and often passed a night in each other's rooms, a few roomed together." He recalled that there "were a few girls on like terms," but these friendships were not reflected in women's living arrangements.[55] Until Ladies' Hall opened in 1873, white women declined to live with Black women in the farmhouse that doubled as the women's dormitory, choosing instead to board in private homes.[56] Perhaps some white women felt they had sacrificed enough by deigning to take classes with African Americans; "It must cost these young people a terrible struggle to do this," a Freedmen's Bureau agent remarked of the southern white women studying at Berea.[57] Cohabitation was more "practical recognition" of Black equality than some whites were prepared to give.

Even if it was incomplete, visitors marveled at the extent of the campus's integration. An official with the Freedmen's Bureau visited in 1870 and remarked: "It is a novel sight to witness all colors in the same class-room vigorously competing."[58] An attendee at Berea's commencement the same year said he had never witnessed such a remarkable display: "To see in the heart of K[entuck]y . . . equal numbers of white and colored, intermingled without constraint, was in itself enough to kindle the enthusiasm of a lover of liberty."[59] Another described the "singular" scenes he observed on campus: "all shades and color, all ages and conditions" gathering in the chapel for instruction, "two bright, intelligent white boys waiting on the pupils at the table . . . in order that they might get money to pay their board," "great, stalwart black fellows, who had served their term of enlistment during the war," and "white girls sitting in the same class with black ones."[60] To the outside world, anyway, Berea was peaceful and harmonious, almost heavenly. Faculty meeting minutes reveal that students' behavior still left something to be desired, however, particularly the men's.

Faculty records never indicate racial antipathy as a source of student misconduct in Berea's first several years. In fact, many of the misdemeanors adjudicated before the fall of 1871 involved racially mixed groups getting into trouble together.[61] Black and white denizens of Howard Hall were charged in similar frequency, and their offenses—smoking, horseplay, truancy—were usually trifling. One incident particularly disturbed the faculty, however. Alexander Pearce, a Black student, was accused of "having repeatedly excused, justified or defended lewd intercourse with women."[62] An investigation revealed that Pearce had initiated bawdy discussions with his white and Black male dorm mates "on the character of the girls" at Berea, implying some might be open to being propositioned.[63] According to his Howard Hall neighbor John Robinson, Pearce had said fornication was blameless so long as it was consensual.[64] Other students corroborated Robinson's testimony.

Pearce's statements particularly alarmed the recent Oberlin graduates on the faculty. The AMA had sent several more to Berea since President Fairchild had taken office.[65] Counting him and longtime teacher J. A. R. Rogers, eight of Berea's thirteen faculty members were Oberlinites by the fall of 1871.[66] Their deep-seated anxieties over matters of sexual morality accompanied them to the South.[67] Premarital sex was a cardinal sin at evangelical Oberlin. As an undergraduate, Henry Fairchild was among those who horsewhipped a classmate for refusing to repent over propositioning a young woman. Dubbed the "Oberlin Lynching," the 1840 white-on-white assault contributed to the school's reputation for moral extremism, especially after five of the twelve faculty members sided with the "lynchers."[68] Apprehension over fornication persisted long after. Adding race to the equation amplified these anxieties by an order of magnitude, as Edmonia Lewis's Spanish Fly trial had made plain.

Details of the Pearce case came to light while President Fairchild was away on college business. When the student body gathered to celebrate Thanksgiving, the principal of the preparatory department, an Oberlin alumnus named Henry Chittenden, publicly addressed the allegations against Pearce. Chittenden's comments do not survive, but John Robinson remembered the principal's alarm: "Who would have believed that a professor, educated at Oberlin[,] would proclaim from that platform that 'Brother Fee's notions [were] leading to another Oneida.'" Chittenden's reference was not to the Oneida Institute but to the free love community in Madison County, New York, where residents practiced group marriage. His allusion connoted a concern for fornication, but what Chittenden really abhorred was the interracial aspect. It seems he felt the students' embrace of social equality had started to exceed the bounds of racial propriety. According to Robinson, the principal evoked the stereotype of Black men as sexual predators when he fretted that white women were being "exposed to insult from the attention of colored students." The "people at the North did not intend this" for Berea, he supposedly said. Perhaps he was referring to the AMA, which quickly got word of the episode.[69] The principal's provocative remarks were met with outrage by the students. They would have been in open rebellion "but for my presence," Fee informed the association's liaison Erastus Cravath.[70]

Never one to mince words, Fee probably told the students something similar to what he wrote Cravath: "The school must be kept as pledged—impartial 'as to caste.'" But where did this impartiality end? Chittenden had accepted his position as principal knowing full well that Berea was an anticaste institution. His alma mater was, too, after all. Yet Fee indicated that the principal and another Oberlin-educated professor, Professor Henry Clark, had exhibited "repellencies" to expressions of intimacy across the color line.[71] "No doubt this is surprising to you that teachers from Oberlin should proscribe, on account of color," he wrote Cravath, who had himself studied at Oberlin (and before that, briefly at New York Central). Fee had been told by Fairchild that "those who have grown up [at Oberlin] lately have not matured [in] the matter"—an early indication that interracial solidarity was flagging there.[72] Don Carlos submitted his editorial to the *New National Era* around this same time and made a similar observation: "Oberlin is not zealously laying hold of this great national prejudice, as she once threw herself against the bulwarks of slavery."[73] As undergraduates, Clark and Chittenden would have been immersed in abolitionism, yet their contact with African Americans at Oberlin would have been far more limited than at Berea. Oberlin's Black enrollment increased after the Civil War but never topped 8 percent.[74] On Berea's campus, African Americans outnumbered whites. Clark and Chittenden found themselves in the minority, likely for the first time in their lives.

After Chittenden's Thanksgiving sermon questioned Berea's egalitarianism, Black students mounted a defense of the college's values. On December 13, 1871, Angus Burleigh, his African American classmate John Henry Jackson, and eighteen other students remonstrated against the principal in a petition to the faculty, who voted to prepare a formal response. It took two more meetings for them to agree on a reply.[75] Again, the text does not survive, but their response seems to have admonished students not to question the character or judgment of their professors. The students replied that they reserved the right to rebuke any behavior they deemed un-Christian and would appeal to the trustees for redress.[76] On his return to campus, Fairchild attempted to mediate the dispute, but the matter remained unsettled into the new year. Three more faculty meetings were held in the span of a week in January to discuss "the relation of white and colored students in the institution" and "the general social problems suggested by the attitude of the young men."[77] The students' experience on campus had led them to question the basis of racial norms. In the process, they had grown more inclined to obey their consciences than school authorities. Toward the end of January, Fairchild wrote Cravath that "the storm that arose in my absence has not entirely abated."[78]

In light of the tumult surrounding the Pearce case, the activities of the Phi Delta Society came under scrutiny. Organized in 1868, the literary society maintained an integrated, coed membership from the start, with Black and white men and women serving in leadership positions. Students of different races paired up to debate one another. Women did not participate in debates, which were considered a masculine arena, but they did offer critiques and read essays. Nonmembers regularly sat in on meetings.[79] This arrangement went unquestioned until early 1872, when the faculty appointed Fee and Fairchild to investigate "the advisableness of young ladies continuing their attendance."[80] Again, it seems their concerns were for both sexual impropriety and race mixing. In conducting the inquiry, Fairchild wrote Cravath to ask his and other AMA leaders' opinions on this hypothetical question: "If two students of suitable age, one white and the other colored, should become engaged to be married, and should conduct themselves with as much propriety as discreet young people usually do under such circumstances, ought we to sever their connexion [*sic*] with the school on that account?"[81] Fairchild reiterated that while the administration had not encountered a case like this to date, he desired guidance should one arise.

Berea could not afford to lose the AMA's sponsorship by clashing with them over the issue, yet the missionary organization's own position on interracial marriage and the larger question of social equality was ambivalent. White southerners routinely accused the northern organization of promoting miscegenation because it hired Black and white teachers and sometimes permitted them to board together. Although these practices looked a lot like social equality to critics, in reality the AMA was averse to endorsing the principle unequivocally. Some of its white teachers were forward-thinking in their views; others were not.[82] Most recoiled at the prospect of interracial marriage. The AMA condemned southern legislation that prohibited such unions but not because the organization endorsed them. Instead, they felt antimiscegenation laws effectively promoted extramarital sex.[83] As a rule, the organization did not want to take a position on race that would undermine its teacher recruitment efforts or its schooling mission. Neutrality produced contradictory positions across AMA jurisdictions. A superintendent in North Carolina denied his educators were "teaching the blacks that they have a right to demand from the whites social equality."[84] Another in Georgia claiming his teachers were "of most benefit to the colored people at large as pioneers in securing to them their social rights."[85]

As his comments on Georgiana Mitchem's marriage indicated, Fairchild's support for social equality did not extend to its furthest expression in the form of interracial marriage. Still, he was reticent to dismiss the matter altogether. "My mind is clear on the subject," he told the AMA, but added: "I have sometimes found myself wrong when I was clear."[86] He certainly appreciated the risks involved, not only after Georgiana Mitchem's travails but also from the scandal he himself had triggered in 1836 when he treated a young Black woman at Oberlin to a carriage ride. On his and Fee's recommendation, Berea's faculty passed a resolution permitting only young women who were members to attend Phi Delta meetings and only then if at least two female teachers were present. Rules for women's future membership were to align with the rules for courtship: women would need the permission of the lady principal and the president.[87] Although these rules dealt with the issue of sexual impropriety, the interracial side of the equation went unaddressed for the time being.

The courtship rules had been broken before, but never by students of different races—that is, until April 1872, when Fee's young cousin John Fee Gregg was brought before the faculty.[88] Gregg had escorted John Robinson's sister Mary to a lecture over the lady principal's objection and without asking permission of Fairchild as was required. Mary Robinson mistakenly assumed Gregg had received the president's consent. Accounting for his disobedience, Gregg claimed "he had been provoked to it by what he considered wrong treatment," implying, it seems, that the lady principal had disapproved on racial grounds. John Robinson came to his sister and his classmate's defense. He did not share the lady principal's objections, he said, nor did his and Mary's parents.[89] Students of the same race regularly received permission to accompany each other to campus events as long as their character was upstanding. Fee explained to the AMA that his cousin was "a first[-]class young man of rare virtue." And, for what it was worth, he said, Mary Robinson was "so near white that the difference is not greater than between my wife and myself."[90] All the same, the faculty required Gregg to sign an acknowledgement of wrongdoing. A letter they received the same day may have influenced their ruling. The parents of a Black student wrote the faculty to ask that she "not receive the attentions of white young men" for fear of the trouble that might arise if she did.[91]

The closing of the Gregg case did not bring peace to Berea. Fairchild's niece, an Oberlin alumna and AMA teacher named Rhoda Lyon, was appointed acting lady principal around that time. On April 19, she wrote to the faculty "asking instructions as to whether she should allow free social intercourse between the white and colored students." Until the faculty could agree on "a more definite answer," they deferred to her judgment. A month later, a committee was appointed to compose a reply to Lyon. It was another three weeks before they presented "a form of answer" to the full faculty, who promptly tabled the draft for the upcoming meeting of the trustees.[92] In the nine weeks since Lyon's initial request, students had begun to test her authority and the faculty's. Three Black women, including the young woman whose parents had written the faculty, had stayed out after hours to meet male classmates without permission.[93] A white student repeatedly disturbed Lyon's class through a window and insulted her when asked to stop. The president's son was brought before the faculty for drinking (on the Sabbath, no less). Angus Burleigh skipped Principal Chittenden's final exam and spoke out of turn when summoned. Julia Britton, a student and skilled musician who had been named the school's first Black instructor in 1870, confessed to "licentious intercourse" with a Black classmate. Both were dismissed.[94]

As Berea descended into turmoil, Fee and Lyon wrote letters to Cravath at the AMA. Their correspondence illustrated the opposing attitudes within the school's leadership over the limits of anticaste ideology. On June 8, Fee reported that amid the faculty's continued abstention, Lyon was forbidding students of different races from escorting each other. "We have reason to believe that a majority of our faculty will sustain her action," he wrote, "[and] will not say her decision was wrong." Since Cravath could not be present for the trustee meeting, where the matter appeared to be headed, Fee asked for his opinion in writing: "In view of what you understand to be right in the sight of God—the example of Jesus Christ, and the declared position of Berea College as set forth in her constitution—the actions of its officers shall be "anti-caste"—are you ready as one to reaffirm that in the treatment of our students in their social relations *we will treat white as colored & colored as white, make no distinction on account of color?* Please answer." Fee's loaded framing made his own position clear. In the founder's opinion, Berea's credo of impartial love struck at the root of racial difference, exploding social boundaries and taboos in "the example of Jesus Christ." If the administration disallowed interracial relationships, it should only be because the couple was "of doubtful virtue" or "[desired] to do some indiscreet thing." For Fee, "ground of color" was never grounds for judgment.[95]

Lyon expressed the opposite sentiment in her letter to Cravath, composed only days before the trustees' June 27, 1872, meeting. Her reason for writing was to ask the AMA for a job that would take her away from Berea. Lyon knew Cravath had heard about "the great excitement that has existed in this school . . . caused by the question of *social equality* coming up in a practical way." She freely admitted that she "opposed the offering and accepting of social attentions between the respective sexes of the two races." Absent guidance from the faculty, she had enforced that view in her role as lady principal, much to the students' dismay. Now she said: "I am tired of the whole question and want and *need* a change." Lyon retained "a strong desire" to teach, but the ambiguities of integration were more than she could bear. Like many other white teachers of freed people from Oberlin and elsewhere, Lyon saw the education of African Americans as encouraging racial uplift without inviting interracial intimacy. "My interest in the colored people is not a particle lessened by my feeling in regard to intermarriage between them and the white race," she said. Lyon could distinguish between the work of benevolence and the recognition of absolute equality in a way that Fee could not. She implored Cravath to be sent "further South," presumably to someplace where the color line was better defined.[96]

A third party provided Cravath some insight into the controversy midway through the trustees' five-day meeting. A white AMA teacher in Lexington happened to be passing through Berea in late June and dispatched a letter to Cravath about the scene at the college. He reported that "considerable difference of opinion among the faculty" had prompted "disregard for authority and a spirit of insubordination" among the students. Of late, their minds had been "turned . . . more to *discussion* than to study." While the teacher denounced students' unruly behavior, as an educator working in a Black school, he appreciated the dilemma facing the trustees. "The anti-caste feature of the college ought not to be let down one jot," he opined, "but whether anti-caste implies indiscriminate mixture of the races on any and every occasion is by no means clear to me." Under the circumstances, he felt that the "principle of highest good" should decide the matter.[97] But highest good for whom? Who was to decide where anticaste ended and impropriety began?

Such a knotty issue would benefit from external mediation, and the AMA was the most obvious referee. "*They needed you there*," the teacher told Cravath.[98] Four years earlier, the AMA had pressured Berea into giving it a seat on the college's board of trustees, which was otherwise composed of current and former residents of the community. Fee had resisted the appointment out of a desire to preserve local control.[99] Now Fee and the trustees present—ten white and one Black—would be left to decide this weighty matter by themselves.[100] If Fee or Fairchild ever received word from Cravath, the letter does not survive (he had not communicated to the board by June 17, at least).[101] Cravath did respond to Principal Lyon regarding her application for reassignment. Evidently, he explained that her request put the AMA in a "compromising" position. To remove her from Berea would seem to "uphold [her] in the position [she] had taken."[102] Cravath preferred that the AMA keep its distance from the controversy. He did not hear about the trustee meeting again until after its adjournment. Professor Rogers, secretary of the board, reported that the gathering had "ended very satisfactorily." Papering over what had in fact been a tense few days, he presented a cheerful synopsis to Berea's sponsor. "The brethren were very harmonious in their conclusion and all are full of hope. The outlook never seemed brighter."[103] The meetings had indeed produced a decision. It was one the AMA could appreciate, if only for its ambiguity.

Berea's leadership reached a compromise on "the question of social intimacy" that preserved social equality per se while discouraging interracial romance. Contradictions within the nine resolutions have led historians to disagree over the extent of the measures' progressiveness.[104] The first points were faithful to Fee's position. The trustees held that "persons of the opposite races and sexes should not be universally prohibited from attending each other to and from social gatherings and public lectures." Indiscretion, impurity, or personal safety were the only valid objections that might be made to such liaisons; "If no obstacle but simply that of complexion exists[,] they should have permission." The sixth point warned of the dangers to which intermarriage would expose students and their parents but did not expressly object to it. In fact, the trustees added that "the mere fact that persons of different colors are engaged to be married is not sufficient cause for removing them."[105] Had the resolutions ended there, they would have represented a triumph for Fee's vision, not to mention a remarkable (and possibly illegal) gesture of racial egalitarianism for 1870s Kentucky.

Yet the trustees felt compelled to include three more points, which blunted if not negated the impact of the preceding six. These final resolutions seemed

directed toward the faculty and spoke to present realities rather than to hypothetical situations. One advised "special caution . . . to guard against such consequences as would not arise in a different state of society," that is, where the
sexes and the races were not as evenly represented. Berea's peculiarity, in other
words, was cause for caution as much as pride. The next resolution counseled
against young women "receiving habitual acts of attention from persons whom
it would clearly be undesirable for them to marry." Difference in color was the
source of their discomfort, as the last point made clear: "It does not seem to us
that under existing circumstances it is desirable in general for those of either
race to cultivate the most intimate social relations with those of the other sex
and a different race, especially when the difference in race is quite marked." [106]
The trustees' reasoning mirrored Kentucky's antimiscegenation statute: the
more Black ancestry in an interracial relationship, the less "desirable" the pairing. Such reasoning placed a stigma on Blackness at Berea by suggesting the
persistence of a racial hierarchy within humanity's "one blood." In a nutshell,
the trustees concluded that while interracial marriage was not sinful, it was to
be avoided like sin.

The board's deliberations pitted Berea's ideals against its livelihood in a
dynamic reminiscent of the debate over William Allen's marriage at Central
College. Some on Berea's board considered the regulations a concession to the
antebellum racial order. John Hanson, Fee's cousin who had taught at Berea
with Rogers before the war, voted against the measures "on the ground that he
did not think any paper on the subject desirable." [107] Social norms had to be
realized in community, not imposed by committees. Other trustees worried for
the safety of Berea were it to endorse interracial marriage, whether explicitly
or implicitly. The dangers of practicing social equality were well known. Only
a year earlier, while on college business in Lexington, a white trustee had been
dragged from a hotel and beaten by a mob after dining with a Black family
and praying at a Black church. [108] That man voted in favor of the regulations.
So did Gabriel Burdett, the board's first and only Black member. [109] An AMA-
sponsored teacher and preacher, he may have felt pressured to support a compromise. But like the parents of the young Black woman, Burdett's more immediate worry may have been for his daughter, a preparatory student.

As president of Berea's board, Fee did not have a vote, but he was likely behind a resolution introduced at the last moment. Taking issue, it seems, with
the board's judgment of what relationships were and were not "desirable," a

motion was made "declaring amalgamation desirable." It was a provocative attempt at collapsing the racial divisions implicit in the regulations. Unsurprisingly, the motion failed, and the other rules carried. The board also refused Henry Chittenden's proffered resignation, deciding instead to admonish him.[110] He would remain principal of the preparatory department for another four years. Daniel Cain, a Black alumnus of the class of 1877, recalled that when he left Berea, there was "racial antagonism . . . not among the students so much as around the faculty."[111] Chittenden departed in 1876, possibly in response to "some difference [he had] with Mr. Fee."[112] Owing to the events of 1872, it appears the fragile consensus between Fee's faction and the AMA appointees had given way to suspicion and rancor. In the wake of the social equality controversy, Fee told Berea's donors that "no school in the land has been more harmonious," and Fairchild claimed there was "perfect harmony among us at present, and . . . no discussion on these subjects."[113] Yet historian Richard Sears notes that of the Berea faculty hired from Oberlin in the late 1860s and early 1870s, all but President Fairchild had left by 1880.[114] By then, AMA liaison Erastus Cravath had resigned his seat on Berea's board. The trustees and the association did not agree on a replacement until 1892.[115]

Berea's Ideals in the Aftermath, 1873–80

On the face of things, student life changed little in the immediate wake of the social equality controversy. Berea enrolled 287 students in 1873 and averaged that many through the end of the decade. Black enrollment dipped briefly but rebounded to 67 percent by 1880.[116] Students of different races continued taking the same classes, eating at the same tables, attending the same meetings, and participating in the same activities. Fee counted it a victory when "12 young white ladies . . . from excellent families of good character and manner" opted to board with around eighty Black women in the opulent new women's dormitory, which opened in 1873. Berea's Ladies' Hall was modeled precisely on Oberlin's.[117] Chittenden told the AMA it was the building that had drawn them, and Fee admitted to Cravath it took "some efforts to get young white ladies to go."[118] White and Black women were still not as chummy as the college men, who continued making mischief together. A group of male students—two Black and five white—were brought before the faculty in January 1873 for smoking. A few months later, Daniel Cain and another Black student were disciplined along with two white peers for wearing women's clothing as part of a "dancing frolic" in Howard Hall.[119] Episodes like these suggested that camaraderie persisted across the color line. In 1873, the administration reprinted an account of commencement that attested to "the peaceful association of the two races in this school" and also noted that the school was "gaining in favor with the [white] mountain population."[120] Strong supporters of the Union cause and opponents of the planter elite, mountaineers were seen as natural allies in the fight against caste.[121]

Beneath this tranquil veneer, a number of Black students felt betrayed by the administration's actions. As historian Hannah Rosen has argued, during Reconstruction, white southerners routinely used public distaste for interracial marriage as a pretext for undermining African American citizenship and enforcing antebellum racial strictures.[122] As a Union veteran, Angus Burleigh could not abide any reversals of the freedoms the war had brought about. And as one of Berea's first African American pupils, Burleigh saw himself as a steward of the college's principles and bristled at any violation of these ideals. In his junior year, he was brought before the faculty for testing their authority on several occasions. Burleigh used an assignment for Professor Clark's rhetoric class as an opportunity to upbraid professors and administrators, then repeated those passages in a class exhibition after being told to remove them.[123] He also clashed with Clark's mother, who replaced Rhoda Lyon as lady principal.[124] She charged him with insubordination for loitering in Ladies' Hall, while Professor Clark accused him of insolence for talking back.[125] Burleigh stood up to each of them, refusing to bow to perceived prejudice. "Mrs. Clark has violated the principles of this institution and she or somebody ought to answer for it," he declared.[126] Among other things, Burleigh told Professor Clark: "I want you to know what you're about when you talk so to me"; "I don't care for your iron rules"; and "How are you going to help yourself? You've got to hear it."[127] With the last, Burleigh reminded his professor that he, too, could learn something at Berea. It was Clark whom Fee had identified with Chittenden as Oberlinites with "repellencies" toward complete racial equality. Fairchild indicated privately that Clark was too proud to forgive freely and too callous to see when he had hurt others' pride.[128] Still, the president was obliged to formally reprimand Burleigh's misbehavior before the student body. Afterward, Burleigh immediately stood up and declared his intention to appeal his case to the trustees. He earned himself another scolding but got the last word.[129] Likely it was Fee's influence that spared Burleigh from expulsion.

John Robinson explained to Fee that other African American students shared Burleigh's indignation. They stayed up nights in Howard Hall discussing "how best to maintain the principles of the College from being diverted by injurious influences," hoping to address the problem from within. Whatever encouragement they found in these gatherings, they still feared "the result that would follow when the last of us were gone" and no witnesses to Berea's halcyon days were left to hold the college to account. Robinson graduated in 1874, Burleigh the next year. Robinson remained distraught about his alma mater's fall from grace as Reconstruction itself collapsed with the Compromise of 1877. Writing to Fee that year, the alumnus reminisced about Berea's early days and "the progress and harmony which existed among the students at that time." He and his friends had delighted in helping enact "that which [Fee] had prayed and worked for so long . . . a living demonstration of the brotherhood of mankind . . . the true idea of manhood." But their experiment had advanced so quickly that some "were not prepared to receive it" and began "aiming to nip the thing in the bud." When "the harmony seemed too real," the administration intervened, and the students' "bright summer was clouded." Robinson declared that the regulations passed in 1872 "would forever place a stigma upon, and underrate manhood," the dignity every person deserved as a child of God.[130] "The spirit that inspired that 'color-line' compromise," he would later write, "was simply the outcropping of a deep, black prejudice against 'color'—unconsciously in the hearts of person in authority in the school."[131]

Robinson placed the blame on the Oberlin-AMA contingent. Chittenden had sown "the first seed of discord" with his Thanksgiving discourse. Ever since, Robinson mused, "that plant has constantly grown, and is fast assuming the same shape as in Oberlin."[132] He had probably never been to Berea's sister school when he wrote these words. Most of what Robinson knew—and resented—about Oberlin came from its missionary graduates, who represented over half the faculty at Berea between 1866 and 1883.[133] Robinson and fellow Black Bereans feared their alma mater had traded radical egalitarianism for the AMA's moderate paternalism. The missionary organization viewed anticaste ideology as a matter of rights but also of rules. If the Old South's racial order was unacceptable, so was the prospect of no racial order at all. Fee's circle preferred to let reform unfold organically, but the Oberlin-AMA network believed in regulation.[134] According to historian Joe Richardson, they were "determined to direct and control." Northern missionaries' "greatest weakness" was being "impatient with and intolerant of those upon whom they were trying to impose their views . . . never able to appreciate or fully comprehend other lifestyles."[135] To the AMA, starting from a premise of absolute equality would only end in anarchy.

As the 1870s progressed and Reconstruction stalled, the association shed its activist mantle and became a more conventional benevolent organization. Formerly nondenominational, it officially allied with the Congregational Church, prompting Fee, a vocal nonsectarian, to disassociate.[136] The organization distanced itself from Berea, in turn, by downplaying its own anticaste credo. Sociologist Christi Smith describes how the AMA shifted its mission in this period "from one of political activism to charity."[137] Campaigns for racial reconciliation were replaced by fundraisers for Black uplift. Respectability was once again put forth as the means of eradicating prejudice, placing the burden of ending bigotry on African Americans. And when the organization finally took a position on the social significance of race in 1878, it was cagey: "This Association does not affirm that races, any more than individuals, are equal in physical or mental fibre and development. Some races, as well as individuals, are manifestly below others in some respects. All that we claim is, that all men shall be regarded as equal before God and the Law."[138] The statement made clear the AMA had fully embraced the postbellum liberal paradigm, which privileged individual merit over collective responsibility. Any sense of mutual obligation across the color line now ended at the recognition of basic rights. It was certainly a far cry from Berea's motto: "God hath made of one blood all nations of men."

President Fairchild invoked that verse when describing campus life in a brief history of the college he published in 1875. The book characterized Berea's anticaste experiment as an unqualified success, achieved "by constant exhibition of perfect equality and perfect harmony," and "without the least friction, or the least sense of impropriety." The sight of racially mixed crowds at graduation, "mingling without distinction and with perfect order, [made] the words on the College seal seem wonderfully appropriate."[139] Yet a visitor to the 1876 commencement observed students and spectators voluntarily segregating by race. Although they took equal part in the day's events, sharing the podium or singing together in choruses, during break periods Black and white students "seemed naturally to separate and group themselves on the color line."[140] Fellowship between the races was fading. Given the choice of socializing or maintaining respectful distance, more and more Black and white Bereans chose the latter after 1875. An alumnus who grew up in Berea referred to the late 1870s as a time when "the relations of the two races were probably more quiet than either before or after. Early experiments in completely ignoring the color line had been discontinued, and a later disturbing element was not yet present."[141] Of the dozens of disciplinary infractions that came before the faculty in that period, few involved parties of both races compared to Berea's early years. Smoking, horseplay, and other hijinks remained commonplace, but rarely among racially mixed groups, suggesting an estrangement between Black and white students.[142]

This same period witnessed an increased policing of campus space. The faculty approved a new set of disciplinary regulations in 1873, and most of the new rules concerned students' whereabouts. Specific policies governed leaving town, going for a walk, receiving social calls, and being in bed at the appropriate hour. Women's movements were more supervised and restricted than men's, as was commonplace in coeducational settings well into the twentieth century.[143] While gendered, none of Berea's rules of conduct was expressly racialized. The behaviors they regulated were some of those at issue during the social equality controversy, however. Sometime around 1875, women were required to form their own literary society separate from the Phi Deltas. Fairchild cited this and other stipulations regarding the "social intercourse" of the sexes as evidence of propriety and decorum on campus.[144] Further restrictions on men's visits to the Ladies' Hall parlor were added in 1882 and again in 1890.[145] The Ladies' Board of Care strictly enforced these protocols. While their records do not survive in full, available minutes indicate that nearly every meeting they conducted between 1880 and 1889 included deliberations over female students' movements.[146] The faculty was responsible for disciplining men, including in instances involving women.

Two cases that came before the faculty hinted at racial and gender tensions simmering beneath Berea's surface. The 1877–78 school year was the only time between 1866 and 1894 when whites outnumbered African Americans on campus, albeit by only fourteen students.[147] In May 1878, a white student named Edwin Smith struck a Black classmate named George Baker. Both drew knives before being separated.[148] According to the faculty's report, Baker had told classmates that he heard Lena Sayers, a white student, use "invidious language concerning colored people, calling them 'prowling negroes.'" Sayers had denied saying so, although she "apologized for the *manner* in which she had spoken."[149] Baker agreed to let the matter drop but continued telling classmates what he had heard. A white alumnus from this period later claimed his Black classmates "were sensitive and ready to see any real or suspected slight."[150] Evidently, white students were sensitive too, however, because Smith "rebuked Mr. Baker for contradicting a lady." "Do you take it up?" Baker retorted. "You can take it up if you want to." Smith hit him in reply. The faculty chastised Baker for not taking a young lady at her word. And they reprimanded both men for their "readiness to shed blood on any trivial offense." Such rash behavior was "a relic of that barbarism fostered by slavery." Traditionally, honor was maintained through bloodshed in the South, especially when a white woman's reputation was involved. College leaders contended this culture of violence "should be repudiated by all lovers of law and order."[151] If there was to be a paradigm shift, Berea had to lead by example.

The second incident occurred in May 1880. The exact details are unclear from the record. By the faculty secretary's admission, it was a "complicated case of cross accusations."[152] Addie Mitchell, a Black student in the grammar department, and Cassius Rawlings, a white student in the literary course, attempted a late-night rendezvous on the lower floor of Ladies' Hall. John Lillie, a Black student in the intermediate school, seems to have discovered the plan and decided to follow Rawlings, or else he happened to be out late and saw him. All three were apparently caught being out after curfew. Lillie testified that Rawlings was at the window of Ladies' Hall, presumably trying to make contact with Mitchell, who was seen in her night clothes on the lower floor of the dormitory. Mitchell retaliated by claiming Lillie had visited her room, a grave violation of the school's code of conduct. And Rawlings confessed to carrying a pistol "with the avowed purpose of seeking revenge on Mr. Lillie because of his testimony." The faculty determined that Mitchell was lying and suspended her. Rawlings was expelled for intent to harm. No punishment was recorded for Lillie.[153]

Far apart in their circumstances, the two incidents told similar stories about the state of race and gender relations at Berea in the long shadow of the 1872 social equality controversy. These later episodes showed how readily violations of racial norms could lead to violence. Smith intervened to defend Sayers against Baker, while Rawlings threatened Lillie to avenge the damage done to his reputation. Both cases involved allegations of Black men trespassing in female space. Sayers's alleged slur against "prowling negroes" evoked the trope of Black men preying on white women, while Mitchell hoped the faculty would believe a Black man was the real interloper, not her white boyfriend. And both cases exposed the stagnation of racial reform at Berea. Baker did not accept Sayers's apology and would sooner have fought Smith than concede the issue. Rawlings and Mitchell met clandestinely rather than seek the administration's permission to date. Once their tryst was discovered, their mutual act of defiance gave way to individual acts of desperation. In the end, each conflict was resolved in so much as order was restored. But neither case prompted a substantive conversation about race on campus, nor did the rulings push back against caste except to discourage violence. Instead, like the trustees' 1872 resolutions, they reinforced racial divisions by admonishing students to keep to their places. Strict attention to social boundaries limited opportunities for meaningful interracial exchanges, which had proven so revelatory in Berea's early years.

As intriguing as these two incidents were, they were also isolated. Faculty meeting minutes record only three other disputes between Black and white students from 1873 to 1880, and none was so obviously racially charged as these two.[154] Racial strife was much more the exception than the rule on campus. Berea's experiment in impartial education remained an outward success, made all the more singular in the South as Reconstruction collapsed and racial pluralism waned. But into the 1880s, accord was increasingly achieved through distance rather than dialogue. The proportion of Black to white students held steady, still averaging three to two. But the trend toward separation also continued. Black and white interaction grew even less frequent, at least according to the disciplinary records. There were more interracial incidents in the eight years after 1872 than in the ten years after 1880.[155] The administration published a second edition of Fairchild's *Interesting History* in 1883. The updated version added ardent denunciations of the racial injustices that had arisen in the South since the so-called Redemption era of white supremacy began.[156] Yet the original paeans to interracial harmony on campus went unchanged in the new edition. Berea still considered itself insulated from racial retrenchment, unconformed to the ways of the world as it always had been.

Lulled into a false sense of security, Fairchild and the faculty were shocked in 1889 when white students began refusing to share tables with Black peers in the dining hall. Such a brazen, coordinated act of discrimination was unprecedented on Berea's campus. It was reflective in part of the emergence of Jim Crow segregation, which began taking hold in the late 1880s. Yet in hindsight, the seeds had been sown much earlier in the social equality controversy and had taken root in the racial dissociation that followed. The school's leaders remained committed to keeping the college free from racial strife. But Berea need not have looked any further than Oberlin, which experienced its own seating crisis in 1882, to see that anticaste ideals alone would not inoculate their campus from intolerance.

5

THE UNRAVELING
OF INTERRACIAL OBERLIN
1874–1892

"Is there a color line at Oberlin?" an editorial in the *Oberlin Review* asked in February 1883.[1] Over the last year, many students, alums, and friends of the institution had posed the same question. In the spring of 1882, the principal of the preparatory department caused a stir when he discouraged a white and a Black student from rooming together. That fall witnessed an even larger uproar when some white students excluded Black women from their table in the dining hall. Oberlinites wondered whether these were isolated incidents or evidence of a larger, more sinister trend. And if bigotry was a new reality on campus, what was its source?

Oberlin was then in the early stages of a campaign to raise its national standing by recruiting students from across the country, especially from affluent backgrounds.[2] Beginning in 1881, the Oberlin catalog included a "Summary by States" advertising the cosmopolitan composition of its student body. A majority came from Ohio that year, but one-third hailed from one of thirty-seven other states and eight foreign countries.[3] The next year, the share of out-of-state students rose 7 percent.[4] The 1883 *Review* editorial attributed recent incidents of intolerance to the "class prejudice" of wealthier matriculates.[5] In the editors' analysis, racism was a sin of pride: snobbish white students did not deign to consort with African Americans, whom they more readily saw as servants than schoolmates. Black observers assessed the situation differently. An editorial from self-described "negro students who love their Alma Mater and revere her principles" asserted that while class status played a role in racism's rise, it was unfair to "stigmatize the wealthy."[6] The problem cut deeper than means.

Fewer and fewer whites recognized an obligation to treat Black peers with respect. A greater sin than pride was at work: indifference.

Since 1835, Oberlin had welcomed students irrespective of race.[7] Now, more and more colleges were admitting African Americans on an impartial basis. The Black proportion of Oberlin's student body fell from a postbellum peak of one in thirteen to about one in twenty after 1875.[8] Between the founding of several Black colleges in the South and the desegregation of many northern and western colleges and universities, some of which began admitting women, African American students had far more options for higher education by the end of Reconstruction. But as the Black editorialists noted, "There are supposed to be some advantages in studying at Oberlin."[9] For one thing, African Americans received scholarship funds from the estate of Charles Avery.[10] But more fundamentally, matriculates of color came to Oberlin for its principles. They believed that equality there would mean more than access to the same education. The added benefit of Oberlin was social: the chance to be treated with dignity in every corner of a predominantly white space.

This guarantee of social acceptance was not written in any handbook. As alumnus John Mercer Langston explained, "Social equality was a matter of individual choice."[11] The Black respondents of 1883 concurred: "These advantages will increase as only the students can increase them."[12] Interracial fellowship at Oberlin had formerly arisen from the goodwill of a community pledged to membership in one another and mutually dedicated to the abolition of slavery. Now, acts of discrimination exposed a shortage of grace on campus. Fewer white students felt called to commune across the color line. Esprit de corps suffered as whites turned their attention from African American freedom to humanitarian causes like temperance and foreign missions. Oberlin leaders remained confident that proximity and the passage of time would remedy prejudice. If any whites arrived inclined to "look scornfully on the colored fellow-student," before long "a kindly feeling" would supplant their ill will and they would become "friends of the colored people, and champions of their rights."[13] In practice, by the early 1880s, some whites who were far advanced in their studies did not seem "imbued with the principles of the place," according to their Black classmates.[14] Friends of the college echoed these alarms and lamented the shift in whites' mentality from sympathy to sufferance. Why had Oberlin's atmosphere changed circa 1882 if its admissions policies had not, and if no one was arguing that they should?

Incidents of intolerance reflected the workings of larger social and intellectual currents on campus. The Thirteenth and Fourteenth Amendments enshrined the liberal principles of personal freedom and individual rights by ending slavery and extending citizenship to all Americans. Like many white northerners, white Oberlinites tended to believe that with former constraints to achievement removed, African Americans' advancement was assured. Confident in the chances for racial progress, they invested their moral energies elsewhere.[15] Moreover, they ignored persistent forms of racism. Many minimized intolerance as a relic of a prejudiced past, failing to appreciate bigotry's potency in the present, including in their own hearts. White students indulged in racist humor, kept African American peers at arm's length, and generally upheld whiteness as the standard for respectability. Black students' experiences from this period reveal how unspoken ideas of inherent difference circumscribed their supposedly equal rights.

School leaders were caught flatfooted when some whites began claiming that individual freedom included the freedom to discriminate. African Americans, along with an old-guard white professor, responded to acts of racism by exhorting their community to recommit to egalitarianism. They called for reclaiming a stake in Black livelihood as white Oberlinites had during slavery. By acknowledging the imminence of a color line, they highlighted the insufficiency of equal access for achieving racial justice. That argument bordered on blasphemy to whites who came of age in the postbellum era, convinced of the unfettered possibilities of their times and the guaranteed rewards of self-sufficiency. Seemingly unable to fathom how freedom could still be racialized after slavery, they doubled down on liberty as the solution to social ills. "Each individual white is left to decide and act as he deems best," a visitor to campus wrote in 1895, making clear whose prerogative took precedence where race relations were concerned. Blind fidelity to this laissez-faire paradigm opened the door to Jim Crow. The same observer noted the de facto segregation of student life: "The two races, though on the best of terms, and dwelling side by side, remain socially each a class apart by itself."[16] Oberlin's color line was, by then, beyond dispute.

Currents and Eddies in Oberlin Thought: 1874–80

1874 marked the founding of a new student journal, the *Oberlin Review*. Still in regular circulation today, it is one of the oldest college newspapers in the

United States. It originated in magazine form and was edited by representatives of each of the college's male and female literary societies, first four in total, later five: Alpha Zeta, the Aeolian Society, the Ladies' Literary Society, Phi Delta, and Phi Kappa Pi. The *Review*'s purpose was to publish the best orations and essays produced by each society, as determined by its members, along with commentary and campus notes composed by the editors. Its pages provide the most comprehensive picture of Oberlin student life and thought in the late nineteenth century. Contributors and editors opined on most all the pressing issues and ideas of the moment. In the *Review*'s first two decades, only one Black student served on the editorial board.[17] African Americans' underrepresentation on the staff of the *Review* stemmed in part from their declining rate of membership in literary societies. Theoretically, any student enrolled in the bachelor's or ladies' degree course qualified for membership in a literary society. But by the mid-1870s, either fewer African Americans were seeking to join or fewer were being admitted. Neither boded well for interracial accord. Seventy-eight percent of eligible Black men who were enrolled in 1870 eventually joined a literary society, but from the mid-1870s to the mid-1880s, that figure averaged 50 percent. Forty-five percent of eligible Black women who were enrolled in 1870 eventually joined a literary society compared with just 29 percent of the same in 1874. Black women's membership did, however, rebound to 50 percent in the early 1880s around the time Mary Church (Terrell) (Fig. 5.1) was appointed an editor of the *Review*.[18]

The inaugural issue of the *Review* appeared in April 1874, a few weeks after the death of Charles Sumner. The Massachusetts senator used his last breaths to urge the passage of a civil rights bill he had first introduced in 1870.[19] Drafted with the help of John Mercer Langston, the legislation would guarantee Americans equal access to hotels, theaters, schools, cemeteries, and churches regardless of race. Sumner believed the law would be the crowning achievement of Reconstruction. Staggering in its scope, the bill stalled in Congress until the senator's death, when his admirers made it their mission to see it passed in a tribute to the civil rights stalwart. Oberlin followed the bill's progress closely. Members of the Alpha Zeta literary society debated the proposed legislation among themselves, and the affirmative side won handily.[20]

In May 1874, the town of Oberlin put on an anniversary celebration of the Fifteenth Amendment, which had been ratified four years earlier. Oberlin alumnae Antoinette Brown and Lucy Stone had broken with fellow women's

FIG. 5.1. Mary E. Church (Terrell).
Courtesy Oberlin College Archives.

rights activists Elizabeth Cady Stanton and Susan B. Anthony in supporting the amendment, which provided for universal male suffrage only. To rebut the argument that illiterate Black men did not deserve the franchise over educated white women, Stone recalled one of her Oberlin Liberty School pupils whose enslavement had deprived him of an education but had not diminished his dignity.[21] She went on to help organize the American Woman Suffrage Association. A chapter was organized in Oberlin in 1870 but did not gain traction.[22] The Fifteenth Amendment celebration of 1874 made clear that the focus remained on securing equal rights for African Americans, at least for the moment. The day's festivities began with a parade. Thirty-seven women of color, representing each of the states, marched the parade route dressed in white. Another was costumed as the goddess of liberty. Other marchers carried banners emblazoned with Republican slogans, including "We Want Civil Rights" and "'Take care of my Civil Right's Bill'" (reportedly Sumner's last words). A commemorative program at First Congregational Church was attended by a Black and white audience and presided over by alumnus Sabram Cox, who reprised the master of ceremonies role he had played at the First of August festivities in 1842. The featured speaker was Langston, then dean of law and acting president of Howard University. Oberlin's most illustrious Black graduate used his keynote to survey the remaining obstacles to equality before the law and advocate for the passage of his and Sumner's bill.[23]

Langston described how African Americans continued to be denied "the full exercise and enjoyment" of their rights by whites who felt that such "recognition would result in social equality." Sharing once exclusive spaces meant whites would have to accept Black counterparts not merely as equivalent citizens but as peers. As long as whites refused to respect African Americans, legal remedies were necessary to ensure equal treatment. Absent one's full civil rights, Langston said, "Citizenship loses much of its value, and liberty seems little more than a name."[24] His speech elicited "loud and protracted" applause.[25] Several months later, President Ulysses S. Grant signed a watered-down version of the Civil Rights Act. Provisions for school and cemetery integration were removed, and enforcement mechanisms were blunted. It was left to injured parties to file complaints, rather than the federal government acting on behalf of those wronged.[26] Oberlin's Black townspeople had sent a resolution to Congress protesting these concessions, but sympathetic lawmakers had been unable to prevent the bill's attenuation.[27]

While African American citizens endorsed Langston's call for robust federal intervention to effect social change, student contributors to the *Review* took a more philosophical view of prejudice and the prospects for progress. Essayists asserted that true liberation must begin with mastery of the self. "The present age is styled the Era of Emancipation," a freshman wrote in 1874. "It is a period of unrestrained license. But its freedom is an almost perfect type of servitude. . . . That man alone is free who rules his own mind." Only through self-possession, he claimed, could anyone truly overcome "the distinctions of wealth and caste" and achieve "the freedom of the sons of God."[28] Another contributor maintained that individuals' "goodness is in direct ratio to their knowledge." Learning bred liberality, she argued: "Those who grow wiser become more charitable. . . . They come to understand far better . . . the class or caste bias; and they make allowances which they once did not—hence justice is generated."[29] A senior avowed that "the true grandeur, as well as only test of manhood, is victory over self, and all that is low and unworthy."[30] The most obvious outlet for this ethic of self-discipline was the movement for temperance and prohibition. Oberlin students participated in the local "temperance wars" of the late 1870 and early 1880s by confronting saloonkeepers, preaching to their patrons, and holding prayer meetings.[31]

To bolster arguments for individual initiative as the fountainhead of morality, students cited the Charles Darwin's ascendant theory of natural selection. Darwin described how a single organism's struggles against circumstances could eventually alter an entire species. His ideas were the subject of regular discussion on campus into the 1880s.[32] One student extrapolated from Darwin that with enough willpower, humankind would be able to "stand erect over the dust of buried prejudices . . . , and the true dignity of his nature receive its most sublime exemplification."[33] He and other *Review* contributors equated evolution with progress (which Darwin did not intend) and celebrated free will as both a product and a driver of that process.[34] They also understood his theory as confirming humankind's common ancestry (which Darwin did intend). In 1875, an alumnus published an essay in the *Review* arguing for natural selection's consistence with revealed religion. He praised Darwin for debunking Louis Agassiz's theory of polygenesis and conforming with scripture "with respect to the unity of the race and the locality of man's origin."[35] In 1880, a senior in the ladies' course wrote a forceful defense of human equality. The different races are but branches of one great family," she observed, "sharing the same parentage, rightfully inheriting the same patrimony." Rehashing Darwin's evidence, she showed that physical differences among humans did not signal a difference in species. The world's peoples might vary in appearance, but they shared a "moral nature" and were endowed with the same potential. Recognizing the unity of the races could help begin to resolve inequities between them. "If the belief in the common brotherhood of mankind were more earnest and more wide-spread, liberty, equality and the preservation of the rights of all human beings, would find more champions than now," she concluded.[36]

Review authors might reject stratifications within the species, but some wrote openly about supposed differences in sophistication across races. Their claims resembled those of period sociologists like Lewis Henry Morgan, Edward Burnett Tylor, and Lester Frank Ward, who described how the world's peoples progressed through stages of civilization. Because all humans were fundamentally the same, the process of social evolution was considered universal across peoples, though not consistent. While history did not determine a race's destiny, its past was believed to shape its present.[37] A young woman who would go on to become assistant principal of the Women's Department explored this topic in an 1877 essay.[38] Entitled "Character Building," her composition compared the cultural development of her Anglo-Saxon forbearers with that of "the colored race of the South." To fellow whites who questioned African Americans' progress since slavery, she argued that their own race only began to develop into a "higher civilization" in the Elizabethan era, after generations of medieval doldrums. Newly emancipated African Americans had not been afforded the same grace period: "The world expects them to do in a few years, what took the white man centuries to do." She declared that with time, enlightenment would come to "all races and peoples" and reminded whites "by what long and toilsome labor . . . what centuries of heroic endeavor—we possess our birthright."[39] She and other white commentators described themselves as inheriting refinement, whereas African Americans had to earn it.[40]

Review contributors occasionally incorporated racial stereotypes as evidence or just for laughs. These essentialist caricatures implied temperament was a product of race rather than of circumstance. An 1875 account of a barroom brawl between a Black man and an Irishman, for instance, suggested the African American was brutish by nature. "The negro's blood was up, and he fought so savagely that he succeeded in escaping," described the article.[41] A few years later, an essay titled "National Particularities" took as a given "that the Irishman is not compatible with the Negro and the Chinaman is the enemy of both."[42] The campus notes section of the *Review* occasionally featured racist one-liners recorded by the editors or reprinted from other papers. Most drew on the trope of African American ignorance or mocked Black dialect. "One of the colored students from the South states that things there are in a terrible state or 'Arnica,'" read one from 1875.[43] Another, from 1880: "A superannuated specimen of our colored population hunting for the museum accosted one of our Freshmen the other morning: 'Sah, whar is de amusement?'"[44] Wisecracks like these, belittling African Americans' intellect or appearance, recurred over the years.[45]

While Oberlin College held itself to a higher moral standard, the *Review* revealed that its students remained far from immune to racial prejudice. Just as whites were not insulated from racism, they were also not removed from contemporary trends in American thought. The *Review* printed racist jokes next to lofty disquisitions on political theory, biology, and sociology. Student essayists showed great affinity for the tenets of liberal individualism and Darwinism as well as social evolutionism and racial essentialism. While their erudite critiques drew frequent allusions to history and literature, white contributors to the *Review* rarely if ever placed contemporary social theories in the specific context of student life at Oberlin. Prior to the discriminatory episodes of 1882–83, some of the only insight into their views of race on campus comes refracted through the *Review*'s coverage of racial tensions at another college, West Point.

In a case of desegregation gone tragically awry, a Black cadet named Johnson Chesnut Whittaker was assaulted at the US Military Academy in the spring of 1880. Whittaker had been born into slavery in South Carolina. He eventually came under the tutelage of Richard Greener, the Oberlin preparatory alumnus whose snubbing from the exhibition had prompted Fanny Jackson's 1864 editorial in the *National Anti-Slavery Standard*. Greener had gone on to become Harvard's first Black graduate and a professor at the University of South Carolina. His recommendation helped Whittaker secure admission to West Point in 1876. A few other African Americans had previously been enrolled, although by 1880 Whittaker was the only Black cadet on campus. Whites ostracized their African American classmate, refusing to room or dine with him. When another cadet struck him in the face, Whittaker reported him to the administration. Because he had not fought back, his peers branded him a coward. One Sunday in early April, he received a threatening note telling him: "You will be fixed. Better keep awake." The next morning, he was discovered in his room unconscious, bloodied, and hogtied to the bed. Clumps of his hair were missing, and his earlobes were lacerated. An Indian club, pocketknife, and smashed mirror lay beside him. When he came to, Whittaker reported he had been assailed by three masked men. The officer investigating the affair concluded otherwise: Whittaker's wounds were self-inflicted. He was accused of faking the assault to avoid taking his exams the next month. Whittaker appealed this judgment to West Point's superintendent, who arranged a court of inquiry.[46]

The case became a cause célèbre, covered by news outlets across the country including the *Oberlin Review*. Its editors chastised West Point authorities for their hasty presumption of Whittaker's guilt. They called Oberlin readers' attention to the testimony of Professor Greener, who bore witness to his former student's upstanding character and academic ability. Contemptible as the charges against Whittaker were, the affair was unsurprising to the *Review* staff. Two years earlier, they noted, West Point's first Black graduate, Henry Ossian Flipper, had published a memoir of his trying college years. The isolation Whittaker described in his testimony mirrored Flipper's experience: "No fellow cadet dared to recognize him as a human being and he was invariably alluded to as 'it' or 'the thing.'" Such degradation flew in the face of scriptural and scientific understandings of the unity of the human race. Although they deplored the two cadets' abuse at West Point, *Review* editors considered it predictable. A "sentiment rooted and nourished by years of slavery, prejudice and oppression" could not be expected to disappear overnight, they said: "It will only pass away, in time, under the influence of action and opinion that is deliberate and persistent, but withal, just, humane and charitable."[47] Here again, Oberlin students advised patience, confident that small-scale efforts, in the aggregate, would effect change over time.

The court of inquiry reached its decision in late May. It found Whittaker guilty of all charges: falsifying the note, maiming and then restraining himself, and feigning unconsciousness. Similarities between Whittaker's handwriting and the script on the note sealed the case against him. Forgery was supposedly true to form for a cadet too craven to defend himself in a fight. No one could explain how he managed to tie himself up so effectively. But combined with the handwriting analysis, the fact that no one reported hearing Whittaker struggle against his assailants was proof enough for the court that there were none. "He has no enemies, because the other students have had no intercourse with him," West Point's superintendent opined, not recognizing that Whittaker's ostracism was itself an act of animus. With his campus turned against him, Whittaker still managed to pass all but one of his exams. Owing to that single failure, however, he was placed on probation that summer.[48]

In the fall, the *Review* followed up on the Whittaker case in an editorial. Now they sided with West Point. "The evidence against Whittaker is without doubt fully convincing," they declared, before reflecting on the inconsistencies of that very same evidence. Editors were thoroughly persuaded by the handwriting experts' testimony, but they remained "at a loss to account for the inflicted cruelties."[49] Nevertheless, they sustained West Point's response to the incident and referred readers to a defense recently published by one of its professors, George Andrews, in the *International Review*. To those who questioned Whittaker's treatment prior to the attack, the professor asserted that cadets' place "in ranks, at the table, in the recitation-room, at church, and elsewhere" were governed by "impartial rules." At the same time, he said, school leaders "always left each cadet free as to association with his fellows." Friendships formed based on merit, and African Americans had to earn whites' esteem. Andrews claimed: "A superior colored youth would probably find himself isolated at first; but it would depend upon himself to command in the end the respect and confidence of his comrades." Flipper had earned that respect, Andrews thought, and Whittaker might have too had he persevered. Regardless, the professor defended white students' personal prerogatives. To insist instead that Black cadets be treated as social equals perforce was to infringe on a white student's "liberty whatever in his choice of associates"—in essence, their freedom to discriminate.[50] Whites brought their prejudices with them to West Point. While contact with worthy Black peers might dispel bigotry, Andrews maintained it was not the academy's purpose to enforce forms of social equality alien to mainstream American society.

Andrews's reasoning satisfied the editors of the *Review*, who declared "that the opprobrium thrown on the Academy by this affair was unjust because [it was] unfounded."[51] He had couched his defense of West Point in liberal terms, and the rhetoric of individual choice and laissez-faire would have resonated with Oberlinites who saw personal liberty as the best means to reform society. Upholding Andrews's position on the case meant disavowing Greener's. Initially, *Review* editors had deferred to the Oberlin alumnus in his assessment of racism at West Point. But Whittaker's trial and Andrews's rebuttal may have persuaded them it was actually illiberal of whites to accept African Americans unconditionally. The West Point professor dismissed inclusivity as unrealistic, even uncouth. Implying both Whittaker and Greener were uppity, he claimed that "obtruding oneself upon others and reviling them for extending a cold reception" would never result in social equality.[52] Racial amity could not be imposed, Andrews reasoned. It would come about naturally if it came about at all.

Oberlin's legacy of interracial education gave its students confidence in the long-term prospects for equality. They were more sympathetic to racial justice than Andrews. At the same time, the *Review* displayed some of his same insensitivities. In December 1880, the editors included this racist wisecrack among the magazine's notes: "A scientist tells us that 'the skulls of the African negroes are dolicho-cephalous, prognathous, platyrhine, and mesoseme.' We are not surprised that West Point officers think that Whittaker clubbed himself."[53] Cribbed from another college magazine, the joke made reference to craniometry, then an active branch of physical anthropology.[54] Darwin had incorporated skull studies in *The Descent of Man* (1871) to show the diversity of human physiognomy. Protoeugenicists, however, used cranial measurement to justify racial hierarchy and white supremacy. This particular joke drew on those schemes to suggest African heads like Whittaker's were misshapen by nature—so much so that they appeared bashed in. The *Review* had never been above printing racist humor, but this quip flirted with notions of inherent racial difference that no amount of personal honor could overcome.

Three years later, in 1883, an African American freshman at Oberlin won admission to West Point. John Hanks Alexander, like Flipper and Whittaker before him, was socially ostracized as a cadet. Faculty and upperclassmen assigned him an extraordinary number of demerits, and he and his only Black classmate were made to sit apart from white cadets in the chapel.[55] That West Point's atmosphere remained unwelcoming to African Americans was to be expected, given its administration's handling of the Whittaker case. What is surprising is how Alexander's time at Oberlin may have prepared him for less than equal treatment. In the early 1880s, racial lines were being drawn at the abolitionist college as well.

Race in Reminiscence: Personal Narratives of 1880s Oberlin

The life writing of two students, one of them white and the other Black, afford glimpses into race's role on campus in the early 1880s, when Black enrollment hovered around 5 percent.[56] Decades after leaving Oberlin, an anonymous white woman and Mary Church Terrell each published narratives of their college years. Sometimes contrasting, sometimes consonant, these two accounts point to the precariousness of Black student life, the contingencies of white acceptance, and the indignities of racial prejudice at Oberlin post-Reconstruction.

In 1926, educator and children's literature author Margaret White Eggleston worked with a white woman who had attended Oberlin in the early 1880s to compile her teenage letters for publication as a memoir.[57] Apparently, they hoped that the text would reassure young women that teen angst was not unique to the Jazz Age. *Kathie's Diary* disguises names and locations that would identify its characters, including the author herself, who assumed the pseudonym Katharine "Kathie" Gray.[58] Whether she or Eggleston amended the text in other ways is impossible to know. Its details are too accurate to have been invented whole cloth, but certainly the diarist and her editor had the power to idealize the story or stylize the dialogue. However mediated, her reminiscences represent one of the only documents of racial norms at Oberlin in the early 1880s.

According to *Kathie's Diary*, she arrived at Oberlin in the spring of 1881, a semester later than most preparatory students. Two weeks into the term, she discovered that her new friend Irene was not in fact white. "Irene Warren" was clearly Isabel ("Bel") Irene Wall, a member of a distinguished African American family with Oberlin roots. Two generations earlier, a North Carolina planter had several children with an enslaved woman, including a son, Orindatus Simon Bolivar (O.S.B.) Wall. He and his siblings were freed as children and sent to Ohio. Several attended Oberlin between 1850 and 1861. O.S.B.'s sister Caroline married John Mercer Langston. O.S.B. married Amanda Ann Thomas, Caroline's best friend and Oberlin classmate. Like the Wall siblings, Amanda Thomas was also a light-skinned Black southerner. During the Civil War, O.S.B. became the first African American to be commissioned a captain in the US Army. Amanda became a civil rights and women's suffrage activist. After the war, O.S.B. studied law at Howard. President Grant appointed him Washington, DC's, first Black justice of the peace in 1869.[59] In 1880, his daughter Bel enrolled in Oberlin's preparatory department.[60] Kathie's memoir recounts how she was immediately drawn to "Irene" for her taste in clothes, her musical talent, her sense of humor, and her beauty. "She is the Whitest White and so pretty and dear," Kathie wrote her mother.[61]

Even before learning her friend's background, Kathie sensed that her roommate Delia treated Irene differently than the other girls in the boarding hall. When Delia saw Kathie put her arm around Irene, she could not contain her disgust. "'How can you fondle a NEGRO?'" Delia asked her roommate incredulously. Shocked, Kathie "[curled] up on the bed and [began] to cry, just heart sick for the tragic secret in that sweet friend's life." Her tears recalled those of Fanny Jackson's white housemate weeping upon learning Jackson had once been enslaved. Yet crying over someone's life story was different than weeping for her racial identity. Kathie worried Irene's race would impinge on her prospects, including at college. Delia, meanwhile, feared for Kathie's reputation. "You wouldn't want the word to go back to your lady mother that you had made friends with a Darkie!" she told her roommate. "You can draw right away from her—be kind but sufficiently distant—and no harm will be done." Delia articulated the same principle of free association as West Point's apologists, but Kathie disagreed vehemently: "Oberlin glories in being broadminded and I don't believe it will make the difference with my 'standing in the class.' . . . *And I don't care if it does.*" She castigated her roommate for her hypocrisy, demanding to know "what sort of Christian and Junior Class Prayer Meeting Leader . . . would urge me to cut poor Irene when we were already such friends?"[62]

For all her valor, Kathie did not consider Irene's racial identity incidental. She judged her friend's Black ancestry a "terrable [*sic*] secret," an "Awful affliction" for someone so otherwise lovely. Three times in four pages she labeled Irene's story "tragic" or a "tragedy," evoking the archetype of the "tragic mulatto" whose racial ambiguity alienates her from both Black and white society. "Irene is a beautiful octorroon [*sic*]!!" she wrote her mother. "Isn't that the saddest thing you ever knew?" After her fight with Delia, Kathie hurried to the hall matron, who told Kathie "just every thing [*sic*] about Irene . . . even the delicate part (which was one of the most terrable [*sic*] things about slavery)." The matron went on to explain the Walls' history at Oberlin and indicated Irene's mother was white, when, in fact, both Amanda Thomas and O.S.B. Wall were people of color.[63]

Kathie characterized Irene's parents' marriage as a "runaway match" and called it "a sad mistake" contrary to the college community's custom. "Oberlin has stood so splendidly for 'equal rights in education without regard to race or color,'" she wrote her mother, "but of course they stop short of intermarriage." Perhaps Kathie or her editor altered Irene's story for effect here, hoping to add some titillation to the story. If the diary is to be believed on its face, Kathie was satisfied with the matron's story and never sought the real truth. Later when "fine and honest" Irene began to tell Kathie her family's story, Kathie cut her off and related her conversation with the matron. Irene explained that "she hadn't spoken about it right away because she supposed every one [*sic*] here knew." In light of Delia's revulsion, she asked if Kathie wanted to remain friends, which she did. The next year, the two boarded in town in the home of a local family. They lived in adjacent rooms, Kathie with another friend and Irene by herself.[64]

Kathie denied Irene agency in shaping her own story. Not only was she content with learning her friend's history secondhand; she took it on herself "to tell some of the others who don't know (so they won't have the shock of finding it out as I did)." Once Irene's Blackness was discovered, she became subject to a respectability test not unlike what George Andrews prescribed for Black cadets seeking white acceptance at West Point. Kathie made sure to "tell them all the lovely things Miss W—said of her," accolades she shared with Irene as well. The matron's testimonial to Irene's character and deportment mattered more to Kathie than her own impressions of her friend. The matron's endorsement convinced Kathie that "she shant make any blunder going right along with the happy friendship." She felt that fate had wronged Irene, but

Kathie's narrative portrays *Delia* as the most aggrieved party. "I did not mean to seem to be finding fault with Delia as I talked with Miss W [the matron]," Kathie told her mother. "I spoke of her as very thoughtful for me and anxious to help the new comer [*sic*] not to make mistakes." The matron helped the white roommates bury the hatchet. When Kathie and Delia kissed and made up, Irene was absent from the scene.[65]

If this portion of *Kathie's Diary* is more or less faithful to her experience, her uncertainty suggests that Oberlin's racial mores were changing in the early 1880s. Racism among white students was nothing new. Black students had been subject to slurs and epithets since the antebellum period. Coeducation with African Americans made some whites reconsider their prejudices and become more accepting. Yet Kathie's memoir indicates that by 1881, that pattern was changing. Rather than second-guess her own bigotry, this white student questioned her benevolent impulses. The same young woman who appreciated Oberlin for "being broadminded" and standing "so splendidly for 'equal rights in education without regard to race or color'" wondered if befriending a Black classmate would run counter to campus mores. The matron reassured her it would not, but only because Bel Irene Wall had proven herself worthy. The Black woman's acceptance was conditional on conformity to white standards of refinement, not to mention beauty. Here was the actual tragedy of Wall's life: that she could not always live on her own terms. She went on to study acting in New York and marry a German engineer. Afterward, Bel Wall Elterich spent the rest of her life passing for white. Eventually, all four of her siblings did too.[66]

In 1910, Bel's nine-year-old niece and namesake was kicked out of a Washington, DC, school when it was discovered that her father was Black. Stephen Wall appealed his daughter's dismissal to the city school board, but only one of its members voted in favor of the girl's reinstatement: Mary Church Terrell.[67] By then, Terrell was among the most prominent African American women in the nation. She was a founding member of the NAACP and a past president of the National Association of Colored Women. Terrell was born in Memphis to elite, light-skinned Black parents who sent her north for schooling, first to a reform-oriented primary school affiliated with Antioch College, then to Oberlin. She entered the college's preparatory department in 1879, a year before Bel Wall. In 1880, she enrolled in the college course. She was the only African American woman in her class initially, but two others later enrolled, Ida Gibbs Hunt and Anna Julia Cooper. They went on to lead overlapping careers as educators, activists, and feminists. John Hanks Alexander was another of her Oberlin classmates. They dated before his departure for West Point at the end of her junior year.[68]

Terrell published her autobiography, *A Colored Woman in a White World,* in 1940. The title and the text expressed the mixture of pride and frustration she felt at being Black and female in Jim Crow America. Terrell had spent her career as an activist fighting racial segregation and Black and women's disenfranchisement. In her autobiography, she celebrated a time before Jim Crow when a young woman of color could flourish at a place like Oberlin. "It would be difficult for a colored girl to go through a white school with fewer unpleasant experiences occasioned by race prejudice than I had," she claimed. "If I attended Oberlin College today, I am told, I would not be so free from annoyances and discriminations caused by race prejudice as I was fifty-six years ago."[69] On the eve of the modern civil rights movement, Terrell related her college experience to show how Black women could thrive both intellectually and socially given an equal chance.

Mary Church Terrell was enthusiastically involved in campus and community life while enrolled at Oberlin. A skilled vocalist, she sang in the choir of First Church for seven years, participated in the Musical Union, and led the singing at the weekly women's prayer meeting. Her peers unanimously voted her class poet for the freshman exhibition. She was in demand as a tablemate in the dining hall and was invited to join the lawn tennis club and the Aeolian Literary Society, whom she twice represented as a disputant in campus debates. As a senior, she was elected the Aeolians' representative on the editorial board of the *Oberlin Review,* making her its first African American coeditor.[70] "If I were white, it might be conceited for me to relate [all] this," Terrell wrote of her achievements. "But I mention these facts to show that, as a colored girl, I was accorded the same treatment at Oberlin College at that time as a white girl under similar circumstances."[71] Not only did she accentuate her acceptance, she dismissed any suggestion of discrimination. Paraphrasing President Fairchild's assessment of prejudice at Oberlin, she wrote: "Occasionally, a colored girl would complain about something which she considered a 'slight,' but, as a rule, it was either because she was looking for trouble, or because she imagined something disagreeable which was not intended."[72]

These disclaimers suggest her time at Oberlin departed markedly from Bel Wall's, but Terrell's account goes on to reveal how race shaped her college experience in some of the same ways. She boarded in Ladies' Hall three years—twice with Black classmates, once alone, never with a white classmate. Like Wall, she was mistaken for white by newcomers to campus, including Matthew Arnold, the English poet and critic. He observed her Greek class on an 1884 visit to Oberlin. It was taught by future Berea president William Goodell Frost. Afterward, Arnold commended her linguistic abilities to Frost, who informed him she was "of African descent." Arnold was stunned: "He said, he thought the tongue of the African was so thick he could not be taught to pronounce the Greek correctly."[73] Years later, she retold the story with relish; she was proud to have disabused a pretentious white man's assumptions of Black people's deficiency.

Her autobiography recalled a freshman Bible study in which she took issue in with verses on inherited sin used elsewhere to justify racial subjugation. Exodus 20:5 states that God will punish sinners' progeny for generations to come. White supremacist theologians and racial scientists used the passage as proof that African peoples were congenitally deficient. Black people supposedly descended from Noah's son Ham, who was stricken with dark skin for his sins.[74] Oberlin rejected this "curse of Ham" argument, but the institution strongly upheld the overall inerrancy of the scripture. When it came to the Exodus verses, she struggled to accept her college's orthodoxy: "The injustice of the law of heredity stunned me."[75] She could not accept the determinism of Exodus 20 any more than she could tolerate the presumption of Black inadequacy. That this passage of the memoir immediately follows her encounter with Matthew Arnold underscored the racial subtext of her response to "the problem of heredity." Even Mary Church Terrell, the most celebrated woman of color at Oberlin since Fanny Jackson, confronted racist obstacles in her pursuit of knowledge. Her college years coincided with what historians Gary Kornblith and Carol Lasser describe as a "racialization of respectability" in the town of Oberlin brought about by the local temperance campaign. Antisaloon activists, many of them faculty or faculty spouses, declared alcoholism a symptom of poverty. Since African Americans made up a disproportionate share of the community's underclass, the association of low income with intemperance effectively stigmatized Blackness.[76]

Terrell invoked heredity again when describing the one Oberlin experience she regarded as patently discriminatory. In the spring of 1883, she was again put forward as a candidate for class poet. She was considered a shoo-in for the honor. This time, however, some classmates endeavored to scuttle her bid. Her primary challenger was "a young [white] man who had previously exhibited not talent or skill in that direction at all." His supporters successfully prevented her from receiving a majority. Her friends stood by her for five or six ballots, criticizing her opponent for not withdrawing "as he probably would have if his rival had been a white girl." Eventually, however, some of them switched their votes to break the deadlock. She appreciated "how many of my classmates stood by me so long," but she resented how race "prevented me from receiving the honor which many members of my class thought . . . I deserved."[77] As an Oberlin student, she expected to be judged on her merits.

As it happens, merit dominated the national conversation in 1883 with the passage of the Pendleton Civil Service Reform Act. The long-anticipated law aimed to reduce cronyism in government by instituting competitive exams for some government positions. Oberlin had followed the issue closely. A professor lectured on repealing the spoils systems during Terrell's freshman year.[78] Between 1881 and 1883, four of Oberlin's five literary societies discussed the legislation at their meetings.[79] When Phi Delta members debated whether a merit-based system would prove beneficial, its judges sided unanimously with the affirmative.[80] Now, only a few months later, Mary Church Terrell's peers were voting for an unqualified classmate over her. She considered the episode a foretaste of the racism she would regularly encounter in adulthood: "I know now better than I did then that 'blood is thicker than water' when several racial groups come together to elect a representative for the whole."[81] Ironically, it was at her abolitionist alma mater that she became acquainted with notions of racial pedigree and fealty that would come to circumscribe her life as a Black woman in the Jim Crow era.

Racism Comes to the Fore, 1882–83

The timing of Mary Church Terrell's snubbing for class poet was no coincidence. Spring 1883 capped a tumultuous year at Oberlin, as simmering racial tensions rose to a boil. Two highly visible instances of discrimination against African Americans sparked debates over the meaning of equal rights and the limits of tolerance post-Reconstruction. By pitting fairness against laissez-faire and righteousness against individual rights, these contests exposed a growing fissure between egalitarianism and liberalism on campus.

In the early months of 1882, a Black student made plans to room with a white classmate. George Washington Davis hailed from Baxter Springs, Kansas. There, Oberlin alumna Julia Wilson ran a freed people's school under the auspices of the Woman's Home Missionary Association, an auxiliary of the AMA.[82] Wilson was so impressed with Davis's work ethic that she paid part of his way at Oberlin, where he also received support from the Avery Fund.[83] He seems to have entered the preparatory department midyear. Late arrival may have made it difficult for Davis to find housing. By the early 1880s, fewer and fewer private homes were admitting boarders of color for fear "white students will not come, or if already in the family, will leave."[84] Perhaps owing to a lack of other options, Davis decided to room on campus with a white student surnamed Clark. The principal of the preparatory department, George H. White, objected. Black and white students had never roomed together in campus housing at Oberlin.[85] A note in the *Review* that semester indicated white students were increasingly sensitive about public misperceptions "that Oberlin students are in the main colored or at least the proportion of colored students is very large."[86] Principal White may have been eager to avoid any controversy the pairing might generate.

An ad hoc committee of students—five Black and one white—wrote the faculty to protest White's actions. While prejudice from their peers might be expected, prejudice from their professors was unacceptable, they wrote: "We feel exceedingly grieved to know that such a spirit so unworthy of your body, should even be entertained, much less find expression." When white faculty did not set a positive example, their failures of tolerance could become ammunition for bigotry: The committee warned: "Such discrimination on the part of any of the faculty, especially of one holding such an important position as Proff. [*sic*] White, cannot but prove disastrous to our welfare."[87] Davis met with President Fairchild to discuss the issue and also wrote his teacher Julia Wilson about the incident. Defying Davis's request for discretion, Wilson dashed off a letter to Fairchild. "I do not think you imagine however how keenly and how painfully they feel any treatment which sets them on one side as 'colored,'" she wrote, "nor do you know how intensely such treatment reacts in prejudicing their mind against white men." Wilson had been advising African Americans to choose Oberlin over Black colleges for the chance "to mingle as men of equal power and standing with the best eliments [*sic*] of the white race." Any deviation from that egalitarian standard ran counter to Oberlin's creed. Wilson implored her alma mater to live up to its legacy, foreswear worldliness, and "show us how Christians now ought to treat this color-line."[88]

Fairchild's reply appears to have assuaged her concerns. The text of his response does not survive, but Wilson considered it "entirely consonant with what I had always supposed to be the Oberlin idea."[89] Most likely Fairchild's letter reiterated that all students were judged by their merits alone and were free to associate with whomever they liked. As the president proclaimed in his history of Oberlin, published the next year, "Every [white] student was left to determine for himself whether he would recognize his colored fellow-pupil. . . . Each [student of color] has found the place that belonged to him, in the regard of his fellows, irrespective of color."[90] Was Davis's rightful place as Clark's roommate? Whether or not the two ultimately roomed together is unclear. They may well have made other plans to avoid further controversy. Davis told Wilson he preferred "the matter be kept as private as possible."[91] Neither he nor Clark signed the petition to the faculty. The matter did not rise to the attention of the *Review.* Instead, its fall issue opened with an essay extolling "modern civilization" as an agent of moral progress. The author admitted to the persistence of prejudice in society but denied its staying power: "Today the principle of human rights is established upon our planet beyond the power of oppression to overthrow it."[92] Because liberal societies supposedly learned from their failures, the essay maintained that their futures were guaranteed to be bright.

Black students' experiences of racism left them unconvinced that a rising tide would lift all boats. A transfer student recalled the lukewarm reception he received upon arriving in the fall of 1882: "I, with other colored students, while not treated as an outsider, was held within definite boundaries upon the outer fringes of college life which embraces mental, social, and recreational contacts."[93] Reverdy Ransom was a close friend of John Hanks Alexander.[94] He had come to Oberlin through the support of the Avery Fund and at the suggestion of Wilberforce professor William Sanders Scarborough, Oberlin class of 1875.[95] Scarborough had only fond memories of his time at the college. He would later write: "Such was the spirit of [Oberlin] that I found myself helped at every turn. . . . I forgot I was a colored boy in the lack of prejudice and the genial atmosphere that surrounded me."[96] Ransom's experience, however, more closely resembled Bel Wall's. "I resented the outward friendliness [of white students] which subtly, but firmly, closed so many doors . . . to colored students," he later wrote.[97] Had he lived on campus that year, Ransom may have encountered more overt forms of racism, as some of his Black female classmates did in the dining hall.

Since Oberlin's integration in 1835, students of different races had sat side by side in the dining room, located in Ladies' Hall. The common table was an emblem of Oberlin's interracial character. In 1866, the longtime principal of the Ladies' Department proudly noted that: "colored ladies . . . have been seated at different tables by the side of white ladies, and if it so happened opposite white young men." While she indicated there was "occasionally a manifestation of prejudice against color," earlier incidents of discrimination did not compare to the shamelessness of white students who arrived a generation later.[98] By 1882, dining arrangements at Oberlin had changed somewhat from years past. Shortly after the Civil War, the original Ladies' Hall was replaced with a larger brick structure. The new building included an airy dining room complete with gas-lit chandeliers. Circular tables replaced the old rectangular ones sometime in the 1870s. Whereas the former tables sat eighteen (typically nine men and nine women on opposite sides), the round ones sat only eight. Possibly as a result of this more restrictive seating, students began choosing their tablemates for three-month increments, submitting their preferences to the matron.[99]

At the start of the fall term, some Black women were assigned to a table of white students, presumably because it had vacant places. Their tablemates complained bitterly, and the women of color moved to an empty table. Adelia Field Johnston, principal of the Ladies' Department and a graduate of Oberlin in its antislavery heyday, strongly disapproved of the white students' behavior. Her first response was to join the exiles' table, hoping to shame their white classmates.[100] Black women had been stereotyped as licentious since the days of slavery and were especially invested in displaying their respectability.[101] Johnston's presence at their table suggested it was in fact the white students who were undignified. When her attempt at shaming them failed, Johnston was forced to overhaul the seating policy. With President Fairchild's backing, she instituted a new arrangement that accounted for students' preferences but reserved one place at each table for her to assign.[102]

"This created a great deal of stir," white senior Henry Castle reported. His peers took exception to the policy as an infringement on their social prerogatives. According to Castle, "seniors & others" came to Johnston "requesting that no colored person be seated at their tables." The principal "made no promises," although she consulted Castle and possibly others before adding Black classmates to their tables. While Castle "had not the slightest objection," thereafter he found it "exceedingly difficult to get anyone" to fill the other vacancies at his table. "They all seem to have a color prejudice," Castle remarked. "The whole thing has been a revelation to me."[103] Others shared Castle's surprise. As rumors of segregation spread, friends and alums of Oberlin wrote Fairchild with their concerns. "Are the colored students in the Ladies' Hall required to sit at a table by themselves?" queried Mary Keep, whose late father-in-law had cast the deciding vote for integration in 1835. "This question is frequently asked."[104] L. A. Roberson, father of two current students of color, prepared a letter protesting racial "'proscription'" as an affront to the abolitionist legacy. African Americans, he explained, "have a 'race pride' in Oberlin on account of past history. Therefore we had sincerely wished that this *color line* would not be drawn."[105]

Benjamin A. Imes, an Oberlin-educated reverend and civil rights leader, likewise condemned the episode as a "precedent so contrary to Oberlin's good history." As he informed Fairchild in a letter in October 1882, "The sting of 'our strong provocations' is driven deeper when there is but a *seeming* lapse among the vanguard of those who lead the march of our manhood's hopes." Imes admired the president as an old abolitionist and knew from their conversations he remained a "sincere advocate of our rights." Still, he feared some of Fairchild's generation were losing enthusiasm for racial equality: "There are those who since the romance of opposition to slavery has died away, betray a love of humanity less than was their hatred of slavery."[106] Oberlin could not rest on its abolitionist laurels. The rising generation had only secondhand knowledge of the movement, and their attentions were elsewhere. The same month Roberson wrote Fairchild, an editorial in the *Review* implored the campus community to support the "Oberlin Band," a group of alums who had lately established a Christian mission in China's Shanxi Province. With gusto reminiscent of the antislavery era, the *Review* declared: "Oberlin students will not let such an enterprise fail."[107] According to one estimate, by 1898, there were 237 Oberlin graduates working in foreign mission fields, almost as many as became freed people's teachers in the South during Reconstruction.[108]

The dining hall incident marked a sea change in Oberlin's respectability politics. The college had historically been a place where African Americans could expect to "be treated as men, and not as colored men," as Julia Wilson put it.[109] Deportment was supposed to be the only measure of an Oberlin student. According to the *Review*, "A large number of colored students['] . . . worth and common sense have disarmed prejudice against their race." African Americans of "ability and gentlemanly conduct" could reasonably expect the respect of their peers.[110] Oberlin was celebrated as a place where "no man is above his brother, except as he proves superiority of brain or power of character. Nor does it matter whether the 'brother' be white or black."[111] Yet the seating controversy portended a new racial paradigm. A greater number of whites reserved the right not to recognize refined African Americans as social equals, effectively excluding them from respectability altogether. Roberson warned that this overall trend would "[crush] all the womanhood and manhood in our young people" by destroying their sense of self-worth. Equal educational opportunities aside, he asked, what had African American matriculates "to hope for, if the midst of those who have invited us to come and have bid us look up, we are shown a place beyond which we must not hope to pass, to simply pamper the prejudices of a few[?]"[112] Black students shared Roberson's indignation. In an editorial to the *Review*, some prayed "that the day will soon dawn when it will not require so much forbearance as brotherly love and charity to tolerate the negroes' presence."[113] Promoting empathy would be difficult, however, when even sympathy was moving beyond the pale.

What was the source of this shift in white attitudes? The white editors of the *Review* attributed the change to class dynamics. They noted that the student body comprised a growing proportion of those "who have their means supplied them and whose surroundings at home are not what they are here."[114] In Oberlin's first few decades, a much larger proportion of students came from humble families and were drawn to the college for the cost savings of its work-study curriculum. Popular yet inefficient, the manual-labor requirement was phased out in the 1850s.[115] Still, a great number of students continued to work part time, with as many as 80 percent of students wholly supporting their studies through manual labor or school teaching during the long winter break. After the war, the economic profile of the student body moved closer to that of other midwestern colleges. An 1875 survey found that only 25 percent of the students in the college course paid their own way, although 40 percent paid a portion.[116] The *Review* claimed it was among the remaining 35 percent "that we find the class prejudice which gives rise to the color line." Affluence supposedly made these students disdainful of social inferiors. But for this demographic change, the editors believed, campus culture was unchanged: "The principles upon which the institution was founded and maintained pervade the institution to-day." It was up to "the students, and the students alone" to "eradicate the evil" and revive the spirit of the reform. "The faculty have done all they can do."[117]

Black students disputed this analysis on multiple counts. They were unconvinced that class was the source of racial animus. "Wealth is generally supposed to bring with it refinement," they reasoned. Years earlier, they noted, whites conspired to deny a student of color (they were probably referring to Richard Greener) a role at the literary exhibition, but "the wealthy and more refined students were those who vigorously opposed such an unfair scheme and exposed the plot." African Americans also disagreed about the place of school leaders in preserving Oberlin's ideals. While the faculty could not "change each student's heart," they played a critical role in promoting tolerance and equality. It was their duty to "maintain those principles at any hazard," never compromising with prejudice. Black writers considered most faculty faithful to these values, although they recalled Principal White's objection to Davis and Clark being roommates. What made the steadfastness of school authorities so vital these days was racism's intransigence. White students had always found "various little ways" to discriminate, but now fewer were outgrowing their pettiness during their time on campus.[118] College juniors prevented Mary Church Terrell's reelection to class poet, and Henry Castle counted seniors among those objecting to African American tablemates. Even master's students in the divinity program—Oberlin's most advanced—were advocating a color line in the dining hall and elsewhere. "What are we to expect from the younger students when a gentleman who is now a theologue refused to sit beside a colored man in the church choir[?]" Black observers asked.[119] They could not explain why whites so steeped in Oberlin culture continued to discriminate, but they knew it boded poorly for the progress of racial justice.

At least one commentator denied that separate seating violated the values of the institution. Responding to "misrepresentations" printed elsewhere, an anonymous editorial in the Oberlin town newspaper claimed "extremists" had fabricated the dining hall controversy and that "interference . . . from without" had unduly forced the administration's hand. This author stridently rejected arguments that "Oberlin principles are a thing of the past." Yet the editorial admitted no contradiction between educational equality and social segregation. Students of color enjoyed "the same waiters and same food and same everything as their neighbors" in the dining hall. As members of a common race, the article claimed, it was only natural that they should share a table: "Had there been a number [of] Frenchmen or Germans or Irishmen instead, each would have plead most earnestly that all of their own nationality might sit together."[120] To this, Black readers retorted: "There is some difference in being granted a privilege to do something and in being compelled to do it . . . for so slight a cause as having a dark skin."[121] While the article did not suggest African Americans belonged to a separate species, the segregationist author characterized them as foreign to Oberlin society, members of a different nation. Like immigrants, students of color were entitled to basic rights but not the full privileges of citizenship.

Even the most reactionary voices did not advocate denying African Americans an equal opportunity to learn. There was precedent for an institution reverting to white-only admissions. In the antebellum era, Cornell College (Iowa), Harvard Medical School, Otterbein University, Wesleyan University, and Williams College all offered Black students admission only to rescind the invitation.[122] For all intents and purposes, New York Central abandoned its open admissions policies when it reopened in 1860. The University of South Carolina briefly admitted Black students in the mid-1870s and became a predominantly Black college until Democrats regained control of the state legislature and closed the university.[123] Maryville College in the mountains of east Tennessee began admitting African Americans after the Civil War, but school leaders gave serious thought to ending racial coeducation after Reconstruction. During the debate, a professor wrote Oberlin's president for guidance. "What does the providence of God teach respecting the co-education of whites & blacks?" he asked. "Have the Faculty or Trustees of [Oberlin] ever doubted the wisdom or Christian expediency of admitting colored youth into the Institution?"[124] There is no evidence that Oberlin had, at least not since John Shipherd first proposed color-blind admissions in late 1834.

Although whites did not propose ending Oberlin's interracial experiment, few expressed concern for its health. Henry Castle claimed segregation made him "'ashamed of his species,'" yet his indignation was more intellectual than personal.[125] "No person with the least pretension to philosophy can entertain such a prejudice for a moment," he claimed. To Castle, bigotry was a product of "imbecility" rather than hatred. "The whole community sinks in my estimation," he concluded. "Not in character indeed, but in intellect."[126] He expressed no sympathy for the Black women wronged. An oration by one of his white classmates appeared even more oblivious to the plight of African Americans around him. Published in the same issue of the *Review* as the editorial on Oberlin's class and color lines, the speech exalted the modern triumph of conscience over "the relations of caste." Freedom of thought had proven sufficient to "render society self-corrective, and liberty self-sustaining and permanent." The author pointed to the antislavery movement as evidence. Abolitionists derived "irresistible power" from their faithfulness to truth, strength enough to vanquish "the enormity of slavery" in time. "Is your skin black?" the student orator asked his listeners. "To-night you sit in the sweet assurance of perfect safety." His words overlooked the lesson of the recent seating controversy, namely that whiteness privileged some people's liberty over others. Although he acknowledged that "obligation is the only security of the weak against the strong," he asserted that freedom would naturally lead to mutuality.[127]

Oberlin celebrated its fiftieth anniversary that summer. Scores of alums descended on the campus for several days of festivities. The program included numerous speeches, but none by a Black graduate. Of the white speakers at the semicentennial, only Lucy Stone noted the "ripple of discontent" of late at Ladies' Hall in her report on the event for the *Woman's Journal*. Yet she characterized the controversy as an anomaly, informing readers there was presently "no trouble on account of color" at her alma mater.[128] Other speakers made frequent allusions to Oberlin's antislavery days but no mention of more recent strivings for equal rights. Five alumni offered reflections on the college's character and evolution through the decades. The speaker for 1873 to 1883 identified temperance and foreign missions as the primary areas of Oberlinites' concern in the last ten years, making no mention of Langston's Civil Rights Act. The alumnus representing 1853 to 1863 rejoiced that the principles that had once made the college abhorrent to many Americans—abolitionism, women's education, teetotalism—had now become mainstream. "The world is simply coming to Oberlin," he exulted. Given the way worldly attitudes had recently contaminated the campus, it was an ironic choice of words.[129]

Although he did not address recent episodes of discrimination on campus, Michael Strieby, class of 1841 and general secretary of the American Missionary Association, was one of the few at the anniversary to acknowledge that obstacles to Black people's progress remained after emancipation: "Slavery was a cancer . . . but caste prejudice, its tap root, is still left." To remedy racism, he advised a program of racial uplift that would make African Americans "equal in property, intelligence and character." Strieby predicted that once the Black man was "no longer degraded" or the object of "our sympathy or pity," he would "take his place among his fellow-men, not by sufferance, but by right." This mission warranted the same devotion as abolition, declared Strieby: "With all the zeal of the anti-slavery era of 1833, I call out here in Oberlin, demanding that what was begun shall not be lost sight of until it be accomplished."[130] Strieby's call to arms contrasted the congratulatory tone of other speakers at the jubilee. Yet his solution to racial inequality still presumed Black deficiency was the source of white prejudice. By his logic, African Americans who were educated and respectable should not expect to encounter discrimination. Recent events at Oberlin suggested otherwise.

Soon after the 1883 jubilee, the Supreme Court ruled on a group of five related lawsuits known as the Civil Rights Cases. Responding to alleged violations of the Civil Rights Act of 1875, the justices deemed the law itself an infringement on the rights of private citizens and organizations and declared it unconstitutional. African Americans nationwide witnessed the removal of federal protections on their access to public accommodations. Oberlin's Black townspeople gathered to express their outrage at the ruling.[131] The *Review* did not cover the meeting, nor even the law's rescission. Whether its silence spelled acceptance, indifference, or ignorance toward the court's decision, the upshot was the same: Oberlin whites had divested from the cause of Black equality. In their view, if the battle was not already won, it was African Americans' to fight. Victory over prejudice was assured in time, thanks to the inexorable advance of liberalism. In the meantime, aggressions against Black students were regrettable but incidental. What African Americans considered cracks in the levy, most whites saw as water over the dam. "'Oberlin is the only college in the United States where there is absolutely no caste,'" ran one tribute from a jubilee publication. "There was never any 'color line.'"[132]

In the November 1883 issue of the *Review*, where they might have published a defense of the Civil Rights Act, editors instead featured a sampling of quotes from Black schoolchildren. These were meant expressly to provide "a good, hearty laugh."[133] The student who compiled them would go on to become a teacher at Fisk University and later a leading missionary to China.[134] In the freed people's schools of the South, she wrote, a student "learning how to shoot, often misses the mark." Her essay used Black students' misspellings and malapropisms to spoof "Sambo's superiority as a letter writer" and lampoon

African Americans' pretentions to literacy and respectability.[135] To her and other white students, the Black race remained developmentally adolescent. Freedom would nurture it into adulthood. In the meantime, African Americans were evidently fair game for parody.

"Who Will Take the Initiative?": 1884 and Thereafter

Oberlin introduced a Thursday lecture series in the 1870s, and it quickly became an unofficial fixture of the curriculum. Intended as a venue for sermons, the event expanded to include speeches on an array of topics, delivered by visiting scholars and preachers or faculty.[136] In an 1884 lecture entitled "The True Character of Slavery as It Existed in This Country," Fairchild did his best to recollect the features of the peculiar institution and the movement to abolish it. Still, he knew current students were too far removed from that era to fully grasp its significance. "The Oberlin student of fifty years ago, and less, was brought up under a pressure, political and ethical, which the present generation cannot comprehend," Fairchild mused. "It will be difficult to raise up again a generation so well grounded in the elementary principles of government & the rights of man." While the lessons of the slavery era were being lost, its legacies persisted. Fairchild predicted white southerners would continue to mourn the Lost Cause for at least a century. Black freedom accounted for some of the "cup of bitterness" they carried. "The race or color problem, the present source of exasperation throughout large portions of the South . . . will help to keep alive the sense of wrong," he claimed. White southerners interpreted racial tensions "as the result of emancipation, rather than of slavery" and opposed African Americans' claims to civil rights as a disruption of white supremacy.[137] "Time and forbearance are the only remedies for such antagonism," he said characteristically. "We can afford to be patient, & wait." Oberlin's president was convinced that slavery, not race, had been "the grand cause of all the alienation" and that after a "necessary lapse of time" its effects would cease.[138]

Another frequent Thursday speaker was Giles Waldo Shurtleff, professor of Latin at the college and graduate of the class of 1859. Shurtleff was sober in every sense, a paragon of self-discipline and austerity in the old Oberlin mold. His temperament had made him well-suited for military service. At the Civil War's outbreak, he was elected captain of Oberlin's volunteer infantry company. Later, John Mercer Langston and O.S.B. Wall persuaded him to apply to help lead Ohio's first Black regiment, the 5th US Colored Troops. Commanding an African American unit subjected Shurtleff to ridicule but also earned him recognition. Four of his sergeants won Congressional Medals of Honor for taking charge of the assault at New Market Heights after he and other officers were wounded. For his part, Shurtleff was promoted to full colonel and eventually brevetted brigadier general. In peacetime, Oberlinites continued referring to him as "the General," a moniker that suited the straitlaced professor.[139] After the war, he helped lead the charge against alcohol as a leader of the Oberlin Temperance Alliance.[140]

In January 1884, Shurtleff gave a lecture concerning the "departure from the old and better standards" he had observed on campus of late. Students' uncouth habits were "affecting that symmetrical development of mind and heart." His first target was baseball, which had lately become an obsession at Oberlin. A source of exercise had ballooned to an undue spectacle, distracting students from more important pursuits. "We writhed around considerably under his remarks upon baseball," the *Review* reported, "and were disposed to think he was taking a needlessly severe view of the case." Among the other behaviors the General attacked were careless talking and idle whistling, throwing snowballs in the street, and eating peanuts in the chapel. He addressed all of these with trademark seriousness, deeming each a threat to Oberlin's integrity. "The force of the suggestions offered by the Professor on other points must be apparent to everyone who has his eyes open," the *Review* wrote.[141] Shurtleff reserved the most stirring language for his final subject, "the duty we owe to fellow students who are colored."[142]

His war record gave him as much authority as any white person to speak on the subject, and he treated the issue of Black dignity more solemnly than any other. Racial equality, he said, warranted "the careful attention of every student, every teacher, and every citizen in this community." Still, by his own admission, Shurtleff struggled to diagnose the source of African Americans' "social ostracism." He was ready to deem many students rude or reckless but reluctant to judge any racist. "Perhaps there is not one here who can be justly charged with consciously cherishing wrong sentiments respecting our duty to colored students," he said. "If such an unreasonable and cruel sentiment as this has grown up among us I am sure you have drifted into it unawares and . . . will be ready to do the right thing when the matter is fully understood." The abolitionist veteran endeavored to educate his listeners about the special severity of anti-Black prejudice. "No race of men since the beginning of history has been subjected to governmental tyranny and social obloquy so terrible," the General explained. In the face of such hatred, "any other race" would have cursed God in despair. Racial antipathy represented "a refinement of cruelty such as no one can comprehend without feeling it."[143]

If whites could never truly know African Americans' suffering, they could at least acknowledge it through their treatment of Black peers. Shurtleff asked rhetorically: "Does not this unspeakable wrong, which is patent to us all, lay some special obligation upon us toward those of our number who belong to this race?" White Oberlinites' responsibility to their counterparts of color extended beyond "mere cold recognition and permission to remain among us . . . more than a seat in the chapel and recitation room." Sufferance was insufficient. Black students deserved "to know from our treatment of them that they have our warm sympathy," he said, echoing Fanny Jackson and other Black alumnae's admonitions to empathy. White students may have been inclined to keep Black peers "at arm[']s length or look upon them as your inferiors," but the General commanded listeners "to welcome them to all the advantages of a Christian culture." To those who claimed equal access was all anyone was due, Shurtleff argued, but the scales of racial justice were weighted differently. Equality must extend beyond opportunity to include reciprocity. "Anything less than this is not a 'fair chance,'" he concluded.[144] Righting the historical wrongs of racism asked special effort of the entire community.

For all the ardor of his address, Shurtleff could not singlehandedly rally the troops. His own campaigns for temperance may have helped ingrain prejudice against African Americans. Moreover, laissez-faire had become an article of faith for most whites and was too entrenched to dislodge readily. In the ensuing years, the *Review* published yet more panegyrics to liberalism as the Anglo-Saxons' great gift to the world, an unstoppable force for human progress.[145] Student commentators remained confident that the free exercise of liberty would heal the festering wounds of the Civil War. They admired "New South" exponents like Henry Grady who contended that the growth of commerce, industry, and civil society would alleviate the region's racial tensions in time. "A repetition of those bloody years between '65 and '75 is now an impossibility in Dixie's land," read one student's essay from 1887. "'Let the dead past bury its dead.'"[146] The rising threat of racial retrenchment appeared nowhere in white writers' sight.

In the ensuing years, as lynching ran rampant and segregation laws began to be passed, Black graduates and students urged whites to remember their stake in Black livelihood. Stumping for the Republican Party on campus in 1889, John Mercer Langston warned of the growing assault on African American rights, especially from "Redeemer" Democrats promising to roll back Reconstruction reforms. Langston told his audience: "The colored men of the South were depending upon [the Republicans'] victory for their freedom. If the negro must thus vote so also this is the duty of the white man."[147] Returning to campus in 1890, alumnus Benjamin Imes raised alarms about voter suppression in the South and its implications for American democracy writ large. "It is not a question . . . of 'what is to be done with the Negro?'" he averred. "Rather what is to be done with the Republic itself [?]"[148] Charles Borrican, a Black member of the class of 1894, despaired of Jim Crow's rise: "The present condition of the colored man belies the statement that there is no higher station than to be an American citizen and a child of God."[149]

Literary society speakers and *Review* editors acknowledged the growing "race problem" but advised forbearance.[150] Like most northerners in the 1890s, these white student commentators privileged sectional harmony over racial equality. Self-determination seemed the most democratic option for the South, racial injustices notwithstanding.[151]

As they had since the 1870s, the new generation of *Review* contributors viewed Black uplift through the lens of racial essentialism. A Phi Delta speaker compared African Americans' three decades of freedom with "the fifteen centuries of free ancestry behind the Anglo-Saxons. He showed the need of faith, patience, and sympathy in the treatment of the Negro and concluded with a glowing tribute to the characteristics of the race."[152] Others were more hateful than hopeful. An Alpha Zeta "orator of the first magnitude," delivered "a fearless attack upon the character of the Negro race" at an 1888 meeting.[153] At a subsequent exhibition, he condemned Reconstruction as a "decade of misrule" riddled with corruption and fraud stemming from the empowerment of African Americans. Their alleged incompetence was, this student claimed, "abundant provocation" for the reassertion of white hegemony.[154] In a similar vein, an 1892 speaker described Black suffrage as "a menace to the nation" for "[teaching] the Negro to view himself as entitled to social, mental, and moral equality with whites."[155] All told, the advisability of Black male suffrage was the subject of at least seven literary society debates between 1889 and 1895, while it had been debated only twice between 1874 and 1888, according to *Review* reports. Rather than rally to the imperiled cause of Black civil rights, some white students began to wonder aloud if it was worth the trouble.[156]

How did Black students fare as the tone of the debate shifted? One source paints a troubling picture. In 1891, an African American newspaper published an account of discrimination in Oberlin's dining hall. According to the *Cleveland Gazette,* "Two colored students . . . occupy seats at a table apart from the other students, and are forced to sit in a corner with the matron's family. They must either accept that alternative or leave." This ostracism had gone on "for nearly two terms" and showed no signs of abating. White students and faculty displayed no remorse, and President Fairchild's successor did not take action. The injured parties also appeared resigned "to sit alone all the time to come" rather than protest. The article lamented that "the days of abolition" when a Black student "mingled with his white brothers in every phase of life" were a far distant memory. Once "colored students had enjoyed every privilege and realized every desire," now Black students waited in vain for acceptance. "Who will take the initiative in this demand for equality of rights to all?" the *Gazette* asked.[157]

The answer was not forthcoming. Instead, as Christi Smith has shown, Oberlin took steps to diminish Black enrollment. As part of its effort to compete with the nation's elite liberal arts colleges and universities, the administration sought to make its student body more male and more white. It invested in new men's athletic facilities and awarded merit scholarships to white male students. The college could have balanced these initiatives with grants for African Americans from the Avery Fund. Instead, over Black townspeople's objections, it stopped tapping that bequest in 1892. Charles Avery's trust was not exhausted, but more and more, white sympathies were.[158]

6

BEREA'S RACE PROBLEM
1889–1895

The tables in Berea's dining hall sat ten each, four on either side and one on each end (Fig. 6.1). On New Year's Day 1889, ten white students proceeded en masse to an empty table. "Whites only" was their unspoken message. At the next meal, a Black student got there first, and an altercation ensued. Word of the dustup spread to the nearby town of Richmond. The local paper's account was reprinted in the *Louisville Courier-Journal*.[1] In less than two weeks, the *New York Times* had picked up the story. The *Times* had been publishing Berea's appeals for donations since 1868. Each notice boasted of the school's color-blind admissions standards and its success in fostering racial reconciliation.[2] Now that commitment seemed compromised. "A disturbance which may cause further trouble is reported from Berea College, the school founded . . . for the coeducation of whites and blacks."[3] The article's title, "The Color Line at College," hinted at the wider racial division at work in the South as segregation was becoming law.

The *Times* added that Berea's faculty were quick to declare a whites-only table "contrary to the principles of the school." Indeed, the incident awakened them to the clear and present danger racism posed to the college's values. In forceful terms, an ailing Henry Fairchild condemned its rise on campus and across the South. Berea's president had always presumed that under the right conditions, whites would naturally learn to treat African Americans as social equals. He taught by example by inviting Black waitstaff to join his family at the dinner table.[4] When white students stopped extending their African American classmates the same courtesy, Fairchild was disturbed. He began to realize what Oberlin's president, his brother James, did not: the old approach to race relations had become inadequate to promoting African Americans' equality,

FIG. 6.1. Dining Room in Ladies' Hall, Berea College.
Courtesy Berea College Special Collections and Archives.

much less to advancing interracial fellowship. In June 1889, at the Alumni Association's urging, Fairchild and the trustees rescinded the social equality regulations of 1872. The president continued speaking out against racial injustice until his death that October. Egalitarianism began to revive on campus in the years that followed, but the college itself fell on hard times. Enrollment and donations had begun deteriorating along with Fairchild's health. They continued to slide thereafter. There was said to be "an air of dilapidation about the place" by 1893.[5]

The next time the *Times* covered Berea was in 1897, when it reported on a fundraiser for the college in Manhattan. The featured speaker was Fairchild's successor, William Goodell Frost. Since taking Berea's helm five years prior, Frost had revitalized the school through his philanthropic prowess and sheer force of will. His address that evening contrast two strains of "civilization" in the American South, one based in racial and class hierarchy and the other based "not by any circumstance of birth, but by merit." Education, he declared, was the best means of breaking down caste barriers and recovering the individual's right to rise. Berea was laboring toward this end, as it had been for thirty years. But Frost put a new spin on the college's anticaste vision. "Most of the educational plans and efforts had been for the negro," he said. "The white people also need education."[6] Berea had traditionally recruited whites from the mountains and African Americans from the Bluegrass in roughly equal measure. Frost's strategy was to prioritize white admissions from Appalachia.

Scholars have shown that by the late 1880s, enthusiasm for the work of racial reconciliation had dried up among northern reformers. The spread of white supremacists' "Redemption" agenda for the South significantly dampened expectations for change. White philanthropists increasingly deemed separate institutions of higher learning the most sensible option for Black education in the South. Rather than trying to compete for donations with schools like Shaw or Fisk, Frost opted to reinvent Berea as the premiere school for the whites of Appalachia. The new president played up the charms of these mountain folk, whose Anglo-Saxon roots and wartime support for the Union made their education a unique and appealing charity case.[7] Berea's rebranding bore fruit. Frost managed to double the endowment in five years.[8] In the same period, white enrollment ballooned from 166 to 455, while Black enrollment fell from 184 to 144. The president's goal became matching the student body's demographics to Kentucky's, where African Americans made up one-sixth of the population. If Berea became a microcosm of the state, he reasoned, its success could pose a powerful counterargument to Jim Crow, whose constitutionality the Supreme Court had lately affirmed in *Plessy v. Ferguson.*

Frost did nothing to restrict Black admissions, but he did nothing to encourage them either. Like Fairchild before him, he had come from Oberlin, where he had been both a student (class of 1876) and a professor. He absorbed the racial thinking of postbellum Oberlin and championed respectability as the key to African American uplift. Frost accepted Berea's presidency believing that the college's mission was to promote racial coeducation as a means of Black advancement. He also knew Berea was struggling financially and was convinced the school's future depended on attracting more white students. In his view, Berea would be seen as little more than a regional Black high school unless whites were recruited from beyond the vicinity, either from the North or from the mountains.[9] And once Frost grew acquainted with Appalachian culture, he came to view the welfare of its people as a worthy aim in and of itself. Unlike presidents past, he refused to make any decision that might jeopardize the recruitment and retention of so-called "mountain whites." Their wishes now took precedence.

While a few Black Bereans supported Frost, many took exception to his presidency and accused him of promoting prejudice on campus. They argued preferential treatment toward whites devalued African Americans' standing at Berea. Consanguinity had been Berea's watchword, preached by its aging founder and affirmed by its late president. Instead of carrying that egalitarian doctrine forward, Frost's white recruitment strategy made racial justice seem more incidental than integral to the college mission. African Americans warned the president's rebranding would fracture the campus, possibly for good. Seizing the initiative, Black alums mobilized against the threat of retrenchment at their alma mater. But as at Oberlin, their appeals to Christian kinship fell more and more on deaf ears.

Moments of Reckoning, 1889–92

After "unpleasant feelings" and "harsh language" arose in Berea's dining hall early in 1889, the faculty appointed a committee to meet with the students involved and restore "an amicable state of affairs." The faculty also tasked President Fairchild with replying to the *Richmond Register,* which they said had "misrepresented" the incident in a recent editorial.[10] The county newspaper had long been critical of Berea for "[forcing] the equality of the whites and blacks" and operating under the "false principle that 'of one blood are all nations of the earth.'" It gloated over the college's recent misfortune: "The not unexpected has happened, and the race war has broken out at Berea College." The *Register* alleged that Black and white students and even "some of the subordinate teachers" had brandished weapons before the faculty intervened. Predicting further clashes, the paper contended that integration made strife all but certain.[11]

Around the same time, the *Louisville Times* wrote Berea to ask whether Black and white students ever roomed together. Fairchild responded that they did not. The exchange incensed John T. Robinson, class of 1874. He was aggravated that the president had answered the question at all, let alone the way he did. "Is it to allay fears that too amicable relations exist?" Robinson asked.[12] The alumnus had possibly roomed with a white classmate his sophomore year. A Black student who matriculated more recently noted that the races did not date or room together as a rule.[13] Robinson wondered whether prejudice had become "so great that no such relation is possible." Expressions of egalitarianism had not always been so taboo. Before the social equality deliberations of

1872, Robinson recalled "at least fifteen young men, white and colored, who were chums and often passed a night in each other[']s rooms" and another "few girls on like terms."[14] He himself went a step further after graduation, becoming engaged to a white woman. She died before they could wed, but he married her sister years later.[15]

Race relations remained on the minds of Berea alums, administrators, and trustees into the summer. At commencement in June, Fairchild took as the theme of his baccalaureate sermon "the treatment due all men in all relations of life." Most of his remarks concerned the dignity of labor, but he surprised the audience by "[taking] advanced ground in the matter of social equality and denied the argument that it is to be settled by being let alone."[16] It was a marked departure from his past comments on race, when he had stuck to the language of equal rights. Berea was not promoting amalgamation, he declared in an 1878 campus address; it was merely fulfilling its Christian duty to afford "equal privileges, equal opportunities, equal possibilities." Whether fidelity to the Golden Rule would lead to interracialism was up to God.[17] In an 1885 editorial, the president again denied accusations that Berea was "forcing social equality against nature." As he explained, "We simply give the opportunity for an education to those that want it, opening the college doors to all persons of good moral character." Students were free to socialize with whomever they liked and were "not required [to] associate with any that are not agreeable to them."[18] Fairchild's stance was consistent with his brother's at Oberlin's. Now, however, Henry realized what James had not: a laissez-faire approach had become insufficient to ensuring African Americans' equal treatment, let alone inspiring interracial fellowship.

The president's baccalaureate remarks do not survive, but presumably he reiterated many of the same sentiments that September when he published an editorial on the "Race Question in the South" in a national reform newspaper. With his health in rapid decline, Fairchild may have sensed this would be his last opportunity to comment publicly on the issue. "It is the custom . . . of some very good and wise men, to ignore the social question entirely," he wrote, "and leave it to be settled by the righteous disposal of other matters involving negroes' rights and interests." Fairchild explained that this line of argument presumed that the civil rights of African Americans were accepted "as a self-evident principle . . . to which every act of state or church or society must conform." Since the end of Reconstruction, however, that basic guarantee had disappeared. Whites restricted African Americans' exercise of the privileges of citizenship with the argument that integrated juries, schools, and public facilities implied the absolute equality of the races. At present, Fairchild observed, "All the rights, interests and opportunities of the colored people are endangered, curtailed, and sometimes, utterly denied by fraud and violence, through pretended fear of social equality."[19] It was not only Redeemer Democrats who were at fault.

Jim Crow was changing the calculus of racial reform in the South. Before, whites could express indifference or even resistance to the prospect of absolute racial parity while still supporting some degree of Black advancement. Chastened by the dining hall dustup, Fairchild now asserted that any denial of the eventuality of social equality lent credence to reactionary efforts to "keep the colored race in subjection." If whites did not affirm that social equality was as much a right of African Americans as political and legal equality, all Black exercises of equality would be threatened. To eschew social equality was to approach race relations on white supremacists' terms. The president admitted that Christians working toward the elimination of "permanent divisions among the peoples of God" did not expect changes in southern culture to "take place suddenly." Still, Fairchild believed scripture's promise that "there shall be neither Greek or Jew, Scythian, bond nor free" would be fulfilled in the fullness of time.[20]

President Fairchild's change of heart caught the AMA by surprise. Michael Strieby, the organization's general secretary who had exhorted his fellow Oberlin graduates at the 1883 jubilee, wrote Fairchild's brother James with his concerns. Strieby wondered what exactly Henry meant by "social," noting that "the word is a slippery one." At the AMA, he said, "We do not insist on *social* equality for the Negro." Committing to such "delicate points" posed a "danger" to a missionary society like his.[21] According to historian Joe M. Richardson, the AMA stopped promoting "social contact" across the color line by the 1880s in an effort to mollify southern whites.[22] The sentiments Strieby expressed to Fairchild reflected that shift: "It seems to me our best fight now is on the recognition of equal manhood and rights of the Negro before the law, in the church, in the school, in the public conveyance, and in the public hotels, etc., leaving the question as to technical *social* equality to take care of itself."[23] Henry Fairchild had made similar comments in years past, but now he disagreed. Conceding the social equality issue invited the very forms of discrimination Strieby enumerated.

Back in June, the spectacle of the frail president issuing such a "forcible" call had greatly moved many in the audience at Berea's baccalaureate.[24] Three days later, the first Black woman to earn Berea's bachelor's degree addressed a reunion of Black and white alums in the college chapel. Fannie B. Miller, class of 1888, was a star student, the best Fairchild said he had ever taught. A Berea education emboldened her to stand up to discrimination. Not long after graduating, she was fined for disorderly conduct after refusing to sit in a theater's "colored" section.[25] When she returned to Berea in June 1889, Miller exhorted her alma mater to keep up the fight against caste and recommit to "the great idea . . . that there is but one family, and God is the Father of all; 'that he hath made of one blood all nations.'"[26] Inspired by Miller's and Fairchild's messages, the Berea Alumni Association adopted a series of resolutions for presentation to the trustees concerning "the great principle of the equality of man." They expressed their devotion to the ideal of racial kinship and pledged their support in seeing it upheld. Knowing that Fairchild's health was failing, they asked that Berea's next president also be "in full sympathy with this principle." Finally, they requested that the trustees rescind the "objectionable" social equality regulations of 1872.[27] Although the Alumni Association did not elaborate on the rationale behind this request, the dining hall controversy seems to have touched a nerve, especially with those who had been on campus during the upheavals of 1871–72. John Henry Jackson, one of Berea's first two Black graduates along with John Robinson, signed the petition as president of the association. Also present at the 1889 meeting were Angus Burleigh, the Union Army veteran, and Eugene Fairchild, the president's son. So was John Fee Gregg, now a college trustee, whose date with Mary Robinson had helped precipitate the regulations' passage seventeen years prior.

When the trustees received the Alumni Association's petition, they put the resolution to a vote. The minutes do not record any debate on the measure, only that "the resolutions of the Board of Trustees passed in 1872 in regard to the social relations of the sexes were rescinded." Fairchild had briefed the board on the "difficulty between some white and colored students at the Boarding Hall."[28] Between his report and the Alumni Association's appeal, they were apparently compelled to act swiftly. The president was the only member present who had voted for the regulations originally. Fee's cousin John Hanson, who had voted against them, was still a trustee, and Fee himself remained the board's nonvoting chairman. While the trustees' reversal was consequential, their wording was amiss. The minutes referred to the "social relations of the sexes" rather than the races. Perhaps the guidelines around interracial dating, while symbolically significant, had lost their immediacy by 1889, making them easier to rescind. The faculty had not formally adjudicated any violation of the regulations since 1883, when two white women had invited three Black men for a walk without permission.[29] Another Black undergraduate, James S. Hathaway, expressed interest in a white woman, but she refused him sometime before she graduated in 1883.[30]

In his autobiography, James O. Bond, class of 1892, recalled that his first love interest was a white woman, whom he met sometime between 1889 and 1891. Their abortive relationship reflected the indelibility of the color line at Berea even after the rescission of the 1872 rules. Bond, the father of historian Horace Mann Bond and grandfather of Civil Rights leader Julian Bond, counted his brief romance with a "Miss F." as among the most formative experiences of his college career. The two used to chat between classes and in the library about their favorite books and authors. Eventually he asked if he could escort her to a lecture. She was flattered but told Bond "that because of conditions we both knew quite well, she would have to take the matter up with her uncle." Her family, in consultation with the faculty, deemed the pairing risky "for reasons which to anyone at all familiar with the race problem in the South will appear obvious, if not convincing." Bond reported no ill will between them thereafter, but the relationship had a lasting effect on him. Born into slavery in 1863, Bond was his master's son. He struggled to reconcile the two halves of his racial identity as a young man. After his short-lived relationship with Miss F., he made a "resolution to be loyal to my mother's people and to make my life count for the most in their uplift." Bond accepted a color line in love but counted several white peers as "loyal and staunch friends."[31] He would dedicate his life to promoting interracial cooperation.[32]

Jim Crow was on the rise in Kentucky by the time Bond graduated in 1892. A month before, over vociferous objection from Black Kentuckians, the legislature passed a Separate Coach Bill that mandated racially segregated seating in train cars. The law was part of a wave of Jim Crow legislation sweeping the South. State lawmakers were moving quickly to segregate not only transportation but schools, parks, theaters, hospitals, and other public accommodations. Bond alluded to this growing threat to African American livelihood in his commencement address. Although dark clouds mounted, Bond took the long view and saw a silver lining. "Wrong for a time seem to prevail and the good already accomplished seem to be overthrown," he conceded, but right would prevail in the end. Adversity would advance civilization just as it always had. Like so many student commentators at Oberlin, where he would go on to study, Bond took a progressive view of history. His speech's title, "Hope for the Future," captured his optimism. Educational and material advances had created an indomitable "liberal spirit," which Bond credited with driving social reform. Liberalism enabled self-making by checking prejudice and upholding individual rights. It made character, not caste, the new measure of "manhood." As citizens received an equal chance to show their "worth," Bond said, Christ's admonition "All ye are brethren" came to pass.[33]

Alumna Mary Britton assessed matters differently. She had studied at Berea in its radical heyday, but her parents' deaths forced her to leave in 1874 before finishing her degree. She found work as a teacher and in 1877 became one of the first of many Berea alums to join the State Association of Colored Teachers.[34] Although the organization was nominally focused on education, it advocated for civil rights in many spheres. Berea alumnus John Henry Jackson, the state association's first president, helped lead the movement against the Separate Coach Bill. So did James Hathaway, the first Black man to be appointed an instructor at Berea, and Jordan C. Jackson Jr., a Black businessman and Berea trustee.[35] Britton and fellow Berea alumna Lena Tibbs were also among the activists who campaigned against the legislation. They testified before the railroad committee of the General Assembly in April 1892, and Britton's remarks were printed in the newspaper. Surveying the political landscape, her speech warned of a future far more foreboding than the one Bond foresaw.

Britton told the committee in no uncertain terms that Jim Crow laws represented a grave threat to Black livelihood. Fake fears of Black predation on white women were being used to promote segregation. Britton deemed legislation like the Separate Coach Bill "an assassination of Afro-American manhood and citizenship." It connoted that, categorically, "To be white means to be virtuous, intelligent, and aesthetic in taste, and to be of African descent means to be uncleanly ignorant and vicious in habits." By giving notions of inherent difference the force of law, Jim Crow made a mockery of liberalism, to say nothing of egalitarianism. Color, not merit, would order society if racial retrenchment went unchecked. Britton reminded the committee how her race had survived generations of bondage to prosper in freedom. Instead of their rights being "held sacred as reparation for the wrongs done the ancestors," Black people were being oppressed anew.[36] The racist logic of Dred Scott had resurfaced in the legal stigmatization of Blackness, Britton declared. History was headed backward. Twice as many African Americans were lynched in 1892 as in 1888.[37]

Berea's campus appeared a refuge from the rising menace of Jim Crow (Fig. 6.2). The college newspaper denounced racism in the same terms as the school's founders had: "All caste, whether it be that of color, or wealth, or rank, or birth, is contrary to the purpose of God, and alien to the spirit of Christ. In Him all race and Class distinctions disappear."[38] Fee was proud. Now in his mid-seventies and preparing to step down as president of the trustees, he boasted of the strides Berea had made toward his dream of racial accord. At a time "when there is so much commotion over the Southern Problem," Berea was the "object lesson" that it was "possible and practicable for colored and white to live in peaceful, happy relations."[39] African Americans remained a slight majority of the student body through 1893.[40] James Hathaway received voting rights on the faculty in 1889 and served as its secretary through 1892. He and his white colleagues adjudicated only one case of racial animosity among students in that time. In 1890, a white student was dismissed for provoking two of his Black peers. Other incidents hinted at camaraderie across the color line. After a white

FIG. 6.2. Class at Berea College, 1889.
Courtesy Berea College Special Collections and Archives.

classmate was expelled for insulting the faculty, two of his Black peers came to his aid. They petitioned the faculty for his reinstatement, even "promising their assistance to [him] to secure proper conduct from him in the future." When a Black and a white student took an impromptu trip to Richmond together, they defied both school rules and southern customs around interracial friendship.[41]

Black alums attested that the college's founding principles were upheld faithfully in the years between President Fairchild's death in 1889 and William Goodell Frost's inauguration in 1892, when Baptist minister and educator William B. Stewart led the college.[42] James O. Bond reported "no serious incidents involving race antagonism" during his college years. His classmate Henry Tinsley remembered there being "as little prejudice and friction between the races as [he had] seen anywhere" in the early 1890s.[43] But if the racial climate was sunny through 1892, the college's religious atmosphere and financial prospects were not. Like Oberlin, most of Berea's donors, boosters, and faculty were Presbyterians or Congregationalists. The school itself had no formal church affiliation. Fee was the pastor of Berea's nondenominational Union Church and advocated restoring elements of early Christianity such as baptism by immersion. Later in life, he stepped up his criticism of Congregationalists and the AMA, whom he accused of promoting sectarianism.[44] By the early 1890s, his writings had become so strident that he himself was accused of sectarianism and Berea along with him. Donors threatened to take their money elsewhere or withhold support until AMA-approved trustees could be appointed to the board. Others called for Stewart's resignation. Because Fee had championed his candidacy, the founder's opponents called the president's leadership into question.[45]

The college could not afford for dissension to continue. Expenditures surpassed receipts for 1891. Many of the wealthy northeastern abolitionists who were once reliable donors to the college had died or had begun supporting Black colleges instead. Fairchild had been too feeble in his last years to travel and make new friends for Berea. His successor Stewart was an earnest teacher but not an accomplished fundraiser. Matters came to a head at the trustees' annual meeting in 1892. After three days, they reached a consensus. The AMA's representatives were added to the board along with the Black alumnus and educator John Henry Jackson. Stewart resigned in protest of the AMA appointments but remained a trustee. William Goodell Frost was offered the presidency. His resumé made him the natural choice for the job: dynamic Oberlin professor, committed social reformer, and scion of an abolitionist family (his grandfather was among those whose names James McCune Smith floated for a professorship at the imagined Gerrit Smith College in 1859). Berea's trustees were unsure Frost would accept, however. He had turned down the job once before, in 1889.[46]

Frost was much more receptive this time around. If wary donors could be brought back into the fold and the college's books balanced for the near term, he would accept. But his reply did more than state his terms. Frost offered his interpretation of Berea's mission and outlined his plans for revitalizing the school. He identified the education of "the colored race" as the college's raison d'être. Berea's work taught the nation to place character over color. Like Bond, he defended the doctrine that all individuals should be judged on their merits, calling it "a principle of absolute righteousness." And like Fee, he described the integrated campus as "an object lesson" in racial accord, distinct from other minority-serving institutions in the South. Still, Frost felt Berea had not yet reached its full potential. For one thing, he said, the college's impact would remain limited until it offered more than a "second class education." Berea's calling card should not be that "it is a school for both races, or that it is cheap," he insisted, but that it offered a first-rate education.[47] He did not expect Berea to become an elite liberal arts college or research university. Rather he hoped the college would develop a state-of-the-art industrial program for skilled trades and the mechanic arts to complement its classical offerings.

Recruitment was the other key factor keeping Berea's influence provincial in Frost's view. Three hundred fifty students had been enrolled during the 1891–92 school year, a 6 percent drop from the previous year. Black students made up 53 percent of the student body, down from 70 percent ten years prior.[48] Still, Frost wrote the trustees: "We must get more students, and especially more white students." A majority Black institution with a mostly preparatory curriculum could not capture the public imagination, he felt, being too similar to southern Black colleges. If Berea was to exert its fullest "moral influence," it needed to resemble a northern college. In effect, it needed to look more like Oberlin: many more white students and drawn from further afield. The greater the number of whites enrolled from beyond Berea's environs, the broader the college's influence. Frost suggested recruiting underserved whites from southern Ohio, whom he thought could be enticed with a low-cost chance at higher education. "Northern students will give a good tone to the school," Frost contended, adding, "As the number of white students from the North increases it will become more easy to draw white students from the South."[49] A groundswell of white southern matriculates would represent a forceful rebuttal of Jim Crow.[50]

Frost did not advocate restricting Black enrollment, nor did he suggest Black students be proscribed from any area of campus life. For the time being, however, he felt their interests were best served indirectly. Putting white students first would put Berea ahead, and once prosperous, the college would be better able to support African Americans as intended. The board did not dis-

FIG. 6.3. "Colored Graduates" of Berea College, 1904.
Courtesy Berea College Special Collections and Archives.

pute Frost's reasoning. But it was not long before he met opposition from Black alums (Fig. 6.3). They saw something ominous in his revision of Berea's racial norms. As one Black graduate wrote, "His methods seem to require a continual emphasis upon the color question. This I claim is contrary to the principles of the institution."[51] What Frost and his allies considered a prudent course correction, African Americans considered a reckless concession to white supremacy. Battle lines would be drawn as the two parties contended for Berea's future.

Black Professors and White Recruitment: 1892–94

The first dispute over Frost's plan concerned the promotion case of James S. Hathaway, Berea's only Black instructor. By 1892, Hathaway had spent over half of his life on the campus. Born into slavery in Mount Sterling, Kentucky, he enrolled in Berea's grammar school in 1875 at age sixteen. Upon completing the college course in 1884, he was appointed tutor of Latin and mathematics in recognition of his academic prowess. Hathaway served as an instructor in the preparatory and collegiate departments for the next nine years. He was awarded an honorary master of arts degree in 1891, a recognition nineteenth-century colleges bestowed on graduates who made good. In an era when few college faculty held PhDs, Hathaway's credentials were even with those of his colleagues.[52] Hathaway did not encounter significant resistance teaching at Berea. One white student's father may have forbidden her from taking Hathaway's classes, but the only documented instance of disrespect toward him came in 1887 from a Black student, who was publicly reprimanded for the offense. Otherwise, his teaching progressed without major incident, and his responsibilities increased over time. After two years he was requested to help conduct morning prayers, placing him in a position of conspicuous authority before the student body. The faculty appointed him to "work in the interests of the college among the colored people" in between semesters.[53] In 1886, he began conducting summer institutes for training Black school teachers, also at the faculty's recommendation.[54]

Hathaway was an activist as well as an academic, and the faculty supported his advocacy against Jim Crow. In 1891 and again in 1892 Hathaway and his colleague Levant Dodge traveled together to Lexington to represent Berea at the Republican State Convention. With the faculty's blessing, Hathaway went to Frankfort in the winter of 1892 to protest the Separate Coach Bill, as contrary to the values of the Berea community.[55] After the bill passed in May, Hathaway cofounded a newspaper, the *Lexington Standard,* to give greater voice to the Black community and begin the fight for repeal. He was granted a leave of absence without pay for the fall semester in order to undertake the venture. The trustees referred the question of his promotion to assistant professor—"without increase of salary"—to a review committee to be chaired by Frost, who had assumed the presidency of the board from Fee.[56]

A few months into his first year, Frost drafted a speech to the campus community expounding on the leading aims of Berea. Impartial admissions was the second of his four precepts after quality instruction. Frost reiterated that the college welcomed all people of good character and was intended for no one group in particular. But his concern for white admissions was already beginning to contradict his commitment to racial equality. He told whites he only expected them to tolerate their African American peers, not risk any stigma that came with treating them as full equals. "We don't compel you to make any colored person your intimate friend," Frost wrote. "But we do say that as you work beside a colored man in the field, so you may recite with a colored man in the class-room with no loss of self-respect." What concern he showed for African Americans' dignity was tinged with condescension. Frost advised whites students to "make due allowance for the colored man if he does not come up to our standard in every respect." After all, he said, it was a "wonder" that the children of slaves and the grandchildren of "savages" were "not all just as boorish" as their ancestors.[57] White paternalism was not new to Berea; nods to hereditary racial hierarchy were.[58]

Frost's feelings on race came into even greater relief with the advice he composed for Black students. Counseling restraint in the face of discrimination, he anticipated Booker T. Washington in his claim that African Americans' displays of respectability would, in time, cure whites of their prejudice. Assertiveness, on the hand, would only worsen matters, he said. As an example, Frost recalled an incident from Oberlin's dining hall. A table of white students "beginning to feel quite reconciled to the presence of the colored, and quite friendly toward them," were "suddenly dashed back in to all their old prejudices when a rough Negro boy planted himself at their table," declaring it his right to join them. Frost blamed the Black student for the altercation that followed. The "rough Negro . . . [made] enemies for himself and his race" with such "uncalled for and ungentlemanly" behavior. Deference and patience were the only proper remedies for prejudice, he said; African Americans' merits would do the rest. In the meantime, Frost wrote that they ought not question the motives of their white "best friends" as some had begun to do: "These crazy colored people smell around to see if they can't find some evidence that the people who have sacrificed everything for the Negro race are not after all their enemies."[59] Whether he delivered these words precisely as written is unknown, although he made similar statements in an editorial for the *Lexington Standard* around the same time.[60] What is clear is that his sentiments did not bode well for Hathaway's case.

Frost publicly expressed his "desire . . . to see a 'Mixed' faculty" in due course.[61] But Hathaway was evidently not his preferred candidate. That the tutor had spent his entire academic career at Berea made him unsophisticated in the president's eyes, although Berea had hired white graduates as professors before. Hathaway taught as many or more courses as his colleagues, but Frost told him he was not yet qualified for a professorship. "The mere fact that he could come to such a conclusion . . . without ever entering my class-room must make his bias and prejudice apparent," Hathaway later remarked.[62] The trustees granted him leave to pursue graduate study, but even if he received further training, Frost would not guarantee his rehiring as a tutor, let alone his promotion.[63] The president made no secret of the fact that he considered the professoriate a rarefied order. "Not many men of any race are born to be professors," he told the *Lexington Standard*. Technical or professional fields required less of a pedigree, perhaps, but when it came to the liberal arts, "A college professor ought to be the descendant of generations of culture." The president's logic reinforced the idea that racial differences were congenital and that African Americans were developmentally delayed. "The colored race" Frost concluded, "will produce orators, statesmen, inventors, and authors long before it will produce men qualified for the higher work of education." If there were "some such [Black] men already" out there fit for the professoriate, the timing had to be right to hire them without jeopardizing Berea's fundraising.[64]

Hathaway knew the president's opinions put his place at the college in doubt. Like George Vashon had in his last year at New York Central, Hathaway saw the writing on the wall. The assumption that "'a colored instructor keeps away students'" was gaining traction at Berea, especially after the president's repeated assurances to prospective whites that they would not have to associate with Black classmates. If this was his alma mater's new ethos, he wanted no part of it. The last straw for Hathaway were Frost's statements about African Americans and the professoriate. His words ignored the college teaching careers of "a host of Negro graduates from Oberlin."[65] Anna Julia Cooper and Mary Church Terrell (who were Frost's students at Oberlin), John Mercer Langston, William Sanders Scarborough (a fellow classicist who was a year ahead of Frost at Oberlin), George Vashon, and Sarah Jane Woodson had all gone on to teach at Black colleges like Wilberforce and Howard. In disregarding their accomplishments, Frost made whiteness, not wisdom, appear the foundation of the ivory tower. Hathaway resigned in disgust in the fall of 1893 and joined the faculty of the State Normal School for Colored Persons (now Kentucky State University), a teacher's college in Frankfort. Its president since 1887 was the outspoken Berea alumnus and trustee John Henry Jackson.

Berea's board appointed Jackson to a part-time professorship of pedagogics around the time Hathaway left. Frost had recently revived the teacher education program, and he praised Jackson as being "eminently fitted" to teach in it.[66] A veteran teacher, principal, and now normal school president, Jackson was as qualified as anyone for the position. But Frost may have also tapped Jackson to placate African American alums, from whom he was beginning to draw fire. The leader of the loyal opposition was Jackson's college classmate John T. Robinson, who had also been a critic of Fairchild. Robinson took Frost to task in a series of editorials in the *Lexington Standard*. Besides protesting Hathaway's rejection, Robinson accused Frost of flouting Berea's anticaste tradition. The alumnus charged the president with coddling white prejudice to further his admissions goals. Frost gave the impression that "the Negro's whole tenure in Berea College is merely that of SUFFERANCE" on whites' part rather than a long-standing partnership between races. The school belonged as much to African Americans as to whites, Robinson insisted. Everyone should enjoy equal acceptance on campus.[67]

Frost and Robinson parted ways in their views on race and individual rights. Robinson advocated personal choice and believed freedom of association should prevail on campus. He had opposed the social equality regulations of 1872 precisely because he felt they interfered with students' prerogatives. "Character and merit should be the one test for all," he said. Yet Robinson added that prejudice "must cease to operate where another's rights begin." Berea should demand every student extend "ordinary courtesy and civility to all" and denounce any suggestion of "the supremacy of any class." To countenance such bigotry "educates caste in and never out." Robinson recalled that racist white students "received no encouragement" in the past; they either reformed or restrained themselves.[68] In reply, Frost reiterated his commitment to disabusing whites of their prejudice. But he added that rumors of radical equality on campus jeopardized white enrollment. Frost found it "useful" to deny such rumors outright where Robinson had advised ignoring them.[69] As for intolerance on campus, Frost maintained that African Americans' dignity would be enough to bring prejudiced white students around. Black students at Berea were "privileged" to be "demonstrating to the world that a Negro can be a gentleman and a scholar."[70] It was unnecessary, he said, to ask anything of white students in return—unwise, too, if it risked their not enrolling. Robinson would dub Frost's approach "condoning caste prejudice as a means of overcoming it."[71] Later that school year, Berea would experience its first incidents of interracial strife among students since 1890. In one case from March 1894, a white student was expelled over his "assault and wounding" of a Black classmate.[72]

Amid these tensions, employing Black professors took on heightened importance to African Americans. Jackson's presence on the faculty reaffirmed the college's anticaste tradition. But Jackson struggled to balance his time between Frankfort and Berea and resigned after only a year.[73] Eager to see another African American appointed, twenty-six Black students and graduates petitioned the trustees in June 1894. They requested that alumnus Frank Williams and his wife Fannie Miller Williams, who had delivered the impassioned address for equality in 1889, be hired as professor and matron, respectively. Petitioners noted that the college had appointed white alumni as professors in the past. And they emphasized that African American faculty would validate Black membership in the campus community: "In as much as the college is sending forth as many colored graduates as it is white . . . we feel that this recognition of its colored graduates is due the race."[74] Frank Williams once told John Fee: "Berea will never complete her great work for the colored people of this state until she is willing to have them represented by a worthy man in the faculty."[75]

In response to the petition, Frost reiterated the college's commitment to interracial education and noted the ridicule Berea endured for maintaining that position. "Our colored friends do not know how many burdens we bear for their sakes," the president wrote, then expressed his "grief and disappointment at the ingratitude and narrow-mindedness" of his Black critics. As for the issue at hand, Frost reiterated that any new hire had to meet the institution's high standards. Apparently Williams, like Hathaway before him, did not. Moreover, the president stressed that appointing a Black professor by popular acclaim would make him seem the "special representative of the colored element" on campus, thereby "drawing a color line" antithetical to Berea's principles.[76] Forty years earlier, Oberlin's trustees had made a similar argument in response to calls for hiring a Black professor. In principle, it was an impartial standard; in practice, it preserved the status quo. African Americans understood how appeals to color blindness could exclude as well as include. In that same letter to Fee, Frank Williams had clarified: "I do not ask that a colored man be employed because he is colored, but, being colored and efficient, color should not prevent employment."[77] Hiring someone simply for his color was illiberal, but so was not hiring him for that reason.

Williams maintained that an accomplished, charismatic professor could be "potent in bringing the two races together," and make everyone "think less of the color of teacher and student."[78] But Frost did not believe a Black professor would readily gain white students' esteem, nor did he see any benefit in them being taught by an African American. Instead, he judged Williams's hiring a liability that would provoke public backlash. Until society "more widely approved" of Berea's integration, the time was "not ripe" for Black faculty. For the moment, the president was convinced that the best means of "doing the work against caste" was "to secure white students." Apart from claiming that some Black female students "consider it an advantage to have a white lady as Principal," his response made clear the interests of Black students were of secondary concern.[79]

Frost did not speak for all the trustees with his statement. John Henry Jackson remained a trustee, and he and Jordan C. Jackson introduced a resolution at the same meeting in favor of "immediately employing a colored professor at Berea" as "just representation and proper recognition" of Berea's Black constituency.[80] To them, the appointment symbolized African Americans' integral role in the college's legacy. It was "a matter of justice" to African Americans, past and present, who had "contributed their means to help make Berea College what it is today."[81] Yet Frost opposed the resolution as written, and it was rephrased. "Immediately employing" became "as soon as practicable."[82] When printed in the *Berea College Reporter,* it grew more innocuous still: "'when it may be done naturally and without impairing the efficiency of the school.'" An editorial in a Louisville newspaper asked: "When will this time come? Who is to decide when it may be done[?]"[83] Apparently the president would choose.

Frost's imperiousness exasperated both Jacksons, who resigned from the board and accused him of stifling Black voices at Berea. Frost, they said, seemed "bent upon making Berea a second Oberlin, where colored students are admitted, more as a matter of sufferance or sympathy than as a matter of right."[84] In their view, the president encouraged condescension and entitlement by prioritizing white admissions.

Bloodlines and the Color Line, 1894–95

Frost saw the question of Black faculty through the lens of his white recruitment plans, which were in full swing by the summer of 1894. The previous school year, alumnus and Ohio pastor William Barton had enlisted over two dozen white students to study at Berea.[85] Their arrival helped put African Americans in the minority on campus for the first time in decades, with whites outnumbering them roughly nine to seven.[86] To Frost, this was a promising start, but more whites—especially more white southerners—were needed to fully realize his vision. The college had been trying to make inroads with the white population of the Cumberland Mountains for some time. In the past, Fairchild and other faculty had traveled to the region to recruit students.[87] Prejudice against African Americans may have kept some mountaineers from enrolling at a college ostensibly committed to racial equality, just as it did the poor whites of the Bluegrass. The son of Berea's most active recruiter alleged that the "the aloofness of the mountain people might have been broken down ten years sooner" were it not for Berea's employing Hathaway, for example. But with Hathaway gone, Black students now in the minority, and the president downplaying interracial exchange, campus mores were changing. The recruiter's son claimed these developments made it easier for potential white students to think, "'Little as I wish to treat niggers as equals and friends, I think I can to a great extent ignore the minority of them who are there, and keep them pretty nearly outside the circle of my real school life.'"[88] Disciplinary records bear out that estrangement. None of the infractions adjudicated by the faculty during the 1894–95 school year involved racially mixed groups of students.[89]

The president's admiration for Appalachian culture also flattered prospective students. Frost toured Appalachia in the summer of 1893, and he quickly became enamored with the region and its people. They had set themselves apart from other white southerners by remaining loyal to the Union during the war.

Moreover, their folkways seemed to preserve the noble simplicity of Anglo-Saxon civilization. A cult had already been forming around this white ethnic identity, with exponents like Theodore Roosevelt justifying imperialism by preaching the supremacy of his racial stock.[90] Frost dubbed Appalachians "our contemporary ancestors" and extolled the virtues of this forgotten white population.[91] They seemed to him a people frozen in time, uncorrupted by modern society but also deprived of its benefits. If Berea could position itself as their leading protector, the college could carve out a niche in the increasingly competitive marketplace of higher education. Berea would offer northern white philanthropists something Black colleges could not: the chance to do good and celebrate their ethnicity simultaneously. Growing xenophobia toward eastern and southern European immigrants only amplified donors' enthusiasm for uplifting their Anglo-Saxon kin.[92]

In capitalizing on the novelty of Appalachians, Frost's fundraising strategy worked hand in glove with new AMA initiatives pleading the cause of the mountaineer. Sociologist Christi Smith has shown how the association "differentiated its mission and aims" in the nineteenth century in order to compete with other Gilded-Age benevolent organizations. The AMA's advocacy for Appalachian Americans reflected its attempt to "draw status and resources" by "[creating] new markets for philanthropy."[93] Pitching to a Republican donor base, the association marketed mountain whites as an important constituency with which to counteract the voting power of white southern Democrats. Sociologists were enlisted to show that Appalachians descended from a loftier racial lineage than the South's "poor white trash." Academics and reformers alike claimed that Reconstruction had failed mountain whites by concentrating solely on African Americans. Appalachians also deserved recompense, they claimed, because they too had been dominated by the slaveholding oligarchy of the antebellum South. Were mountaineers' needs not addressed through a program of industrial education comparable to what Booker T. Washington prescribed for African Americans, this worthy white population might be outpaced in its social evolution. Frost helped launch a media campaign to spread these ideas through the popular press as well as in academic journals.[94]

Starting in November 1894, Frost went on the road to cultivate "a new constituency" of college boosters.[95] On return visits to the East, Frost lectured on Appalachia and the needs of its people flanked by prominent exponents of Anglo-Saxonism and eugenics, including Theodore Roosevelt, Woodrow Wilson, and the Harvard scientist Nathaniel Shaler.[96] On these occasions, anticaste ideals were eclipsed by Berea's mission to the mountaineers. Elsewhere Frost asserted that the interests of Appalachians and African Americans were not mutually exclusive and that serving the former would advance the latter. But Black alums like John Robinson rejected the idea that one race would ride another's coattails. "All that we contend for is that the colored people receive the same consideration or attention at Berea that white people receive. Manhood is the standard and not numbers or position." Many of the college's first donors contributed to the endowment expressly to support Black education. As such, African Americans had as much "right or claim on [Berea]" as whites. If the college was to be true to its roots as a "mixed school," then "[it] should make no difference whether white or colored students are in the majority." To think otherwise was to betray "the germinal principle (equality) which gives the school a right to exist." Around that time, an explosive device was planted on campus, presumably an outsider's attempt at terrorizing the interracial community. Fortunately, it was discovered before it could detonate, but Robinson declared that the "real Berea bomb," the danger of retrenchment, was still ticking. Should Berea not return to its abolitionist roots, Robinson warned, it would turn "into a white school with a Negro annex" before long.[97]

Not all African Americans affiliated with Berea shared these criticisms. J. W. Hughes, a student, believed Berea would be a success so long as its doors remained open to all. "Is it wise and expedient for the colored people of this south-land . . . to ignore the privilege of obtaining the advantages of these opportunities . . . simply because they don't like its President?" he asked. In his view, the college's principles were larger than any one person and would prevail in the end.[98] James O. Bond went further. Writing from Oberlin, where he was now a seminary student, he defended the president's dedication to Berea's values. When critics appealed to Black pride, Bond said, it was they who displayed a "spirit of caste" contradictory the college's ideals. "Let me suggest that as we are all descendants of one common parent, citizens of one common country and members of one common church, [we] cease . . . to talk about 'white' or 'colored' and simply speak of men as men and treat all according to merit." White recruitment efforts were a nonissue for Bond since character, not color, was ultimately what mattered on campus.[99] A minister of a Colored Methodist Episcopal Church visited Berea around the same time. In talking with students and touring the college, he found no evidence of antipathy toward African

Americans' presence on campus: "My honest conviction is that colored students will be fairly treated." But when he reported that "three-fourths of the faculty" showed compassion and concern for Black students, he allowed that the feeling was not universal.[100]

One thing that was indisputable was the change in Berea's student body. The number of white students increased from 269 in 1893–94 to 305 the following school year, while the number of Black students fell from 217 to 156.[101] The increase in white matriculation was in line with Frost's plans, but the net decline in enrollment reflected poorly on the institution. The president attributed the drop to the scathing editorials Black graduates had written about their alma mater. The president crafted his own message to the Black community with the help of William Barton, the alumnus and trustee who had recruited white students from Ohio. The appeal they published defended the administration's actions as consistent with the school's traditions. Entitled "Berea's Invitation Is to All" and emblazoned with photos of both Fee and Frost, the broadside stressed that the college's welcome remained universal. Those "who wished to make the most of themselves" would find satisfaction at Berea. African Americans were respected and content on campus, but "misrepresentations" in the press were keeping others away. Black critics were hurting their own race by preventing Berea from doing all it could for African Americans. Dissent strained the institution, which was already struggling financially following the Panic of 1893.[102]

Although Frost and Barton's statement declared it was "time for the friends of race progress to stand together," their supplement was more a defense of liberalism than a call for racial communion. Each individual deserved the opportunity "to make the most of every educational advantage within their reach," their appeal read. Berea had endured "ridicule and reproach" since emancipation for extending its welcome regardless of race. For Black "agitators" now to expect the college's attention to be "confined to the colored people"—a misrepresentation of his critics' position—would be as illiberal as the college's excluding African Americans. "Whosoever will make come" was Berea's standard. But to Frost and Barton, whether African Americans felt comfortable enough to enroll was apparently beside the point. "If you wish to stay away from Berea," their supplement told Black readers, "you will not be hurting the College, but you will be hurting yourself." Berea would be "marching on" with or without them. In the administration's view, as long every individual continued to be extended the same opportunities, the college was living up to its creed.[103]

Frost dismissed his detractors, but some students sought to give them voice. In the spring of 1895, members of Berea's oldest literary society, the Phi Delta, invited alumnus Frank Williams to be the keynote speaker at their annual spring exhibition. The society had been conspicuously integrated since its founding, and a majority of members that year were Black. By asking Williams to speak, the Phi Deltas fired a shot across the bow of the administration. Not only had Frost rejected the petition to make Williams a professor a year earlier, but Williams had also published a trenchant critique of the president's handling of the Hathaway case only few months prior.[104] Instead of honoring the literary society's choice as was customary, the faculty wrote Williams and rescinded his invitation, claiming that his "'attacks upon the management of the College'" forced their hand.[105]

The Phi Deltas cried foul, passing a resolution of protest which subsequently appeared in the *Lexington Standard*. Their remonstrance accused the faculty of suppressing free speech in a manner inconsistent with the liberal paradigm. The professors' actions seemed calculated to shield Frost "from serious suspicions of unsoundness charged against him relative to the principles of the College." It was not the Phi Deltas' invitation or Williams's words that were at issue: "The basis of this whole controversy is President Frost's attitude toward the colored people." J. W. Hughes, the Black student who had earlier advised looking past Frost's foibles, was among the signatories. An overwhelming majority of members supported the resolution, yet the vote was not unanimous. In fact, it fell out along racial lines. At least seventeen of the nineteen names in favor were Black and all seven of those opposed were white.[106] It appears even white students open-minded enough to socialize across the color line did not dare cross the president, at least not publicly. As for Williams, he would not apologize for criticizing Frost. He considered it his duty as an alumnus to mount "a brave and honest stand" against any deviation from Berea's principles.[107] Yet Berea's white alums did not seem to feel the same obligation. As historian Meg Gudgeirsson observes, they kept silent during this period when their Black classmates spoke up.[108]

Besides trying to protect the president from public censure, the faculty were also determined that the 1895 commencement go smoothly because a special guest had been invited. Daniel K. Pearsons was a Chicago physician, real estate mogul, and college philanthropist. Frost had paid him a call that winter and invited him to visit Berea. Pearsons agreed. Upon his arrival, Pearsons made a thorough inspection of the campus. Frost would later recall how he "investigated the institution from the library to the kitchen, and took great delight in the stalwart mountaineers who filled our Tabernacle on Commencement Day."[109] Enamored with the school and its students, the doctor pledged $50,000 on the spot, conditional on the college raising $150,000 from other sources. It was the largest private gift Berea had ever received. Black listeners present heard Pearsons say: "I make this gift to the colored people and mountain whites."[110] But the *Berea College Reporter* recorded his words as "to all humanity, and especially to the loyal people of these mountains."[111] The philanthropist donated to many American colleges but not to historically Black institutions, suggesting African American advancement was not his priority.[112] Pearsons would go on to donate a total of $225,000 to Berea. He conditioned his gifts on the raising of matching funds. Between his largesse and others', the college's endowment grew tenfold between 1892 and 1912.[113]

After Frost secured Pearsons's donation, it became harder to indict his leadership. Nevertheless, a "Citizens Committee" composed of some of Frost's most outspoken Black alumni critics—Hathaway, Hughes, Robinson, and Williams—appeared at the trustees' annual summer meeting to issue a formal complaint. Besides their usual condemnations of the "mental color line running through [Frost's] policy," they added their denunciation of the president's nascent campaign for Appalachian education. His prioritization of white admissions was already marginalizing Black interests, contrary to Berea custom. They were disturbed by "the 'good blood' theory" that Frost now invoked when speaking of mountain whites' Anglo-Saxonism. The authors had no quarrel with mountaineers; they considered them far more open-minded than their poor white counterparts from the Bluegrass. What distressed African Americans were the eugenic undertones of his homages to Appalachians' "superior lineage and eminence." Caste rhetoric flew in the face of the college's tradition of consanguinity. "We do not believe, gentlemen, that President Frost hates negroes," the petitioners explained, "but we do charge that his white policy tends to a white dominance."[114] Frost had lately been promoting Berea's ability to ease lingering tensions between North and South by educating white students from both regions.[115] African Americans knew sectional rapprochement would come at the cost of Black rights. And so long as Frost's agenda presumed whites' "birth, blood, and station" was a cut above, condescension would rule the day on campus.[116] Segregation, they feared, was not far behind.

Frost's critics made two requests of the trustees. They asked that as a show of good faith in the college's principles, Hathaway be acquitted from all insinuations of inadequacy as a teacher. And they implored that a Black professor be permanently appointed to the faculty. In response, the trustees declined to "defend every word the President has uttered," but they affirmed their confidence in him.[117] Having never formally charged Hathaway with incompetence, they declined to act on the first request, although Frost personally retracted any insulting comments he may have made.[118] To the renewed call for a Black professor, the trustees reiterated their unwillingness to appoint anyone to the faculty by acclamation or for reasons of race. The vote on this measure was not unanimous, however. The dissenting voice was none other than John G. Fee.[119] Berea's founder had begun to lament the administration's effort to establish a "white majority," telling the *Standard* in 1895 that "such a policy would not meet the design of the founders of the institution."[120] Fee had viewed Hathaway's presence on the faculty as a blessing: "The faculty rejoiced that they could exemplify their principles with the presence of a colored member."[121] Now at the June 1895 meeting of the trustees, Berea's founder hoped the college might reaffirm those principles by appointing a Black professor. He was outvoted.

Privately, Fee had expressed concerns to Frost about the "vigorous language" the president had lately used in response to Black critics, particularly John T. Robinson. Just prior to the trustees' meeting, Frost wrote Fee to explain himself. He apologized for "any harsh name" he may have called Robinson. The president viewed his chief critic much the same way Robinson viewed him, as "a demagogue who appeals to the prejudice and ignorance of his hearers." Frost recognized the irony. Responding to Robinson's allegations of racism, the president avowed: "These false statements are doing exactly what I am accused of doing!"—namely discouraging Black enrollment. Frost believed Robinson's actions were rooted in "ignorance and insanity" and that the critic was as senseless as his criticisms. "I do not believe he is a liar," he told Fee, "but a monomaniac."[122] The moniker was curious given Frost's upbringing. In the antebellum period, abolitionists like his grandfather William Goodell were branded monomaniacs for their single-minded pursuit of Black freedom.[123] Forty years later, Frost was accusing Robinson of exhibiting a pathological concern for racial equality.

The "Cause of Christ" at Berea, 1895

Berea's letterhead went through several iterations from the late 1860s through the mid-1890s. The earliest version simply bore the college's name and location. But Berea soon graduated to something more elegant, with the college seal appearing at the top of the page. Designed in time for the 1870 catalog, the circular emblem featured a gleaming cross at the center with "Berea College" below it. Behind the cross appeared the slogan "Vincit Qui Patitur" ("He conquers who endures"), taken from the family crest of one of Berea's first teachers.[124] Around the outer ring were the words of Acts 17:26: "God Hath Made of One Blood All Nations of Men." The seal made its final appearance in the college catalog in 1873–74, although it served as the frontispiece for President Fairchild's 1875 history of the college. Stationary emblazoned with the emblem remained in use through at least 1880. Thereafter, the college resorted to a more sedate letterhead with only "Berea College" and the names of the faculty. Further rebranding accompanied Frost's investiture. While his administration saw fit to add more header text, it did not reinstate the college's former motto (Fig. 6.4).

Frost's letter to Fee about Robinson was written on the new stationary. The right column of the letterhead listed the trustees, the left some facts about the institution: its founding by antislavery Kentuckians, its bargain tuition, and information about its student body ("from good Kentucky families, and from the North"). Proudly it claimed Berea was the "only college with this providential opening to efface sectional lines, and to educate the white people of the South without excluding the colored." In the center of the header was printed a different motto, the first words of Berea's charter: "In Order to Promote the Cause of Christ" (Fig. 6.5) The phrase had appeared in promotional materials for years. An 1878 pamphlet, for instance, encapsulated Berea's mission with the same words, but added: "As such it will be impartial in conferring its privileges and benefits upon all, without distinction of race."[125] By contrast, Frost's letterhead—and his policies more broadly—invoked whiteness and Blackness explicitly. Moreover, the pledge to "educate the white people of the South without excluding the colored" made African American admissions into an afterthought. Indeed, according to Christi Smith, "no mention was made in the college's publicity materials of its anti-caste history or integrated classrooms after 1895."[126] Over the next two years, white enrollment rose 69 percent while Black enrollment remained flat. The student body was 75 percent white by 1896; by 1901, it was 83 percent white.[127]

Berea College.

Berea, Ky. June 29th 1878.

To the Board of Trustees
of Berea College,
Dear Brethren,

In my work as agent I left Berea a few days before the opening of the fall term, purposing to spend from five to six weeks in the smaller towns of Connecticut and Massachusetts. Nearly two weeks however was occupied in New York City by questions arising from the settlement of the estates of C. F. Doty and Barnard Nellis. On account of the death of Bro. Whipple a large mass of papers had to be searched into and legal advice obtained before a satisfactory settlement with the A.M.A. could be reached. I visited Bridgeport, Waterbury, Holyoke, Northampton, Florence, Pittsfield, Westfield, Dalton &c, and gathered $234 - in money besides some subscriptions and general pledges.

Berea, Ky., June 30th 1895

FIGS. 6.4 AND 6.5. Berea College Letterhead, 1878 (*top*) and 1895.
Courtesy Berea College Special Collections and Archives.

The generic "Cause of Christ" held a wider appeal than the more radical motto "of One Blood." In 1893, Robinson reported hearing rumors that of late, some on campus were invoking the verse from the Acts of the Apostles in its entirety: "God hath made of one blood all nations of men, and set the bounds of their habitation." The alumnus claimed the latter portion was "not relevant to the purpose of the founders," noting that it had once been used as justification for segregation by Berea's enemies. "Is it possible that they have reformed the reformers?" he asked.[128] Frost remarked on the verse in his letter to Fee, claiming the "bounds" clause "set no limit upon the progress of any people." African Americans, the president said, deserved as much respect as whites if both parties were "of the same degree of culture and moral worth."[129] His liberalism taught that everyone deserved a chance at respectability. Yet his rhetoric around Anglo-Saxonism suggested that while refinement was attainable for all, it came more naturally to some. African Americans were not excluded, but mountain whites were grandfathered in. Ranking one person's heritage over another's denied humanity's essential sameness, its consanguinity. Was this the Berea way, African Americans asked.

Later in the summer of 1895, Robinson and company published their petition to the trustees as a pamphlet, which they titled *Save Berea College for Christ and Humanity*. Their introduction avowed that the college's mission was indeed the cause of Christ but that "the evil of caste . . . militates against the Christ spirit." African Americans refused to be treated as "objects of charity" when scripture taught that equality was everyone's birthright. "No accidental superiority or birth gives one class a right to dominate and control another," they affirmed.[130] Berea's founders had risked life and limb for that creed. Although the trustees compromised on color in 1872, they had redeemed themselves by overturning the interracial dating restrictions in 1889. Fairchild had come to realize there could be no equivocation on the issue: full equality must be the foundation of racial reform. But Frost saw the matter differently. A common campus and curriculum need not imply complete cooperation across the color line. Provided opportunity remained open to all, the races could pursue the cause of Christ in parallel rather than in unison. As long as Frost's philosophy was paying dividends, his vision would carry the day.

EPILOGUE

Matters worsened at Berea in the ensuing years. In January 1896, a group of Black and white students was discovered playing cards in the dorm. Cardplaying was expressly forbidden, but it was not considered a grave offense. Generations prior, such mischief had been commonplace among the residents of Howard Hall. Yet this was the first interracial incident of any kind since March 1894. Six of the young men involved—four Black and two white—were reprimanded. The seventh, an African American named John H. Mingo, was expelled. Classmates petitioned the faculty to reconsider, but Mingo's dismissal was upheld. He had come to Berea after graduating from normal school and briefly serving as principal of the Oliver Street Colored School in Winchester, Kentucky.[1] Mingo had recently served as recording secretary of the Phi Delta Society and had been among those who challenged the administration by advocating Frank Williams as the exhibition speaker. Now the faculty singled him out for "unwholesome influence among the students," a charge they had never before applied. They told Mingo's friends his expulsion was "in the best interests of the institution."[2]

As the doctrine of "separate but equal" became the law of the land in the wake of *Plessy v. Ferguson,* racial divisions widened on campus. Around 1898, twenty-three white students wrote the administration to ask that Black student-teachers "be removed at once" from the primary schools sponsored by Berea's teacher education program. "We do not have any prejudice toward any such teachers," their petition said, "but we do not want our friends and relation [*sic*] in these schools to be taught and trained by the colored race."[3] From their perspective, the request was not racist. It did not deny African Americans' ability to teach, just their suitability to teach whites. President Frost reiterated the virtue of racial separation when he told white families their children could "attend school

at Berea and have no more to do with the colored people than at their home."[4]
His administration's policies encouraged the belief that Black and white people
were equal so long as Black equality did not impose on white prerogative. The
student petitioners of 1898, for instance, tried to disabuse any notion that they
had embraced social equality by enrolling at Berea: "We do not want to go back
to our homes and tell that we had Negroe [*sic*] teacher[s] in Berea College. This
would cause us to suffer much ridicule and also would injure the school."[5] The
next year, some refused to be photographed with Black classmates.[6]

Watching events unfold, John Fee could not contain his indignation. The
college's patriarch was especially exasperated in 1900 when the administration
rejected a Black candidate, Thomas W. Talley, for a science professorship. Talley
had been specially recommended by Fisk University president Erastus Cravath,
the AMA's former liaison to Berea, but the administration opted instead for a
less qualified white applicant. To Fee, his snubbing was another missed opportunity for Berea "to complete a well-begun work, of the co-education of the so-
called races."[7] The human race was the only one that mattered to the aging abolitionist. He also took exception to Berea's new mission of "effacing sectional
lines." The founders did not intend for the college to reconcile North and
South through the cause of Appalachian education, Fee said. Rather, he and the
others had established Berea for the purpose of "effacing the barbarous spirit of
caste between colored and white at home." Frost's recruitment efforts among
the mountaineers threatened to "run [Berea] down to a mere white school."
Only when Black and white students were represented in "fair proportion"
could the college teach "the brotherhood of the race."[8] His beloved Berea was
at a crossroads. As the old reformer wrote in 1900, just months before his death:
"Our province is to convert the world . . . [or we] shall be converted by it."[9]

His words were more prophetic than he could have known. Early in 1904,
Kentucky state legislator Carl Day proposed a bill to ban racial coeducation in
private colleges. The so-called Day Law was aimed expressly at Berea, it being
the only interracial college in the state. Tennessee had passed a similar law tar-
geting Maryville College in 1901. Day and other lawmakers believed integration promoted intermarriage and encouraged racial strife. Berea's faculty tried
to disabuse these allegations in a remonstrance to the legislature.[10] Meanwhile,
fifty Black students petitioned Frost to defend the college's ideals.[11] As lawmakers deliberated in Frankfort, Frost preached a passionate sermon on racial solidarity in Berea using a favorite abolitionist scripture, Hebrews 13:3: "Remember

them that are in bonds, as bound with them."[12] Once the law passed, the trustees challenged it in court. The college's lawyers argued the Day Law violated due process by abridging freedom of contract and the privileges and immunities of Berea trustees.[13] Frost made a different argument, however. Historian David Nelson claims the president did not publicly dispute the Day Law's "constitutionality or justice but the fact that, given Berea's totally segregated nature, it was wholly unnecessary."[14] Testifying before the Senate Committee on Education, Frost stated that while the college was opposed to "repressing the Negro and calling him by humiliating names," there was a "Berea way of preventing the mingling of the races." As he explained, "We put such character and self-respect into the Negro that he keeps himself in order."[15] The statement endorsed the logic of segregation, albeit in a de facto manner. Furthermore, it suggested that African Americans were by nature unruly and insecure.

Although Frost's comments twisted Berea's founding principles beyond recognition, it was largely true that students of different races no longer socialized together on campus. Black observers claimed the Day Law "simply legalized what had already taken place in spirit" at Berea.[16] A visitor to campus in 1904 reported there was more "prejudice and friction between the races . . . than anywhere" he had been. "The bitterest feeling you can imagine was brought about."[17] Some organizations like the Phi Delta Society remained integrated.[18] But Black alums received reports that "colored students were [being] 'jim-crowed'" elsewhere on campus. Separate tables were becoming the norm in the dining hall. African Americans were no longer finding welcome on college sports teams or in the brass band, and there were purportedly attempts to exclude them from student lounges. Frost allegedly tried to persuade Black women to board someplace other than in Ladies' Hall so as to satisfy the prejudices of its white residents.[19] The faculty denied a white male student's request to escort a Black female classmate to a concert.[20] Segregation was becoming the unwritten rule on campus. The historian Carter G. Woodson, one of Berea's last Black graduates before the Day Law, bemoaned the toll racist treatment took on African Americans' self-worth. As he wrote in his classic 1933 critique, *The Mis-Education of the Negro,* "If you make a man think that he is justly an outcast, you do not have to order him to the back door. He will go without being told; and if there is no back door, his very nature will demand one."[21]

Black enrollment was the same at Berea in 1904 as it was in 1895, yet white students now outnumbered them five to one.[22] With African Americans now a small minority, it was easier for the administration to imagine the college's future without them. As the college's case against the Day Law wound its ways through the courts, Frost began making arrangements for African Americans' education elsewhere. Tuition exchanges were temporarily set up with Black institutions so that African Americans enrolled at Berea could continue their studies during the lengthy appeals process. In 1906, Kentucky's highest court upheld the Day Law, only striking down a provision that forbade the races from being educated within twenty-five miles of each other. Berea appealed to the US Supreme Court. As the case awaited final adjudication, the trustees made plans to establish a separate Black vocational school. The Lincoln Institute was to be located near Louisville, almost one-hundred miles from Madison County but home to a greater concentration of African Americans. Its curriculum was modeled on that of Hampton and Tuskegee. The new school would offer industrial education but no liberal arts coursework.[23]

Berea transferred $200,000 of its endowment to the Lincoln Institute, half of the pre-Frost endowment plus one-sixth of the amount raised since his arrival. The proportions were based on African Americans' share of the school's enrollment in each period. A donation from Andrew Carnegie promptly replenished Berea's depleted coffers. Frost committed to raising an additional $200,000 for the Lincoln Institute. James O. Bond helped spearhead the campaign among the Black community, but it made little headway there owing to loud opposition from other African American graduates.[24] They were insulted that college leaders gave no thought to Berea becoming a Black institution. "It would seem that in the name of justice, to say nothing of humanity . . . it should have been given to the colored people," some contended. "Had it not been for the colored people, there would have been no Berea College." To them it was further evidence of the Frost administration's "'freeze out policy'" toward African Americans.[25] The Kentucky State Teachers' Association, an organization dominated by Black Berea alums, drafted a final statement of protest. Its authors included Mary Britton, the alumna who had eloquently testified against the Separate Coach Bill in 1892; Jordan Jackson, the trustee who had resigned in protest in 1894; and Teachers' Association president Frank Williams, whose speaking invitation had been rescinded in 1895. Their memorial was published in 1907 as a pamphlet entitled *President Frost's Betrayal of the Colored People in his Administration of Berea College.* It was as much a lament as a censure.

In 1908, as the campaign for the Lincoln Institute was underway, the Supreme Court handed down its ruling in *Berea College v. Kentucky*. The majority opinion sidestepped the civil liberties issue and characterized the case as a question of corporate oversight. Because Berea was chartered by an act of the Kentucky legislature, it was the state's right to regulate its activities, including by prohibiting racial coeducation. Justice John Marshall Harlan, a native Kentuckian, wrote the dissent. Having famously opposed the Court's ruling in *Plessy,* he now took aim at racial segregation in higher education. Harlan branded the Day Law a "hostile state action" against the constitutional rights of Berea and its students. "Have we become so inoculated with prejudice of race," he asked, "that an American government, professedly based on the principles of freedom . . . can make distinctions between such citizens . . . simply because of their respective races?"[26] The question would hang like a pall over American jurisprudence for the rest of the Jim Crow era. It had been forty-two years since 1866, when the first African Americans had enrolled at Berea. After 1908, it would be forty-two years before any more could.

The Lincoln Institute opened in 1910. The same year racial issues once again came to a head at Oberlin. The alumni magazine published an article in March about a new literary society, Phi Sigma. "The reason for the formation of this society is that it has become generally understood that colored men are not wanted in Alpha Zeta, Phi Delta, or Phi Kappa Pi." Two African Americans had been refused membership in recent years because of their race.[27] There was now talk of creating separate YMCA Bible studies as well.[28] News of whites-only student organizations at Oberlin shocked and outraged some older alums. An 1851 graduate told alumni magazine editors that their report was "too extreme even for our fairly developed credulity."[29] Lucien Warner, a prominent member of the class of 1865, also wrote in dumbfounded. "Oberlin during its early history stood out from other Colleges for two fundamental principles, the higher education of women, and the brotherhood of man including the black man," he reasoned. "Is one of these two principles now to be abandoned, or kept only in the letter and nullified in the spirit?" Warner predicted that if the logic of separate but equal continued in extracurricular settings, it was "only a short step" toward segregation in all aspects of college life.[30]

Oberlin faculty condemned discrimination in college life, but current students and school leaders appeared more resigned to the presence of prejudice on campus, even if they opposed it in principle.[31] In a letter to the alumni magazine, a senior deplored racism as the epitome of illiberalism. But he understood how some classmates' desire for "fellowship and comradeship" could lead them to shun Black peers: "In what seemed to be a choice, one good has been chosen at the expense of a far greater good."[32] Oberlin's acting president. Azariah Smith Root, echoed that theme in a memo to Oberlin trustees, noting: "It is this social side of the society life which brings into existence the colored question."[33] The chair of Phi Delta's membership committee was unashamed to admit that fact. Accounting for the society's recent rejection of William Warwick, a Black applicant, he explained: "the presence of a colored man in our ranks would for many of us spoil utterly the social side of society life." Warwick was otherwise qualified, but "few of us would have been able to give him the glad hand of fellowship and the social equality which would be his due." In this white student's estimation, color prejudice was a forgone conclusion, insurmountable regardless of any individual's merits. Moreover, he said, it was unfair to Warwick to raise his hopes for white acceptance "outside Oberlin wal[l]s" by treating him as an equal on campus.[34] The circumstances seemed to him beyond dispute. But to the alumni of Phi Delta, whose ranks once included the likes of John Mercer Langston and George Vashon, racial proscription violated the tradition and spirit of their society.[35] They insisted current members reconsider Warwick's application. When he was eventually admitted, he became the only African American, male or female, to join any of Oberlin's six "white" literary societies.[36]

The literary society scandal coincided with an uproar over the treatment of Oberlin's Black athletes. Every year, the college competed in Ohio's "Big Six" track and field championships, which were held in Columbus. In 1909, the Oberlin team had opted to stay in second-rate accommodations there rather than see its African American members refused at one of the city's finer hotels. In 1910, however, white athletes chose comfort over solidarity, claiming that the "service and food [had] been very unsatisfactory" the previous year and "the opportunity for success at the meet [had] suffered" as a result.[37] They told sprinter Joseph Jones and high jumper Henry Williams that they would have to find someplace else to stay during the event. Jones and Williams intended to boycott, but acting president Root persuaded them to go.[38] He informed the trustees that the separate arrangements for Black athletes were "not due at all to any opposition on the part of our boys to the colored men." White athletes would have "gladly take[n] them to the best hotel in the city" if it admitted

African Americans. Root, an alumnus of the class of 1884, characterized the issue as being "not an Oberlin difficulty but a Columbus difficulty." Like the Phi Delta student, he placed the blame with the outside world. But his phrasing revealed his own racial bias; "the colored men" were somehow distinct from "our boys."[39]

President Henry Churchill King returned from overseas that autumn and addressed the controversies that arose in his absence. Like Root, King had attended Oberlin in the twilight of its reform years, graduating in 1879. He admired the abolitionist generation but was committed to modernizing his alma mater. While King championed liberal ideals at home and abroad, he accepted that times had changed where race was concerned. "I think the attitude of the students toward the colored question as a whole is merely representative of the attitude of the whole north," he told the press in September 1910. "Of course they are not zealous advocates of equal rights for negroes as were the early students."[40] His administration managed to condemn racism while countenancing it. King, like his friend and correspondent Frost, preached "self-respect" as the solution to the race problem. Oberlin's president staked out his position in a lecture he delivered late that fall. Just as self-respecting whites knew there was no shame in acting justly toward African Americans, he asserted, self-respecting African Americans had pride enough in their race not to demand social equality with whites. "In King's view," historians Gary Kornblith and Carol Lasser explain, "by embracing their racially distinct character, Oberlin's people of color would willingly submit to their own segregation." The president's object was "to keep the peace, not to achieve social justice."[41] A debate over dormitory assignments a few years later put his priorities on full display.

Into the twentieth century, fewer and fewer Black women found welcome in Oberlin campus housing. Some classmates continued to balk at sitting next to them in the dining hall and at lectures. The issue became concerning enough that the dean of women, Florence Fitch, held a special meeting in 1908 chiding everyone to be courteous.[42] The next year, Fitch floated the idea of a separate Black dormitory as a compromise, but her proposal did not gain traction. The dean began directing Black women to "colored" boarding houses in town instead, arguing they would find a warmer welcome there.[43] Between white students' prejudice and Fitch's guidance, by 1913 it had become an unwritten rule than no more than two African Americans would be housed in the women's dormitory per term.[44] That fall, Mary Church Terrell enrolled her two daughters at Oberlin. Terrell was by then one of Oberlin's most distinguished living alums; among her many accomplishments, she was former president of the National Association of Colored Women, a charter member the NAACP, and a cofounder of the Colored Women's League and the National Association of College Women. She credited her success to her education at Oberlin and intended for her children to enjoy the same advantages she did.

Quickly, however, she learned that the Oberlin of 1913 was a different place from the one she left in 1884. When she met with the dean of women in June to discuss her daughters' enrollment, Fitch tried to explain that the campus's racial climate had changed. For one thing, Terrell's girls would not be able to live in the women's dormitory because the two spaces reserved for African Americans were already taken. When Fitch would not guarantee them places in their second year, Terrell was indignant.[45] She would not stand for them being "forced to live in a boarding house kept exclusively for Colored girls . . . deprived of one of the very greatest benefits" of an Oberlin education. Segregation, Terrell said, excluded African Americans from "many phases of college life experienced only when a number of students live together." She knew those benefits firsthand and wanted them for her children. "I brought my daughters to Oberlin so that they might measure arms with white boys and girls, for I felt this would give them an outlook upon life . . . which they could secure in no other way." Among her own life's greatest blessings had been the chance "to pursue my course thru Oberlin College as a human being," accorded equal opportunity and treated with equal respect. She told Fitch it would be better for the college to lose "a few hundred prejudice ridden students" by recommitting to racial equality than to lose its soul by indulging Jim Crow.[46]

Terrell visited campus again that winter. This time, she sought the help of the secretary of the college, Fitch's superior, in securing rooms for her daughters on campus. He told her point-blank that he was "strongly against allowing them to board in any of the college dormitories and thus be brought into social contact with white students." Stunned at the frankness of his racism, Terrell appealed to President King as a last resort. This housing issue illuminated a deeper moral crisis at Oberlin, she told King, who was a personal friend. Their alma mater had lost its moorings when Black students were "really persuaded to believe that by flocking together all the time and never mingling at all with the white students, they are exhibiting a tremendous amount of 'self respect.'" In her day, "It was quite possible to conceive of a white girl's having a genuine friendship for a Colored girl without the latter's having to force herself upon the former for recognition." In the "trying years" since, when Terrell had been "beaten and buffeted about by American race prejudice," her relationships with white classmates had sustained her faith in the prospect of racial harmony. She was devastated that interracial contact, let alone friendship, was becoming officially discouraged on campus. "Altho[ugh] I try to be optimistic in this wicked and cruel country, in which everything is done to . . . break the heart of my unfortunate race," she wrote King, "nothing has come so near forcing me to give up hope . . . than the heart-breaking back-sliding of Oberlin College."[47]

While the president was moved by the alumna's plea and shocked by the college secretary's prejudice, he defended his administration's approach to race. "I can guess a little how hard the general situation in the country must often seem to colored people," King wrote Terrell, "but I hope that they will not make the mistake of turning against those who want to be their genuine friends." Oberlin was still capable of doing "valuable work for a limited number of colored students." White mindsets being what they were, however, King said African Americans' integration could not be as complete as it once was. Separate boarding houses were unavoidable. So was some whites' "lack of consideration" for Black peers.[48] Sixty years earlier, Professor Henry Cowles had informed prospective applicants: "We believe in treating men according to their intrinsic merits—not according to distinctions over which they can have no control. If you are a young gentleman of color, you may expect to be treated here according to your real merit."[49] Now President King told Terrell that Black students should anticipate whites excluding them from certain areas of campus life. If they wanted to study at Oberlin, African Americans would have to accept some degree of ostracism because any resistance on their part would only make matters worse. "I want to have the colored students as careful as possible not to give needless offense," he wrote Terrell.[50] She withdrew her daughters at the end of their first year, but not before notifying the NAACP of her alma mater's retrenchment.[51]

Oberlin had always been a predominantly white institution. African Americans made up less than 5 percent of enrollment around the turn of the twentieth century.[52] That was a smaller proportion than during Reconstruction but comparable to their share in the antebellum period. Back then, the college was synonymous with Black freedom. African Americans exercised outsized influence over the reputation of their alma mater and over the course of reform on campus. Their minority standing did not translate to a minority interest. They had the ear of school leaders and the attention of their peers. Although their advocacy did not fully convert the institution to egalitarianism, it pushed many whites to take a stake in Black lives. If Oberlin's interracial experiment was conceived in liberty, African Americans helped dedicate the college to the proposition of equality. They knew that realizing that ideal would not be easy. Righting racial inequity was far more difficult than granting rights irrespective of race. Oberlin's Black female graduates, in particular, knew that biases against Blackness ran deep. To shift the racial paradigm, they entreated whites to reset their understandings of race and gender and appreciate Black men and women for their common humanity.

Liberalism was compatible with egalitarianism so long as an attack on one person's freedom was understood as an attack on everyone's. In the post–Civil War period, however, championing equal rights and self-sufficiency became a pretext for avoiding the harder work of dismantling white supremacy. Racial discrimination remained liberals' enemy, but as national support for Reconstruction waned, more and more white reformers abandoned racial reconciliation as an end goal. Individual liberty came to be seen by groups like the AMA as the race problem's one and only solution. That logic made it easier for some whites at Oberlin and Berea to downplay prejudice and for others to indulge in it, claiming personal prerogative. African Americans and some aging white allies continued challenging racial caste and asserting the kinship of the human family, but abolitionist campuses turned their attention to other reforms. Absent a collective, sustained dialogue around race, Oberlin and Berea fractured along color lines. The emergence of social evolutionism compounded Black and white estrangement by placing heredity before mutuality. With fellowship forsaken and laissez-faire ascendant, the chances for egalitarianism's revival on campus grew slim. The door was open for Jim Crow's entry. Black students at both schools fell victim to the tyranny of a white majority whose racism even school leaders declined to oppose. Catering to prejudice was deemed more expedient than trying to dismantle it. By the start of World War I, New York Central had faded into legend, Berea was all white, and Oberlin, the prototypical abolitionist college, was beholden to the very bigotry its experiment had once contested.

The irony of this history makes it that much more tragic but also, perhaps, that much more relevant as a cautionary tale for our own time. Since the 1960s, civil rights legislation has banned discrimination in higher education and other institutions. Formal barriers to higher learning have fallen, and millions of African Americans and other historically disadvantaged groups can ostensibly pursue dreams their grandparents could not. At the same time, however, half a century's worth of opportunity has not yielded racial equity in higher education. According to recent figures from the National Center of Education Statistics, the rate of African Americans' immediate enrollment in college after high school was 8 percent lower than for white Americans, while the percentage of African Americans ages eighteen to twenty-four who were neither enrolled nor working was 11 percent higher. Forty-five percent of whites ages twenty-five to twenty-nine had earned a bachelor's degree or higher compared with 29 percent for their Black counterparts. In the fall of 2018, when African Americans made up 13 percent of the US population, they accounted for just 6 percent of all full-time faculty in degree-granting postsecondary institutions.[53] According to the most recent national study from the American Council on Education and TIAA Institute, 8 percent of college presidents in 2016 were Black compared with 80 percent who were white.[54] For each of these measures, the statistics for Hispanic Americans and Native Americans also diverge unfavorably from white averages.

Nearly all universities now express some degree of support for diversity and inclusion on campus. But inclusivity cannot be assumed merely because a university admits students from a wide array of backgrounds or counts multiculturalism among its values. The climate at many institutions today remains unwelcoming to African Americans and other minorities. A recent study finds that those who attend historically Black colleges and universities (HBCUs) were over one-third less likely to develop high blood pressure or high cholesterol as adults compared with those who attend predominantly white institutions.[55] For a possible explanation as to why, visit the website of the *Journal of Blacks in Higher Education* and peruse its running log of news stories on campus racial incidents.[56] Accounts include everything from racist graffiti and noose hangings, to verbal abuse and profiling, to white supremacist demonstrations and blackface incidents. Reports arrive regularly from every region of the country and from institutions of every stripe—public and private, secular and religious, research universities and small liberal arts colleges.[57] Scrolling through them, it is hard to say which is more disturbing, the incidents themselves, their frequency, or their pervasiveness. But what is also striking is the courage of the student activists who document and protest the hate they encounter on campus. By articulating how their admission has not equated to their full acceptance, these collegians of color join a brave line of truth tellers stretching back to the Oberlin Black student committee of 1841 and including figures like Mahommah Baquaqua, Angus Burleigh, and Fanny Jackson.

The first experiments in interracial education make it abundantly clear that colleges are not ipso facto collegial, even if they espouse racial tolerance and mutual respect. Whether a university chooses to dedicate itself to the work of racial justice is that institution's decision to make. But if it makes that commitment, it must fully honor it. Lip service can be as detrimental as disregard. Hesitancy and half measures can demoralize the distressed without actually addressing the problem. It was probably not a coincidence that New York Central's Black enrollment fell by half the year after its administration forced out William Allen. And the long shadow of Berea's social equality controversy demonstrated how deeply the trustees' resolutions wounded that generation of students. If antiracism and inclusion are genuinely among an institution's priorities, then those in power must be direct and proactive about promoting them. As one recent study concludes, "Mitigating racial incidents on campus requires the same level of anticipation, monitoring, and attention, as does enrollment management, course registration, fundraising, or any other operational procedure."[58] To address this imperative like the others means expending resources. New York Central learned the hard way what happens when the best intentions rest on unstable funding.

Actions speak louder than money or words, especially when it comes to building trust. As the late social psychologist Larry E. Davis exhorted higher education leaders, "If we are to ever make our colleges and universities resemble more closely the America to which we aspire, we must at some point have the courage to seek change."[59] Good faith leadership in the cause of racial justice entails taking time, making sacrifices, showing humility. One of the more striking moments in the abolitionist college saga came in 1889 when Henry Fairchild publicly acknowledged the blind spots in his own racial thinking and embraced social equality when other white leaders feared to do the same. That episode, which helped inspire a brief renaissance of egalitarianism at Berea, illustrated an important point. College presidents are more than wardens of educational bureaucracies. Historian Eddie R. Cole points out that the leadership of a university comes with "moral authority."[60] How and when presidents and administrators opt to exercise their power matters. But responsibility for equity and inclusion should not rest solely with them. Of late, diversity task forces at Harvard, Stanford, Wisconsin, and other institutions have reached a similar conclusion: Because everyone contributes to a campus's climate, all members of the community must take responsibility for its welfare.

College viewbooks advertise racial diversity as a selling point, and despite repeated legal challenges, the Supreme Court has, as of this writing, upheld it as being among "those intangible characteristics . . . that are central to [a university's] identity and educational mission."[61] However, while the benefits of living and learning in a multicultural community are considered universal, the burdens tend to fall disproportionately on students of color. Most enter colleges that are much less diverse than the high schools they attended, owing to the influence of race, income, and residential segregation on secondary school demographics. For these same reasons, many white matriculates attend colleges that are much *more* racially diverse than their high schools were. This disconnect can be a recipe for conflict or, more likely, indifference. History shows white students can more easily disregard racist incidents on campus. And as early experiments in racial coeducation made clear, white apathy poses a grave threat to racial justice. If students of color are the only ones actively fighting racism on campus, it will be construed as "their" pet problem. To combat this tendency, institutions that commit to this work should talk about inclusivity the way they do academic honesty, as a collective obligation all members must accept and uphold. Giles Shurtleff said as much in 1884. When the general-turned-professor spoke of Oberlin's "duty" to its most vulnerable members, he excused no one from service: "This matter . . . needs the careful attention of every student, every teacher, and every citizen in this community."[62]

As colleges and universities search for ways of making themselves more welcoming and affirming, there is one final lesson they might draw from the abolitionist college legacy. It is difficult to pinpoint the precise moment when nineteenth-century experiments in interracial education went awry, but trouble tended to arise *after* college leaders and boosters claimed their institutions had solved the race problem. Their mistake was in thinking of racial diversity as a deliverable. In fact, it is a dialogue, a dialectic of ideals and experience, much like faith. Robert Maynard Hutchins, who grew up in Oberlin and went on to become president of the University of Chicago, famously described liberal education as "the great conversation" between minds of the past and the present.[63]

Students engaging with big ideas is indeed one of higher education's critical functions. But so is students engaging with one another—as discussants, lab partners, or teammates, yes, but firstly as people. On campus or off, all humans are fully human, equally deserving of dignity and respect. Only by honoring and protecting that equality can universities live up to their name and truly be communities of the whole.

EPILOGUE

Students engaging with big ideas is indeed one of higher education's critical functions. But so is students engaging with one another—as discussants, lab partners, or teammates, yes, but firstly as people. On campus or off, all humans are fully human, equally deserving of dignity and respect. Only by honoring and protecting that equality can universities live up to their name and truly be communities of the whole.

ACKNOWLEDGMENTS

I began this research in graduate school. Generous financial support from the Ashford Dissertation Fellows Program, the Center for American Political Studies, and the Charles Warren Center for Studies in American History at Harvard; the Bentley Historical Library at the University of Michigan; Oberlin College Archives; and the Spencer Foundation and National Academy of Education made it possible for me to visit far-flung archives and finish writing my dissertation. I was especially grateful for the moral support of my dissertation committee. They have remained in my corner since then, offering advice, reading revisions, and writing letters on my behalf. I cannot hope to repay the kindness of Ronald Butchart, Julie Reuben, John Stauffer, and Laurel Thatcher Ulrich, but I try to pay it forward to my own students. James Brewer Stewart belongs in this category as well. He believed in the significance of this project before I could fully articulate it myself.

My graduate school buddies have been there for me, too. Celebrations and commiserations with Christopher Allison, Carla Cevasco, Dan Farbman, and Rebecca Scofield have helped get me through the last five years, just as they did the previous six. As a cohort, we've gone from sharing general exam notes to sharing parenting tips. They are remarkable historians and even better friends. I'm grateful for other friendships that have extended beyond the walls of the Barker Center. Zach Nowak has been a mensch for all seasons. Conversations with him, Collier Brown, Chloe Chapin, Bradley Craig, Holger Droessler, Amy Fish, Elizabeth Jemison, Theresa McCulla, and Arthur Patton-Hock have encouraged me to stay the course and keep things in perspective. I could say much the same of education history friends, including Eddie Cole, Jon Hale, Michael Hevel, Alex Hyres, Mike Jirik, Alisha Johnson, Erika Kitzmiller, and Campbell Scribner.

A postdoctoral fellowship at Boston University's Kilachand Honors College gave me the headspace to reconceive this project as a book. My fellow postdocs inspired me daily with their creativity as teachers and scholars. Trent Masiki remains a regular and valued conversation partner. The KHC staff and leadership set a shining example of what it means to serve students (and how to be good officemates). Special thanks to Carrie Preston for her mentorship. Since leaving KHC, I have been immensely grateful for the support of my Assumption University colleagues, who have welcomed me to campus, encouraged my research, and inspired me with their deep commitment to teaching and mentoring. There are simply too many wonderful people at Assumption for me to name here (and risk leaving someone out!), but I would specifically like to thank the my intrepid department chairs Carl Keyes and Irina Mukhina. I am also grateful to the Center for Purpose and Vocation, the D'Alzon Library, the Division for Student Success, the History Department, the Honors Program, the Office of the Provost, and the Women's Studies Program. Interest and input from students has meant a great deal, too, especially from members of the ALANA Network and the Black Student Union.

Research funds from Kilachand and Assumption helped me hire outstanding student research assistants. Jared Flippen and Catalina Zamarano scoured college catalogs to compile extensive databases I still refer to regularly. Samantha Surowiec relied on their handiwork in completing her painstaking analysis of literary society memberships as part of a summer research fellowship. Olivia Burke put great care and good cheer into compiling the bibliography. Tim Bell worked overtime proofreading the entire manuscript. He was never my student, nor was he paid, but he's my dad.

Many of the librarians and archivists who made my dissertation possible reprised their roles for this iteration. Mary Kimberly is a faithful caretaker of McGraw and New York Central College history. I wish her late husband and fellow historian Carl could have seen this book come out. At Oberlin, Ken Grossi and Louisa Hoffman fielded numerous inquiries and requests with alacrity. I am grateful for their help these many years. Roland Baumann has also given generously of his time and his extensive knowledge of Oberlin history, and Jack and Kathy Secrist were gracious hosts during my 2018 research trip. Tim Binkley, Sharyn Mitchell, Lori Myers-Steele, and Rachel Vagts at Berea were a pleasure to work with. I am especially indebted to Sharyn and her intern Ian Paine for conscientiously locating and scanning many valuable documents

I could not access from afar during the pandemic. True to form, the American Antiquarian Society held a number of sources for this project that were unavailable anywhere else. I thank Kimberly Toney and her colleagues for making the Antiquarian Society such a hospitable place to do research and bring students.

As I completed the manuscript, I received generous feedback from a number of senior scholars whose research has inspired my own. Nina Silber offered comments and encouragement on my book proposal. Carol Lasser and Gary Kornblith greatly enriched this project with their critiques and advice at multiple points. Steve Gowler gave helpful feedback on chapter 4. Adam Nelson kindly read the entire manuscript and offered insightful edits. Richard Blackett and Ed Rugemer welcomed me to this book series and suggested important fixes and additions to the manuscript, as did the anonymous outside reviewer. LSU Press editor in chief Rand Dotson patiently answered numerous questions about publication and stewarded my manuscript through the process along with his hardworking colleagues Neal Novak, Sunny Rosen, and James Wilson. I thank George Roupe for copyediting the manuscript and Jake Raabe for compiling the index.

Ultimately, my family is most to thank for helping me write this book. The love and support of my parents, Tim and Peggy Bell; my in-laws, Eric Giles and Cathy Rens; my sister-in-law, Hannah Giles; and especially my wife, Leah Giles, have carried me through years of research, writing, and hand-wringing. Their faith in me has made all the difference—more than they know and more than I can express. Among their many, many graces, in recent years they repeatedly assumed my share of childcare responsibilities so that I could see this monograph through to completion. Juniper, this book is dedicated to your extraordinary mommy. I'll keep you in mind for the next one.

NOTES

Preface

1. *Catalogue of Trustees, Officers, and Students of the Oberlin Collegiate Institute; Together with the Second Annual Report,* 17; "Catalogue and Record of Colored Students, 1834–1972," Office of the Secretary Records, Alumni Records, Minority Student Records, Box 1, OCA.

2. Horton, "Black Education at Oberlin College: A Controversial Commitment," 483n12.

3. On more recent incarnations of this phenomenon, see hampton, *Black Racialization and Resistance at an Elite University;* Johnson, *Undermining Racial Justice: How One University Embraced Inclusion and Inequality.*

Introduction

1. Slater, "The Blacks Who First Entered the World of White Higher Education," 47.

2. Baumgartner, *In Pursuit of Knowledge: Black Women and Educational Activism in Antebellum America,* 45, Appendix D.

3. *Minutes of the Fifth Annual Convention for the Improvement of the Free People of Colour,* 17. According to the report, these were the Mount Pleasant Classical Institution (which had, in fact, closed in 1832); the Noyes Academy in Canaan, New Hampshire; the Oneida Institute in Whitesboro, New York; Western Reserve College in Hudson, Ohio (which is only known to have admitted one African American in this period); a Black girls school run by the Philadelphia Female Anti-Slavery Society; and an unnamed school in Gettysburg, probably the one recently started by Daniel Alexander Payne, future African Methodist Episcopal bishop. Apparently, they had not learned of Oberlin's new admissions policy.

4. Goodman, *Of One Blood: Abolitionism and the Origins of Racial Equality,* 45–51; Litwack, *North of Slavery: The Negro in the Free States, 1790–1860,* 123–26; Moss, "Education's Inequity: Opposition to Black Higher Education in Antebellum Connecticut"; Stewart, "The New Haven Negro College and the Meanings of Race in New England, 1776–1870."

5. Baumgartner, "Love and Justice: African American Women, Education, and Protest in Antebellum New England," 659, 664; Baumgartner, *In Pursuit of Knowledge,* 13–45; Goodman, *Of One Blood,* 51–53; Litwack, *North of Slavery,* 126–31.

6. Duane, *Educated for Freedom: The Incredible Story of Two Fugitive Schoolboys Who Grew Up*

to Change a Nation, 54–59; Moss, *Schooling Citizens: The Struggle for African American Education in Antebellum America,* 1–3; Wilder, *Ebony and Ivy: Race, Slavery, and the Troubled History of America's Universities,* 271–72.

7. Cross, *The Burned-Over District: The Social and Intellectual History of Enthusiastic Religion in Western New York, 1800–1850;* Ryan, *Cradle of the Middle Class: The Family in Oneida County, New York, 1790–1865.*

8. Baumgartner, *In Pursuit of Knowledge,* 46–47; Sernett, *Abolition's Axe: Beriah Green, Oneida Institute, and the Black Freedom Struggle,* 52.

9. Archer, *Jim Crow North: The Struggle for Equal Rights in Antebellum New England,* 57–75; Boonshoft, "From Property to Education: Public Schooling, Race, and the Transformation of Suffrage in the Early National North"; Demos, *The Heathen School: A Story of Hope and Betrayal in the Age of the Early Republic;* Field, *The Struggle for Equal Adulthood: Gender, Race, Age, and the Fight for Citizenship in Antebellum America;* Hines, "Learning Freedom: Education, Elevation, and New York's African-American Community, 1827–1829"; Kaestle, *Pillars of the Republic: Common Schools and American Society, 1780–1860,* 171–79; Moss, *Schooling Citizens;* Neem, *Democracy's Schools: The Rise of Public Education in America,* 162–68.

10. Archer, *Jim Crow North,* 31–42, 76–90; Jones, *Birthright Citizens: A History of Race and Rights in Antebellum America,* 1–34; Horton, "From Class to Race in Early America: Northern Post-Emancipation Racial Reconstruction"; Horton and Horton, *In Hope of Liberty: Culture, Community, and Protest among Northern Free Blacks, 1700–1860,* 168–70; Stewart, "Modernizing 'Difference': The Political Meanings of Color in the Free States, 1776–1840."

11. Wilder, *Ebony and Ivy,* 3.

12. Harris, Campbell, and Brody, eds., *Slavery and the University: Histories and Legacies;* Wilder, *Ebony and Ivy.*

13. Irvine, *The African American Quest for Institutions of Higher Education before the Civil War: The Forgotten Histories of the Ashmun Institute, Liberia College, and Avery College.*

14. Davis, *The Problem of Slavery in the Age of Emancipation,* 83–104; Goodman, *Of One Blood,* 11–22; Guyatt, *Bind Us Apart: How Enlightened Americans Created Racial Segregation,* 197–306; Horton and Horton, *In Hope of Liberty,* 177–202; Jones, *Birthright Citizens,* 35–49.

15. Jirik, "Combating Slavery and Colonization: Student Abolitionism and the Politics of Antislavery in Higher Education, 1833–1841"; Sumner, *Collegiate Republic: Cultivating an Ideal Society in Early America,* 161–63, 177–78; Wilder, *Ebony and Ivy,* 241–74.

16. Fairchild, *Oberlin: The Colony and the College,* 62.

17. John Keep to Charles Finney, Mar. 10, 1835, Charles Grandison Finney Presidential Papers, Reel 3, OCA.

18. Rosen, *Terror in Heart of Freedom: Citizenship, Sexual Violence, and the Meaning of Race in the Postemancipation South,* 153.

19. Keep to Finney, Mar. 10, 1835.

20. Dain, *A Hideous Monster of the Mind: American Race Theory in the Early Republic,* 165.

21. Davis, *The Problem of Slavery in the Age of Emancipation,* 3–44, 144–61; Guyatt, *Bind Us Apart,* 17–114; Melish, "The 'Condition' Debate and Racial Discourse in the Antebellum North"; Fredrickson, *The Black Image in the White Mind: The Debate on Afro-American Character and Destiny, 1817–1914,* 12–21, 28–29, 35–36, 40.

22. 2 Corinthians 5:17. Like most nineteenth-century Americans, the actors in this story, both Black and white, were well versed in the King James Bible. Since it was their preferred translation, all biblical quotations in this book are taken from that version.

23. Kendi, *Stamped from the Beginning: The Definitive History of Racist Ideas in America,* 120– 34, 161–76; Melish, "The 'Condition' Debate and Racial Discourse in the Antebellum North"; Stewart, "The Emergence of Racial Modernity and the Rise of the White North, 1790–1840."

24. Ball, *To Live an Antislavery Life: Personal Politics and the Antebellum Black Middle Class;* Dain, *A Hideous Monster of the Mind,* 153–54; Horton, *In Hope of Liberty,* 125–54, 220–23; Rael, *Black Identity and Black Protest in the Antebellum North,* 118–208; Stewart, "The Emergence of Racial Modernity and the Rise of the White North"; Stewart, "Modernizing 'Difference.'" The foundational study on the "politics of respectability" is Higginbotham, *Righteous Discontent: The Women's Movement in the Black Baptist Church, 1880–1920.*

25. "For a' That and a' That," in Currie, ed., *The Entire Works of Robert Burns; with an Account of His Life, and a Criticism on His Writings,* 296.

26. Genesis 1:27, 2:7; Acts 17:-26; Romans 2:11; 1 Corinthians 15:22.

27. 1 Corinthians 12:12; Galatians 3:28.

28. Bay, *The White Image in the Black Mind: African-American Ideas about White People, 1830– 1925,* 13–37; Goodman, *Of One Blood,* 246–51; Kantrowitz, *More Than Freedom: Fighting for Black Citizenship in a White Republic, 1829–1889,* 3–9; Stauffer, *The Black Hearts of Men: Radical Aboli- tionists and the Transformation of Race,* 134–81.

29. Sollors, ed., *Interracialism: Black-White Intermarriage in American History, Literature, and Law,* 1–14.

30. Moulton, *The Fight for Interracial Marriage Rights in Antebellum Massachusetts,* 6, 146–76. See also Lemire, *"Miscegenation": Making Race in America,* 82–86.

31. Lemire, *"Miscegenation,"* 59–75.

32. *History of Pennsylvania Hall, Which Was Destroyed by A Mob On the 17th of May, 1838,* 170.

33. Walters, "The Erotic South: Civilization and Sexuality in American Abolitionism."

34. Cheek and Cheek, *John Mercer Langston and the Fight for Black Freedom, 1829–65,* 11–18.

35. Dailey, *White Fright: The Sexual Panic at the Heart of America's Racist History;* Hodes, *White Women, Black Men: Illicit Sex in the Nineteenth-Century South;* Lemire, *"Miscegenation."*

36. *The First Annual Report of the Oberlin College Institute,* 12.

37. Fairchild, *The Joint Education of the Sexes: A Report Presented at a Meeting of the Ohio Teachers' Association, Sandusky City,* 8–11.

38. Fairchild, *Oberlin: The Colony and the College,* 56.

39. *The First Annual Report of the Oberlin College Institute,* 12; *Catalogue of Trustees, Officers, and Students of the Oberlin Collegiate Institute,* 7–17.

40. Baumann, *Constructing Black Education at Oberlin College: A Documentary History,* 20–21.

41. Fairchild, *Oberlin: The Colony and the College,* 75.

42. Ballantine, ed., *The Oberlin Jubilee: 1833–1883,* 91.

43. John Keep to Gerrit Smith, Jan. 16, 1836, Robert S. Fletcher Papers, Box 9, OCA.

44. Cheek and Cheek, *John Mercer Langston and the Fight for Black Freedom,* 85; Fairchild, *Oberlin: The Colony and the College,* 219.

45. Allport, *The Nature of Prejudice,* 261–81, 488–91.

46. Dixon, Durrheim, and Tredoux, "Beyond the Optimal Contact Strategy: A Reality Check for the Contact Hypothesis," 697–711;" Dovidio, Glick, and Rudman, eds., *On the Nature of Prejudice: Fifty Years after Allport;* Pettigrew and Tropp, "How Does Intergroup Contact Reduce Prejudice? Meta-Analytic Tests of Three Mediators"; Pica-Smith, Contini, and Veloria, *Social Justice Education in European Multi-Ethnic Schools: Addressing the Goals of Intercultural Education.*

47. Smith, *Reparation and Reconciliation: The Rise and Fall of Integrated Higher Education,* 65.

48. Two other important historical test cases for contact theory were the Port Royal experiment in Civil War–era South Carolina and the interracial Moravian communities of the Early Republic. See Mann, "The 'Contact of Living Souls': Shepard Gilbert's Civic Education in Reconstruction South Carolina"; Sensbach, *A Separate Canaan: The Making of an Afro-Moravian World in North Carolina, 1763–1840.*

49. Anderson, *The Education of Blacks in the South, 1860–1935;* Baumgartner, *In Pursuit of Knowledge;* Butchart, *Schooling the Freed People: Teaching, Learning, and the Struggle for Black Freedom, 1861–1876;* Givens, *Fugitive Pedagogy: Carter G. Woodson and the Art of Black Teaching;* Moss, *Schooling Citizens;* Snyder, *Great Crossings: Indians, Settlers, and Slaves in the Age of Jackson;* Williams, *Self-Taught: African American Education in Slavery and Freedom.*

50. A number of excellent studies that focus primarily on white women who were associated with Oberlin have shaped my thinking on the role of gender on that and other abolitionist campuses. See, for instance, Ginzberg, "Women in an Evangelical Community: Oberlin 1835–1850"; Hogeland, "Coeducation of the Sexes at Oberlin College: A Study of Social Ideas in Mid-Nineteenth-Century America"; Kelley, *Learning to Stand and Speak: Women, Education, and Public Life in America's Republic;* Kenny, *Contentious Liberties: American Abolitionists in Post-Emancipation Jamaica, 1834–1866;* Lasser, ed. *Educating Men and Women Together: Coeducation in a Changing World 1833–1908;* Morris, "'I Have at Last Found My 'Sphere': The Unintentional Development of a Female Abolitionist Stronghold at Oberlin College"; Turpin, *A New Moral Vision: Gender, Religion, and the Changing Purposes of Higher Education, 1837–1917,* 63–87. On Black women at abolitionist colleges and academies, see Baumgartner, *In Pursuit of Knowledge;* Lasser, "Enacting Emancipation: African American Women Abolitionists at Oberlin College and the Quest for Empowerment, Equality, and Respectability"; Lawson and Merrill, ed., *The Three Sarahs: Documents of Antebellum Black College Women;* Perkins, "The Impact of the 'Cult of True Womanhood' on the Education of Black Women"; and chapter 3 of this book.

51. I use the terms "interracial education" and "racial coeducation" interchangeably to describe students of different races receiving equal educational opportunities in the same institution. I reserve the term "integration" for instances of interracial education that achieved at least proportional representation of African Americans.

52. "Colored Students in Berea—All Schools," Associated Items: Blacks and Berea College, Box 1, Berea College Archives (hereafter BCA).

53. Hofstadter, *Academic Freedom in the Age of the College,* 260–61.

54. Colleges like Antioch, Bates, Hillsdale, Knox, and Wheaton as well as Oberlin spinoffs such as Benzonia, Olivet, and Tabor admitted students irrespective of sex and race, but few if any African Americans matriculated in the Civil War and Reconstruction eras. Eleutherian College in Jefferson County, Indiana, enrolled at least eighteen African Americans, but only scant records of student life survive. See Furnish, "A Rosetta Stone on Slavery's Doorstep: Eleutherian College and

the Lost Antislavery History of Jefferson County, Indiana"; Thompson, "Eleutherian Institute." Maryville College (Tennessee) admitted about sixty Black men during and after Reconstruction, but its administration never identified as abolitionist nor did its white students. See Burnside, "A 'Delicate and Difficult Duty': Interracial Education at Maryville College, Tennessee, 1868–1901"; Lamon, "Ignoring the Color Line: Maryville College, 1868–1901."

55. For statistics on African Americans' college enrollment in the late nineteenth and early twentieth centuries, see W. E. B. Du Bois and Augustus Granville Dill, eds., *The College-Bred Negro American*. Du Bois and Dill's study indicates (p. 35) that the University of Kansas was a notable exception. It had enrolled 211 black students by 1910, with most entering after 1890.

56. Catherine Hanchett, "New York Central College Students: A List," New York Central College Collection, MHS; "Catalogue and Record of Colored Students, 1834–1972," OCA; "Addendum to 'The Catalogue and Record of Colored Students,' 1862–1899," Minority Students Records, Oberlin College Archives website, accessed Dec. 31, 2020, https://libguides.oberlin.edu/c.php?g=1103249&p=8043468. To determine Berea students' races, I have relied on an annotated copy of *Historical Register of the Officers and Students of Berea College, from the Beginning to June, 1904*, available at Berea College Archives.

57. On the ways in which African Americans understood and enacted their citizenship in the Early Republic, see Gosse, *The First Reconstruction: Black Politics in America from the Revolution to the Civil War*; Masur, *Until Justice Be Done: America's First Civil Rights Movement, from the Revolution to Reconstruction*; Spires, *The Practice of Citizenship: Black Politics and Print Culture in the Early United States*.

58. I use the gender-inclusive "alums" instead of "alumni" except when referring specifically to multiple male graduates. I use "alumnae" to refer to multiple female graduates.

59. See, for instance, Crummell, *The Race-Problem in America*.

60. My thinking on gradations of equality in the Early Republic and Civil War era has been especially shaped by Huston, *The American and British Debate over Equality, 1776–1920*; Masur, *An Example for All the Land: Emancipation and the Struggle over Equality in Washington, DC*; McMahon, *Mere Equals: The Paradox of Educated Women in the Early American Republic*; Postel, *Equality: An American Dilemma, 1866–1896*.

61. Bigglestone, "Oberlin College and the Negro Student, 1865–1940"; Gudgeirsson, "'We Do Not Have Any Prejudice . . . but . . .': Racism in the Interracial Berea Literary Institute, 1866–1904"; Harris, *The State Must Provide: Why America's Colleges Have Always Been Unequal and How to Set Them Right*; Horton, "Black Education at Oberlin College"; Nelson, "Experiment in Interracial Education at Berea College, 1858–1908"; Sears, *A Utopian Experiment in Kentucky: Integration and Social Equality at Berea, 1866–1904*; Waite, *Permission to Remain among Us: Education for Blacks in Oberlin, Ohio, 1880–1914*.

62. Baumann, *Constructing Black Education at Oberlin College*; Morris, *Oberlin, Hotbed of Abolitionism: College, Community, and the Fight for Freedom and Equality in Antebellum America*; Short, "New York Central College: A Baptist Experiment in Integrated Higher Education, 1848–1861"; Smith, *Reparation and Reconciliation*.

63. Bonilla-Silva, *Racism without Racists: Color-Blind Racism and the Persistence of Racial Inequality in the United States*; Carr, *"Colorblind" Racism*; Pollock, *Colormute: Race Talk Dilemmas in an American School*.

64. J. Brent Morris makes a similar argument about political pragmatism at antebellum Oberlin. See Morris, "'All the Truly Wise or Truly Pious Have One and the Same End in View': Oberlin, the West, and Abolitionist Schism."

65. Allport, *The Nature of Prejudice*, 489. Original emphasis. For a historical analysis of this "brothers in arms" effect on American race relations, see Klinkner and Smith, *The Unsteady March: The Rise and Decline of Racial Equality in America*.

66. Kenny, *Contentious Liberties*, 30–32.

67. Among the many titles that take up this question are Blight, *Race and Reunion: The Civil War in American Memory*, 98–139; Blum, *Reforging the White Republic: Race, Religion, and American Nationalism, 1865–1898*; Cumbler, *From Abolition to Rights for All: The Making of a Reform Community in the Nineteenth Century;* Foner, *Reconstruction: America's Unfinished Revolution, 1863–1877;* Gillette, *Retreat from Reconstruction, 1869–1879;* McPherson, *The Abolitionist Legacy: From Reconstruction to the NAACP;* Richardson, *The Death of Reconstruction: Race, Labor, and Politics in the Post–Civil War North, 1865–1901*.

68. Butchart, *Schooling the Freed People;* Jones, *Soldiers of Light and Love: Northern Teachers and Georgia Blacks, 1865–1873*.

69. Frederickson, *The Black Image in the White Mind*, 178; Richardson, *The Death of Reconstruction*, 122–55.

70. Butler, *Critical Americans: Victorian Intellectuals and Transatlantic Liberal Reform*, 98–109; Cohen, *The Reconstruction of American Liberalism, 1865–1914*, 61–76; Hartman, *Scenes of Subjection: Terror, Slavery, and Self-Making in Nineteenth-Century America*, 115–206; Horton, *Race and the Making of American Liberalism*, 15–36; Frederickson, *The Black Image in the White Mind;* 178–83.

71. Waite, "The Segregation of Black Students at Oberlin College after Reconstruction," 351–352.

72. Cumbler, *From Abolition to Rights for All*, 155–57; Leonard, *Illiberal Reformers: Race, Eugenics, and American Economics in the Progressive Era*, 89–107; Sanderson, *Social Evolutionism: A Critical History*, 10–35; Stocking, *Race, Culture, and Evolution: Essays in The History of Anthropology*, 2nd ed., 110–33, 234–70. On the prevalence of social evolutionism in American sociology into the twentieth century, see Fredrickson, *The Black Image in the White Mind*, 311–19.

73. Davis, *"We Will Be Satisfied with Nothing Less": The African American Struggle for Equal Rights in the North during Reconstruction;* Kantrowitz, *More Than Freedom;* Rael, *Black Identity and Black Protest in the Antebellum North;* Sinha, *The Slave's Cause: A History of Abolition*, 299–338.

74. hooks, *Killing Rage: Ending Racism*, 263–72.

75. "Theme for English B," in Rampersad, ed., *The Collected Works of Langston Hughes*, 3:53.

1. Oberlin College and the Trial of Interracial Education, 1835–1853

1. Fletcher, *A History of Oberlin College: From Its Foundation through the Civil War*, 2:521.

2. Cowles to "S.B., Esq.," 151.

3. Cowles to "S.B., Esq.," 151.

4. Fletcher, *A History of Oberlin College*, 2:678–79.

5. Ballantine, *The Oberlin Jubilee, 1833–1883*, 285.

6. Langston, *From the Virginia Plantation to the National Capitol,* 138.

7. Cheek and Cheek, *John Mercer Langston and the Fight for Black Freedom, 1829–1865,* 104.

8. Langston, *From the Virginia Plantation to the National Capitol,* 138.

9. F. A. Collester to her mother, Apr. 19, 1852, Oberlin File, Box 4, OCA.

10. John C. Leith to J. S. Leith, May 6, 1861, John C. Leith Papers, Box 1, OCA.

11. For larger context on Black education and civil society in this period, see Baumgartner, *In Pursuit of Knowledge;* Kelley, *Learning to Stand and Speak: Women, Education, and Public Life in America's Republic.*

12. Remond, "The First Settlers: Native Peoples of the Vermilion Watershed," 96. For a critique of Oberlin and other colleges' histories of settler colonialism, see Boggs et al., "Abolitionist University Studies: An Invitation."

13. DeRogatis, *Moral Geography: Maps, Missionaries, and the American Frontier,* 157–79; Fletcher, *A History of Oberlin College,* 1:85–117; Kornblith and Lasser, *Elusive Utopia: The Struggle for Racial Equality in Oberlin, Ohio,* 9–19; Morris, *Oberlin, Hotbed of Abolitionism,* 15–18.

14. Abzug, *Cosmos Crumbling: American Reform and the Religious Imagination;* McLoughlin, *Modern Revivalism: Charles Grandison Finney to Billy Graham,* 3–64.

15. Covenant of the Oberlin Colony, photocopy in Robert S. Fletcher Papers, Box 19, OCA. The scriptural reference is to Romans 12:5.

16. Oberlin was chartered as a collegiate institute in 1833. It became a college in 1850, although it had been issuing bachelor's degrees since 1836.

17. *The First Annual Report of the Oberlin Collegiate Institute,* 12. Between 1833 and 1840, approximately 361 women and 744 men studied at Oberlin. "Catalogue of the Oberlin Collegiate Institute," *Oberlin Evangelist* (Nov. 18, 1840): 190.

18. *Catalogue of Trustees, Officers, and Students of the Oberlin Collegiate Institute,* 18.

19. *The First Annual Report of the Oberlin Collegiate Institute,* 6.

20. Nash, *Women's Education in the United States, 1780–1840,* 6–7, 40.

21. Malkmus, "Small Towns, Small Sects, and Coeducation in Midwestern Colleges, 1853–1861," *History of Higher Education Annual* 22 (2002): 33–65. Malkmus omits Eleutherian College, which, other than the three colleges studied here, was the only one to attract sizable numbers of both black and female students in the mid-nineteenth century.

22. Geiger, *The History of American Higher Education: Learning and Culture from the Founding to World War II,* 246.

23. Fletcher, *A History of Oberlin College,* 1:373.

24. *The First Annual Report of the Oberlin Collegiate Institute,* 6. The teacher's college existed in name only and was short-lived.

25. Turpin, *A New Moral Vision,* 63–87.

26. *The First Annual Report of the Oberlin Collegiate Institute,* 4.

27. Alice Welch Cowles, Notebook (1838–1840), 9, Robert S. Fletcher Papers, Box 4, OCA.

28. *Catalogue of Trustees, Officers, and Students of the Oberlin Collegiate Institute,* 24.

29. Ginzberg, "Women in an Evangelical Community," 78–88.

30. Goodman, "The Manual Labor Movement and the Origins of Abolitionism," 355–88; Sernett, *Abolition's Axe,* 49–107.

31. *The First Annual Report of the Oberlin Collegiate Institute,* 11–12; "List of Unrecorded Stu-

dents, 1834–1845," Office of the Secretary Records, Box 4, OCA; Fairchild, *Oberlin: The Colony and the College,* 37, 103, 216–17.

32. Nathan Fletcher, "Critical Letters #2," Office of the Treasurer Records, Miscellaneous Archives, Box 4, OCA.

33. Lesick, *The Lane Rebels: Evangelicalism and Antislavery in Antebellum America,* 25–73.

34. McLoughlin, *Modern Revivalism,* 36–39.

35. Moorhead, "Social Reform and the Divided Conscience of Antebellum Protestantism," 416–30; Ryan, *Cradle of the Middle Class,* 60–144; Hardesty, *Women Called to Witness: Evangelical Feminism in the Nineteenth Century,* 86–95.

36. Kornblith and Lasser, *Elusive Utopia,* 36.

37. Lesick, *The Lane Rebels,* 70–115.

38. *Fifth Annual Report of the Trustees of Cincinnati Lane Seminary,* 36–37.

39. Fletcher, *A History of Oberlin College,* 1:160.

40. Taylor, *Frontiers of Freedom: Cincinnati's Black Community, 1802–1868,* 50–79, 109–12.

41. Abzug, *Passionate Liberator: Theodore Dwight Weld and the Dilemma of Reform,* 98–122; Fletcher, *A History of Oberlin College,* 1:154–65; Lesick, *The Lane Rebels,* 116–32.

42. Lesick, *The Lane Rebels,* 160n96.

43. *A Statement of the Reasons Which Induced the Students of Lane Seminary, to Dissolve Their Connection with That Institution,* 26.

44. Lesick, *The Lane Rebels,* 132.

45. John Shipherd to John Keep, Dec. 13, 1834, Robert S. Fletcher Papers, Box 9, OCA; Henry Stanton and George Whipple to Charles Finney, Jan. 10, 1835, Robert S. Fletcher Papers, Box 9, OCA.

46. John Shipherd to Nathan Fletcher, Dec. 15, 1834, Office of the Treasurer Records, Correspondence, Box 1, OCA. See also Bigglestone, "Irrespective of Color," 35–36.

47. Fairchild, *Oberlin: The Colony and the College,* 342.

48. Shipherd to Fletcher, Dec. 15, 1834.

49. Fletcher, "Critical Letters #3," Office of the Treasurer Records, Miscellaneous Archives, Box 4, OCA.

50. Baumann, *Constructing Black Education at Oberlin College,* 20–21. The men voted twenty to seventeen in favor. The women voted fifteen to six against.

51. Sollors, *Interracialism,* 1–14.

52. Fletcher, *A History of Oberlin College,* 1:377.

53. *Catalogue of Trustees, Officers, and Students of the Oberlin Collegiate Institute,* 24. A student was expelled for the offense in 1836. See Fletcher, *A History of Oberlin College,* 2:686.

54. Benjamin Woodbury to John Shipherd, Mar. 26, 1835, Office of the Treasurer Records, Miscellaneous Archives, Box 2, OCA.

55. John Shipherd to Board of Trustees, Jan. 19, 1835, Robert S. Fletcher Papers, Box 9, OCA. See also Finney, *Memoirs of Rev. Charles G. Finney, Written by Himself,* 333.

56. Morris, *Oberlin, Hotbed of Abolitionism,* 65; Perry, *Radical Abolitionism: Anarchy and the Government of God in Antislavery Thought,* 40–46.

57. Kornblith and Lasser, *Elusive Utopia,* 23.

58. On Fayette, see DeCaro, *"Fire from the Midst of You": A Religious Life of John Brown,* 114.

59. Shipherd to Board of Trustees, Jan. 19, 1835.

60. Demos, *The Heathen School: A Story of Hope and Betrayal in the Age of the Early Republic*.

61. Shipherd to Board of Trustees, Jan. 19, 1835.

62. 2 Corinthians 8:11.

63. Fairchild, *Oberlin: The Colony and the College*, 59.

64. Matthew 18:6; Mark 12:31; Acts 17:26.

65. Fairchild, *Oberlin: The Colony and the College*, 59.

66. John Keep to Charles Finney, Mar. 10, 1835, Finney Papers, Reel 3, OCA.

67. Board of Trustees Minutes, Feb. 10, 1835, Board of Trustees Records, Box 2, 28, OCA.

68. Grimsted, *American Mobbing, 1828–1861: Toward Civil War*, 3–32; Stewart, *Holy Warriors: The Abolitionists and American Slavery*, 3–32.

69. Kornblith and Lasser, *Elusive Utopia*, 27.

70. *Catalogue of Trustees, Officers, and Students of the Oberlin Collegiate Institute; Together with the Second Annual Report*, 7–17.

71. *Oberlin College: Alumni Catalogue, 1833–1936*, 18–20; Fairchild, *Oberlin: The Colony and the College*, 67.

72. Sheffield Manual Labor Institute Catalog, June 1836, Oberlin College Library Records, Autograph File, Box 4, Document 181, OCA.

73. Constitution of the Oberlin Anti-Slavery Society, Oberlin College Library Records, Historical Files, Autograph File, Box 3, Doc. 146, OCA. The use of nicknames and initials makes a precise count difficult. At least six opponents of integration signed the OASS constitution, and another, Angeline Tenney, became secretary of the Young Ladies' Anti-Slavery Society.

74. Theodore Dwight Weld to Lewis Tappan, Nov. 17, 1835, in Barnes and Dumond, eds., *Letters of Theodore Dwight Weld, Angelina Grimké Weld and Sarah Grimké, 1822–1844*, 1:244.

75. Fairchild, *Oberlin: The Colony and the College*, 75.

76. *Third Annual Report of the American Anti-Slavery Society*, 98; Fletcher, *A History of Oberlin College*, 1:236–37.

77. Fairchild, *Oberlin: The Colony and the College*, 155.

78. Morris, "'I Have at Last Found My "Sphere,"'" 206.

79. Fairchild, *Oberlin: The Colony and the College*, 155; Smith, *A History of Oberlin; or New Lights of the West*, 59.

80. Morris, *Oberlin, Hotbed of Abolitionism*, 70, 85–86.

81. Morris, "'All the Truly Wise or Truly Pious Have One and the Same End in View'," 234–67.

82. J. A. Thome to Theodore Dwight Weld, Feb. 9, 1836, in Barnes and Dumond, eds., *Letters of Theodore Dwight Weld*, 1:257.

83. Constitution of the Oberlin Anti-Slavery Society.

84. Morris, *Oberlin, Hotbed of Abolitionism*, 48.

85. Bartanen and Littlefield, *Forensics in America: A History*, 281; Shumway and Brower, *Oberliniana: A Jubilee Volume of Semi-Historical Anecdotes Connected with the Past and Present of Oberlin College, 1833–1883*, 154.

86. Kelley, *Learning to Stand and Speak*, 14; see also 117–32.

87. Alice Cowles to Henry Cowles and Zilpah Grant, Jan. 16, 1836, Henry Cowles Papers, Box 2, OCA.

88. Lott, *Love and Theft: Black Face Minstrelsy and the American Working Class;* Rogin, *Blackface/White Noise: Jewish Immigrants in the Hollywood Melting Pot.*

89. Cowles and Cowles to Grant, Jan. 16, 1836.

90. Ibid.

91. Wyatt-Brown, *Lewis Tappan and the Evangelical War against Slavery,* 177–78, 183n38; McLoughlin, *Modern Revivalism,* 110.

92. "Due to the O.C. Institute from the Oberlin Professorship Association," Office of the Treasurer Records, Correspondence, Box 3, OCA; Fletcher, *A History of Oberlin College,* 1:453.

93. Charles Finney to Arthur Tappan, Apr. 30, 1836, Finney Papers, Reel 3, OCA.

94. *Catalogue of the Officers and Students of Oberlin College for the College Year 1852–53.* For the college's entire history, the Black portion of the student body peaked in 1974 at 11.9 percent. See Bok, "Activists Concerned over Black Student Enrollment Numbers."

95. Fletcher, *A History of Oberlin College,* 2:536.

96. Quarles, *Black Abolitionists,* 114.

97. Blodgett, "Oberlin College: Early Decisions," 360.

98. Fairchild, *Oberlin: The Colony and the College,* 113.

99. Blodgett, *Oberlin History: Essays and Impressions,* 135; Morris, *Oberlin, Hotbed of Abolitionism,* 68. In 1836 the faculty voted to allow women to have morning devotionals in the boarding house, most likely to save time. Fletcher, *A History of Oberlin College,* 2:752.

100. Cheek and Cheek, *John Mercer Langston,* 85.

101. Theodore Weld to Lewis Tappan, Oct. 24, 1836, in Barnes and Dumond, *Letters of Theodore Dwight Weld, Angelina Grimké Weld and Sarah Grimké, 1822–1844,* 1:345.

102. Cape, *We Sit Together: Utopian Benches from the Shakers to the Separatists of Zoar;* Fletcher, *A History of Oberlin College,* 2:612.

103. Smith, *A History of Oberlin,* 28, 58.

104. Smith, *A History of Oberlin,* 30, 58.

105. Edward Henry Fairchild to his children (n.d.), typescript, 8, in E. H. Fairchild Papers, Box 1, BCA; James Fairchild to Mary Kellogg, Dec. 21, 1840, in Fairchild and Graham, eds., *Where Liberty Dwells: The Letters of James Harris Fairchild and Mary Fletcher Kellogg from the Western Reserve,* 3:422; Smith, *A History of Oberlin,* 58.

106. Ellsworth, "Ohio's Legislative Attack upon Abolition Schools."

107. Smith, *A History of Oberlin,* 60.

108. Bigglestone, *They Stopped in Oberlin: Black Residents and Visitors of the Nineteenth Century,* 59–61.

109. Kornblith and Lasser, *Elusive Utopia,* 38–39.

110. "Catalogue of the Oberlin Collegiate Institute," *Oberlin Evangelist* (Nov. 18, 1840): 190.

111. Baumann, *Constructing Black Education at Oberlin College,* 38.

112. Fletcher, *A History of Oberlin College,* 1:438–62.

113. Horton, "Black Education at Oberlin College," 484–85.

114. Bell, "Confronting Colorism," 248–49.

115. "An Expression of the Sentiments of the Colored Students of the Oberlin Institute," in Baumann, *Constructing Black Education at Oberlin College,* 43–44.

116. *Catalogue of the Officers and Students of the Oberlin Collegiate Institute, 1840–1,* 22.

117. Phi Kappa Pi Roll of Members, 1883, 22–26, Phi Kappa Pi Records, Box 1, OCA; *Constitution, By-Laws and Roll of Members of the Phi Delta Society,* 22–24, Phi Delta Society Records, Box 1, OCA.

118. McDaniel, "The Fourth and the First: Abolitionist Holidays, Respectability, and Radical Interracial Reform," 129–51.

119. "First of August—Colored People," *Oberlin Evangelist* (Aug. 17, 1842), 133; Hannah Tracy to Elizabeth Lord, Aug. 12, 1842, Oberlin File, Box 1, OCA.

120. "First of August—Colored People," 134.

121. *Proceedings of the General Anti-Slavery Convention, Called by the Committee of the British and Foreign Anti-Slavery Society, and Held in London from Tuesday, June 13 to Tuesday, June 20, 1843,* 206.

122. *Proceedings of the General Anti-Slavery Convention,* 206.

123. "First of August—Colored People," 133.

124. Tracy to Lord, Aug. 12, 1842.

125. "The First of August," *Oberlin Evangelist* (Aug. 16, 1843), 7.

126. "The First of August," *Oberlin Evangelist* (Aug. 14, 1844), 7.

127. *Proceedings of the General Anti-Slavery Convention,* 206.

128. B. D. Wright to Dear Sisters, May 1, 1846, Robert S. Fletcher Papers, Box 10, OCA.

129. Aptheker, ed., *A Documentary History of the Negro People in the United States,* 287.

130. Morris, *Oberlin, Hotbed of Abolitionism,* 148–56.

131. James Monroe, "Human Brotherhood," James Monroe Papers, Box 25, OCA.

132. Fairchild, *Oberlin: The Colony and the College,* 181. The policy originated in their interpretation of 1 Timothy 2:11–12, which forbids women from teaching men. Oberlin women were permitted to address mixed audiences at events like literary exhibitions because men were absent from the program. See, for instance, "Young Ladies' Literary Society," *Oberlin Evangelist* (Mar. 18, 1841), 46.

133. Woods, *Debating Women: Gender, Education, and Spaces for Argument, 1835–1945,* 29–39.

134. Morris, "'I Have at Last Found My "Sphere,"'" 197–214.

135. Stone, "Why Do We Rejoice To-day?" 3.

136. Program of the August First Celebration (1846), Oberlin File, Box 1, OCA.

137. Lawson and Merrill, *The Three Sarahs,* 13.

138. Füllberg-Stolberg, "From the *Amistad* Slave Rebellion to the Christian Mendi Mission in West Africa: The *African* American Career of Sarah Margru Kinson," 156.

139. "Reminiscences of Early Oberlin" (Feb. 1918), 3, Blackwell Family Papers, Schlesinger Library, Radcliffe Institute, Harvard University.

140. Lawson and Merrill, *The Three Sarahs,* 192.

141. *Catalogue of the Officers and Students of Oberlin College, for the College Year 1850–51,* 30.

142. Fletcher, *A History of Oberlin College,* 2:762; Lasser, "Enacting Emancipation," 328.

143. "List of Members in 1846" and "Members of the Ladies' Literary Society, June 25th, 1850," Young Ladies' Society, Association Minutes, Ladies' Literary Society Records, Box 1, OCA.

144. Holley and Chadwick, *A Life for Liberty: Anti-Slavery and Other Letters of Sallie Holley,* 45.

145. "Commencement Exercises," *Oberlin Evangelist* (Nov. 6, 1850), 180; Woods, *Debating Women,* 40.

146. "Commencement Exercises," *Oberlin Evangelist* (Nov. 6, 1850), 180.

147. "Negro Graduates of Oberlin College," 1844–1972, Minority Student Records, OCA.

148. "Commencement at Oberlin," *Oberlin Evangelist* (Sept. 11, 1844), 151.

149. Allen and Allen. *Reluctant Reformers: Racism and Social Reform Movements in the United States*, 31–39; Pease and Pease, "Ends, Means, and Attitudes: Black-White Conflict in the Antislavery Movement."

150. Mary Sheldon, "Our Duty to the Oppressed," Composition Book, Mary Sheldon Papers, RG 30, Box 1, OCA.

151. Stanton, "A Plea for the Oppressed," *Oberlin Evangelist* (Dec. 17, 1850), 208.

152. Cowles to "S.B., Esq.," 151.

153. *Catalogue of the Officers and Students of Oberlin College for the College Year 1852–53*, 11–13, 27–33; *Constitution, By-Laws and List of Members of the L.L.S. Society*, 18–19; *Constitution, By-Laws and Roll of Members of the Phi Delta Society*, 24–25; List of Members by Class, 1853–1910, Aeolian Literary Society, Ladies' Literary Society Records, Subgroup II, Box 1, OCA; Members Roll, Records of the Young Men's Anti-Slavery Society, Activist/Political Organizations, Box 3, OCA; *Constitution, By-Laws and Roll of Members of the Phi Kappa Pi Society* (1883), Phi Kappa Pi Records, Box 1, 25–27, OCA.

154. James Thome to Theodore Weld, Apr. 13, 1841, in Barnes and Dumond, eds., *Letters of Theodore Dwight Weld, Angelina Grimké Weld and Sarah Grimké*, 2:864.

155. Board of Trustees Minutes, Feb. 18, 1852, 162, OCA.

156. "Colored Professorship," *Voice of the Fugitive* 2:11 (May 20, 1852): 2.

157. Morris, *Oberlin, Hotbed of Abolition*, 164.

158. Cheek and Cheek, *John Mercer Langston and the Fight for Black Freedom*, 181; Morris, *Oberlin, Hotbed of Abolition*, 167, 170.

159. Holley and Chadwick, *A Life for Liberty*, 61.

160. Blackwell, *Lucy Stone: Pioneer of Woman's Rights*, 56.

161. Board of Trustees Minutes, Feb. 18, 1852, 162, OCA.

162. Langston, *From the Virginia Plantation to the National Capitol*, 137–39.

163. Cheek and Cheek, *John Mercer Langston and the Fight for Black Freedom*, 103.

164. Leonard, *The Story of Oberlin: The Institution, the Community, the Idea, the Movement*, 425.

165. Fairchild, "Are Negroes Susceptible of High Cultivation?" *Oberlin Evangelist* (June 4, 1862): 94.

166. Lawson and Merrill, *The Three Sarahs*, 249–51.

167. Guyatt, *Bind Us Apart*, 174–75.

168. Fairchild, "Are Negroes Susceptible of High Cultivation?" 94.

169. Board of Trustees Minutes, Aug. 25, 1852, 168, OCA.

170. Fletcher, "Against the Consensus: Oberlin College and the Education of American Negroes, 1835–1865," 216.

171. Fairchild, *Oberlin: The Colony and the College*, 252–54; James Harris Fairchild, "Letter from the President of Oberlin College," *New National Era* (Dec. 14, 1871); 1. Sources do not specify how many students were chosen for tutorships in the antebellum years, but Fairchild's later letter indicates that the figure was between thirty and forty in 1871. The preparatory department's

enrollment in 1853 was nearly the same as in 1871 (661 versus 678), so it seems likely that the number of tutors needed was similar in each time period. Fairchild's letter also stated that roughly one in five eligible students was chosen.

172. Between the fall of 1853 and the spring of 1862, there were twelve African Americans who attained at least junior standing in the college department or studied in the theology department: George F. T. Cook, John F. Cook, John H. Cook, Charles A. Dorsey, John C. Jones, Elias T. Jones, John G. Mitchell, Mary Jane Patterson, Benjamin F. Randolph, Benjamin Sampson, Charles H. Thompson, and Thomas D. Tucker.

173. Jackson-Coppin, *Reminiscences of School Life, and Hints on Teaching,* 19.

2. The Rise and Fall of New York Central College, 1848–1860

1. "To the Trustees of New York Central College," 1853, New York Central College Collection, CCHS.

2. *Catalogue of the Officers and Students of New York Central College for the Year 1852–3,* 11.

3. *Sixth Annual Report of American Baptist Free Mission Society,* 2.

4. Wright, *Cornell's Three Precursors,* 68.

5. "To the Trustees of New York Central College," 1853, New York Central College Collection, CCHS.

6. Fletcher, *A History of Oberlin College,* 2:888; Horton, "Black Education at Oberlin College," 487.

7. "To the Trustees of New York Central College," 1853, New York Central College Collection, CCHS; Fairchild, *Oberlin: The Colony and the College,* 192.

8. Burke, *American Collegiate Populations: A Test of the Traditional View,* 11–52, esp. 14.

9. The discussion of antebellum college failure rates began with Tewksbury, *The Founding of American Colleges and Universities before the Civil War: With Particular Reference to the Religious Influences Bearing upon the College Movement,* and was revived by Hofstadter, *Academic Freedom in the Age of the College.* Revisionist theses have been advanced in Burke, *American Collegiate Populations;* McLachlan, "The American College in the Nineteenth Century: Towards a Reappraisal," 287–306; Naylor, "The Ante-Bellum College Movement: A Reappraisal of Tewksbury's Founding of American Colleges and Universities," 261–74.

10. Sernett, *Abolition's Axe,* 93–107.

11. 2 Corinthians 6:17.

12. *Fifth Annual Report of the American Baptist Free Mission Society, May 1848,* 19; McKivigan, *The War against Proslavery Religion: Abolitionism and the Northern Churches, 1830–1865,* 89–90, 96, 99–101.

13. Foss and Mathews, *Facts for Baptist Churches,* 370.

14. G.G.R., "Education—Moral, Intellectual, and Physical—Woman," *New York Daily Tribune* (Aug. 1, 1848), 5.

15. Foss and Mathews, *Facts for Baptist Churches,* 370, 399–401. Another interracial, manual-labor school, the Albany Manual Labor Academy, was founded by Oberlin-educated abolitionists around this time. It later became an all-Black institution, the Albany Enterprise Academy. See

Randolph, "Building upon Cultural Capital: Thomas Jefferson Ferguson and the Albany Enterprise Academy in Southeast Ohio, 1863–1886."

16. Grosvenor, *A Review of the "Correspondence" of Messrs. Fuller & Wayland: On the Subject of American Slavery,* 142.

17. Acts 17:6; Foss and Mathews, *Facts for Baptist Churches,* 28, 93; Mahommah Baquaqua to [W. Walker?], Sept. 28, 1850, in Baquaqua, *The Biography of Mahommah Gardo Baquaqua: His Passage from Slavery to Freedom in Africa and America,* 238.

18. Foss and Mathews, *Facts for Baptist Churches,* 400.

19. Porter, "Radicalism: An Oration Delivered at the New York Central College Commencement," *Liberator* (Aug. 6, 1852), 128.

20. G.G.R., "Education—Moral, Intellectual, and Physical—Woman," 5.

21. Foss and Mathews, *Facts for Baptist Churches,* 400. Emphasis added.

22. McMahon, *Mere Equals.*

23. Hall, *An Astronomer's Wife,* 48.

24. "The Institution, Public Meeting, &c," *McGrawville Express* (Nov. 25. 1847), 2.

25. Johnson, *Islands of Holiness: Rural Religion in Upstate New York, 1790–1860,* 49, 65, 121–25, 130–33.

26. Cross, *The Burned-Over District,* 13, 329–31.

27. "The Institution, Public Meeting, &c," *McGrawville Express* (Nov. 25, 1847), 2.

28. Short, "New York Central College," 251, 255.

29. On patterns of Baptist college fundraising in this period, see Potts, *Baptist Colleges in the Development of American Society, 1812–1861.*

30. Weierman, *One Nation, One Blood: Interracial Marriage in American Fiction, Scandal, and Law, 1820–1870,* 105; Wright, *Cornell's Three Precursors,* 10, 39.

31. Baumgartner, *In Pursuit of Knowledge,* 120–21.

32. Dunn, "The Early Academies of Cortland County," 60–61, 64–65; Beadie, "Female Students and Denominational Affiliation: Sources of Success and Variation among Nineteenth-Century Academies," 75–115.

33. Seventh Census of the United States, 1850, National Archives Microfilm Publication M432, Records of the Bureau of the Census, Record Group 29, National Archives, Washington, DC.

34. Stauffer, *The Black Hearts of Men,* 141.

35. Quarles, *Black Abolitionists,* 98.

36. Ibid.

37. Frederick Douglass, "McGrawville College," *North Star* (Apr. 26, 1850): 2.

38. Foss and Mathews, *Facts for Baptist Churches,* 402; "Female Labor List for January 1850," New York Central College Collection, CCHS.

39. Blackett, *The Captive's Quest for Freedom: Fugitive Slaves, the 1850 Fugitive Slave Law, and the Politics of Slavery;* Sinha, *The Slave's Cause,* 500–542.

40. Harrold, *The Rise of Aggressive Abolitionism: Addresses to the Slaves,* 117–39; Stauffer, *The Black Hearts of Men,* 163–64; "Wm. L. Chaplin," *Liberator* (Oct. 4, 1850), 1.

41. Hanchett, "New York Central College Students: A List"; Male and Female Labor Lists for January, March, May, and June 1850, New York Central College Collection, CCHS; *Seventh*

Annual Meeting of the American Baptist Free Mission Society, 33. Cumulatively, between 1849 and 1858, Black and Native men made up about 4 percent of the cumulative student population of New York Central College, while Black and Native women represented 1 percent.

42. Bacon, *But One Race: The Life of Robert Purvis,* 110, 187.

43. Hanchett, "New York Central College Students."

44. Invitation to Literary Anniversaries of Central College, 1855, Box 152, NYCC Printed Material, Gerrit Smith Papers (hereinafter GSP), Syracuse University Archives.

45. "Education—Moral, Intellectual, Physical," *New York Tribune* (Aug. 1, 1848).

46. Abzug, *Cosmos Crumbling,* 5.

47. "Cayuga Chief's Visit," *Cortland County Express* (Mar. 14, 1850): 2.

48. Ott, *Pumpkin: The Curious History of an American Icon.*

49. *The Pumpkin Pie Offering. To Which Are Added the Proceedings of the Great Pumpkin Pie Jubilee,* 3–4.

50. *The Pumpkin Pie Offering,* 6, 7, 5. Original emphasis.

51. Edith Phillips to her brother, June 4, 1850, Phillips Family Papers, Box 1, OCA.

52. "Death by Smallpox. Progress of the Disease," *Cortland County Express* (June 6, 1850): 2.

53. Catherine M. Hanchett, "Smallpox at Central College (Parts I and II)," New York Central College Collection, MHS.

54. Tacie Townsend, "The Student's Burial," Miscellaneous Scrapbook: New York Central College at McGraw, CCHS.

55. Edith Phillips to her brother, June 4, 1850, Phillips Family Papers, Box 1, OCA.

56. William Allen to Frederick Douglass, June 16, 1851, *Frederick Douglass' Paper* (June 26, 1851), 3; Winch, *A Gentleman of Color: The Life of James Forten,* 357. Allen's letter notes that Anna Pierce and Joseph Purvis were buried "upon the hill-side, but a few rods from the College."

57. Purvis, *Hagar: The Singing Maiden, with Other Stories and Rhymes,* 113.

58. "Layout and Epitaphs of College Students in Graveyard," New York Central College Collection, CCHS. Catherine Hanchett lists both Elliot Blake and Chauncey Powell as black in "New York Central College Students," 3, 17. But the 1850 Censuses for Kingsville, Ohio, and Pittsfield, Vermont (their hometowns), list both men as white.

59. "Subscription for Building College Burial Ground Fence," n.d., Folder 5, New York Central College Records, CCHS.

60. Lewis Spaulding, "Culture as Duty," *Liberator* (July 24, 1857): 4.

61. Faulkner, *Lucretia Mott's Heresy: Abolition and Women's Rights in Nineteenth-Century America;* Friedman, *Gregarious Saints: Self and Community in American Abolitionism, 1830–1870,* 107–10; McKivigan, "The American Baptist Free Mission Society," 342–43, 348.

62. "Letter from C.A. Hammond," *Frederick Douglass' Paper* (Mar. 11, 1853): 1.

63. "The Fourth," *Cortland County Express* (July 11, 1850): 2.

64. Palmer, ed., *Selected Letters of Lucretia Coffin Mott,* 206.

65. Edith Phillips to her brother and sister, July 9, 1850, Phillips Family Papers, Box 1, OCA.

66. Stauffer, *The Black Hearts of Men,* 16–18.

67. "The Fourth," *Cortland County Express* (July 11, 1850), 2.

68. Palmer, *Selected Letters of Lucretia Coffin Mott,* 206.

NOTES TO PAGES 63–67

69. Edith Phillips to her brother and sister, July 23, 1850, Phillips Family Papers, Box 1, OCA.

70. Catherine Hanchett, "Charles Lewis Reason, 1818–1893: The Nation's First Black Professor," 9, New York Central College Records, MHS.

71. Blackett, "William G. Allen: The Forgotten Professor," 39–52.

72. "Resolutions of Central College," *Liberator* (Oct. 11, 1850): 1.

73. "Letter from Wm. G. Allen," *Frederick Douglass' Paper* (Nov. 12, 1852): 3; Welch, *"Grip's" Historical Souvenir of Cortland,* 217.

74. Lasser and Merrill, *Friends and Sisters,* 118.

75. Ford, "Honor to Whom Honor Is Due," *The Herald of Gospel Liberty* (Nov. 9, 1909): 1543. According to one letter to *Frederick Douglass' Paper,* when a previous visiting speaker made "an attack on those ladies who wear the Bloomer Costume," he showed "most clearly that he had mistaken . . . the character of his hearers." Timothy Stow, "McGrawville College," *Frederick Douglass' Paper* (July 30, 1852): 3.

76. Wayne, "Lydia Sayer Hasbrouck (1827–1910)," 88–89.

77. Baumgartner, *In Pursuit of Knowledge,* 55.

78. Stauffer, *The Black Hearts of Men,* 120.

79. Gerrit Smith to Samuel Aaron and T. B. Hudson, Sept. 16, 1852, Schlesinger Library, Radcliffe College.

80. Stephen Jones to Asa Caldwell, Jan. 3, 1852, Folder 6, New York Central College Collection, CCHS.

81. "A Blow to Color-Phobia," *Liberator* (July 18, 1851): 114.

82. Allen, *A Short Personal Narrative,* 15.

83. *Laws of the State of New York, Passed at the Seventy-Fourth Session of the Legislature,* 423–24.

84. "From the *Albany State Register.* New York Central College," *Liberator* (July 18, 1851): 1.

85. Report of the Board of Trustees to the New York Central College Association, July 16, 1851, New York Central College Collection, CCHS.

86. Kenyon, "Sermon Delivered before the Association," in *Minutes of the Fifth Annual Meeting of the New York Central College Association,* 14, 15.

87. Porter, "Radicalism," 128.

88. *Minutes of the Fifth Annual Meeting of the New York Central College Association,* 5, 7; Timothy Stow, "McGrawville College," *Frederick Douglass' Paper* (July 30, 1852): 3.

89. Asa Caldwell, "New York Central College," *Frederick Douglass' Paper* (Feb. 18, 1853): 3.

90. *Catalogue of the Officers and Students of New York Central College for the Year 1852-3,* 10.

91. Allen, *A Short Personal Narrative,* 23.

92. Weierman, *One Nation, One Blood,* 111.

93. "Cayuga Chief's Visit," 2.

94. Stafford Green to Asa Caldwell, Sept. 24, 1852, New York Central College Collection, CCHS.

95. Allen, *American Prejudice against Color: An Authentic Narrative, Showing How Easily the Nation Got into an Uproar;* Blackett, "William G. Allen," 39–52; Weierman, *One Nation, One Blood,* 112–17.

96. Asa Caldwell to Frederick Douglass, Mar. 21, 1853, *Frederick Douglass' Paper* (Apr. 1, 1853): 3.

97. Allen, *A Short Personal Narrative,* 23.

98. Ibid., 23.

99. Weierman, *One Nation, One Blood*, 116.

100. L. D. Tanner to Frederick Douglass, Apr. 17, 1853, *Frederick Douglass' Paper* (Apr. 29, 1853): 3.

101. Weierman, *One Nation, One Blood*, 124.

102. Allen, *A Short Personal Narrative*, 43–44.

103. Ibid., 48.

104. Elbert, "An Inter-Racial Love Story in Fact and Fiction: William and Mary King Allen's Marriage and Louisa May Alcott's Tale, 'M.L.,'" 17–42.

105. *Catalogue of the Officers and Students of New-York Central College for The Year 1853–4.*

106. Hall, *An Astronomer's Wife*, 48.

107. Kezia King to the Board of Trustees, July 11, 1853, New York Central College Records, CCHS.

108. Bell, "Confronting Colorism: Interracial Abolition and the Consequences of Complexion," 253–62.

109. Baquaqua, *The Biography of Mahommah Gardo Baquaqua*, 187–90.

110. Mahommah G. Baquaqua to George Whipple, Oct. 26, 1853, in Baquaqua, *The Biography of Mahommah Gardo Baquaqua*, 247.

111. *Minutes of the Seventh Annual Meeting of the New York Central College Association*, 3.

112. *Catalogue of the Officers and Students on N.Y. Central College for the Collegiate Year 1854–55*, 12.

113. Langston, *From the Virginia Plantation to the National Capitol*, 75.

114. *Commencement Exercises of New York Central College; N.Y. Central College: Prize Declamation.*

115. *Minutes of the Seventh Annual Meeting of the New York Central College Association*, 3.

116. *Sixty-Ninth Annual Report of the Regents of the University of the State of New York*, 173. The report to the regents indicates income exceeded expenditures by $666.

117. S. H. Potter, Report to the Trustees, 1855, New York Central College Collection, CCHS.

118. George Vashon to Gerrit Smith, Apr. 22, 1855, Box 37, GSP, Syracuse University Archives.

119. Elbert, "An Interracial Love Story in Fact and Fiction," 38.

120. *Catalogue of the Officers and Students on N.Y. Central College for the Collegiate Year 1854–55; Catalogue of the Officers and Students of N.Y. Central College for the Collegiate Year 1855–56; Catalogue of the Officers and Students of N.Y. Central College for the Collegiate Year 1856–57.*

121. Judgment in US Supreme Court, *Dred Scott v. John F. A. Sanford*, Mar. 6, 1857, Case Files 1792–1995, Record Group 267, Records of the Supreme Court of the United States, National Archives.

122. Leonard Calkins, Theodore Parker, and Gerrit Smith, "New York Central College," *Liberator* (Mar. 6, 1857): 40.

123. Azariah Smith, "Please to Read This Aloud," *Liberator* (Mar. 6, 1857): 40.

124. Brown, *The Black Man: His Antecedents, His Genius, and His Achievements*, 2nd ed., 224.

125. George Vashon to Gerrit Smith, Oct. 20, 1856, and Apr. 25, 1857, Box 37, GSP, Syracuse University Archives.

126. Vashon to Gerrit Smith, Oct. 20, 1856.

127. Vashon to Smith, Apr. 25, 1857.

128. Ibid.

129. Vashon to the Board of Trustees, June 24, 1857, CCHS.

130. Hanchett, "George Boyer Vashon, 1824–1878: Black Educator, Poet, Fighter for Equal Rights (Part One)," 217.

131. Smith, *Reparation and Reconciliation*, 93.

132. Azariah Smith, Metcalf Smith, Howard Gilbert, and Alonzo Armour to Stafford Green, Aug. 21, 1857, Folder 11, New York Central College Collection, CCHS.

133. Samuel J. May to his wife, June 25, 1857, Samuel J. May Family Papers, Box 1, Cornell University Archives.

134. Spaulding, "Culture as Duty."

135. Leonard G. Calkins, "The Charges Denied," *Liberator* (Aug. 14, 1857): 131.

136. "Testimonial," *Liberator* (Oct. 30, 1857): 176.

137. *Catalogue of Eleutherian College, 1857–8*, 7. Metcalf Smith was appointed professor of science and mathematics. Judson Smith served as instructor in languages before completing his bachelor's degree at Amherst. He went on to earn his master's in divinity at Oberlin, where he subsequently joined the faculty.

138. Furnish, "A Rosetta Stone on Slavery's Doorstep," 363.

139. Thomas Craven to Gerrit Smith, Feb. 20, 1856, Box 8, GSP, Syracuse University Archives. Eleutherian shed its collegiate character and became a primary school after 1861. See Furnish, "A Rosetta Stone on Slavery's Doorstep," 364–65.

140. Program of N.Y. Central College Commencement Exercises (June 23, 1858), Folder 12, New York Central College Collection, CCHS. It has been suggested that Grace Mapps, an African American from New Jersey and cousin of the Black artist and educator Sarah Mapps Douglass, graduated from New York Central in 1852. However, there were no recipients of Central College's bachelor's degree until 1855, and Mapps was not among them. See Jessie Carney Smith, ed., *Notable Black American Women*, book 2 (Detroit: Gale Research, 1996), 427.

141. Richardson, "Edmonia Lewis at McGrawville: The Early Education of a Nineteenth-Century Black Woman Artist."

142. The others were Benjamin Kellogg Sampson and brothers Charles and George Dorsey. See "Catalogue and Record of Colored Students, 1834–1972," Office of the Secretary Records, Alumni Records, Minority Student Records, Box 1, OCA.

143. *Seventy-First Annual Report of the Regents of the University of the State of New York*, 137.

144. Warranty Deed of the Trustees of New York Central College to Gerrit Smith, July 28, 1858, Box 152, GSP, Syracuse University Archives.

145. "Debts Due from Trustees of NY Central College," Jan. 1, 1859, Folder 13, New York Central College Collection, CCHS.

146. Gerrit Smith to S. S. Hayward, July 11, 1859, Box 152, GSP, Syracuse University Archives.

147. James McCune Smith to Gerrit Smith, Jan. 29, 1859 (Gerrit Smith's draft reply is on the reverse), Box 34, GSP, Syracuse University Archives. The letter containing Smith's original proposition to McCune Smith does not survive.

148. Baumgartner, "Gender Politics and the Manual Labor College Initiative at National Colored Conventions in Antebellum America"; Mabee, *Black Education in New York State*, 165.

149. Irvine, *The African American Quest for Institutions of Higher Education before the Civil War*, 335–56.

150. McCune Smith to Gerrit Smith, Jan. 29, 1859.

151. Ibid.

152. James McCune Smith to Gerrit Smith, Mar. 9, 1859, Box 34, GSP, Syracuse University Archives.

153. Stauffer, *The Black Hearts of Men*, 236–81.

154. Noah Osbourn to Gerrit Smith, Apr. 4, 1860, Box 152, GSP, Syracuse University Archives.

155. New York Central College Circular, July 1860, Folder 14, New York Central College Collection, CCHS.

156. Mary Backus to her brother, Aug. 26, 1860, Folder 15, New York Central College Collection, CCHS.

157. 1860 US census, population schedule. NARA microfilm publication M653. Washington, DC: National Archives and Records Administration.

158. Cyrus Grosvenor to Gerrit Smith, Nov. 12, 1860, Box 20, GSP, Syracuse University Archives.

159. Victor Kingsley to Gerrit Smith, Oct. 22, 1860, Box 152, GSP, Syracuse University Archives.

160. Trustee Minutes, June 18, 1861, Folder 15, New York Central College Collection, CCHS.

161. Victor Kingsley to Gerrit Smith, Nov. 5, 1860, Box 24, GSP, Syracuse University Archives.

162. New York Central College Association Complaint against Israel Palmer, Dec. 1860, New York Central College Collection, CCHS.

163. Victor Kingsley to Gerrit Smith, Dec. 18, 1860, Box 24, GSP, Syracuse University Archives.

164. Smith to Hayward, July 11, 1859.

165. McPherson, *The Struggle for Equality: Abolitionists and the Negro in the Civil War and Reconstruction*, 3rd ed., 40–51.

166. Woodson, *The Education of the Negro Prior to 1861*, 276–80.

167. "College Cemetery Is Subject of Much Controversy," *Cortland Standard* (Aug. 25, 1944) and associated clippings in Miscellaneous Scrapbook: New York Central College at McGraw, CCHS.

3. Oberlin's Black Alumnae and the New Birth of Freedom, 1852–1867

1. McKivigan, ed., *The Frederick Douglass Papers.* Series 3, *Correspondence*, vol. 1, *1842–1852*, 289n2, 290, 320–23.

2. Henle and Merrill, "Antebellum Black Coeds at Oberlin College," 8.

3. Baumgartner, "Love and Justice," 652–76; Baumgartner, *In Pursuit of Knowledge;* Lasser, "Enacting Emancipation," 319–45.

4. Collins, *Black Feminist Thought: Knowledge, Consciousness, and the Politics of Empowerment*, 2nd ed., 12, 201–26.

5. On teaching as a form of African American activism, see Baumgartner, *In Pursuit of Knowledge*, 79–106, 177–204; Butchart, *Schooling the Freed People*, 120–54; Williams, *Self-Taught*, 96–125.

6. Morris, *Oberlin, Hotbed of Abolitionism*, 132–86; Davis, *The Problem of Slavery in the Age of Emancipation*, 193–225; Sinha, *The Slave's Cause*, 500–542.

7. Shipherd, *History of the Oberlin-Wellington Rescue*, 178.

8. Gilroy, *The Genuine Article: Race, Mass Culture, and American Literary Manhood*, 37–66.

9. Bay, *The White Image in the Black Mind*, 38–74; Dain, *A Hideous Monster of the Mind*, 227–64; Horsman, *Race and Manifest Destiny: The Origins of American Racial Anglo-Saxonism*, 139–57; Fredrickson, *The Black Image in the White Mind*, 71–96, 98–100, 135–36; Jacobson, *Whiteness of a Different Color: European Immigrants and the Alchemy of Race*, 31–55.

10. Lasser, "Enacting Emancipation," 327–28.

11. Hodes, *White Women, Black Men*, 5, 147.

12. Lasser, "Enacting Emancipation," 330.

13. *Record of the Proceedings of the Ladies Board, 1851–1852* (typescript), Fletcher Papers, Box 12, OCA, 2.

14. Lawson and Merrill, *The Three Sarahs*, 47–54.

15. "Festival of the Young Men's Literary Association," *Weekly Anglo-African* (Apr. 19, 1862). Among the other black women honored were Mary Shadd Cary, Sarah Mapps Douglass, and Frances Ellen Watkins Harper.

16. Bigglestone, *They Stopped in Oberlin*, 97–98; Butchart, *Schooling the Freed People*, 18; Lawson and Merrill, *The Three Sarahs*, 223–24.

17. *Annual Catalogue of the Officers and Students of Oberlin College for the College Year 1859–60*, 8–14; 32–37; *Constitution, By-Laws and List of Members of the L.L.S. Society*, 19–20; *Constitution, By-Laws and Roll of Members of the Phi Delta Society*, 25–26; List of Members by Class, 1853–1910, Aeolian Literary Society; Phi Kappa Pi Roll of Members,1883, 27–30.

18. Jackson-Coppin, *Reminiscences of School Life, and Hints on Teaching*, 17.

19. L. Maria Child, "Edmonia Lewis," *Broken Fetter* (Mar. 3, 1865): 1.

20. "Letter from Lydia M. Child," 31.

21. *Record of Standing, Conduct, Attendance, and Scholarship of the Students in the Various Classes of New York Central College*, MHS.

22. Henry Wreford, "A Negro Sculptress," *Athenaeum* (Mar. 3, 1866): 302.

23. Keep to Finney, Mar. 10, 1835, Finney Papers, Reel 3, OCA.

24. "Meeting of the Colored People," *Lorain County News* (Feb. 17, 1870): 2.

25. John Keep and Henry Cowles, "To the Friends of the African Race" (1862), Oberlin File, Box 1, OCA.

26. Langston, *From the Virginia Plantation to the National Capitol*, 172.

27. Langston, *From the Virginia Plantation to the National Capitol*, 171.

28. "Mysterious Affair at Oberlin," *Cleveland Plain Dealer* (Feb. 11, 1862): 3.

29. Jackson-Coppin, *Reminiscences*, 14.

30. Perkins, *Fanny Jackson Coppin and the Institute for Colored Youth, 1865–1902*, 26.

31. Ibid., 12.

32. Henle and Merrill, "Antebellum Black Coeds at Oberlin College," 9–10; Frances Josephine Norris, Alumni and Development Records, OCA.

33. Cowles to "S.B., Esq." Original emphasis.

34. Fairchild, *Oberlin, Its Origin, Progress, and Results: An Address Prepared for the Alumni of Oberlin College Assembled August 22, 1860*, 29.

35. Fanny Jackson, "Prejudice at Oberlin," *National Anti-Slavery Standard* (July 9, 1864): 2.

36. Jackson-Coppin, *Reminiscences*, 15.

37. Ibid., 14.

38. Ibid., 15. This page lists eight white students whose names can be found in the Oberlin catalog. The ninth was Mary Ann Southard, Jackson's tearful housemate. Jackson mistakenly recorded Southard's surname as "Sutherland" and noted she was from Maine. While no female student named Sutherland studied at Oberlin in the 1860s, the catalog does list a Mary Ann Calista Southard, hailing from Exeter, Maine. *General Catalogue of Oberlin College, 1833–1908,* 911.

39. Cheek and Cheek, *John Mercer Langston and the Fight for Black Freedom,* 300–301.

40. Jackson-Coppin, *Reminiscences,* 18.

41. Weisenburger, "William Sanders Scarborough: Early Life and Years at Wilberforce," 211.

42. "A Trial in Prospect," *Lorain County News* (Feb. 19, 1862): 2.

43. "Mysterious Affair at Oberlin"; "A Trial in Prospect"; Langston, *From the Virginia Plantation to the National Capitol,* 171–74.

44. "The Oberlin Poisoning Case," *Cleveland Morning Leader* (Mar. 3, 1862): 3; Blodgett, "John Langston and the Case of Edmonia Lewis, 1862," 212; Langston, *From the Virginia Plantation to the National Capitol,* 174–76.

45. "Mysterious Affair at Oberlin."

46. Parrish, *American Curiosity: Cultures of Natural History in the Colonial British Atlantic World,* 259–306.

47. Langston, *From the Virginia Plantation to the National Capitol,* 176–77; "The Oberlin Poisoning Case"; "A Trial in Prospect."

48. Langston, *From the Virginia Plantation to the National Capitol,* 172. On her family, see "Letter from Lydia M. Child," 31.

49. Langston, *From the Virginia Plantation to the National Capitol,* 177, 172.

50. Leith to Leith, May 6, 1861.

51. "A Trial in Prospect."

52. "A Trial in Prospect."

53. "The Poisoning Affair," *Lorain County News* (Mar. 5, 1862): 2.

54. "The Oberlin Poisoning Case."

55. Bearden and Henderson, *A History of African-American Artists, from 1792 to the Present,* 58; "The Oberlin Poisoning Case."

56. Langston, *From the Virginia Plantation to the National Capitol,* 179.

57. Fairchild, "Are Negroes Susceptible of High Cultivation?" *Oberlin Evangelist* (June 4, 1862), 94.

58. Langston, *From the Virginia Plantation to the National Capitol,* 180.

59. Langston, *From the Virginia Plantation to the National Capitol,* 179; Kornblith and Lasser, *Elusive Utopia,* 113–15; Smith, *Reparation and Reconciliation,* 75–76.

60. Fred Allen to A. A. Wright, Jan. 30, 1863, Fletcher Papers, Box 1, OCA. Webster's 1844 *American Dictionary* defined "wench" as both "a young woman of ill fame" and "a black or colored female servant." Webster, *An American Dictionary of the English Language,* 922.

61. "How We Received It," *Lorain County News* (Jan. 7, 1863): 2.

62. Bearden and Henderson, *A History of African-American Artists,* 60; "Once More," *Lorain County News* (Feb. 25, 1863): 3.

63. Clara Hale to "Dear Folks at Home," Feb. 26, 1863, Fletcher Papers, Box 3, OCA.

64. Bearden and Henderson, *A History of African-American Artists,* 60.

65. "A Colored Artist," *Lorain County News* (Mar. 28, 1866): 3.

66. Jackson-Coppin, *Reminiscences,* 12.

67. Fanny M. Jackson, "To the 54th Mass. Volunteers," *Lorain County News* (June 10, 1863): 1.

68. Perkins, *Fanny Jackson Coppin and the Institute for Colored Youth,* 37.

69. Besides Central College's three Black professors, there was Charlotte Forten, who taught at the Epes School in Salem, Massachusetts, beginning in 1856. See Baumgartner, *In Pursuit of Knowledge,* 202. Aaron Molyneaux Hewlett directed Harvard's gymnasium and taught physical education. See Cohen, *Reconstructing the Campus,* 6.

70. Fairchild, "Are Negroes Susceptible of High Cultivation?"

71. Don Carlos, "Letter from Oberlin, Ohio," *New National Era* (Nov. 23, 1871): 1.

72. One Who Has Suffered, "Oberlin," *New National Era* (Nov. 30, 1871): 1.

73. Fairchild, "Letter from the President of Oberlin College," 1.

74. Anna Julia Cooper to Alfred Churchill, Jan. 21 and Feb. 9, 1941, Anna Julia Cooper Alumni Files, OCA.

75. Leonard, *The Story of Oberlin,* 309.

76. Sterling, *We Are Your Sisters: Black Women in the Nineteenth Century,* 203.

77. Fairchild, "Letter from the President of Oberlin College," 1.

78. Perkins, *Fanny Jackson Coppin,* 31.

79. Jackson-Coppin, *Reminiscences,* 18, 19, 12.

80. "A Fortnight in Oberlin," *National Anti-Slavery Standard* (Mar. 11, 1865): 3.

81. Jackson-Coppin, *Reminiscences,* 12.

82. "A Fortnight in Oberlin."

83. Perkins, *Fanny Jackson Coppin and the Institute for Colored Youth,* 33.

84. "Prejudice at Oberlin College," *Commonwealth* (May 27, 1864): 4.

85. Perkins, *Fanny Jackson Coppin and the Institute for Colored Youth,* 40.

86. John 5:1–4.

87. Jackson, "Prejudice at Oberlin."

88. Ibid. Original emphasis.

89. Stauffer, *The Black Hearts of Men,* 39.

90. Ibid. Original emphases.

91. Jackson, "Prejudice at Oberlin."

92. Sara Stanley to George Whipple, Jan. 19, 1864, in Lawson and Merrill, *The Three Sarahs,* 79, 80.

93. Sara Stanley to George Whipple, Mar. 4, 1864, in Lawson and Merrill, *The Three Sarahs,* 81.

94. Sara Stanley to William Woodbury, July 21, 1864, in Lawson and Merrill, *The Three Sarahs,* 86–90.

95. Lemire, *"Miscegenation,"* 116–33.

96. Sara Stanley to William Woodbury, July 21, 1864, in Lawson and Merrill, *The Three Sarahs,* 88–89.

97. Sara Stanley to William Woodbury, Aug. 29, 1864, in Lawson and Merrill, *The Three Sarahs,* 92; Weisenfeld, "'Who Is Sufficient for These Things?' Sara G. Stanley and the American Missionary Association, 1864–1868," 496–97.

98. Sara G. Stanley to George Whipple, Oct. 6, 1864, in Lawson and Merrill, *The Three Sarahs*, 95–97.

99. Stanley to Whipple, Oct. 6, 1864, in Lawson and Merrill, *The Three Sarahs*, 96–98.

100. Blanche Harris to the AMA, Mar. 30, 1864, in Lawson and Merrill, *The Three Sarahs*, 233.

101. On Litts's background, see Baumann, *Constructing Black Education at Oberlin College*, 318n145.

102. Span, *From Cotton Field to Schoolhouse: African American Education in Mississippi*, 38–39.

103. Blanche Harris to George Whipple, Jan. 23, 1866, in Lawson and Merrill, *The Three Sarahs*, 236–37.

104. Ervin and Sheer, eds., *A Community of Voices on Education and the African American Experience*, 76.

105. Blanche Harris to George Whipple, Mar. 10, 1866, in Lawson and Merrill, *The Three Sarahs*, 238–39.

106. Harris to Whipple, Mar. 10, 1866.

107. Lawson and Merrill, *The Three Sarahs*, 227.

108. L. Maria Child, "Edmonia Lewis," *Broken Fetter* (Mar. 3, 1865): 1.

109. "Letter from Lydia M. Child," 31; Wreford, "A Negro Sculptress."

110. Omi and Winant, *Racial Formation in the United States*.

111. Child, "Edmonia Lewis."

112. "Letter from Lydia M. Child."

113. Wreford, "A Negro Sculptress."

114. Atkins, *Stone Mirrors: The Sculpture and Silence of Edmonia Lewis*; Buick, *Child of the Fire: Mary Edmonia Lewis and the Problem of Art History's Black and Indian Subject*; Henderson and Henderson, *The Indomitable Spirit of Edmonia Lewis: A Narrative Biography*; Nelson, *The Color of Stone: Sculpting the Black Female Subject in Nineteenth-Century America*, 159–78; Wolfe, *Edmonia Lewis: Wildfire in Marble*.

115. Revo, "Edmonia Lewis," in Henry Louis Gates Jr. and Evelyn Brooks Higginbotham, eds., *African American Lives*, 530.

116. Wreford, "A Negro Sculptress."

117. Revo, "Edmonia Lewis," 530.

118. Mitchell, *Raising Freedom's Child: Black Children and Visions of the Future after Slavery*, 1–10, 51–90.

119. Wolfe, *Edmonia Lewis*, 63.

120. "Edmonia Lewis," *Freedmen's Record* (Jan. 1867): 3; Buick, *Child of the Fire*, 15, 60; Wolfe, *Edmonia Lewis*, 63.

121. "Edmonia Lewis," *Freedmen's Record* (Jan. 1867): 3.

122. Nelson, *The Color of Stone*, 162. Original emphasis.

123. "Edmonia Lewis," *Freedmen's Record* (Jan. 1867): 3.

124. Fredrickson, *The Black Image in the White Mind*, 107.

125. Buick, *Child of Fire*, 16.

126. Hannaford, *Women of the Century*, 264, 266.

127. Henderson and Henderson, *The Indomitable Spirit of Edmonia Lewis*, 18.

128. "Commencement at Oberlin," *Anglo-African* (Sept. 9, 1865).

129. "Fanny M. Jackson," *Liberator* (Oct. 6, 1865): 159; "All Sorts," *New Haven Daily Palladium* (Oct. 10, 1865); "Miscellaneous Items," *Vermont Chronicle* (Sept. 23, 1865): 5.

130. Jackson-Coppin, *Reminiscences,* 13, 14.

131. Data courtesy of Ronald E. Butchart and the Freedmen's Teacher Project. Communication with the author, Sept. 9, 2019.

132. Butchart, *Schooling the Freed People,* 78–119; Butchart, "Mission Matters: Mount Holyoke, Oberlin, and the Schooling of Southern Blacks, 1861–1917."

133. Bay, *The White Image in the Black Mind,* 32–33; Pease and Pease, "Ends, Means, and Attitudes."

134. Don Carlos, "Letter from Oberlin, Ohio" 1.

4. Berea College and the Boundaries of Equality, 1866–1880

1. Burleigh, *John G. Fee: Founder of Berea College,* 10.

2. Foner, *Reconstruction,* 77–123; Masur, *An Example for All the Land,* 87–126.

3. Webb, *Kentucky in the Reconstruction Era.*

4. Wallenstein, "Pioneer Black Legislators from Kentucky, 1860s–1960s," 533–57.

5. *Historical Register of the Officers and Students of Berea College, from the Beginning to June, 1904,* BCA.

6. Smith, *Reparation and Reconciliation,* 2–5. On anticaste jurisprudence, see Horton, *Race and the Making of American Liberalism,* 15–36.

7. Apart from some abortive instances, public universities in the South did not integrate until the mid-twentieth century. Arkansas Industrial University's attempt in 1872 ended after only a year. When the University of South Carolina integrated in 1873, most whites withdrew. The school became a white institution again after 1877. Cohen, *Reconstructing the Campus,* 118–27.

8. Smith, *Reparation and Reconciliation,* 6.

9. "The Races in the Colleges," *New York Times* (Dec. 2, 1883): 6; Bennett, *Religion and the Rise of Jim Crow in New Orleans,* 54; Richardson, *Christian Reconstruction: The American Missionary Association and Southern Blacks, 1861–1890,* 124, 232; Smith, *Reparation and Reconciliation,* 189–92. Smith demonstrates that Howard leaders were committed to integration but provides few examples of social encounters between students of different races on campus.

10. "Colored Students in Berea—All Schools."

11. Ernest G. Dodge to William Frost, Apr. 11, 1925, William G. Frost Papers, Box 13, BCA.

12. Acts 10:34, 17:26.

13. Fee, *Autobiography of John G. Fee, Berea, Kentucky,* 56–57.

14. Reprinted in "Anti-Slavery Missions in Slave States," *Oberlin Evangelist* 12:26 (Dec. 19, 1855), 208.

15. Wilson, *Berea College: An Illustrated History,* 11–12.

16. Fairchild, *Berea College, Ky.: An Interesting History,* 1st ed. 107–8; Fee, *Autobiography,* 185–90; Peck, *Berea's First Century,* 26–28, 141–42.

17. Richardson, *Christian Reconstruction,* 157, 189–234.

18. Acts 17:11; Freehling, *The Road to Disunion,* vol. 2, *Secessionists Triumphant,* 227–30; Peck,

Berea's First Century, 1–2; Sears, *The Day of Small Things: Abolitionism in the Midst of Slavery, Berea, Kentucky, 1854–1864,* 1–26.

19. John G. Fee to Gerrit Smith, Jan. 4, 1856, Box 18, GSP, Syracuse University Archives.

20. Freehling, *Road to Disunion,* 222–24, 233; Peck with Smith, *Berea's First 125 Years, 1855–1980,* 1–12; Sears, *The Day of Small Things,* 27–112, 229–64; Wilson, *Berea College: An Illustrated History,* 9–15.

21. Freehling, *Road to Disunion,* 232, 234–35; Peck with Smith, *Berea's First 125 Years,* 12–25; Sears, *Day of Small Things,* 229–34, 265–88; Wilson, *Berea College: An Illustrated History,* 16–21.

22. Report of W. W. Wheeler to the Trustees, Mar. 31, 1866, Board of Trustee Records, Box 1, BCA.

23. John G. Fee, "The Induction of Colored Pupils into Berea College," Aug. 2, 1900, 5–6, John G. Fee Papers, Box 7, BCA.

24. Fee, *Autobiography,* 183; Smith, *Reparation and Reconciliation,* 78.

25. Angus Burleigh to Edwin S. Fee, Dec. 1924, Angus A. Burleigh Student File, Box 1, BCA.

26. Angus Burleigh to Berea Alumnus, May 7, 1934, Burleigh Student File, Box 1, BCA.

27. Sears, *A Utopian Experiment in Kentucky,* 42, 47.

28. "Berea Literary Institute: Grounds for Encouragement (1867)," 2, Office of Information Records: Publications, Box 14, BCA.

29. Sears, *A Utopian Experiment in Kentucky,* 71–76, 159–60.

30. Sears, *A Utopian Experiment in Kentucky,* 120.

31. Alvord, *Letters from the South,* 37–38; Richardson, *Memoirs of Berea,* 16; Sears, *A Utopian Experiment in Kentucky,* 115–20.

32. John Fee to Gerrit Smith, Apr. 9, 1868, Box 18, GSP, Syracuse University Archives.

33. "Berea Literary Institute," 4.

34. Peck, *Berea's First Century,* 141.

35. Baumann, *Constructing Black Education at Oberlin College,* 34, 59.

36. "Berea Literary Institute," 4.

37. "A Letter from John G. Fee to the People of Lexington," Oct. 16, 1869, Fee Papers, Box 7, BCA.

38. John G. Fee to Erastus Cravath, Jan. 25, 1867, AMA #45056, *American Missionary Association Papers,* BCA.

39. J. H. Fairchild, "Berea, KY.: Commencement Exercises," *American Missionary* 12:8 (Aug. 1868): 172.

40. "Berea College, Berea Kentucky. Normal and Collegiate Education under Christian Influences (1868)," Office of Information (Development) Records: Publications, Box 14, BCA.

41. *Inauguration of Rev. E. H. Fairchild; Address of Rev. John G. Fee and the President,* 12–13.

42. Guyatt, *Bind Us Apart,* 161–75; Walters, "The Erotic South," 177–201.

43. *Inauguration of Rev. E. H. Fairchild,* 13, 10; *Records of the Faculty of Berea College,* vol. 1, *May 4, 1869 to Dec. 1, 1880,* 9, Academic Divisions: Faculty Minutes, Box 5, BCA.

44. Fee, "A Letter from John G. Fee to the People of Lexington."

45. Sears, *A Utopian Experiment in Kentucky,* 200n33.

46. Fowler, *Northern Attitudes toward Interracial Marriage: Legislation and Public Opinion in the Middle Atlantic and the States of the Old Northwest, 1780–1930,* 373.

47. Adams and Nelson, "President E. Henry Fairchild and Berea College's Commitment to Women's Education," 10.

48. Peck, *Berea's First Century,* 83.

49. *First Catalogue of the Officers and Students of Berea College for 1866–7,* 5; *Catalogue of the Officers and Students of Berea College, 1867–8,* 5. Belle A. Pratt was the daughter of Almon Bradley Pratt and sister of Hattie Pratt, a Latin teacher at Berea and an alumna of Oberlin. Frederick Hall to W. G. Frost, Oct. 14, 1925, Frost Papers, Box 13, BCA; "Congregational Necrology: Almon Bradley Pratt," *Congregational Quarterly* 19:2 (Apr. 1877), 317–18.

50. *Catalogue of the Officers and Students of Berea College, 1871–1872,* 6–7. The Berea College Archives file copy of this catalogue has the races of the students annotated. Thirteen of the forty-three bachelor's degree recipients between 1873 and 1889 were African American. Peck, *Berea's First Century,* 43.

51. Peck, *Berea's First Century,* 43.

52. The Berea student catalogues for 1870–71, 1871–72, and 1873–74 (there was no catalog printed for 1872–73) indicate college students' residences as well as their hometowns. The catalog does not list the residences of women enrolled in the ladies' department, although it does list their hometowns. Half were from the vicinity and likely lived at home.

53. John Fee to Gerrit Smith, Nov. 18, 1873, Box 18, GSP, Syracuse University Archives; Peck, *Berea's First Century,* 28.

54. The *Catalogue of the Officers and Students of Berea College, 1871–1872,* 6. The catalog indicates that Roberts died that school year. Whether he and Robinson were roommates prior to that or Robinson inherited his room is unclear.

55. John T. Robinson, "His Alma Mater," *Lexington Standard* (Oct. 1893), clipping in Associated Items: Blacks and Berea College, Box 1, BCA. Despite Robinson's assertion that "a few roomed together," there are no other documented cases of black and white roommates apart from him and Roberts.

56. Fee to Smith, Nov. 18, 1873.

57. Extract from Report of Gen. Ben. P. Runkle, Assistant Commissioner for Kentucky, to Gen. O. O. Howard, in "Testimonies on Behalf of Berea College: 1872," Publications, Box 14, BCA.

58. Alvord, *Letters from the South,* 38.

59. John A. R. Rogers, "Our College Record: Berea College," *American Missionary* 14:9 (Sept. 1870): 207.

60. "Extract from Report of Gen. Ben. P. Runkle, Assistant Commissioner for Kentucky to Gen. O. O. Howard," in "Testimonials on Behalf of Berea College (1872)," Office of Information (Development) Records, Box 14, BCA.

61. *Records of the Faculty of Berea College,* 1:12–13, 56, 70, and 74.

62. *Records of the Faculty of Berea College,* 1:75.

63. "Evidence Taken in case of Alex. Pearce (Nov. 25th '71): Charge 1," 2, Academic Divisions: Faculty Minutes, Inserts, Box 5, BCA.

64. Ibid., 5.

65. They were Henry Clark (who was on leave during the 1871–72 school year), Henry Chittenden, Alice Peck, Hattie Pratt, Charles Starbuck, and Albert Wright. Rhoda Lyon arrived a short while later to replace the lady principal.

66. *Catalogue of the Officers and Students of Berea College, 1871–1872,* 5. On the backgrounds of Berea employees, see Fairchild, *An Interesting History,* 1st ed., 65–70. Not included is Alice E. Peck, who also attended Oberlin's Ladies Department. *Annual Catalogue of the Officers and Students of Oberlin College for the College Year 1868–1869,* 34.

67. Gail Kenny describes a similar preoccupation among Oberlin missionaries to Jamaica in the antebellum period. See *Contentious Liberties,* 100–128.

68. Fletcher, *A History of Oberlin College,* 1:444–47.

69. John T. Robinson, "The B.C.Q.," *Lexington Standard* (May 4, 1894), clipping in Associated Items: Blacks and Berea College, Box 1, BCA.

70. John Fee to Erastus Cravath, Jan. 5, 1872, *American Missionary Association Papers,* microfilm, reel 71, roll 4, BCA.

71. Ibid.

72. John Fee to Erastus Cravath, June 8, 1872, *American Missionary Association Papers,* microfilm, reel 71, roll 4, BCA.

73. Don Carlos, "Letter from Oberlin, Ohio," 1.

74. "Relative Number of Colored Students," Annual Report to the President, Mar. 1901, 78, Accessed May 25, 2020. https://www2.oberlin.edu/archive/oresources/minority/nums_black_stu dents.html.

75. *Records of the Faculty of Berea College,* 1:78–80. The names of the other petitioners are not recorded.

76. Ibid., 81.

77. Ibid., 82, 84, quotes on 85, 87.

78. Henry Fairchild to Erastus Cravath, Jan. 24, 1872, *American Missionary Association Papers,* microfilm, reel 71, roll 4, BCA.

79. Peck, *Berea's First Century,* 45; Sears, *Utopian Experiment,* 84–85, 190n8.

80. *Records of the Faculty of Berea College,* 1:85.

81. Fairchild to Cravath, Jan. 24, 1872.

82. Butchart, "Mission Matters"; Butchart, *Schooling the Freed People,* 78–119.

83. Richardson, *Christian Reconstruction,* 254.

84. Butchart, *Northern Schools, Southern Blacks, and Reconstruction: Freedmen's Education, 1862–1875,* 162.

85. Richardson, *Christian Reconstruction,* 223. See also McPherson, *The Abolitionist Legacy,* 180–81.

86. Fairchild to Cravath, Jan. 24, 1872.

87. *Records of the Faculty of Berea College:* 1:88.

88. One white couple and two black couples had previously been disciplined. *Records of the Faculty of Berea College,* 1:71–72, 86; Sears, *Utopian Experiment in Kentucky,* 129.

89. *Records of the Faculty of Berea College,* 1:94.

90. Fee to Cravath, June 8, 1872, *American Missionary Association Papers,* microfilm, reel 71, roll 4, BCA.

91. *Records of the Faculty of Berea College,* 1:94.

92. *Records of the Faculty of Berea College,* 1:94, 97, 98, 104, 112.

93. Rhoda Lyon to the Faculty, Apr. 26, 1872, Administrative Divisions: Dean of Women,

Box 1, BCA. This letter is badly damaged, making it impossible to determine the identities and races of the young men.

94. *Records of the Faculty of Berea College,* 1:98, 103, 107, 114–15. Britton was still allowed to graduate from the ladies' course, making her the first black woman to earn a degree at Berea. She went on to found the Hooks School of Music in Memphis and become a charter member of the NAACP, of which her grandson Benjamin Hooks later served as executive director.

95. Fee to Cravath, June 8, 1872. Original emphasis.

96. Rhoda Lyon to Erastus Cravath, June 25, 1872, *American Missionary Association Papers,* microfilm, reel 71, roll 4, BCA. Original emphases.

97. John G. Hamilton to Erastus Cravath, June 28, 1872, *American Missionary Association Papers,* microfilm, reel 71, roll 4, BCA.

98. Hamilton to Cravath, June 28, 1872. Original emphasis.

99. William E. Lincoln to AMA, Apr. 8, 1868, *American Missionary Association Papers,* microfilm, reel 70, roll 3, BCA; George Whipple to John G. Fee, Apr. 18 and May 11, 1868, Fee Papers, Box 4, BCA.

100. Including Fee, there were fourteen members of Berea's board of trustees for 1871–1872. Cravath and one other, William N. Embree, were absent from that year's meeting. The lone Black trustee, Berea's first, was Reverend Gabriel Burdett, a Union Army veteran who had assisted Fee at Camp Nelson during the war. Afterward, he served as pastor of its church and a teacher in its school, which was sponsored by the AMA. Sears, *Utopian Experiment,* 153–55.

101. On June 17, John A. R. Rogers wrote Cravath asking him to "at least consider the possibility of giving us your counsel and cooperation." See Rogers to Cravath, June 17, 1872, *American Missionary Association Papers,* microfilm, reel 71, roll 4, BCA.

102. Rhoda Lyon to Erastus Cravath, July 5, 1872, *American Missionary Association Papers,* microfilm, reel 71, roll 4, BCA.

103. John A. R. Rogers to Erastus Cravath, July 10, 1872, *American Missionary Association Papers,* microfilm, reel 71, roll 4, BCA.

104. Gudgeirsson, "'We Do Not Have Any Prejudice . . . but,'" 39; Harlow, *Religion, Race, and the Making of Confederate Kentucky, 1830–1880,* 209–10; McPherson, *The Abolitionist Legacy,* 245; Sears, *Utopian Experiment,* 134–35, 200n32; Smith, *Reparation and Reconciliation,* 92.

105. Minutes of the Board of Trustees of Berea College, Board of Trustees Records (hereafter MBTBC), Box 8, BCA, 81–82.

106. MBTBC, 82.

107. MBTBC, 82.

108. Sears, *A Utopian Experiment in Kentucky,* 118.

109. John Robinson would later claim that Burdett voted with Hanson (and Fee) against the resolutions, but the meeting minutes do not indicate that Burdett did, and Fee was ineligible to vote. John T. Robinson, "His Alma Mater," *Lexington Standard* (Oct. 1893), clipping in Associated Items: Blacks and Berea College, Box 1, BCA. Oberlin did not appoint a black trustee until 1950, when Ralph Bunche joined its board. Baumann, *Constructing Black Education at Oberlin College,* 79.

110. MBTBC, 80–82.

111. Violet Tyler, "Race Relations in Berea College According to the Negro Graduates," May 1924, 6, Student Files: Violet Tyler, Box 1, BCA.

112. Hall to Frost, Oct. 14, 1925.

113. John G. Fee, *To the Friends of Christian Education* (Oct. 11, 1873), Office of Information Records: Publications, Box 14, BCA; Fairchild, *An Interesting History,* 1st ed., 47.

114. Sears, *A Utopian Experiment in Kentucky,* 141.

115. Peck, *Berea's First Century,* 143.

116. "Colored Students in Berea—All Schools."

117. Fee to Smith, Nov. 18, 1873. On the design and features of the Ladies' Hall, see Sears, *A Utopian Experiment in Kentucky,* 63–64.

118. John Fee to Erastus Cravath, Sept. 19, 1873, quoted in Sears, *A Utopian Experiment in Kentucky,* 64.

119. *Records of the Faculty of Berea College,* 1:133, 145, 147.

120. John M. Ellis, "Berea College," *Advance* (July 17, 1873), reprinted in "Berea College" (1873), Office of Information Records: Publications, Box 14, BCA.

121. Smith, *Reparation and Reconciliation,* 80.

122. Rosen, *Terror in Heart of Freedom,* 133–78.

123. *Records of the Faculty of Berea College,* 1:166, 173.

124. Fairchild, *Interesting History,* 67.

125. *Records of the Faculty of Berea College,* 1:172–73.

126. *Records of the Faculty of Berea College,* 1:174.

127. *Records of the Faculty of Berea College,* 1:173.

128. E. H. Fairchild to Michael Strieby, June 7, 1877, *American Missionary Association Papers,* Box 1, BCA.

129. *Records of the Faculty of Berea College,* 1:166, 174, 183, 185.

130. John T. Robinson to John Fee, Oct. 29, 1877, Fee Papers, Box 4, BCA.

131. Robinson, "His Alma Mater."

132. Robinson to Fee, Oct. 29, 1877.

133. Fairchild, *Berea College: An Interesting History,* 2nd ed., 54.

134. On this tendency among early AMA/Oberlin missionaries in Jamaica, see Kenny, *Contentious Liberties,* 87–99.

135. Richardson, *Christian Reconstruction,* 157.

136. Peck, *Berea's First Century,* 143.

137. Smith, *Reparation and Reconciliation,* 130.

138. "Principles and Plans," *American Missionary* 32:6 (June 1878): 162.

139. Fairchild, *An Interesting History,* 1st ed., 81, 44, 6.

140. R. L. Breck, "A Visit to Berea," July 14, 1876, reprinted from *Transylvania Presbyterian,* Publications about Berea College, Box 7, BCA.

141. Dodge to Frost, Apr. 11, 1925.

142. For exceptions, see *Records of the Faculty of Berea College,* 1:349, 353, 382, 416–18.

143. *Laws and Regulations of Berea College.*

144. Fairchild, *Interesting History,* 101; Wilson, *Berea College: An Illustrated History,* 44.

145. *Records of the Faculty of Berea College,* vol. 2, *Dec 8, 1880–May 6, 1889,* 53; *Records of the Faculty of Berea College,* vol. 3, *May 27, 1889 to December 29, 1892,* 39, both College, Academy, and Foundation Faculty, Series 2, Box 1, BCA.

146. *Records of the Proceedings of the Ladies' Board of Care of Berea College,* typescript, 1–11, Administrative Divisions: The Ladies' Board of Care, Box 1, BCA. The minutes prior to 1880 do not survive.

147. "Colored Students in Berea—All Schools."

148. *Records of the Faculty of Berea College,* 1:349, 351.

149. *Records of the Faculty of Berea College,* 1:353–54. Original emphasis.

150. Dodge to Frost, Apr. 11, 1925.

151. *Records of the Faculty of Berea College,* 1:353–56.

152. *Records of the Faculty of Berea College,* 1:416.

153. *Records of the Faculty of Berea College,* 1:416–19.

154. *Records of the Faculty of Berea College,* 1:133, 144, 382.

155. *Records of the Faculty of Berea College,* 2:15–17, 94, 167, 255.

156. Fairchild, *Interesting History,* 2nd ed., 61–62.

5. The Unraveling of Interracial Oberlin, 1874–1892

1. "Is There a Color Line at Oberlin?" *Oberlin Review* (Feb 3, 1883): 115–16. Hereafter *OR.*

2. Smith, *Reparation and Reconciliation,* 138–39, 175–76.

3. *Catalogue of the Officers and Students of Oberlin College for the College Year 1881-82,* 54.

4. *Catalogue of the Officers and Students of Oberlin College for the College Year 1882-83,* 58.

5. "Is There a Color Line at Oberlin?" 115.

6. "Communications," *OR* (Mar. 3, 1883): 136.

7. "Communications," 137.

8. Bigglestone, "Oberlin College and the Negro Student," 198; Smith, *Reparation and Reconciliation,* 87; "Relative Number of Colored Students," Annual Report to the President, Mar. 1901, 78, OCA.

9. "Communications," 137.

10. Baumann, *Constructing Black Education at Oberlin College,* 34.

11. Langston, *From the Virginia Plantation to the National Capitol,* 138.

12. "Communications," 137.

13. Fairchild, *Oberlin: The Colony and the College,* 113.

14. "Communications," 137.

15. Cally L. Waite contends that the secularization of Oberlin's curriculum contributed to the segregation of its student body in this period. I argue religious enthusiasm for reform was not reduced so much as redirected and that foreign missions and temperance assumed pride of place over racial justice. See Waite, "The Segregation of Black Students at Oberlin College after Reconstruction," 352.

16. Leonard, *The Story of Oberlin,* 385.

17. "Editorial Board," *OR* 9:12 (Mar. 1, 1884): 133.

18. *Annual Catalogue of the Officers and Students of Oberlin College for the College Year 1869–70,* 9–15, 31–37; *Annual Catalogue of the Officers and Students of Oberlin College for the College Year 1874–75,* 9–13, 29–33; *Annual Catalogue of the Officers and Students of Oberlin College for the College*

Year 1879–80, 10–15, 16–19; *Annual Catalogue of the Officers and Students of Oberlin College for the College Year 1882–83*, 10–16, 17–22; *Constitution and By-Laws and List of Members of the Alpha Zeta Society*, 21–26, Alpha Zeta Literary Society, Box 1, OCA; *Constitution, By-Laws and List of Members of the L.L.S. Society*, 23–27; *Constitution, By-Laws and Roll of Members of the Phi Delta Society*, 28–30; Aeolian Literary Society, List of Members by Class, 1853–1910, Ladies' Literary Society Records, OCA; Phi Kappa Pi Society Membership Roll, 1883, 34–38, Phi Kappa Pi Records, OCA. Of eligible white students enrolled between 1874 and 1883, 82 percent of men and 61 percent of women eventually joined literary societies. From the 1850s to the 1870s, black women's membership rates were on par with white women's or even exceeded them. Black men's membership rates fluctuated in the same period. Theirs were generally lower than white men's rates except in 1860, when they peaked at 100 percent, compared to 65 percent for white men.

19. Lester, *Life and Public Services of Charles Sumner*, 521.

20. "Local Matters," *OR* 1:2 (Apr. 15, 1874): 15.

21. Stanton, Anthony, and Gage, *History of Woman Suffrage*, vol. 2, *1861–1876*, 383–84.

22. "The Advance Movement. Organization of a Woman's Suffrage Association," *Lorain County News* (May 5, 1870): 3.

23. "The Day We Celebrate," *Oberlin Weekly News* (May 21, 1874); Kornblith and Lasser, *Elusive Utopia*, 155–56.

24. John Mercer Langston, "Equality before the Law," in *Freedom and Citizenship: Selected Letters and Addresses of Hon. John Mercer Langston, L.L.D.* (Washington, DC: H. Darby, 1883), 151–52.

25. "The Day We Celebrate."

26. Foner, *Reconstruction*, 556.

27. Kornblith and Lasser, *Elusive Utopia*, 156.

28. J. W. Welsh, "Personal Liberty," *OR* 1:13 (Oct. 7, 1874): 99.

29. Letcher, "Spiritual Dynamics," *OR* 2:17 (Nov. 3, 1875): 197–98.

30. Morris, "Moral Evolution," *OR* 6:3 (Oct. 9, 1878): 26.

31. Barnard, *From Evangelicalism to Progressivism at Oberlin College, 1866–1917*, 31–32.

32. Barnard, *From Evangelicalism to Progressivism at Oberlin College*, 50–51; "Local Matters," *OR* 1:6 (June 10, 1874): 47; "Darwin," *OR* 9:18 (May 20, 1882): 6–7; "Judging by Late Developments," *OR* 10:5 (Nov. 18, 1882): 55; A. Wilford Hall, "The Problem of Human Life," *OR* 10:6 (Dec. 2, 1882): 64; "Society Notes," *OR* 11:1 (Sept. 22, 1883): 10.

33. Morris, "Moral Evolution," 26.

34. Boone, "Social Evolution," *OR* 6:7 (Dec. 11, 1878): 73–74; Fairchild, "Modern Iconoclasm," *OR* 3:16 (Oct. 25, 1876): 181–82; Gates, "Evolution and Free Will," *OR* 5:10 (Jan. 23, 1878): 110–11.

35. Todd, "Evolution and Revelation" *OR* 2:10 (July 7, 1875): 112.

36. Patterson, "The Unity of the Human Race," *OR* 7:13 (Feb. 19, 1880): 147.

37. Sanderson, *Social Evolutionism*, 10–35; Stocking, *Race, Culture, and Evolution*, 111–33, 235–70.

38. *General Catalogue of Oberlin College, 1833[–]1908: Including an Account of the Principal Events in the History of the College, with Illustrations of the College Buildings*, 176.

39. Stratton, "Character Building," *OR* 5:3 (Oct. 17, 1877): 27.

40. Davis, "The Dawn and Development of English Liberty," *OR* 12:1 (Sept. 27, 1884): 3–6; Howland, "A Plea for Restricted Immigration," *OR* 14:16 (Apr. 26, 1887): 182–85; "Society Congress," *OR* 23:5 (Oct. 30, 1895): 69.

41. "De Rebus Temporis," *OR* 2:6 (May 5, 1875): 70.

42. Harrison, "Our National Peculiarities," *OR* 6 :13 (Mar. 5, 1879): 147.

43. "Local," *OR* 2:2 (Mar. 10, 1875), 22.

44. "De Rebus Temporis," *OR* 8:5 (Nov. 20, 1880), 56.

45. "Our Table," *OR* 2:8 (June 9, 1875), 97; "De Rebus Temporis," *OR* 5:14 (Mar. 20, 1878), 165; "De Rebus Temporis," *OR* 8:11 (Feb. 19, 1881), 130; "Society Notes," *OR* 18:26 (Mar. 31, 1891), 379.

46. Marszalek, "A Black Cadet at West Point," *American Heritage* 22:5 (Aug. 1971). Accessed June 7, 2019, https://www.americanheritage.com/black-cadet-west-point.

47. "Some of the Authorities at West Point," *OR* 7:18 (May 6, 1880), 211–12 (quotes on 212).

48. Marszalek, "A Black Cadet at West Point."

49. "Reviews," *OR* 8:4 (Nov. 6, 1880), 41.

50. Andrews, "West Point and the Colored Cadets," *International Review* (Nov. 1880), 480, 483, 484, 482.

51. "Reviews," *OR* 8:4 (Nov. 6, 1880): 41.

52. Andrews, "West Point and the Colored Cadets," 481.

53. "Our Table," *OR* 8:6 (Dec. 4, 1880), 72.

54. The same joke appeared in the University of Minnesota's literary magazine a few months earlier. "Clippings," *Ariel* 4:1 (Oct. 7, 1880), 11.

55. Gatewood, "John Hanks Alexander of Arkansas: Second Black Graduate of West Point," *Arkansas Historical Quarterly* 41:2 (Summer 1982): 103–28 (especially 119–21); Brian Shellum, *Black Cadet in a White Bastion: Charles Young at West Point* (Lincoln: University of Nebraska Press, 2006), 45–47. My thanks to Gary Kornblith and Carol Lasser for bringing the career of John Hanks Alexander to my attention.

56. Smith, *Reparation and Reconciliation,* 87.

57. "Diary of a Nineteenth-Century Girl," *New York Times Book Review* (June 20, 1926): 13.

58. No one by this name is recorded in the college catalog for 1881–82. The catalog does record the hometown of every student. But apart from Oberlin and major cities, place names in *Kathie's Diary* also appear to have been altered.

59. Cheek and Cheek, *John Mercer Langston and the Fight for Black Freedom,* 250–52; Sharfstein, *The Invisible Line: A Secret History of Race in America,* 85–102, 151–67.

60. *Catalogue of the Officers and Students of Oberlin College for the College Year 1880–81,* 37.

61. Eggleston, ed., *Kathie's Diary: Leaves from an Old, Old Diary,* 225.

62. Ibid., 223, 224, 224, 222, 224.

63. Ibid., 223, 224, 222, 224.

64. Ibid., 224, 224–25, 225, 276–77.

65. Ibid., 225.

66. Sharfstein, *The Invisible Line,* 236, 253–71.

67. Ibid., 266–67, 311–14.

68. Ham, foreword to Terrell, *A Colored Woman in a White World,* 7–20; Parker, *Unceasing Militant: The Life of Mary Church Terrell,* 5–30, 34.

69. Terrell, *A Colored Woman in a White World,* 77.

70. Ibid., 74–78.

71. Ibid., 71.

72. Ibid., 71–72. Compare to Fairchild, *Oberlin: The Colony and the College,* 113.

73. Terrell, *A Colored Woman in a White World,* 73.

74. Fox-Genovese and Genovese, *The Mind of the Master Class: History and Faith in the Southern Slaveholders' Worldview,* 521.

75. Terrell, *A Colored Woman in a White World,* 74.

76. Kornblith and Lasser, *Elusive Utopia,* 196–223.

77. Terrell, *A Colored Woman in a White World,* 75.

78. "De Rerus Temporis," *OR* 8:14 (Apr. 2, 1881): 165.

79. "Society Notes," *OR* 8:13 (Mar. 19, 1881), 156; "Society Notes," *OR* 8:15 (Apr. 16, 1881): 180; "Society Notes," *OR* 10:10 (Feb. 3, 1883), 156.

80. "Society Notes," *OR* 8:13 (Feb. 28, 1883): 165.

81. Terrell, *A Colored Woman in a White World,* 76.

82. "Miss Wilson's Work among Refugees in Kansas," *American Missionary* 35:1 (Jan. 1881): 280–81.

83. "Avery Scholarship List, 1879–1898," Minority Student Records, OCA.

84. Giles Shurtleff, "Some Features of Our College Life," 1884, Giles Waldo and Mary E. Burton Shurtleff Papers, OCA. See also "Communications," 137.

85. Notes of Talk with James Harris Fairchild, Feb. 19, 1897, Delevan Leonard Papers, OCA.

86. "College Notes," *OR* 9:14 (Mar. 25, 1882): 64.

87. J. Garnett et al., Petition to the "Hon. Faculty of O.C.," 1882, James Harris Fairchild Papers, OCA.

88. Julia Wilson to James H. Fairchild, Mar. 16, 1882, Fairchild Papers, OCA.

89. Wilson to Fairchild, Mar. 24, 1882.

90. Fairchild, *Oberlin: The Colony and the College,* 112–13.

91. Wilson to Fairchild, Mar. 16, 1882.

92. Bradley, "The Elements of Modern Civilization," *OR* 10:1 (Sept. 23, 1882): 4. A headnote indicates this essay was delivered at an oratorical contest in Mar. 1882.

93. Ransom, *The Pilgrimage of Harriet Ransom's Son,* 33.

94. Gatewood, "John Hanks Alexander of Arkansas," 116.

95. "Avery Scholarship List, 1879–1898"; Gomez-Jefferson, *The Sage of Tawawa: Reverdy Cassius Ransom, 1861–1959,* 14.

96. Ronnick, ed. *The Autobiography of William Sanders Scarborough: An American Journey from Slavery to Scholarship,* 50.

97. Ransom, *The Pilgrimage of Harriet Ransom's Son,* 33.

98. Fletcher, *A History of Oberlin College,* 2:524, 526.

99. Ibid., 2:612–13; Terrell, *A Colored Woman in a White World,* 71.

100. Lucy Stone, "Oberlin College," *Woman's Journal* (July 21, 1883): 226.

101. Ball, *To Live an Antislavery Life;* Baumgartner, *In Pursuit of Knowledge;* Higginbotham, *Righteous Discontent.*

102. Bigglestone, "Oberlin College and the Negro Student," 200–201; "College Notes."

103. Henry Castle to Mary Tenney Castle and Harriet Castle Coleman, Jan. 3, 1883, Henry Northrup Castle Papers, Box 3, University of Chicago Library.

104. Mary Keep to James Fairchild, Nov. 29, 1882, Fairchild Papers, OCA. See also George S. Harrison to James Fairchild, Mar. 5, 1883, Fairchild Papers, OCA.

105. L. A. Roberson to James Fairchild, Oct. 11, 1882, Fairchild Papers, OCA, original emphases; Baumann, *Constructing Black Education at Oberlin College*, 329n152.

106. Benjamin Imes to James Fairchild, Oct. 16, 1882, Fairchild Papers, OCA.

107. "The China Band—Its Object and the Demand," *Oberlin Review* 10:3 (Oct. 21, 1882): 29; Barnard, *From Evangelicalism to Progressivism at Oberlin College*, 30; Fairchild, *Oberlin: The Colony and the College*, 145–46.

108. Leonard, *The Story of Oberlin*, 336. Evangelicalism shaped Oberlin culture long after the Second Great Awakening. Secular and scientific approaches to social reform began to be discussed on campus in the early 1880s, but they did not begin to compete with Oberlin's traditional, faith-based approach until the latter years of the decade. See Barnard, *From Evangelicalism to Progressivism at Oberlin College*, 30–33, 59–68.

109. Wilson to Fairchild, Mar. 16, 1882.

110. "De Rebus Temporis," *OR* 11:1 (Sept. 22, 1883), 12.

111. Shumway and Brower, *Oberliniana*, 174.

112. Roberson to Fairchild, Oct. 11, 1882.

113. "Communications," 137.

114. "Is There a Color Line at Oberlin?" 115.

115. Fairchild, *Oberlin: The Colony and the College*, 186–95.

116. Barnard, *From Evangelicalism to Progressivism at Oberlin College*, 18; Giles Shurtleff, "Shall We Have a Winter Term?" *OR* 2:9 (June 23, 1875): 99–100.

117. "Is There a Color Line at Oberlin?" 115.

118. Ibid.

119. "Communications," 136–37.

120. "College Notes," 3.

121. "Communications," 137.

122. Blackett, *Beating against the Barriers: Biographical Essays in Nineteenth-Century Afro-American History*, 290–92; Cohen, *Reconstructing the Campus*, 97–98; Levine, *Martin Delany, Frederick Douglass, and the Politics of Representative Identity*, 61–62; Malkmus, "Small Towns, Small Sects, and Coeducation in Midwestern Colleges, 1853–1861," 44; Potts, *Wesleyan University, 1831–1910: Collegiate Enterprise in New England*, 53–54, 53–54.

123. Cohen, *Reconstructing the Campus*, 114–27.

124. Alexander Bartlett to James H. Fairchild, Nov. 26, 1878, Fairchild Papers, OCA. Bartlett was an Oberlin graduate. His brother Peter, who was Maryville's president, favored excluding African Americans but was overruled by the college trustees, who were fearful of losing northern donor support. See Burnside, "A 'Delicate and Difficult Duty,'" 234–35.

125. Castle was quoting the political economist Henry V. Poor's book *Money and Its Laws* (1877). Whether Poor or Castle used "species" to mean whites or Anglo-Saxons is ambiguous from either text. In Poor's case, the representative of his "species" is the English philosopher Jeremy Bentham.

126. Henry Castle to Mary Tenney Castle and Harriet Castle Coleman, Jan. 3, 1883.

127. J. W. Dow, "The Security of Liberty," *OR* 10:10 (Feb. 3, 1883): 109–11.

128. Stone, "Oberlin College."

129. Ballantine, *The Oberlin Jubilee*, 224–25, 213.

130. Ibid., 131, 132.

131. "The Civil Rights Bill in Oberlin," *Oberlin Weekly News* (Nov. 2, 1883): 3.

132. Shumway and Brower, *Oberliniana,* 174.

133. The so-called Civil Rights Cases were decided in October 1883. Unlike at Oberlin, the student magazine of nearby Denison College printed an editorial about the ruling in its November issue. "The Decisions of the Supreme Court," *Denison Collegian* 17:3 (Nov. 24, 1883): 36.

134. Wong, "The Legacy of Luella Miner," 253–64.

135. Miner, "The Schoolma'am at Home," *OR* 11:5 (Nov. 17, 1883): 51, 52.

136. Barnard, *From Evangelicalism to Progressivism at Oberlin College,* 26.

137. James Fairchild, "The True Character of Slavery as It Existed in This Country" (1884), Fairchild Papers, Series 8, Box 9, OCA, 1, 3, 4, 5.

138. Fairchild, "The True Character of Slavery," 4, 5.

139. Mercer, "Giles Waldo Shurtleff: A Biography of Oberlin's Favorite Son"; Washington, *Eagles on Their Buttons: A Black Infantry Regiment in the Civil War,* 17–26.

140. Kornblith and Lasser, *Elusive Utopia,* 198, 206, 208, 211.

141. "De Rebus Temporis," *OR* 11:9 (Jan. 19, 1884): 106.

142. Shurtleff, "Some Features of Our College Life."

143. Ibid.

144. Ibid.

145. C.A. Vincent, "Elements of Progress," *OR* 12:2 (Oct. 11, 1884): 16–19; L. H. Davis, "The Dawn and Development of English Liberty," *OR* 12:1 (Sept. 27, 1884): 3–6; E. C. Ritsher, "Conservatism: An Essential Element of Progress," *OR* 13:18 (May 28, 1886): 213–15; L. P. Howland, "A Plea for Restricted Immigration," *OR* 14:16 (Apr. 26, 1887), 185.

146. N. B. Young, "The 'New South' and the Negro," *OR* (Nov. 22, 1887): 51–52. His quote is from Henry Wadsworth Longfellow's poem "A Psalm of Life."

147. "De Alumnis," *OR* 17:6 (Oct. 29, 1889): 74.

148. "De Alumnis," *OR* 17:19 (Feb. 11, 1890): 260.

149. "Jubilee Exhibition," *OR* 20:32 (May 24, 1893): 583–84.

150. "Hayes' Southern Policy," *OR* 16:1 (Sept. 25, 1888): 2–4; "Society Notes," *OR* 17:16 (Jan. 21, 1890): 220; "The Race Problem Has Been Discussed of Late," *OR* 17:32 (May 20, 1890): 447; "Society Notes," *OR* 19:28 (Apr. 26, 1892): 406.

151. Blight, *Race and Reunion,* 338–80; Cohen, *The Reconstruction of American Liberalism,* 79–85; Silber, *The Romance of Reunion: Northerners and the South, 1865–1900,* 93–123.

152. "Society Congress," *OR* 23:5 (Oct. 30, 1895): 69.

153. "Society Notes," *OR* 16:7 (Dec. 18, 1888): 80.

154. "Junior Exhibition," *OR* 17:31 (May 13, 1890): 434–36.

155. "Phi Kappa Special Quarterly," *OR* 19:26 (Apr. 12, 1892): 368.

156. "Society Notes," *OR* 9:13 (Mar. 11, 1882): 149; "De Rebus Temporis," *OR* 3:5 (Nov. 21, 1885), 61; "Society Notes," *OR* 16:17 (May 14, 1889): 242; "Society Notes," *OR* 17:16 (Jan. 21, 1890): 220; "Society Notes," *OR* 17:25 (Mar. 25, 1890): 347; "Junior Exhibition," *OR* 17:31 (May 13, 1890): 434–36; "Society Notes," *OR* 19:21 (Feb. 22, 1892): 304; "Phi Kappa Special Quarterly," *OR* 19:26 (Apr. 12, 1892): 368; "Literary Society Notes," *OR* 23:10 (Dec. 4, 1895): 162.

157. "How Oberlin Has Changed," *Cleveland Gazette* (Mar. 28, 1891): 1.

158. Kornblith and Lasser, *Elusive Utopia,* 225; Smith, *Reparation and Reconciliation,* 180–82.

6. Berea's Race Problem, 1889–1895

1. "In and about Kentucky," *Louisville Courier-Journal* (Jan. 10, 1889): 4.

2. "An Appeal for Aid to a Kentucky College," *New York Times* (Mar. 9, 1868): 5; "Berea College," *New York Times* (Feb. 2, 1878): 6; "Berea College Endowment," *New York Times* (May 8, 1881): 10.

3. "The Color Line at College," *New York Times* (Jan. 14, 1889: 8.

4. Gudgeirsson, "'We Do Not Have Any Prejudice . . . but,'" 41.

5. McPherson, *The Abolitionist Legacy,* 246.

6. "Education in the South; Needs of That Section Set Forth by President Frost of Berea College," *New York Times* (Mar. 22, 1897): 3.

7. Silber, *The Romance of Reunion,* 124–58; Smith, *Reparation and Reconciliation,* 206–33.

8. McPherson, *The Abolitionist Legacy,* 247; Peck, *Berea's First Century,* 145–46.

9. Peck, *Berea's First Century,* 48, 68–69.

10. *Records of the Faculty of Berea College,* 2:330.

11. "In and about Kentucky," 4.

12. Robinson, "His Alma Mater." No copy of Fairchild's editorial can be located, and there are no back issues of the *Louisville Times* available for 1889.

13. Elgetha Brand Bell, *Life Story of a Nonagenarian,* ed. Lelia Smith McBath and Barbara Johnson Green, Self-published, 1985, 13. Student Files: Elgetha Bell, Box 1, BCA.

14. Robinson, "His Alma Mater." No copy of Fairchild's editorial can be located, and there are no back issues of the *Louisville Times* available for 1889.

15. Dodge to Frost, Apr. 11, 1925; Tyler, "Race Relations in Berea College According to the Negro Graduates," 8.

16. "Commencement Sunday," *Berea College Reporter* 1:3 (July 1889): 8. Unfortunately the text of Fairchild's sermon does not survive.

17. Sears, *Utopian Experiment,* 136.

18. E. H. Fairchild, "The Race Question," *Berea College Reporter* 1:1 (Summer 1885): 2.

19. E. H. Fairchild, "Race Question in the South," 652.

20. Fairchild, "Race Question in the South." The relevant scriptures are Galatians 3:28 and Colossians 3:11.

21. Michael Strieby to James Fairchild, Sept. 17, 1889, Fairchild Papers, Box 14, OCA. Emphasis in the original. On the politics of "advancing interracialism," see Moulton, *The Fight for Interracial Marriage Rights in Antebellum Massachusetts,* 142–76.

22. Richardson, *Christian Reconstruction,* 255.

23. Michael Strieby to James Fairchild, Sept. 21, 1889, Fairchild Papers, Box 14, OCA. Original emphasis.

24. "Commencement Sunday," 8.

25. Martha S. Jones, *Vanguard: How Black Women Broke Barriers, Won the Vote, and Insisted on Equality for All* (New York: Basic Books, 2020), 12–13.

26. Fannie B. Miller, "Berea College (Read at the Alumni Reunion)," *Berea College Reporter* 1:3 (July 1889): 6.

27. John H. Jackson to the Board of Trustees, June 20, 1889, Board of Trustees Records, Box 1, BCA.

28. MBTBC, 217, 215.

29. *Records of the Faculty of Berea College,* 2:94.

30. Dodge to Frost, Apr. 11, 1925.

31. Bond, "Autobiography," 26, in *Horace Mann Bond Papers* (microfilm), ed. John H. Bracey Jr., Black Studies Research Sources. Bethesda, MD: University Publications of America, 1989.

32. Nelson, "James Bond," in Gerald L. Smith et al., eds., *The Kentucky African American Encyclopedia,* 55–56.

33. James Bond, "Hope for the Future," *Berea College Reporter* (June 1892), 2. The relevant scripture is Matthew 23:8.

34. McDaniel, "Mary Ellen Britton: A Potent Agent for Public Reform," 52–61.

35. Johnson, *Biographical Sketches of Prominent Negro Men and Women of Kentucky,* 37–38, 63–64; Sears, "John Henry Jackson" and "Jordan C. Jackson, Jr.," in Smith et al., eds., *The Kentucky African American Encyclopedia,* 270–71.

36. Mary E. Britton, "A Woman's Appeal to Members of the Kentucky General Assembly," *Kentucky Leader* (Apr. 19, 1892): 3.

37. Statistics from Project HAL: Historical American Lynching Data Collection Project, University of North Carolina, Wilmington, accessed July 20, 2016, http://people.uncw.edu/hinese/HAL/HAL percent20Web percent20Page.htm.

38. "The Spirit of Caste," *Berea College Reporter* 4:1 (Feb. 1892): 2.

39. John G. Fee, "To the Friends of Berea College," *Berea College Reporter* (July 1890): 4.

40. "Colored Students in Berea—All Schools."

41. *Records of the Faculty of Berea College,* 3:13, 18, 66, 45, 221.

42. *President Frost's betrayal of the Colored People in His Administration of Berea College,* 2.

43. Tyler, "Race Relations in Berea College According to the Negro Graduates," 6, 7.

44. Fee, *The Autobiography of John G. Fee,* 184–211.

45. Peck, *Berea's First Century,* 143; Wilson, *Berea College: An Illustrated History,* 68–70.

46. Peck, *Berea's First Century,* 47, 142–43; Wilson, *Berea College: An Illustrated History,* 67, 70.

47. Frost to "Brethren at Berea," July 16, 1892, Frost Papers, Box 4, BCA.

48. "Colored Students in Berea—All Schools."

49. Frost to "Brethren at Berea," July 16, 1892.

50. William Goodell Frost, "An Answer Made," *Lexington Standard* (Oct. 23, 1893), clipping in Associated Items: Blacks and Berea College, Box 1, BCA.

51. Frank L. Williams to the Faculty, June 14, 1895, College, Academy, and Foundation Faculty Records, Box 4, BCA.

52. *Catalogue of the Officers and Students of Berea College, 1875–1876,* 9; *Catalogue of the Officers and Students of Berea College, 1876–1877,* 9; *Catalogue of the Officers and Students of Berea College, 1880–1881,* 7; Dodge to William Frost, Apr. 11, 1925; MBTBC, 172, 217; Paul David Nelson, "James Shelton Hathaway," in Smith et al., eds. *The Kentucky African American Encyclopedia,* 237–38.

53. *Records of the Faculty of Berea College,* 2:261, 238, 193.

54. B. S. Hunting to Board of Trustees, June 24, 1886, Board of Trustees Records, Box 1, BCA.

55. *Records of the Faculty of Berea College,* 3:138, 182, 174.

56. MBCBT, 247–48.

57. William Goodell Frost, "Berea Ideas," Winter 1893, Frost Papers, Box 14, BCA.

58. J. T. Robinson, "A 'Killing' Frost," *Lexington Standard* (Dec. 7, 1894), clipping in Associated Items: Blacks and Berea College, Box 1, BCA.

59. Frost, "Berea Ideas."

60. William Goodell Frost, "An Answer Made," *Lexington Standard* (Oct. 23, 1893), clipping in Associated Items: Blacks and Berea College, Box 1, BCA.

61. Frost, "An Answer Made."

62. James Hathaway, "The Berea Question," *Lexington Standard* (ca 1893), clipping in Associated Items: Blacks and Berea College, Box 1, BCA. This clipping is labeled 1893, but based on its content and that of other dated items, it may actually have been published in 1894.

63. MBCBT, 263; John T. Robinson et al., *Save Berea College for Christ and Humanity* (1895), 22, in Associated Items: Blacks and Berea College, Box 1, BCA.

64. Frost, "An Answer Made."

65. Hathaway, "The Berea Question." See also Williams to the Faculty, June 14, 1895.

66. Frost, "An Answer Made."

67. Robinson, "His Alma Mater." Original emphases.

68. Robinson, "His Alma Mater."

69. Gudgeirsson, "'We Do Not Have Any Prejudice . . . but,'" 43.

70. Frost, "An Answer Made." Original emphasis.

71. John T. Robinson, "The B.C.Q.," *Lexington Standard* (May 4, 1894), clipping in Associated Items: Blacks and Berea College, Box 1, BCA.

72. *Records of the Faculty of Berea College*, vol 4, *Jan. 2, 1893–Mar. 25, 1896*, 159, Academic Divisions: Faculty Minutes, Box 2, BCA.

73. Burnside, "Suspicion versus Faith: Negro Criticisms of Berea College in the Nineteenth Century," 252.

74. "The Petition of 26," June 28, 1894, Board of Trustees Records, Box 6, BCA.

75. Frank L. Williams to John G. Fee, Sept. 7, 1893, in Fee Papers, Box 4, BCA.

76. "Long Form," 1894, Board of Trustees Records, Box 6, BCA.

77. Williams to Fee, Sept. 7, 1893.

78. Ibid.

79. "Long Form," 1894, Board of Trustees Records, Box 6, BCA.

80. "Berea College," *New South* (July 21, 1894), clipping in Associated Items: Blacks and Berea College, Box 1, BCA; J. C. Jackson and J. H. Jackson, "An Answer: To Mr. M. W. McGowan's Query in Our Last Issue," *Lexington Standard* (Nov. 1894), clipping in Associated Items: Blacks and Berea College, Box 1, BCA.

81. Jackson and Jackson, "An Answer: To Mr. M. W. McGowan's Query."

82. MBTBC, 272.

83. "Berea College," *New South* (July 21, 1894).

84. Jackson and Jackson, "An Answer: To Mr. M. W. McGowan's Query."

85. Peck, *Berea's First Century*, 69.

86. "Colored Students in Berea—All Schools."

87. Peck, *Berea's First Century*, 168.

88. Dodge to Frost, Apr. 11, 1925.

89. *Records of the Faculty of Berea College*, 4:220–322.

90. Jacobson, *Whiteness of a Different Color,* 206–9.

91. William Goodell Frost, "Our Contemporary Ancestors in the Southern Mountains," *Atlantic Monthly* 83 (Mar. 1899): 311–19.

92. Smith, *Reparation and Reconciliation,* 212–20; Wilson, *Berea College: An Illustrated History,* 78, 81.

93. Smith, *Reparation and Reconciliation,* 231.

94. Ibid., 212–25; Wilson, *Berea College: An Illustrated History,* 79–80.

95. W. G. Frost to Eleanor Marsh Frost, Nov. 26, 1894, Box 1, Frost Papers, BCA.

96. Burnside, "Suspicion versus Faith," 244–45; Peck, *Berea's First Century,* 71.

97. J. T. Robinson, "The Real Berea Bomb," *Lexington Standard* (Dec. 1894), clipping in Associated Items: Blacks and Berea College, Box 1, BCA.

98. J. W. Hughes, "Contributed—Berea Question," *The New South* (Nov. 11, 1894), clipping in Associated Items: Blacks and Berea College, Box 1, BCA.

99. James O. Bond, "The Other Side of the Berea Question," *Lexington Standard* (Apr. 1894): clipping in Associated Items: Blacks and Berea College, Box 1, BCA.

100. D. A. Walker, "To Mr. Magowan's Query Concerning Pres. Frost and Berea College," *New South* (Nov. 20, 1894), clipping in Associated Items: Blacks and Berea College, Box 1, BCA.

101. "Colored Students in Berea—All Schools."

102. "Supplement: Berea's Invitation Is to All," *Berea College Reporter* (Winter 1894).

103. "Supplement: Berea's Invitation Is to All."

104. Frank L. Williams, "Berea College and the Colored Professorship," *New South* (Nov. 24, 1894), clipping in Associated Items: Blacks and Berea College, Box 1, BCA.

105. "A Protest Made by Some of the Students of Berea College," *Lexington Standard* (June 21, 1895), clipping in Associated Items: Blacks and Berea College, Box 1, BCA. The original resolutions appear in Phi Delta Literary Society Records, Series IV, Box 4, Recording Secretary Records: Book IV, BCA, 79–82, 84–85.

106. "A Protest Made by Some of the Students of Berea College." Two of the names do not appear in the 1904 *Historical Register,* so their races cannot be verified.

107. Williams to the Faculty, June 14, 1895, College, Academy, and Foundation Faculty Records, Box 4, BCA.

108. Gudgeirsson, "'We Do Not Have Any Prejudice . . . but,'" 44.

109. Williams, *The Life of Dr. D. K. Pearsons, Friend of the Small College and of Missions,* 173.

110. *Save Berea College for Christ and Humanity,* 2, in Associated Items: Blacks and Berea College, Box 1, BCA.

111. Peck, *Berea's First Century,* 71.

112. Williams, *The Life of Dr. D. K. Pearsons.*

113. Peck, *Berea's First Century,* 146–47.

114. *Save Berea College for Christ and Humanity,* 15, 18, 11, 28, in Associated Items: Blacks and Berea College, Box 1, BCA.

115. Frost, *Sectional Lines.*

116. *Save Berea for Christ and Humanity,* 13, 11, in Associated Items: Blacks and Berea College, Box 1, BCA.

117. MBCBT, 280.

118. *Save Berea College for Christ and Humanity,* 31, in Associated Items: Blacks and Berea College, Box 1, BCA.

119. MBCBT, 281.

120. Nelson, "Experiment in Interracial Education at Berea College, 1858–1908," 23.

121. John G. Fee, untitled clipping ca. 1895, in Associated Items: Blacks and Berea College, Box 1, BCA.

122. William G. Frost to John G. Fee, June 25, 1895, Box 4, Fee Papers, BCA.

123. Stauffer, *The Black Hearts of Men,* 43.

124. Grindstaff, "Berea College Seal."

125. "Berea College, Madison County, Ky., Devoted to Christian Education, Offers Its Advantages to All" Office of Information Records: Publications, Box 14, BCA.

126. Smith, *Reparation and Reconciliation,* 214.

127. "Colored Students in Berea—All Schools."

128. Robinson, "His Alma Mater." On the later use of this verse as justification for Jim Crow, see Hawkins, *The Bible Told Them So: How Southern Evangelicals Fought to Preserve White Supremacy,* 43–67.

129. Frost to Fee, June 25, 1895.

130. *Save Berea College for Christ and Humanity,* 5, in Associated Items: Blacks and Berea College, Box 1, BCA.

Epilogue

1. "African American Schools in Clark County, KY," *Notable Kentucky African Americans Database,* accessed Dec. 10, 2020, http://nkaa.uky.edu/nkaa/items/show/2665. My thanks to Sharyn Mitchell for directing me to this website.

2. *Records of the Faculty of Berea College,* 4:379, 377.

3. "To the Faculty" (ca 1898), Board of Trustees Records, Series 1, Box 1, BCA.

4. W. G. Frost to Melissa Parkerson, Mar. 5, 1901, Box 6, Frost Papers, BCA.

5. "To the Faculty."

6. Sears, *A Utopian Experiment in Kentucky,* 149.

7. Sears, *A Utopian Experiment in Kentucky,* 149.

8. Nelson, "Experiment in Interracial Education at Berea College," 23.

9. Sears, *A Utopian Experiment in Kentucky,* 149.

10. Wilson, *Berea College: An Illustrated History,* 83.

11. Smith, *Reparation and Reconciliation,* 229.

12. Peck, *Berea's First Century,* 52.

13. Peck, *Berea's First Century,* 55; Wilson, *Berea College: An Illustrated History,* 84.

14. Nelson, "Experiment in Interracial Education at Berea College," 24.

15. William G. Frost, "To the Educational Committee of the Kentucky Senate," 4, Frost Papers, Box 23, BCA.

16. *President Frost's betrayal of the Colored People in His Administration of Berea College,* 4.

17. Tyler, "Race Relations in Berea College According to the Negro Graduates," 7.

18. Wilson, *Berea College: An Illustrated History,* 85.

19. *President Frost's betrayal of the Colored People in His Administration of Berea College,* 4–5.

20. Tyler, "Race Relations in Berea College According to the Negro Graduates," 7.

21. Woodson, *The Mis-Education of the Negro,* 41.

22. "Colored Students in Berea—All Schools."

23. "Separate Provisions for Colored Students," *Berea Quarterly* 10:2 (Apr. 1906): 21–24.

24. Nelson, "Experiment in Interracial Education at Berea College," 24–25; Peck, *Berea's First Century,* 53–55; Wilson, *Berea College: An Illustrated History,* 87–88.

25. *President Frost's betrayal of the Colored People in His Administration of Berea College,* 10, 5.

26. Berea College v. Kentucky, 211 US 45 (1908), 67, 69.

27. Bigglestone, "Oberlin College and the Negro Student," 202.

28. "Literary Society for Colored Students," *Oberlin Alumni Magazine* 6:6 (Mar. 1910): 224.

29. L. F. Parker to the Editors, *Oberlin Alumni Magazine* 6:7 (Apr. 1910): 253.

30. Lucien C. Warner to the Editors, *Oberlin Alumni Magazine* 6:7 (Apr. 1910): 253.

31. Bigglestone, "Oberlin College and the Negro Student," 204.

32. A. C. Marts to the Editors, *Oberlin Alumni Magazine* 6:7 (Apr. 1910): 252.

33. "Acting President A. S. Root's Circular Regarding Alleged Discrimination to Oberlin's Board of Trustees," June 20, 1910, in Baumann, *Constructing Black Education at Oberlin College,* 96.

34. C. M. Howe to the Editors, *Oberlin Alumni Magazine* 6:7 (Apr. 1910): 251.

35. Langston and Vashon joined Phi Delta under its original name, the Union Literary Society.

36. Baumann, *Constructing Black Education at Oberlin College,* 90.

37. "Acting President A. S. Root's Circular Regarding Alleged Discrimination to Oberlin's Board of Trustees," 93.

38. Baumann, *Constructing Black Education at Oberlin College,* 88–89; "Literary Society for Colored Students."

39. "Acting President A. S. Root's Circular Regarding Alleged Discrimination to Oberlin's Board of Trustees," 93.

40. Bigglestone, "Oberlin College and the Negro Student," 204.

41. Kornblith and Lasser, *Elusive Utopia,* 240.

42. Bigglestone, "Oberlin College and the Negro Student," 201–2.

43. Waite, *Permission to Remain among Us,* 107–8.

44. Bigglestone, "Oberlin College and the Negro Student," 209; Mary Church Terrell to Henry Churchill King, Jan. 26, 1914, Henry Churchill King Papers, Box 72, OCA.

45. Parker, *Unceasing Militant,* 103–6; Waite, *Permission to Remain among Us,* 108.

46. Letter of Mary Church Terrell to Florence Fitch, Oct. 1913, in Baumann, *Constructing Black Education at Oberlin College,* 105, 107, 106.

47. Terrell to King, Jan. 26, 1914.

48. Waite, *Permission to Remain among Us,* 110.

49. Cowles to "S.B., Esq.," 151.

50. Waite, *Permission to Remain among Us,* 110.

51. Kornblith and Lasser, *Elusive Utopia,* 241; Parker, *Unceasing Militant,* 109–11.

52. Kornblith and Lasser, *Elusive Utopia,* 241.

53. Hussar et al., *The Condition of Education 2020,* 122, 209, 206, 151.

54. Carey, "Unlike the Students They Oversee, Most College Presidents Are White and Male."

55. Colen, Pinchak, and Barnett, "Racial Disparities in Health among College Educated African-Americans: Can HBCU Attendance Reduce the Risk of Metabolic Syndrome in Midlife?"

56. "Campus Racial Incidents," *Journal of Blacks in Higher Education* website, accessed Dec. 27, 2020, https://www.jbhe.com/incidents/.

57. Compare to the findings of García and Johnston-Guerrero, "Challenging the Utility of a Racial Microaggressions Framework through a Systematic Review of Racially Biased Incidents on Campus," 49–66.

58. Bonds and Freeman, "Preparing for the Storm in Times of Peace: Strategies for Preparing Higher Education Presidents for Campus Racial Crises," in Toldson, Shockley, and Douglas, eds., *Campus Uprisings: How Student Activists and Collegiate Leaders Resist Racism and Create Hope,* 128.

59. Davis, "Colleges Can Help Resolve Our Racial Crisis."

60. Cole, "Academe's Disturbing Indifference to Racism." See also Cole, *The Campus Color Line: College Presidents and the Struggle for Black Freedom* (Princeton, NJ: Princeton University Press, 2020).

61. Fisher v. University of Texas at Austin, 579 US (2016), 19.

62. Shurtleff, "Some Features of Our College Life."

63. Hutchins, *The Great Conversation: The Substance of a Liberal Education.* Hutchins's father William succeeded Frost as president of Berea College in 1920.

BIBLIOGRAPHY

PRIMARY SOURCES

Manuscript Collections

Amistad Research Center, Tulane University
    American Missionary Association Papers (microfilm)
Berea College Archives (BCA)
    American Missionary Association Papers
    Associated Items: Blacks and Berea College
    Board of Trustee Records
    College, Academy, and Foundation Faculty
    Day Law Files
    Dean of Women
    Edward Henry Fairchild Papers
    John G. Fee Papers
    William G. Frost Papers
    General Faculty Records
    Office of Information Records
    Publications about Berea College
    Recording Secretary Records
    Student Files
Cornell University Archives
    Samuel J. May Family Papers
Cortland County Historical Society (CCHS)
    Miscellaneous Scrapbook: New York Central College at McGraw
    New York Central College Collection
McGraw Historical Society (MHS)
    New York Central College Records
Oberlin College Archives (OCA)

    Alumni and Development Records
    Board of Trustees Records
    Henry Churchill King Papers
    Henry Cowles Papers
    James Harris Fairchild Papers
    Robert S. Fletcher Papers
    Charles Grandison Finney Presidential Papers (microfilm)
    Ladies' Literary Society Records
    John C. Leith Papers
    Delevan Leonard Papers
    Minority Student Records
    James Monroe Papers
    Oberlin College Library Records
    Oberlin File
    Office of the Secretary Records
    Office of the Treasurer Records
    Phi Delta Society Records
    Phi Kappa Pi Records
    Mary Sheldon Papers
    Giles Waldo and Mary E. Burton Shurtleff Papers
    Young Men's Anti-Slavery Society Records
Arthur and Elizabeth Schlesinger Library on the History of Women in America, Radcliffe College
    Blackwell Family Papers
Syracuse University Archives
    Gerrit Smith Papers (GSP)

Newspaper and Magazine Articles

"The Advance Movement. Organization of a Woman's Suffrage Association." *Lorain County News* (May 5, 1870): 3.

"All Sorts." *New Haven Daily Palladium* (October 10, 1865).

William Allen to Frederick Douglass, June 16, 1851. *Frederick Douglass' Paper* (June 26, 1851): 3.

"An Appeal for Aid to a Kentucky College." *New York Times* (March 9, 1868): 5.

Andrews, George L. "West Point and the Colored Cadets." *International Review* (November 1880): 480–84.

"Anti-Slavery Missions in Slave States." *Oberlin Evangelist* (December 19, 1855): 208.

"Berea College." *New York Times* (February 2, 1878): 6.

"Berea College Endowment." *New York Times* (May 8, 1881): 10

"A Blow to Color-Phobia." *Liberator* (July 18, 1851): 114.

Bond, James. "Hope for the Future." *Berea College Reporter* (June 1892): 2.

Boone, G. B. "Social Evolution." *Oberlin Review* 6:7 (December 11, 1878): 73–74.

Bradley, D. F. "The Elements of Modern Civilization." *Oberlin Review* 10:1 (September 23, 1882): 1–4.

Britton, Mary E. "A Woman's Appeal to Members of the Kentucky General Assembly." *Kentucky Leader* (April 19, 1892): 3.

C. M. Howe to the Editors. *Oberlin Alumni Magazine* 6:7 (April 1910): 251.

Caldwell, Asa. "New York Central College." *Frederick Douglass' Paper* (February 18, 1853): 3.

———. Letter to Frederick Douglass, March 21, 1853. *Frederick Douglass' Paper* (April 1, 1853), 3.

Calkins, Leonard G. "The Charges Denied." *Liberator* (August 14, 1857): 131.

Calkins, Leonard G., Theodore Parker, and Gerrit Smith. "New York Central College." *Liberator* (March 6, 1857): 40.

Carlos, Don. "Letter from Oberlin, Ohio." *New National Era* (November 23, 1871): 1.

"Catalogue of the Oberlin Collegiate Institute." *Oberlin Evangelist* (November 18, 1840): 190.

"Cayuga Chief's Visit." *Cortland Country Express* (March 14, 1850): 2.

Child, L. Maria. "Edmonia Lewis." *Broken Fetter* (March 3, 1865): 1.

"The China Band—Its Object and the Demand." *Oberlin Review* 10:3 (October 21, 1882): 29.

"The Civil Rights Bill in Oberlin." *Oberlin Weekly News* (November 2, 1883): 3.

"Clippings." *Ariel* 4:1 (October 7, 1880): 11.

"College Notes." *Oberlin Review* 9:14 (Mar. 25, 1882): 64

"The Color Line at College." *New York Times* (January 14, 1889): 8.

"A Colored Artist." *Lorain County News* (June 10, 1863): 1.

"Colored Professorship." *Voice of the Fugitive* 2:11 (May 20, 1852): 2.

"Commencement at Oberlin." *Anglo-African* (September 9, 1865).

"Commencement at Oberlin." *Oberlin Evangelist* (September 11, 1844): 151.

"Commencement Exercises." *Oberlin Evangelist* (November 6, 1850): 180.

"Commencement Sunday." *Berea College Reporter* 1:3 (July 1889): 8.

"Communications." *Oberlin Review* 10:12 (March 3, 1883): 136–37.

"Congressional Necrology: Almon Bradley Pratt." *Congregational Quarterly* 19:2 (April 1877): 317–18.

Cowles, Henry, to "S.B., Esq." *Oberlin Evangelist* (September 10, 1851): 151.

"Darwin." *Oberlin Review* 9:18 (May 20, 1882): 6–7.

Davis, L. H. "The Dawn and Development of English Liberty." *Oberlin Review* 12:1 (September 27, 1884): 3–6.

"The Day We Celebrate." *Oberlin Weekly News* (May 21, 1874): n.p.

"De Alumnis." *Oberlin Review* 17:6 (October 29, 1889): 74.

"De Alumnis." *Oberlin Review* 17:19 (February 11, 1890): 260.

"De Rebus Temporis." *Oberlin Review* 2:6 (May 5, 1875): 70.

"De Rebus Temporis." *Oberlin Review* 8:5 (November 20, 1880): 56.

"De Rebus Temporis." *Oberlin Review* 5:14 (March 20, 1878): 165.

"De Rebus Temporis." *Oberlin Review* 8:11 (February 19, 1881): 130.

"De Rebus Temporis." *Oberlin Review* 8:14 (April 2, 1881): 165.

"De Rebus Temporis." *Oberlin Review* 11:9 (January 19, 1884): 106.

"De Rebus Temporis." *Oberlin Review* 11:1 (September 22, 1883): 11–12.

"The Decisions of the Supreme Court." *Denison Collegian* 17:3 (November 24, 1883): 36.

"Death by Smallpox. Progress of the Disease." *Cortland County Express* (June 6, 1850): 2.

"Diary of a Nineteenth-Century Girl." *New York Times Book Review* (June 20, 1926): 13.

Douglass, Frederick. "McGrawville College." *North Star* (April 26, 1850): 2.

Dow, J. W. "The Security of Liberty." *Oberlin Review* 10:10 (February 3, 1883): 109–11.

"Edmonia Lewis." *Freedmen's Record* (January 1867): 3.

"Education—Moral, Intellectual, Physical." *New York Tribune* (August 1, 1848).

"Education in the South; Needs of That Section Set Forth by President Frost of Berea College." *New York Times* (March 22, 1897): 3.

Fairchild, E. H. "Are Negroes Susceptible of High Cultivation?" *Oberlin Evangelist* (June 4, 1862): 94.

———. "The Race Question." *Berea College Reporter* 1:1 (Summer 1885): 2.

———. "Race Question in the South." *Advance* (September 12, 1889): 652.

Fairchild, Edward K. "Modern Iconoclasm." *Oberlin Review* 3:16 (October 25, 1876): 181–82.

Fairchild, James H. "Berea K.Y.: Commencement Exercises." *American Missionary* 12:8 (August 1868): 172.

———. "Letter from the President of Oberlin College." *New National Era* (December 14, 1871): 1.

"Fanny M. Jackson." *Liberator* (October 6, 1865): 159.

Fee, John Gregg. "To the Friends of Berea College." *Berea College Reporter* (July 1890): 4.

"Festival of the Young Men's Literary Association." *Weekly Anglo-African* (April 19, 1862): n.p.

"The First of August." *Oberlin Evangelist* (August 16, 1843): 7.

"The First of August." *Oberlin Evangelist* (August 14, 1844): 7.

"First of August—Colored People." *Oberlin Evangelist* (August 17, 1842): 133

"A Fortnight in Oberlin." *National Anti-Slavery Standard* (March 11, 1865): 3.

"The Fourth." *Cortland County Express* (July 11, 1850): 2.

"From the *Albany State Register.* New York Central College." *Liberator* (July 18, 1851): 1.

Frost, William Goodell. "Our Contemporary Ancestors in the Southern Mountains." *Atlantic Monthly* 83 (March 1899): 311–19.

———. *Sectional Lines.* Berea: Students' Press, 1895.

Gates, W. A. "Evolution and Free Will." *Oberlin Review* 5:10 (January 23, 1878): 110–11.

G.G.R. "Education—Moral, Intellectual, and Physical—Women." *New York Daily Tribune* (August 1, 1848): 5.

Hall, Wilford A. "The Problem of Human Life." *Oberlin Review* 10:6 (December 2, 1882): 64–65.

Harrison, B. B. "Our National Peculiarities." *Oberlin Review* 6:13 (March 5, 1879): 147.

"Hayes' Southern Policy." *Oberlin Review* 16:1 (September 25, 1888): 2–4.

"How Oberlin Has Changed." *Cleveland Gazette* (March 28, 1891): 1.

"How We Received It." *Lorain County News* (January 7, 1863): 2.

Howland, L. P. "A Plea for Restricted Immigration." *Oberlin Review* 14:16 (April 26, 1887): 182–85.

"In and about Kentucky." *Louisville Courier-Journal* (January 10, 1889): 4.

"Is There a Color Line at Oberlin?" *Oberlin Review* 10:10 (February 3, 1883): 115–16.

Jackson, Fanny. "Prejudice at Oberlin." *National Anti-Slavery Standard* (July 9, 1864): 2.

———. "To the 54th Mass. Volunteers." *Lorain County News* (June 10, 1863): 1.

Jackson-Coppin, Fanny. *Reminiscences of School Life, and Hints on Teaching.* Philadelphia: AME Book Concern, 1913.

"Jubilee Exhibition." *Oberlin Review* 20:32 (May 24, 1893): 583–84.

"Judging by Late Developments. . . . " *Oberlin Review* 10:5 (November 18, 1882): 55.

"Junior Exhibition." *Oberlin Review* 17:31 (May 13, 1890): 434–36.

Letcher, Minnie H. "Spiritual Dynamics." *Oberlin Review* 2:17 (November 3, 1875): 197–98.

"Letter from C. A. Hammond." *Frederick Douglass' Paper* (March 11, 1853): 1.

"Letter from Lydia M. Child." *Liberator* (February 19, 1864): 31.

"Letter from Wm. G. Allen." *Frederick Douglass' Paper* (November 12, 1852): 3.

"Literary Society for Colored Students." *Oberlin Alumni Magazine* 6:6 (March 1910): 224.

"Literary Society Notes." *Oberlin Review* 23:10 (December 4, 1895): 162.

"Local." *Oberlin Review* 2:2 (March 10, 1875): 22.

"Local Matters." *Oberlin Review* 1: 2 (April 15, 1874): 15.

"Local Matters." *Oberlin Review* 1:6 (June 10, 1874): 46–48.

Marts, A. C., to the Editors. *Oberlin Alumni Magazine* 6:7 (April 1910): 252.

"Meeting of the Colored People." *Lorain County News* (February 17, 1870): 2.

Miller, Fannie B. "Berea College (Read at the Alumni Reunion)." *Berea College Reporter* 1:3 (July 1889): 6.

Miner, Luella. "The Schoolma'am at Home." *Oberlin Review* 11:5 (November 17, 1883): 51–52.

"Miscellaneous Items." *Vermont Chronicle* (September 23, 1865): 5.

"Miss Wilson's Work among Refugees in Kansas." *American Missionary* 35:1 (January 1881): 280–81.

Morris, L. W. "Moral Evolution." *Oberlin Review* 6:3 (October 9, 1878): 25–26.

"Mysterious Affair at Oberlin." *Cleveland Plain Dealer* (February 11, 1862): 3.

"The Oberlin Poisoning Case." *Cleveland Morning Leader* (March 3, 1862): 3.

"Once More," *Lorain County News* (February 25, 1863): 3.

One Who Has Suffered, "Oberlin," *New National Era* (November 30, 1871), 1.

"Our Table." *Oberlin Review* 2:8 (June 9, 1875): 97.

"Our Table." *Oberlin Review* 8:6 (December 4, 1880): 72.

Parker, L. F., to the Editors. *Oberlin Alumni Magazine* 6:7 (April 1910): 253.

Patterson, Mary L. "The Unity of the Human Race." *Oberlin Review* 7:13 (February 19, 1880): 145–47.

"Phi Kappa Special Quarterly." *Oberlin Review* 19:26 (April 12, 1892): 367–69.

"The Poisoning Affair." *Lorain County News* (March 5, 1862): 2.

Porter, J. C. "Radicalism: An Oration Delivered at the New York Central College Commencement." *Liberator* (August 6, 1852): 128.

"Prejudice at Oberlin College." *Commonwealth* (May 27, 1864): 4.

"Principles and Plans." *American Missionary* 32:6 (June 1878): 162.

"The Race Problem Has Been Discussed of Late." *Oberlin Review* 17:32 (May 20, 1890): 447.

"The Races in the Colleges." *New York Times* (December 2, 1883): 6.

Ransom, Reverdy C. *The Pilgrimage of Harriet Ransom's Son.* Nashville: A.M.E. Sunday School Union, 1949.

"Resolutions of Central College." *Liberator* (October 11, 1850): 1.

"Reviews." *Oberlin Review* 8:4 (November 6, 1880): 41.

Ritsher, E. C. "Conservatism: An Essential Element of Progress." *Oberlin Review* 13:18 (May 28, 1886): 213–15.

Rogers, John A. R. "Our College Record: Berea College." *American Missionary* 14:9 (September 1870): 207.

"Separate Provisions for Colored Students." *Berea Quarterly* 10:2 (April 1906): 21–24.

Shurtleff, Giles. "Shall We Have a Winter Term?" *Oberlin Review* 2:9 (June 23, 1875): 99–100.

Smith, Azariah. "Please to Read This Aloud." *Liberator* (March 6, 1857): 40.

"Society Congress." *Oberlin Review* 23:5 (October 30, 1895): 69.

"Society Notes." *Oberlin Review* 11:1 (September 22, 1883): 10.

"Society Notes." *Oberlin Review* 8:13 (March 19, 1881): 156.

"Society Notes." *Oberlin Review* 18:26 March 31, 1891): 379.

"Society Notes." *Oberlin Review* 8:15 (April 16, 1881): 180.

"Society Notes." *Oberlin Review* 9:13 (March 11, 1882): 149.

"Society Notes." *Oberlin Review* 10:10 (February 3, 1883): 156.

"Society Notes." *Oberlin Review* 8: 13 (February 28, 1883): 165.

"Society Notes." *Oberlin Review* 16:7 (December 18, 1888): 80.

"Society Notes." *Oberlin Review* 16:17 (May 14, 1889): 242.

"Society Notes." *Oberlin Review* 17:16 (January 21, 1890): 220.

"Society Notes." *Oberlin Review* 17:25 (March 25, 1890): 347.

"Society Notes." *Oberlin Review* 19: 21 (February 22, 1892): 304.

"Society Notes." *Oberlin Review* 19:28 (April 26, 1892): 406.

"Some of the Authorities at West Point. . . ." *Oberlin Review* 7:18 (May 6, 1880): 211–12.

Spaulding, Lewis. "Culture as Duty." *Liberator* (July 24, 1857), 4.

"The Spirit of Caste." *Berea College Reporter* 4:1 (February 1892): 2.

Stanton, Lucy. "A Plea for the Oppressed." *Oberlin Evangelist* (December 17, 1850): 208.

Stone, Lucy. "Oberlin College." *Woman's Journal* (July 21, 1883): 226.

———. "Why Do We Rejoice To-day?" *Anti-Slavery Bugle* (November 27, 1846): 3.

Stow, Timothy. "McGrawville College." *Frederick Douglass' Paper* (July 30, 1852): 3.

Stratton, Margaret E. "Character Building." *Oberlin Review* 5:3 (October 17, 1877): 25–27.

"Supplement: Berea's Invitation Is to All." *Berea College Reporter* (Winter 1894): n.p.

Tanner, L. D., to Frederick Douglass, April 17, 1853. *Frederick Douglass' Paper* (April 29, 1853), 3.

"Testimonial." *Liberator* (October 30, 1857): 176.

Todd, J. E. "Evolution and Revelation." *Oberlin Review* 2:10 (July 7, 1875): 111–13.

"A Trial in Prospect." *Lorain County News* (February 19, 1862): 2.

Vincent, C. A. "Elements of Progress." *Oberlin Review* 12:2 (October 11, 1884): 16–19.

Warner, Lucien C., to the Editors. *Oberlin Alumni Magazine* 6:7 (April 1910): 253.

Welsh, J. W. "Personal Liberty." *Oberlin Review* (October 7, 1864): 99.

"Wm. L. Chaplin." *Liberator* (October 4, 1850), 1.

Wreford, Henry. "A Negro Sculptress." *Athenaeum* (March 3, 1866): 302.

"Young Ladies' Literary Society." *Oberlin Evangelist* (March 18, 1841): 46.

Young, N. B. "The 'New South' and the Negro." *Oberlin Review* 15:5 (November 22, 1887): 51–52.

Other Published Primary Sources

Allen, William G. *American Prejudice against Color: An Authentic Narrative, Showing How Easily the Nation Got into an Uproar.* London: W. & F. G. Cash, 1853.

———. *A Short Personal Narrative.* Dublin: W. Curry, 1860.

Alvord, J. W. *Letters from the South.* Washington, DC: Howard University Press, 1870.

Annual Catalogue of the Officers and Students of Oberlin College for the College Year 1859–60. Oberlin: Shankland & Harmond, 1859.

Annual Catalogue of the Officers and Students of Oberlin College for the College Year 1868–1869. Springfield, OH: Republic Steam Printing, 1868.

Annual Catalogue of the Officers and Students of Oberlin College for the College Year 1869–70. Oberlin, OH: Richard Butler, Printer, News Office, 1869.

Annual Catalogue of the Officers and Students of Oberlin College for the College Year 1874–75, Oberlin: Pratt & Battle, 1874.

Annual Catalogue of the Officers and Students of Oberlin College for the College Year 1879–80. Oberlin: Mattison's Steam Printing House, 1879.

Annual Catalogue of the Officers and Students of Oberlin College for the College Year 1882–83. Chicago: Blakely, Marsh, 1882.

Ballantine, William Gay, ed. *The Oberlin Jubilee: 1833–1883.* Oberlin: E. J. Goodrich, 1883.

Baquaqua, Mahommah Gardo. *The Biography of Mahommah Gardo Baquaqua: His Passage from Slavery to Freedom in Africa and America.* Ed. Robin Law and Paul E. Lovejoy. Princeton, NJ: Markus Wiener, 2007.

Barnes, Gilbert H., and Dwight L. Dumond, eds. *Letters of Theodore Dwight Weld, Angelina Grimké Weld and Sarah Grimké, 1822–1844.* 2 vols. New York: D. Appleton-Century, 1934.

Berea College v. Kentucky. 211 US 45 (1908).

Bond, James O. "Autobiography." In *Horace Mann Bond Papers* (microfilm), ed. John H. Bracey Jr., Black Studies Research Sources. Bethesda, MD: University Publications of America, 1989.

Brown, William Wells. *The Black Man: His Antecedents, His Genius, and His Achievements.* 2nd ed. New York: Thomas Hamilton, 1863.

Catalogue of Eleutherian College, 1857–8. Madison, IN: Courier Steam Printing, 1858.

Catalogue of the Officers and Students of Berea College, 1867–8. Cincinnati: Elm Street Printing, 1868.

Catalogue of the Officers and Students of Berea College, 1871–1872. Sandusky: Daily Register Printing Office, 1872.

Catalogue of the Officers and Students of Berea College, 1875–1876. New York: G. P. Putnam's Sons, 1876.

Catalogue of the Officers and Students of Berea College, 1876–1877. Cincinnati: Elm Street Printing, 1877.

Catalogue of the Officers and Students of Berea College, 1880–1881. Cincinnati: Elm Street Printing, 1881.

Catalogue of the Officers and Students on N.Y. Central College for the Collegiate Year 1854–55. Homer: Dixon & Case, 1855.

Catalogue of the Officers and Students on N.Y. Central College for the Collegiate Year 1855–56. Homer: Dixon & Case, 1855–56.

Catalogue of the Officer and Students on N.Y. Central College of the Collegiate Year 1856–57. Homer: Jos. R. Dixon, 1857.

Catalogue of the Officers and Students of New York Central College for the Year 1852–3. Homer: Cornelius B. Gould, 1853.

Catalogue of the Officers and Students of New-York Central College for the Year 1853–4. Homer: Dixon & Gould, 1854.

Catalogue of the Officers and Students of Oberlin College, for the College Year 1850–51. Oberlin: James Fitch, 1850.

Catalogue of the Officers and Students of Oberlin College for the College Year 1852–53. Oberlin: James M. Fitch, 1851.

Catalogue of the Officers and Students of Oberlin College for the College Year 1868–1869. Springfield: Republican Steam Printing, 1868.

Catalogue of the Officers and Students of Oberlin College for the College Year 1880–81. Cleveland: Leader Printing, 1880.

Catalogue of the Officers and Students of Oberlin College for the College Year 1881–82. Chicago: Blakely, Marsh, & Co., 1881.

Catalogue of the Officers and Students of Oberlin College for the College Year 1882–83. Chicago: Blakely, Marsh, & Co., 1882.

Catalogue of the Officers and Students of the Oberlin Collegiate Institute, 1840–1. Oberlin: James Steele, 1840.

Catalogue of Trustees, Officers, and Students of the Oberlin Collegiate Institute; Together with the Second Annual Report. Cleveland: Rice and Penniman's Print, 1835.

Commencement Exercises of New York Central College. Cortland: H. G. Crouch, 1855.

Constitution and By-Laws and List of Members of the Alpha Zeta Society. Oberlin: News, Job, and Book Print, 1888.

Constitution, By-Laws and List of Members of the L.L.S. Society. Oberlin: Tribune Print, 1900.

Constitution, By-Laws and Roll of Members of the Phi Delta Society. Oberlin: Oberlin Record Presses, 1891.

Crummell, Alexander. *The Race-Problem in America.* Washington, DC: William R. Morrison, 1889.

Currie, James, ed. *The Entire Works of Robert Burns; with an Account of His Life, and a Criticism on His Writing.* London: Allan Bell, 1836.

Du Bois, W. E. B., and Augustus Granville Dill, eds. *The College-Bred Negro American.* Atlanta: Atlanta University Press, 1910.

Eggleston, Margaret W., ed. *Kathie's Diary: Leaves from an Old, Old Diary.* New York: George H. Doran, 1926.

Fairchild, E. H. *Berea College, Ky.: An Interesting History.* Cincinnati: Elm Street Printing, 1875.

———. *Berea College: An Interesting History.* 2nd ed. Cincinnati: Elm Street Printing, 1883.

Fairchild, James H. *The Joint Education of the Sexes: A Report Presented at a Meeting of the Ohio Teachers' Association, Sandusky City.* Oberlin: James Fitch, 1852.

———. *Oberlin: The Colony and the College, 1833–1883.* Oberlin: E. J. Goodrich, 1883.

———. *Oberlin, Its Origin, Progress, and Results: An Address Prepared for the Alumni of Oberlin College Assembled August 22, 1860.* Oberlin: Shanklan and Harmon, 1860.

Fairchild, James Thome, and Dorothy Kellogg Fairchild Graham, eds. *Where Liberty Dwells: The Letters of James Harris Fairchild and Mary Fletcher Kellogg from the Western Reserve* 3 vols. Oberlin: Self-published, 1939.

Fee, John Gregg. *Autobiography of John G. Fee, Berea, Kentucky.* Chicago: National Christian Association, 1891.

Fifth Annual Report of the American Baptist Free Mission Society, May 1848. Utica: H. H. Curtiss, 1848

Fifth Annual Report of the Trustees of Cincinnati Lane Seminary. Cincinnati: Corey and Fairbank, 1834.

Finney, Charles. *Memoirs of Rev. Charles G. Finney, Written by Himself.* New York: A. S. Barnes, 1876.

The First Annual Report of the Oberlin College Institute. Elyria, OH: Atlas Office, 1834.

First Catalogue of the Officers and Students of Berea College for 1866–7. Cincinnati: Gazette Steam, 1867.

Ford, A. "Honor to Whom Honor Is Due." *Herald of Gospel Liberty* 101:7 (November 9, 1909): 1543.

Foss, A. T., and Edward Mathews. *Facts for Baptist Churches.* Utica: American Baptist Free Mission Society, 1850.

General Catalogue of Oberlin College, 1833–1908: Including an Account of the Principal Events in the History of the College, with Illustrations of the College Buildings. Oberlin: Oberlin College, 1909.

Grosvenor, Cyrus Pitt. *A Review of the "Correspondence" of Messrs. Fuller & Wayland: On the Subject of American Slavery.* Utica, NY: Christian Contributor, 1847.

Hannaford, Phebe Ann. *Women of the Century.* Boston: B. B. Russell, 1877.

History of Pennsylvania Hall, Which Was Destroyed by a Mob on the 17th of May, 1838. Philadelphia: Merrihew and Gunn, 1838.

Holley, Sallie, and John White Chadwick. *A Life for Liberty: Anti-Slavery and Other Letters of Sallie Holley.* New York: G. P. Putnam's Sons, 1899.

Inauguration of Rev. E. H. Fairchild; Address of Rev. John G. Fee and the President. Cincinnati: Elm Street Printing, 1870.

Johnson, W. D. *Biographical Sketches of Prominent Negro Men and Women of Kentucky.* Lexington, KY: Standard Print, 1897.

Kenyon, A. "Sermon Delivered before the Association." In *Minutes of the Fifth Annual Meeting of the New York Central College Association.* De Ruyter, NY: A. C. Hills, 1852.

Langston, John Mercer. *From the Virginia Plantation to the National Capitol; or The First and Only Negro Representative in Congress from the Old Dominion.* Hartford: American Publishing, 1894.

———. "Equality before the Law." In *Freedom and Citizenship: Selected Letters and Addresses of Hon. John Mercer Langston, L.L.D.* Washington, DC: H. Darby, 1883.

Laws and Regulations of Berea College. Cincinnati: Elm Street Printing, 1873.

Laws of the State of New York, Passed at the Seventy-Fourth Session of the Legislature. Albany: Gould, Banks, 1851.

Leonard, Delevan. *The Story of Oberlin: The Institution, the Community, the Idea, the Movement.* Boston: Pilgrim, 1898.

Lester, Charles Edwards. *Life and Public Services of Charles Sumner.* New York: United States Publishing, 1874.

Marts, A. C., to the Editors. *Oberlin Alumni Magazine* 6:7 (Apr. 1910): 252.

Minutes of the Fifth Annual Convention for the Improvement of the Free People of Colour. Philadelphia: William P. Gibbons, 1835.

Minutes of the Fifth Annual Meeting of the New York Central College Association. De Ruyter, NY: A. C. Hills, 1852.

Minutes of the Seventh Annual Meeting of the New York Central College Association. Homer, NY: Dixon and Gould, 1854.

N.Y. Central College: Prize Declamation. Homer: Dixon & Case, 1855.

Oberlin College: Alumni Catalogue, 1833–1936. Oberlin: Oberlin College, 1937.

Parker, L. F., to the Editors. *Oberlin Alumni Magazine* 6:7 (Apr. 1910): 253.

President Frost's betrayal of the Colored People in His Administration of Berea College. Danville, KY: State Teachers' Association, 1907.

Proceedings of the General Anti-Slavery Convention, Called by the Committee of the British and Foreign Anti-Slavery Society, and Held in London from Tuesday, June 13 to Tuesday, June 20, 1843. London: John Snow, 1843.

The Pumpkin Pie Offering. To Which Are Added the Proceedings of the Great Pumpkin Pie Jubilee. McGrawville, NY: A. T. Boynton, 1850.

Purvis, T. T. *Hagar: The Singing Maiden, with Other Stories and Rhymes.* Philadelphia: Walton, 1881.

Rampersad, Arnold, ed. *The Collected Works of Langston Hughes.* Vol. 3. Columbia: University of Missouri Press, 2001.

Richardson, Hiram. *Memoirs of Berea.* Berea: Berea College Press, 1940.

Ronnick, Michele, ed. *The Autobiography of William Sanders Scarborough: An American Journey from Slavery to Scholarship.* Detroit: Wayne State University Press, 2005.

Seventh Annual Meeting of the American Baptist Free Mission Society. Utica: Roberts and Sherman, 1850.

Seventy-First Annual Report of the Regents of the University of the State of New York. Albany: C. Van Benthuysen, 1858.

Shipherd, Jacob R., ed. *History of the Oberlin-Wellington Rescue.* Boston: John P. Jewett, 1859.

Shumway, A. L., and C. D. Brower. *Oberliniana: A Jubilee Volume of Semi-Historical Anecdotes Connected with the Past and Present of Oberlin College, 1833–1883.* Cleveland: Home Publishing, 1883.

Sixth Annual Report of American Baptist Free Mission Society. Utica, NY: W. W. Curtiss, 1849.

Sixty-Ninth Annual Report of the Regents of the University of the State of New York. Albany: C. Van Benthuysen, 1856.

Smith, Delazon. *A History of Oberlin; or, New Lights of the West.* Cleveland: S. Underhill & Son, 1837.

Stanton, Elizabeth Cady, Susan B. Anthony, and Matilda Joslyn Gage, eds. *History of Woman Suffrage.* Vol. 2, *1861–1876.* Rochester: Charles Mann, 1887.

A Statement of the Reasons Which Induced the Students of Lane Seminary, to Dissolve Their Connection with That Institution. Cincinnati: n.p., 1834.

Terrell, Mary Church. *A Colored Woman in a White World.* Edited by Debra Ham Newman. Amherst, NY: Humanity Books, 2005.

Third Annual Report of the American Anti-Slavery Society. New York: William S. Dorr, 1836.

Warner, Lucien C., to the Editors. *Oberlin Alumni Magazine* 6:7 (Apr. 1910): 253.

Webster, Noah. *An American Dictionary of the English Language.* New York: Harper and Brothers, 1844.

Welch, E. L. *"Grip's" Historical Souvenir of Cortland.* Albany: 1899.

Woodson, Carter G. *The Mis-Education of the Negro.* Washington, DC: Associated Publishers, 1933.

SECONDARY SOURCES

Abzug, Robert. *Cosmos Crumbling: American Reform and the Religious Imagination.* New York: Oxford University Press, 1994.

———. *Passionate Liberator: Theodore Dwight Weld and the Dilemma of Reform.* New York: Oxford University Press, 1980.

Adams, Regina, and David Nelson. "President E. Henry Fairchild and Berea College's Commitment to Women's Education." In *Women in Berea's History: A Symposium for Women's History Week,* 5–13. Berea, KY: Berea College, 1985.

"African American Schools in Clark County, KY." *Notable Kentucky African Americans Database.* Accessed December 10, 2020, http://nkaa.uky.edu/nkaa/items/show/2665.

Allen, Robert L., and Pamela P. Allen. *Reluctant Reformers: Racism and Social Reform Movements in the United States.* Washington, DC: Howard University Press, 1974.

Allport, Gordon. *The Nature of Prejudice.* Boston: Addison-Wesley, 1954.

Anderson, James. *The Education of Blacks in the South, 1860–1935.* Chapel Hill: University of North Carolina Press, 1988.

Aptheker, Herbert, ed. *A Documentary History of the Negro People in the United States.* New York: Citadel, 1951.

Archer, Richard. *Jim Crow North: The Struggle for Equal Rights in Antebellum New England.* New York: Oxford University Press, 2017.

Atkins, Jeannine. *Stone Mirrors: The Sculpture and Silence of Edmonia Lewis.* New York: Simon and Schuster, 2017.

Bacon, Margaret Hope. *But One Race: The Life of Robert Purvis.* Albany: State University of New York Press, 2007.

Ball, Erica L. *To Live an Antislavery Life: Personal Politics and the Antebellum Black Middle Class.* Athens: University of Georgia Press, 2012.

Barnard, John. *From Evangelicalism to Progressivism at Oberlin College, 1866–1917.* Columbus: Ohio State University Press, 1969.

Bartanen, Michael, and Robert S. Littlefield. *Forensics in America: A History.* Plymouth, UK: Rowman & Littlefield, 2004.

Baumgartner, Kabria. *In Pursuit of Knowledge: Black Women and Educational Activism in Antebellum America.* New York: New York University Press, 2019.

———. "Gender Politics and the Manual Labor College Initiative at National Colored Conventions in Antebellum America." In *The Colored Conventions Movement: Black Organizing in the Nineteenth Century,* edited by P. Gabrielle Foreman, Jim Casey, and Sarah Lynn Patterson, 230–45. Chapel Hill: University of North Carolina Press, 2021.

———. "Love and Justice: African American Women, Education, and Protest in Antebellum New England." *Journal of Social History* 52:3 (Spring 2019): 652–76.

Baumann, Roland M. *Constructing Black Education at Oberlin College: A Documentary History.* Athens: Ohio University Press, 2010.

Bay, Mia. *The White Image in the Black Mind: African-American Ideas about White People, 1830–1925.* New York: Oxford University Press, 2000.

Beadie, Nancy. "Female Students and Denominational Affiliation: Sources of Success and Variation among Nineteenth-Century Academies." *American Journal of Education* 107:2 (February 1999): 75–115.

Bearden, Romare, and Harry Henderson. *A History of African-American Artists, from 1792 to the Present.* New York: Pantheon Books, 1993.

Bell, John Frederick. "Confronting Colorism: Interracial Abolition and the Consequences of Complexion." *Journal of the Early Republic* 39:2 (Summer 2019): 239–66.

Bennett, James B. *Religion and the Rise of Jim Crow in New Orleans.* Princeton, NJ: Princeton University Press, 2005.

Bigglestone, William. "Irrespective of Color." *Oberlin Alumni Magazine* 17:2 (November 1981): 35–36.

———. "Oberlin College and the Negro Student, 1865–1940." *Journal of Negro History* 56:3 (July 1971): 198–219.

———. *They Stopped in Oberlin: Black Residents and Visitors of the Nineteenth Century.* Oberlin: Oberlin College, 2002.

Blackett, R. J. M. *Beating against the Barriers: Biological Essays in Nineteenth-Century Afro-American History.* Baton Rouge: Louisiana State University Press, 1986.

———. *The Captive's Quest for Freedom: Fugitive Slaves, the 1850 Fugitive Slave Law, and the Politics of Slavery.* Cambridge: Cambridge University Press, 2018.

———. "William G. Allen: The Forgotten Professor." *Civil War History* 26:1 (1980): 39–52.

Blackwell, Alice Stone. *Lucy Stone: Pioneer of Woman's Rights.* Charlottesville: University of Virginia Press, 1930.

Blight, David. *Race and Reunion: The Civil War in American Memory.* Cambridge, MA: Harvard University Press, 2001.

Blodgett, Geoffrey. "John Langston and the Case of Edmonia Lewis, 1862." *Journal of Negro History* 53:3 (July 1968): 201–18.

———. "Oberlin College: Early Decisions." In *Cradles of Conscious: Ohio's Independent Colleges and Universities,* edited by John William Oliver Jr. et al. 358–79. Kent, OH: Kent State University Press, 2003.

———. *Oberlin History: Essays and Impressions.* Kent, OH: Kent State University Press, 2006.

Blum, Edward J. *Reforging the White Republic: Race, Religion, and American Nationalism, 1865–1898.* Baton Rouge: Louisiana State University Press, 2005.

Boggs, Abigail, Eli Meyerhoff, Nick Mitchell, and Zach Schwartz-Weinstein. "Abolitionist University Studies: An Invitation." *Abolition Journal* (August 28, 2019). Accessed May 18, 2021, https://abolitionjournal.org/abolitionist-university-studies -an-invitation/.

Bok, Oliver. "Activists Concerned over Black Student Enrollment Numbers." *The Oberlin Review* (November 21, 2014). Accessed September 28, 2021, https://oberlinreview

.org/6882/uncategorized/activists-concerned-over-black-student-enrollment
-numbers/.

Bonds, Mahauganee Shaw, and Sydney Freeman Jr. "Preparing for the Storm in Times
of Peace: Strategies for Preparing Higher Education Presidents for Campus Racial
Crises." In *Campus Uprisings: How Student Activists and Collegiate Leaders Resist Racism and Create Hope,* edited by Ivory Toldson, Kmt G. Shockley, and Ty-Ron M. O.
Douglas, 116–42. New York: Teachers College Press, 2020.

Bonilla-Silva, *Racism without Racists: Color-Blind Racism and the Persistence of Racial
Inequality in the United States.* 5th ed. New York: Rowman and Littlefield, 2003.

Boonshoft, Mark. "From Property to Education: Public Schooling, Race, and the
Transformation of Suffrage in the Early National North." *Journal of the Early Republic* 41:3 (Fall 2021): 435–69.

Burnside, Jacqueline. "A 'Delicate and Difficult Duty': Interracial Education at Maryville
College, Tennessee, 1868–1901." *American Presbyterians* 72:4 (Winter 1994): 229–40.

———. "Suspicion versus Faith: Negro Criticisms of Berea College in the Nineteenth
Century." *Register of the Kentucky Historical Society* 83:3 (Summer 1985): 237–66.

Burke, Colin. *American Collegiate Populations: A Test of the Traditional View.* New York:
New York University Press, 1982.

Buick, Kirsten Pai. *Child of the Fire: Mary Edmonia Lewis and the Problem of Art History's Black and Indian Subject.* Durham, NC: Duke University Press, 2010.

Burleigh, A. A. *John G. Fee: Founder of Berea College.* Berea: Berea College, 1931.

Butchart, Ronald E. "Mission Matters: Mount Holyoke, Oberlin, and the Schooling
of Southern Blacks, 1861–1917." *History of Education Quarterly* 42:1 (Spring 2002):
1–17.

———. *Northern Schools, Southern Blacks, and Reconstruction: Freedmen's Education,
1862–1875.* Westport, CT: Greenwood, 1980.

———. *Schooling the Freed People: Teaching, Learning, and the Struggle for Black Freedom, 1861–1876.* Chapel Hill: University of North Carolina Press, 2013.

Butler, Leslie. *Critical Americans: Victorian Intellectuals and Transatlantic Liberal Reform.*
Chapel Hill: University of North Carolina Press, 2007.

"Campus Racial Incidents." *Journal of Blacks in Higher Education* website. Accessed
December 27, 2020, https://www.jbhe.com/incidents/.

Cape, Francis. *We Sit Together: Utopian Benches from the Shakers to the Separatists of
Zoar.* New York: Princeton Architectural, 2013.

Carey, Isaac. "Unlike the Students They Oversee, Most College Presidents Are White
and Male." *Hechinger Report* (June 20, 2017). Accessed December 27, 2020, https://
hechingerreport.org/unlike-the-students-they-oversee-most-college-presidents
-are-white-and-male/.

Carr, Lesley. *"Colorblind" Racism.* Thousand Oaks, CA: SAGE Publications, 1997.

Cheek, William, and Aimee Lee Cheek. *John Mercer Langston and the Fight for Black Freedom, 1829–1865.* Urbana: University of Illinois Press, 1989.

Cohen, Michael David. *Reconstructing the Campus: Higher Education and the American Civil War.* Charlottesville: University of Virginia Press, 2012.

Cohen, Nancy. *The Reconstruction of American Liberalism, 1865–1914.* Chapel Hill: University of North Carolina Press, 2002.

Cole, Eddie R. "Academe's Disturbing Indifference to Racism." *Chronicle of Higher Education* (November 24, 2020). Accessed December 29, 2020, https://www.chronicle.com/article/academes-disturbing-indifference-to-racism.

———. *The Campus Color Line: College Presidents and the Struggle for Black Freedom.* Princeton, NJ: Princeton University Press, 2020.

Colen, Cynthia G., Nicolo P. Pinchak, and Kierra S. Barnett. "Racial Disparities in Health among College Educated African-Americans: Can HBCU Attendance Reduce the Risk of Metabolic Syndrome in Midlife?" *American Journal of Epidemiology* (November 5, 2020), advance online publication, https://doi.org/10.1093/aje/kwaa245.

Collins, Patricia Hill. *Black Feminist Thought: Knowledge, Consciousness, and the Politics of Empowerment.* 2nd ed. New York: Routledge, 2000.

Counts, George. *Dare the Schools Build a New Social Order?* New York: John Day, 1932.

Cross, Whitney R. *The Burned-Over District: The Social and Intellectual History of Enthusiastic Religion in Western New York, 1800–1850.* Ithaca: Cornell University Press, 1950.

Cumbler, John T. *From Abolition to Rights for All: The Making of a Reform Community in the Nineteenth Century.* Philadelphia: University of Pennsylvania Press, 2011.

Dailey, Jane. *White Fright: The Sexual Panic at the Heart of America's Racist History.* New York: Basic Books, 2020.

Dain, Bruce. *A Hideous Monster of the Mind: American Race Theory in the Early Republic.* Cambridge, MA: Harvard University Press, 2002.

Davis, David Brion. *The Problem of Slavery in the Age of Emancipation.* New York: Vintage Books, 2014.

Davis, Hugh. *"We Will Be Satisfied with Nothing Less": The African American Struggle for Equal Rights in the North during Reconstruction.* Ithaca, NY: Cornell University Press, 2011.

Davis, Larry E. "Colleges Can Help Resolve Our Racial Crisis." *Inside Higher Ed* (September 24, 2020). Accessed April 22, 2021, https://www.insidehighered.com/views/2020/09/24/colleges-must-work-establish-cultures-are-just-world-they-profess-value-opinion.

DeCaro, Louis A. *"Fire from the Midst of You": A Religious Life of John Brown.* New York: New York University Press, 2002.

Demos, John. *The Heathen School: A Story of Hope and Betrayal in the Age of the Early Republic.* New York: Vintage, 2014.

DeRogatis, Amy. *Moral Geography: Maps, Missionaries, and the American Frontier.* New York: Columbia University Press, 2003.

Dixon, John, Kevin Durrheim, and Colin Tredoux. "Beyond the Optimal Contact Strategy: A Reality Check for the Contact Hypothesis." *American Psychologist* 60:7 (2005): 697–711.

Dovidio, John F., Peter Glick, and Laurie A. Rudman, eds. *On the Nature of Prejudice: Fifty Years after Allport.* Malden, MA: Blackwell Publishing, 2005.

Duane, Anna Mae. *Educated for Freedom: The Incredible Story of Two Fugitive Schoolboys Who Grew Up to Change a Nation.* New York: New York University Press, 2020.

Dunn, Seymour B. "The Early Academies of Cortland County." *Cortland County Chronicles* 1 (1970): 57–76.

Elbert, Sarah. "An Inter-Racial Love Story in Fact and Fiction: William and Mary King Allen's Marriage and Louisa May Alcott's Tale, 'M.L.'" *History Workshop Journal* 53 (Spring 2002): 17–42.

Ellsworth, Clayton. "Ohio's Legislative Attack upon Abolition Schools." *Mississippi Valley Historical Review* 21:3 (December 1, 1934): 379–86.

Ervin, Hazel Arnett, and Lois Jamison Sheer, eds. *A Community of Voices on Education and the African American Experience.* Newcastle upon Tyne, UK: Cambridge Scholars, 2015.

Faulkner, Carol. *Lucretia Mott's Heresy: Abolition and Women's Rights in Nineteenth-Century America.* Philadelphia: University of Pennsylvania Press, 2011.

Feagin, Joe R. *The White Racial Frame: Centuries of Racial Framing and Counter-Framing.* New York: Routledge, 2010.

Field, Corinne T. *The Struggle for Equal Adulthood: Gender, Race, Age, and the Fight for Citizenship in Antebellum America.* Chapel Hill: University of North Carolina Press, 2014.

Fletcher, Juanita. "Against the Consensus: Oberlin College and the Education of American Negroes, 1835–1865." PhD diss., American University, 1974.

Fletcher, Robert S. *A History of Oberlin College: From Its Foundation through the Civil War.* 2 vols. Oberlin: Oberlin College, 1943.

Fowler, David H. *Northern Attitudes toward Interracial Marriage: Legislation and Public Opinion in the Middle Atlantic and the States of the Old Northeast, 1780–1930.* New York: Garland, 1987.

Fox-Genovese, Elizabeth, and Eugene D. Genovese. *The Mind of the Master Class: History and Faith in the Southern Slaveholders' Worldview.* New York: Cambridge University Press, 2005.

Fredrickson, George M. *The Black Image in the White Mind: The Debate on Afro-American Character and Destiny, 1817–1914.* New York: Harper & Row, 1971.

Freehling, William. *The Road to Disunion.* Vol. 2, *Secessionists Triumphant.* New York: Oxford University Press, 2007.

Friedman, Lawrence. *Gregarious Saints: Self and Community in American Abolitionism, 1830–1870.* New York: Cambridge University Press, 1982.

Foner, Eric. *Reconstruction: America's Unfinished Revolution, 1863–1877.* New York: Harper and Row, 1988.

Füllberg-Stolberg, Katja. "From the *Amistad* Slave Rebellion to the Christian Mendi Mission in West Africa: The *African* American Career of Sarah Margru Kinson." In *Critical Voicings of Black Liberation: Resistance and Representations in the Americas,* edited by Kimberley L. Phillips et al.,147–62. Piscataway: Transaction Publishers, 2003.

Furnish, Mark Allen. "A Rosetta Stone on Slavery's Doorstep: Eleutherian College and the Lost Antislavery History of Jefferson County, Indiana." PhD diss., Purdue University, 2014.

García, G., and M. Johnston-Guerrero. "Challenging the Utility of a Racial Microaggressions Framework through a Systematic Review of Racially Biased Incidents on Campus." *Journal of Critical Scholarship on Higher Education and Student Affairs* 2:1 (2015): 49–66.

Gatewood, William B. Jr. "John Hanks Alexander of Arkansas: Second Black Graduate of West Point." *Arkansas Historical Quarterly* 41:2 (Summer 1982): 103–28.

Geiger, Roger L. *The History of American Higher Education: Learning and Culture from the Founding to World War II.* Princeton, NJ: Princeton University Press, 2015.

Gillette, William. *Retreat from Reconstruction, 1869–1879.* Baton Rouge: Louisiana State University Press, 1979.

Gilroy, Paul. *The Genuine Article: Race, Mass Culture, and American Literary Manhood.* Durham, NC: Duke University Press, 2001.

Ginzberg, Lori D. "Women in an Evangelical Community: Oberlin, 1835–1850." *Ohio History* 89 (Winter 1960): 78–88.

Givens, Jarvis R. *Fugitive Pedagogy: Carter G. Woodson and the Art of Black Teaching.* Cambridge, MA: Harvard University Press, 2021.

Gomez-Jefferson, Annetta L. *The Sage of Tawawa: Reverdy Cassius Ransom, 1861–1959.* Kent, OH: Kent State University Press, 2002.

Goodman, Paul. "The Manual Labor Movement and the Origins of Abolitionism." *Journal of the Early Republic* 13:3 (Autumn 1993): 355–88.

———. *Of One Blood: Abolitionism and the Origins of Racial Equality.* Berkeley: University of California Press, 1998.

Gosse, Van. *The First Reconstruction: Black Politics in America from the Revolution to the Civil War.* Chapel Hill: University of North Carolina Press, 2021.

Grimsted, David. *American Mobbing, 1828–1861: Toward Civil War.* New York: Oxford University Press, 1998.

Grindstaff, Katie. "Berea College Seal." Berea College: Hutchins Library. July 2015. Accessed May 2, 2016, http://libraryguides.berea.edu/bereacollegeseal.

Gudgeirsson, Meg Eppel. "'We Do Not Have Any Prejudice . . . but': Racism in the Interracial Berea Literary Institute, 1866–1904." *Ohio Valley History* 20:3 (Fall 2020): 26–50.

Guyatt, Nicholas. *Bind Us Apart: How Enlightened Americans Created Racial Segregation.* New York: Basic Books, 2015.

Hall, Angelo. *An Astronomer's Wife: The Biography of Angeline Hall.* Baltimore: Nunn, 1908.

hampton, rosalind. *Black Racialization and Resistance at an Elite University.* Toronto: University of Toronto Press, 2020.

Hanchett, Catherine. "George Boyer Vashon, 1824–1878: Black Educator, Poet, Fighter for Equal Rights (Part One)." *Western Pennsylvania Historical Magazine* 68:3 (July 1985): 205–19.

Hardesty, Nancy A. *Women Called to Witness: Evangelical Feminism in the Nineteenth Century.* 2nd ed. Knoxville: University of Tennessee Press, 1999.

Harlow, Luke E. *Religion, Race, and the Making of Confederate Kentucky, 1830–1880.* Cambridge: Cambridge University Press, 2014.

Harris, Adam. *The State Must Provide: Why America's Colleges Have Always Been Unequal—And How to Set Them Right.* New York: Harper Collins, 2021.

Harris, Lesley M., James T Campbell, and Alfred Brody, eds. *Slavery and the University: Histories and Legacies.* Athens: University of Georgia Press, 2019

Harrold, Stanley. *The Rise of Aggressive Abolitionism: Addresses to the Slaves.* Lexington: University Press of Kentucky, 2004.

Hartman, Saidiya V. *Scenes of Subjection: Terror, Slavery, and Self-Making in Nineteenth-Century America.* New York: Oxford University Press, 1997.

Hawkins, J. Russell. *The Bible Told Them So: How Southern Evangelicals Fought to Preserve White Supremacy.* New York: Oxford University Press, 2021.

Henderson, Harry Brinton, and Albert Henderson. *The Indomitable Spirit of Edmonia Lewis: A Narrative Biography.* Milford, CT: Esquiline Hill, 2012.

Henle, Ellen, and Marlene Merrill. "Antebellum Black Coeds at Oberlin College." *Women's Studies Newsletter* 7:2 (Spring 1979): 8–11.

Higginbotham, Evelyn Brooks. *Righteous Discontent: The Women's Movement in the Black Baptist Church, 1880–1920.* Cambridge, MA: Harvard University Press, 1994.

Hines, Michael. "Learning Freedom: Education, Elevation, and New York's African-American Community, 1827–1829." *History of Education Quarterly* 56:4 (Fall 2016): 618–45.

Hodes, Martha. *White Women, Black Men: Illicit Sex in the Nineteenth-Century South.* New Haven, CT: Yale University Press, 1997.

Hofstadter, Richard. *Academic Freedom in the Age of the College.* New York: Columbia University Press, 1955.

Hogeland, Ronald W. "Coeducation of the Sexes at Oberlin College: A Study of Social Ideas in Mid-Nineteenth-Century America." *Journal of Social History* 6 (Winter 1972–73): 160–76.

hooks, bell. *Killing Rage: Ending Racism* New York: Henry Holt and Company, 1996.

Horton, Carol A. *Race and the Making of American Liberalism.* New York: Oxford University Press, 2005.

Horton, James Oliver. "Black Education at Oberlin College: A Controversial Commitment." *Journal of Negro Education* 54:4 (Autumn 1985): 477–99.

———. *Free People of Color: Inside the African American Community.* Washington, DC: Smithsonian Institution Press, 1993.

Horton, James Oliver, and Lois E. Horton. *In Hope of Liberty: Culture, Community, and Protest among Northern Free Blacks, 1700–1860.* New York: Oxford University Press, 1997.

Horsman, Reginald. *Race and Manifest Destiny: The Origins of Racial Anglo-Saxonism.* Cambridge, MA: Harvard University Press, 1981.

Horton, Lois. "From Class to Race in Early America: Northern Post-Emancipation Racial Reconstruction." *Journal of the Early Republic* 19:4 (Winter 1999): 629–49.

Hussar, B., et al. *The Condition of Education 2020.* Washington, DC: US Department of Education, National Center for Education Statistics, 2020.

Huston, James L. *The American and British Debate over Equality, 1776–1920.* Baton Rouge: Louisiana State University Press, 2017.

Hutchins, Robert Maynard. *The Great Conversation: The Substance of a Liberal Education.* Chicago: Encyclopedia Britannica, 1952.

Irvine, Russell W. *The African American Quest for Institutions of Higher Education before the Civil War: The Forgotten Histories of the Ashmun Institute, Liberia College, and Avery College.* Lewiston, NY: Edwin Mellen, 2010.

Jacobson, Matthew Frye. *Whiteness of a Different Color: European Immigrants and the Alchemy of Race.* Cambridge, MA: Harvard University Press, 1999.

Jirik, Michael E. "Combating Slavery and Colonization: Student Abolitionism and the Politics of Antislavery in Higher Education, 1833–1841." Master's thesis, University of Massachusetts Amherst, 2015.

Johnson, Curtis D. *Islands of Holiness: Rural Religion in Upstate New York, 1790–1860.* Ithaca, NY: Cornell University Press, 1989.

Jones, Jacqueline. *Soldiers of Light and Love: Northern Teachers and Georgia Blacks, 1865–1873.* Athens: University of Georgia Press, 1980.

Jones, Martha S. *Birthright Citizens: A History of Race and Rights in Antebellum America.* New York: Cambridge University Press, 2018.

———. *Vanguard: How Black Women Broke Barriers, Won the Vote, and Insisted on Equality for All.* New York: Basic Books, 2020.

Johnson, Matthew. *Undermining Racial Justice: How One University Embraced Inclusion and Inequality.* Ithaca, NY: Cornell University Press, 2020.

Kaestle, Carl F. *Pillars of the Republic: Common Schools and American Society, 1780–1860.* New York: MacMillan, 1983.

Kantrowitz, Stephen. *More Than Freedom: Fighting for Black Citizenship in a White Republic, 1829–1889.* New York: Penguin Books, 2012.

Kelley, Mary. *Learning to Stand and Speak: Women, Education, and Public Life in America's Republic.* Chapel Hill: University of North Carolina Press, 2006.

Kendi, Ibram X. *Stamped from the Beginning: The Definitive History of Racist Ideas in America.* New York: Nation Books, 2016.

Kenny, Gale L. *Contentious Liberties: American Abolitionists in Post-Emancipation Jamaica, 1834–1866.* Athens: University of Georgia Press, 2010.

Klinkner, Philip A., with Rogers M. Smith. *The Unsteady March: The Rise and Decline of Racial Equality in America.* Chicago: University of Chicago Press, 2002.

Kornblith, Gary J., and Carol Lasser. *Elusive Utopia: The Struggle for Racial Equality in Oberlin, Ohio.* Baton Rouge: Louisiana University Press, 2018.

Lamon, Lester C. "Ignoring the Color Line: Maryville College, 1868–1901." In *The Adaptable South: Essays in Honor of George Brown Tindall,* edited by Elizabeth Jacoway et al., 64–89. Baton Rouge: Louisiana State University Press, 1991.

Lasser, Carol. "Enacting Emancipation: African American Women Abolitionists at Oberlin College and the Quest for Empowerment, Equality, and Respectability." In *Women's Rights and Transatlantic Antislavery in the Era of Emancipation,* edited by Kathryn Kish Sklar, and James Brewer Stewart, 319–45. New Haven, CT: Yale University Press, 2007.

———, ed. *Educating Men and Women Together: Coeducation in a Changing World 1833–1908.* Urbana: University of Illinois Press, 1987.

Lasser, Carol, and Marlene Deahl Merrill, eds. *Friends and Sisters: Letters between Lucy Stone and Antoinette Brown Blackwell, 1846–93.* Urbana: University of Illinois Press, 1987.

Lawson, Ellen NickKensie. and Marlene Merrill, eds. *The Three Sarahs: Documents of Antebellum Black College Women.* New York: Edwin Mellen, 1984.

Lemire, Elise. *"Miscegenation": Making Race in America.* Philadelphia: University of Pennsylvania Press, 2010.

Leonard, Thomas C. *Illiberal Reformers: Race, Eugenics, and American Economics in the Progressive Era.* Princeton, NJ: Princeton University Press, 2016.

Lesick, Lawrence. *The Lane Rebels: Evangelicalism and Antislavery in Antebellum America*. Metuchen, NJ: Scarecrow, 1980.

Levine, Robert S. *Martin Delany, Frederick Douglass, and the Politics of Representative Identity*. Chapel Hill: University of North Carolina Press, 2000.

Litwack, Leon. *North of Slavery: The Negro in the Free States, 1790–1860*. Chicago: University of Chicago Press, 1960.

Lloyd, Ralph Waldo. *Maryville College: A History of 150 Years, 1819–1969*. Maryville, TN: Maryville College, 1969.

Lott, Eric. *Love and Theft: Black Face Minstrelsy and the American Working Class*. New York: Oxford University Press, 1993.

Mabee, Carleton. *Black Education in New York State: From Colonial to Modern Times*. Syracuse, NY: Syracuse University Press, 1979.

Malkmus, Doris. "Small Towns, Small Sects, and Coeducation in the Midwestern Colleges, 1853–1861." *History of Higher Education Annual* 22 (2002): 33–65.

Mann, Robert G. "The 'Contact of Living Souls': Shepard Gilbert's Civics Education in Reconstruction South Carolina." *New England Quarterly* 88:2 (June 2015): 286–315.

Marszalek, John F., Jr. "A Cadet at West Point." *American Heritage* 22:5 (August 1971). Accessed June 7, 2019, https://www.americanheritage.com/black-cadet-west-point.

Masur, Kate. *An Example for All the Land: Emancipation and the Struggle over Equality in Washington, DC*. Chapel Hill: University of North Carolina Press, 2010.

———. *Until Justice Be Done: America's First Civil Rights Movement, from the Revolution to Reconstruction*. New York: W. W. Norton, 2021.

McDaniel, Karen Cotton. "Mary Ellen Britton: A Potent Agent for Public Reform." *Griot: The Journal of African American Studies* 23:1 (Spring 2013): 52–61.

McDaniel, W. Caleb. "The Fourth and the First: Abolitionist Holidays, Respectability, and Radical Interracial Reform." *American Quarterly* 57:1 (March 2005): 129–51.

McKivigan, John R. "The American Baptist Free Mission Society." *Foundations* 21 (October–December 1978): 340–55.

———. *The Frederick Douglass Papers*. Series 3, *Correspondence*, vol. 1, *1842–1852*. New Haven, CT: Yale University Press, 2009.

———. *The War against Proslavery Religion: Abolitionism and the Northern Churches, 1830–1865*. Ithaca, NY: Cornell University Press, 1984.

McLachlan, James. "The American College in the Nineteenth Century: Towards a Reappraisal." *Teachers College Record* 80:2 (December 1978): 287–306.

McLoughlin, William. *Modern Revivalism: Charles Grandison Finney to Billy Graham*. 2nd ed. New York: Ronald, 1959.

McMahon, Lucia. *Mere Equals: The Paradox of Educated Women in the Early American Republic*. Ithaca, NY: Cornell University Press, 2012.

McPherson, James M. *The Abolitionist Legacy: From Reconstruction to the NAACP.* Princeton, NJ: Princeton University Press, 1975.

———. *The Struggle for Equality: Abolitionists and the Negro in the Civil War and Reconstruction.* 3rd ed. Princeton, NJ: Princeton University Press, 2014.

Meighan, Roland, and Clive Harper. *A Sociology of Educating.* 5th ed. New York: Continuum International, 2011.

Melish, Joanne Pope. "The 'Condition' Debate and Racial Discourse in the Antebellum North." *Journal of the Early Republic* 19 (Winter 1999): 651–72.

Mercer, John L., "Giles Waldo Shurtleff: A Biography of Oberlin's Favorite Son." PhD diss., Kent State University, 2016.

Mills, Charles W. *Black Rights/White Wrongs: The Critique of Racial Liberalism.* New York: Oxford University Press, 2017.

Mitchell, Mary Naill. *Raising Freedom's Child: Black Children and Visions of the Future after Slavery.* New York: New York University Press, 2008.

Moorhead, James. "Social Reform and the Divided Conscience of Antebellum Protestantism." *Church History* 48:4 (December 1979): 416–30.

Morris, Brent J. "'All the Truly Wise or Truly Pious Have One and the Same End in View': Oberlin, the West, and Abolitionist Schism." *Civil War History* 57:3 (September 2011): 234–67.

———. *Oberlin, Hotbed of Abolitionism: College, Community, and the Fight for Freedom and Equality in Antebellum America.* Chapel Hill: University of North Carolina Press, 2014.

———. "'I Have at Last Found My Sphere': The Unintentional Development of a Female Abolitionist Stronghold at Oberlin College." In *Slavery and the University: Histories and Legacies,* edited by Lesley M. Harris, James T Campbell, and Alfred Brody, 197–214. Athens: University of Georgia Press, 2019.

Moss, Hilary J. "Education's Inequity: Opposition to Black Higher Education in Antebellum Connecticut." *History of Education Quarterly* 46:1 (Spring 2006), 16–35.

———. *Schooling Citizens: The Struggle for African American Education in Antebellum America.* Chicago: University of Chicago Press, 2009.

Moulton, Amber D. *The Fight for Interracial Marriage Rights in Antebellum Massachusetts.* Cambridge, MA: Harvard University Press, 2015.

Nash, Margaret. *Women's Education in the United States, 1780–1840.* New York: Palgrave Macmillan, 2005.

Naylor, Natalie. "The Ante-Bellum College Movement: A Reappraisal of Tewksbury's Founding of American College and Universities." *History of Education Quarterly* 13:3 (Fall 1973): 261–74.

Neem, Johann N. *Democracy's Schools: The Rise of Public Education in America.* Baltimore: Johns Hopkins University Press, 2017.

Nelson, Charmaine A. *The Color of Stone: Sculpting the Black Female Subject in Nineteenth-Century America*. Minneapolis: University of Minnesota Press, 2007.

Nelson, Paul David. "Experiment in Interracial Education at Berea College, 1858–1908." *Journal of Negro History* 59:1 (1974): 13–27.

———. "James Bond." In *The Kentucky African American Encyclopedia*, edited by Gerald L. Smith et al., 54–55. Lexington: University Press of Kentucky, 2015.

———. "James Shelton Hathaway." In *The Kentucky African American Encyclopedia*, edited by Gerald L. Smith et al., 237–38. Lexington: University Press of Kentucky, 2015.

Omi, Michael, and Howard Winant. *Racial Formation in the United States*. New York: Routledge, 1986.

Ott, Cindy. *Pumpkin: The Curious History of an American Icon*. Seattle: University of Washington Press, 2012.

Palmer, Beverly Wilson, ed. *Selected Letters of Lucretia Coffin Mott*. Urbana, IL: University of Illinois Press, 2002.

Parker, Alison M., *Unceasing Militant: The Life of Mary Church Terrell*. Chapel Hill: University of North Carolina Press, 2020.

Parrish, Susan Scott. *American Curiosity: Cultures of Natural History in the Colonial British Atlantic World*. Chapel Hill: University of North Carolina Press, 2006.

Pease, Jane H., and William H. Pease. "Ends, Means, and Attitudes: Black-White Conflict in the Antislavery Movement." *Civil War History* 18:2 (June 1972): 117–28.

Peck, Elisabeth S. *Berea's First Century*. Lexington: University Press of Kentucky, 1955.

Peck, Elisabeth S., with Emily Ann Smith. *Berea's First 125 Years, 1855–1980*. Lexington: University Press of Kentucky, 1982.

Perkins, Linda Marie. *Fanny Jackson Coppin and the Institute for Colored Youth, 1865–1902*. New York: Garland, 1987.

———. "The Impact of the 'Cult of True Womanhood' on the Education of Black Women." *Journal of Social Issues* 39:3 (Fall 1983): 17–28.

Perry, Lewis. *Radical Abolitionism: Anarchy and the Government of God in Antislavery Thought*. Ithaca, NY: Cornell University Press, 1973.

Pettigrew, Thomas F., and Linda R. Tropp. "How Does Intergroup Contact Reduce Prejudice? Meta-Analytic Tests of Three Mediators." *European Journal of Social Psychology* 38:6 (2008): 922–34.

Pica-Smith, Cinzia, Rina Manuela Contini, and Carmen N. Veloria. *Social Justice Education in European Multi-Ethnic Schools: Addressing the Goals of Intercultural Education*. New York: Routledge, 2019.

Pollock, Mica. *Colormute: Race Talk Dilemmas in an American School*. Princeton, NJ: Princeton University Press, 2004.

Postel, Charles. *Equality: An American Dilemma, 1866–1896*. New York: Farrar, Strauss, & Giroux, 2019.

Potts, David. *Wesleyan University, 1831–1910: Collegiate Enterprise in New England*. Hanover, NH: Wesleyan University Press, 1992.

Potts, Donald. *Baptist Colleges in the Development of American Society, 1812–1861*. New York: Garland, 1988.

Quarles, Benjamin. *Black Abolitionists*. New York: Oxford University Press, 1969.

Rael, Patrick. *Black Identity and Black Protest in the Antebellum North*. Chapel Hill: North Carolina Press, 2002.

Randolph, Adah. "Building upon Cultural Capital: Thomas Jefferson Ferguson and the Albany Enterprise Academy in Southeast Ohio, 1863–1886." *Journal of African American History* 87: 2 (Spring 2002): 182–95.

Remond, Brian. "The First Settlers: Native Peoples of the Vermilion Watershed." In *Living in the Vermilion River Watershed*, edited by Mary Garvin and Jan Cooper, 96–101. Chardon, OH: POV Communications, 2008,.

Revo, Lisa E. "Edmonia Lewis." In *African American Lives*, edited by Henry Louis Gates Jr. and Evelyn Brooks Higginbotham, 529–31. New York: Oxford University Press, 2004.

Richardson, Heather Cox. *The Death of Reconstruction: Race, Labor, and Politics in the Post–Civil War North, 1865–1901*. Cambridge, MA: Harvard University Press, 2001.

Richardson, Joe M. *Christian Reconstruction: The American Missionary Association and Southern Blacks, 1861–1890*. Athens: University of Georgia Press, 1986.

Richardson, Marilyn. "Edmonia Lewis at McGrawville: The Early Education of a Nineteenth-Century Black Female Artist." *Nineteenth-Century Contexts* 22 (2000): 239–56.

Rogin, Michael. *Blackface/White Noise: Jewish Immigrants in the Hollywood Melting Pot*. Berkeley: University of California Press, 1998.

Rosen, Hannah. *Terror in Heart of Freedom: Citizenship, Sexual Violence, and the Meaning of Race in the Postemancipation South*. Chapel Hill: University of North Carolina Press, 2009.

Ryan, Mary P. *Cradle of the Middle Class: The Family in Oneida County, New York 1790–1865*. New York: Cambridge University Press, 1981.

Sanderson, Stephen K. *Social Evolutionism: A Critical History*. Cambridge, MA: Basil Blackwell, 1990.

Sears, Richard D. *The Day of Small Things: Abolitionism in the Midst of Slavery, Berea Kentucky, 1854–1864*. New York: University Press of America, 1986.

———. "John Henry Jackson" and "Jordan C. Jackson, Jr." In *The Kentucky African American Encyclopedia*, edited by Gerald L. Smith et al., 270–71. Lexington: University Press of Kentucky, 2015.

———. *A Utopian Experiment in Kentucky: Integration and Social Equality at Berea, 1866–1904.* Westport, CT: Greenwood, 1996.

Sensbach, Jon F. *A Separate Canaan: The Making of an Afro-Moravian World in North Carolina, 1763–1840.* Chapel Hill: University of North Carolina Press, 1998.

Sernett, Milton. *Abolition's Axe: Beriah Green, Oneida Institute, and the Black Freedom Struggle.* Syracuse, NY: Syracuse University Press, 1986.

Sharfstein, Daniel, J. *The Invisible Line: A Secret History of Race in America.* New York: Penguin Press, 2011.

Shellum, Brian. *Black Cadet in a White Bastion: Charles Young at West Point.* Lincoln: University of Nebraska Press, 2006.

Short, Kenneth. "New York Central College: A Baptist Experiment in Integrated Higher Education, 1848–1861." *Foundations* 3 (July 1962): 250–56.

Silber, Nina. *The Romance of Reunion: Northerners and the South, 1865–1900.* Chapel Hill: University of North Carolina Press, 1993.

Sinha, Manisha. *The Slave's Cause: A History of Abolition.* New Haven, CT: Yale University Press, 2017.

Slater, Robert Bruce. "The Blacks Who First Entered the World of White Higher Education." *Journal of Blacks in Higher Education* 4 (Summer 1994): 47–56.

Smith, Christi M. *Reparation and Reconciliation: The Rise and Fall of Integrated Higher Education.* Chapel Hill: University of North Carolina Press, 2016.

Smith, Jessie Carney, ed. *Notable Black American Women.* Book 2. Detroit: Gale Research, 1996.

Snyder, Christina. *Great Crossings: Indians, Settlers, and Slaves in the Age of Jackson.* London: Oxford University Press, 2017.

Sollors, Werner, ed. *Interracialism: Black-White Intermarriage in American History, Literature, and Law.* New York: Oxford University Press, 2000.

Span, Christopher M. *From Cotton Field to Schoolhouse: African American Education in Mississippi.* Chapel Hill: University of North Carolina Press, 2009.

Sperry, Kip. "Religion and Ethnicity in the Western Reserve." In *Regional Studies in Latter-Day Saint Church History: Ohio and Upper Canada,* edited by Guy L. Dorius, Craig K. Manscill, and Craig James Ostler, 87–109. Provo: Religious Studies Center, Brigham Young University, 2006.

Spires, Derrick R. *The Practice of Citizenship: Black Politics and Print Culture in the Early United States.* Philadelphia: University of Pennsylvania Press, 2019.

Stauffer, John. *The Black Hearts of Men: Radical Abolitionists and the Transformation of Race.* Cambridge, MA: Harvard University Press, 2002.

Sterling, Dorothy, ed. *We Are Your Sisters: Black Women in the Nineteenth Century.* New York: W. W. Norton, 1984.

Stewart, James Brewer. "The Emergence of Racial Modernity and the Rise of the White North, 1790–1840." *Journal of the Early Republic* 18:2 (Summer 1998): 181–217.

———. *Holy Warriors: The Abolitionists and American Slavery.* New York: Hill and Wang 1997.

———. "Modernizing 'Difference': The Political Meanings of Color in the Free States, 1776–1840." *Journal of the Early Republic* 19:4 (Winter 1999): 691–712.

———. "The New Haven Negro College and the Meanings of Race in New England, 1776–1870." *New England Quarterly* 76:3 (September 2003): 323–55.

Stocking, George W. *Race, Culture, and Evolution: Essays in the History of Anthropology.* 2nd ed. Chicago: University of Chicago Press, 1982.

Sumner, Margaret. *Collegiate Republic: Cultivating an Ideal Society in Early America.* Charlottesville: University of Virginia Press, 2014.

Taylor, Nikki M. *Frontiers of Freedom: Cincinnati's Black Community, 1802–1868.* Athens: Ohio University Press, 2005.

Tewksbury, Donald G. *The Founding of American Colleges and Universities before the Civil War: With Particular Reference to the Religious Influences Bearing upon the College Movement.* New York: Bureau of Publications, Teachers College, Columbia University, 1932.

Thompson, William. "Eleutherian Institute." *Indiana Magazine of History* 19:2 (June 1, 1923): 109–31.

Turpin, Andrea L. *A New Moral Vision: Gender, Religion, and the Changing Purposes of American Higher Education, 1837–1917.* Ithaca, NY: Cornell University Press, 2016.

Waite, Cally L. *Permission to Remain among Us: Education for Blacks in Oberlin, Ohio, 1880–1914.* Westport, CT: Praeger, 2002.

———. "The Segregation of Black Students at Oberlin College after Reconstruction." *History of Education Quarterly* 41:3 (2001): 344–64.

Wallenstein, Peter. "Pioneer Black Legislators from Kentucky, 1860s–1960s." *Register of the Kentucky Historical Society* 110:3/4 (Summer/Autumn 2012): 533–57.

Walters, Ronald G. "The Erotic South: Civilization and Sexuality in American Abolitionism." *American Quarterly* 25:2 (1973): 177–201.

Washington, Versaille F. *Eagles on Their Buttons: A Black Infantry Regiment in the Civil War.* Columbia: University of Missouri Press, 1999.

Wayne, Tiffany K. "Lydia Sayer Hasbrouck (1827–1910)." In *Women's Rights in the United States: A Comprehensive Encyclopedia of Issues, Events, and People,* edited by Tiffany K. Wayne, 88–89. Santa Barbara: ABC-Clio, 2015.

Webb, Ross A. *Kentucky in the Reconstruction Era.* Lexington: University Press of Kentucky, 1979.

Weierman, Karen Woods. *One Nation, One Blood: Interracial Marriage in American*

Fiction, Scandal, and Law, 1820–1870. Amherst: University of Massachusetts Press, 2005.

Weisenburger, Francis P. "William Sanders Scarborough: Early Life and Years at Wilberforce." *Ohio History* 71:3 (October 1962): 203–89.

Weisenfeld, Judith. "'Who Is Sufficient for These Things?': Sara G. Stanley and the American Missionary Association, 1864–1868." *Church History* 60:4 (December 1991): 493–507.

Wilder, Craig Steven. *Ebony and Ivy: Race, Slavery, and the Troubled History of America's Universities.* New York: Bloomsbury, 2013.

Williams, Edward F. *The Life of Dr. D. K. Pearsons, Friend of the Small College and of Missions.* New York: Pilgrim, 1911.

Williams, Heather Andrea. *Self-Taught: African American Education in Slavery and Freedom.* Chapel Hill: University of North Carolina Press, 2005.

Wilson, Shannon H. *Berea College: An Illustrated History.* Lexington: University Press of Kentucky, 2006.

Winch, Julie. *Gentleman of Color: The Life of James Forten.* New York: Oxford University Press, 2002.

Wolfe, Rinna. *Edmonia Lewis: Wildfire in Marble.* Parsippany, NJ: Dillon, 1998.

Woods, Carly S. *Debating Women: Gender, Education, and Spaces for Argument, 1835–1945.* East Lansing: Michigan State University Press, 2018.

Woodson, Carter Godwin. *The Education of the Negro Prior to 1861.* Washington, DC: Associated Publishers, 1919.

Wong, Mary Shepard. "The Legacy of Luella Miner." *International Bulletin of Mission Research* 40:3 (2016): 253–64.

Wright, Albert Hazen. *Cornell's Three Precursors.* Vol. 1, *New York Central College.* Ithaca: New York State College of Agriculture, Cornell University, 1958.

Wyatt-Brown, Bertram. *Lewis Tappan and the Evangelical War against Slavery.* Cleveland: Case Western University Press, 1969.

INDEX

5th US Colored Troops, 167

12th US Colored Troops, 111

54th Massachusetts Infantry, 95

Abolitionism: activists, 43–44, 57–58, 62–64, 82–83, 88, 94, 97, 101, 105–9; colleges, ix–x, 1–7, 11–14, 16–38, 51–53, 66–78, 111–18, 124, 222–23n54; legacies, 160, 170, 196, 206–12

Adams, Joseph, 47

Aeolian Literary Society, 86, 142, 154

Africa, 2, 22, 41, 59, 65, 69–70, 155. *See also* colonization

African Methodist Episcopal Church, 219n3

Agassiz, Louis, 145

Akron (OH), 32

Alabama, 59

Albany (NY), 64

Albany Enterprise Academy, 231n15

Albany Manual Labor Academy, 231n15

Alcott, Louisa May, 68

Alexander, John Hanks, 150, 154, 158

Allegheny Institute, 76

Allen, William G., 20, 50, 63–64, 66–68, 70–71, 74, 79, 130, 211

Allport, Gordon, 6, 11

Alpha Zeta, 142, 169, 204

American Anti-Slavery Society, 30, 38, 41, 58

American Baptist Free Mission Society, 52–55, 58–59, 62, 65, 70, 74

American Council on Education, 210

American Missionary, 118

American Missionary Association: Berea partnership, 123–31, 176, 181, 191; founding, 41; on race, 53, 100–104, 109, 112–114, 118, 125–26, 134, 164, 209; Oberlin partnership, 53, 112–114; personnel, 86, 100–104, 112–115, 121, 126–34, 201

American Revolutionary War, 2

Amherst College, 1, 236n137

Amistad, 41

Andrews, George, 148–49, 151

Anthony, Susan, 143

anticaste movement, 112–14, 119, 124, 127–28, 132–34, 138, 164, 172–73, 177, 180, 187–92, 195, 197, 209

Antioch College, 153, 222–23n54

Appalachia, 14, 173, 190–91, 195, 201

Arkansas Industrial University, 242n7

Arnold, Matthew, 155

Auburn (NY), 59

Avery, Charles, 118. *See also* Avery Fund

Avery College, 76

Avery Fund, 118, 140, 157–58, 170

Baker, George, 135–36

Baltimore (MD), 57

Baptist General Missionary Convention, 52

Baptists, 52–54, 62, 64, 70, 181

Baquaqua, Mahommah Gardo, 57–59, 69–70, 211

Bartlett, Alexander, 252n124

Bartlett, Peter, 252n124

Barton, William, 190, 193

Bates College, 222–23n54

Baumgartner, Kabria, 1

Baxter Springs (KS), 157

Beecher, Catharine, 19

Beecher, Lyman, 21–22

Benin, 57

Bentham, Jeremy, 252n125

Berea College: admissions, 111–16, 121, 172–73, 183–90, 197, 202–3; alumni, 113, 131, 133, 136, 172, 174, 177–184, 187, 190, 194, 204–5; athletics, 205–6; curriculum, 121; demographics, 111–13, 116, 121–24, 131, 180, 182, 190, 193, 202–3, 209; discipline, 122–27, 131–33, 135, 200; faculty, 122–123, 126, 130–32, 135, 174, 181–82, 193–96, 200–201, 204–5, 244n49, 260n63; finances, 117, 131, 172–73, 181–82, 191–93, 195, 203; housing, 121–22, 131; motto, 197–199; property, 115–116; racial integration, ix, 6–9, 12–14, 121–39, 171–99, 200–202; recruitment, 111, 116, 118, 173, 182–93, 201; social equality controversy, 121–131, 138, 174; trustees, 113–14, 116, 124–25, 129–33, 177–78, 181, 185, 187–89, 195–96, 202, 205

Berea College v. Kentucky, 204

Berea College, Ky.: An Interesting History (Fairchild), 134, 137, 158

Berlin (OH), 91

Bible, 3–4, 28, 53, 59, 107, 145, 155, 176, 179, 197, 199, 201–2, 229n139

Binghamton (NY), 54

biracial students, 47, 119

Birmingham (OH), 90–91

Black educators, 10, 12–13, 45, 48–49, 62, 73, 75–78, 82, 95–97, 100–104, 108–10, 119, 179–180, 184–90, 200–201. *See also* Jackson, Fanny M. (Coppin); Vashon, George

Black nationalism, 76

Blair, Bill, 17

Bluegrass region, 115, 173, 190, 195

Bond, Horace Mann, 178

Bond, James O., 178–79, 181–82, 183 (fig. 6.3), 192, 203

Bond, Julian, 178

Borrican, Charles, 169

Boston (MA), 66, 94, 107

Bowdoin College, 1

Bradley, James, 22–24, 27, 30, 36

Britton, Mary, 179–80, 183 (fig. 6.3), 203

Brown, Antoinette, 41, 63, 142–43

Brown, John, 62, 64, 77, 83, 105, 116

Brown, John Mifflin, 34, 36–37, 40, 100

Brown vs. Board of Education, 1, 6

Bunche, Ralph, 246n100

Burdett, Gabriel, 130

Burleigh, Angus, 111–12, 114, 117, 124, 127, 132–33, 177, 211

Burlington, 92–93

Burned Over District, 2, 5, 7, 20, 30, 54

Burns, Anthony, 36

Burns, Robert, 3

Butchart, Ronald, 109, 241n131

Bute Street School, 100

Byberry (PA), 58, 61–62

Cain, Daniel, 131–32

California, 59, 87

Calkins, Leonard, 72–74

Camp Nelson, 111, 116–17, 246n100

Canada, 52, 65, 70

Canaan (NH), 219n3

Canterbury (CT), 2

Caribbean Islands, 65

Carlos, Don, 95, 110, 124

Carnegie, Andrew, 203

Case Western Reserve University. *See* Western Reserve College

Castle, Henry, 159–60, 162

Cayuga tribe, 59

Cazenovia (NY), 57

Chaplin, William, 57, 63

Charleston (SC), 30

Chase, Salmon, 45

Chatham Street Chapel, 22, 34

Chicago (IL), 194

Child, Lydia Marie, 107

China, 160, 165

Chippewa tribe, 87

Chittenden, Henry, 123–24, 131–33, 244n65

Cincinnati (OH), 21–24, 30–31, 36

citizenship, 2, 8, 16, 43, 81, 93, 113, 132, 141, 144, 163, 176, 179, 223n57

Civil Rights Act of 1875, 142–44, 164–65

Civil Rights Cases, 165

Civil War, ix, 1, 7, 11, 14, 19, 34, 51, 58, 68, 84, 86–87, 109–10, 112, 116, 124, 151, 163, 166, 168, 190, 209

Clark, Henry, 124, 132, 244n65

Clay, Cassius, 115–16

Cleveland (OH), 29, 35–36, 42, 86, 100

Cleveland Gazette, 170

Coan, William, 100–101

Cole, Eddie R., 211–12

Colgate University. See Madison University

Collins, Patricia Hill, 81

colonization, 2–3, 21–23, 30–31, 53

Colored Methodist Episcopal Church, 192–93

Colored Woman in a White World, A (Terrell), 154–56

Colored Women' League, 207

color-blindness, 1, 16, 89, 92, 163, 171, 189

Columbus (OH), 205–6

Commonwealth, 97–99

Compromise of 1877, 133

congregationalism, 21, 55, 134, 181

Connecticut, 2, 19

contract hypothesis, 6

Cook, George F. T., 231n172

Cook, John F., 60, 66, 231n172

Cook, John H., 231n172

Cooper, Anna Julia, 95, 153, 187

Copeland, John Anthony, 83

Cornell College, 163

Cornish, Samuel, 37

Cortland (NY), 55

Cortland County (NY), 54–55, 57–59, 71, 77

Cowles, Alice, 15, 20, 33–34

Cowles, Henry, 15, 33, 44, 208

Cox, Jacob Dolson, 16

Cox, Sabram, 36, 39–40

Crandall, Prudence, 2

craniometry, 149

Cravath, Erastus, 123–25, 127–28, 131, 201

Crummell, Alexander, 20

Cumberland Mountains, 7, 190

curse of Ham, 155

Darnes, Josephine, 84–85

Darwin, Charles, 145, 149. See also social evolutionism

Davis, George Washington, 157–58, 162

Davis, Larry E., 211

Day, Carl, 201

Day Law, 201–4

Day, William Howard, 40, 83

Delaware Ladies' Antislavery Society, 86

Democratic Party, 101, 163, 169, 176, 191

Denison College, 253n133

Descent of Man, The (Darwin), 149

Dodge, Levant, 184

Dorsey, Charles A., 231n172

Douglass, Frederick, 32, 43, 56–58, 62–63, 66–67, 76, 80

Douglass, Rosetta, 80

Douglass, Sarah Mapps, 236n140

Dred Scott v. Sanford, 72–73, 83, 180

Edmonson, Mary and Emily, 36, 57, 84

Eggleston, Margaret White, 150

Elements of Logic (Whatley), 38, 42

Elements of Rhetoric (Whatley), 38, 42

Eleutherian College, 34, 74, 222–23n54, 225n21

Ellis, Wade, 96

emancipation, 3, 11, 16, 30, 32, 40–41, 81, 84, 93–94, 96, 110, 111, 117, 144, 146, 166

Emancipation Proclamation, 94, 96, 105

Embree, William N., 246n100

Emerson, Ralph Waldo, 74

England, 66

Epes Grammar School, 240n69

eugenics, 191, 195
evangelicalism, 3–4, 11, 18–20, 22, 30, 41, 52, 123
Exeter (ME), 239n38
Expression of the Sentiments of Colored Students, 100

Fairchild, Eugene, 127, 177
Fairchild, Henry, 35, 47–48, 96–99, 119–20, 123, 171–77, 181, 187, 211
Fairchild, James Harris, 31, 95, 118–21, 123–25, 127, 129, 131, 134–35, 137–138, 154, 157–60, 166, 170, 171, 175
Fayette, John Sykes, 27
Fee, Burritt, 117, 121
Fee, John G., 111–34, 180–81, 188–89, 193, 196–99, 201
Fee, Matilda, 116
Female Anti-Slavery Society, 31
feminism. See women's rights
Ferris, Helen Bisbee, 9 (fig. 0.1)
Fifteenth Amendment, 11, 142–43
Finger Lakes, 59
Finney, Charles Grandison, 22, 24–26, 29–30, 32–37, 45, 95, 108
Fisk University, 165, 173, 201
Fitch, Florence, 206–7
Flipper, Henry Ossian, 147–50
Foreign Mission School, 27
Forever Free, 105–8
Forten, James, 58
Foster, Stephen and Abbey Kelley, 32
Fourteenth Amendment, 11, 141
Forten, Charlotte, 240n69
Frankfort (NY), 184–85, 187–88
Frederick Douglass' Paper, 65
free association, 7, 15, 23, 151
Free Soil Party, 45
free speech, 7, 13, 62–65, 74, 78, 194
Freedman's Bureau, 112, 117–18, 121–22
Freedmen's Teachers Project, 109, 241n131
Freedwoman and Her Child, The (Lewis), 105

Frost, William Goodell, 172–74, 181–97, 200–203, 206, 260n63
Fugitive Slave Act, 43, 45, 57, 63–65, 83

Garnet, Henry Highland, 20
Garrison, William Lloyd, 3, 32, 37, 41, 43, 58, 107
gender roles, 5, 7, 13–14, 19–20, 40, 50, 53–54, 58, 62, 81, 83–85, 96–97, 114–15, 135, 209, 222n50, 229n139
Georgia, 126
Germany, 153
Gerrit Smith College, 75–77, 182
Gettysburg (PA), 219n3
Gilbert, Theodosia, 57
Gillard, Jacob, 60
Goodell, William, 196
Grady, Henry, 168
Grant, Ulysses S., 144, 151
Gray, Katharine. See Kathie's Diary (Eggleston)
Great Awakening. See Second Great Awakening
Greeley, Horace, 63
Green, Beriah, 20
Greener, Richard, 97–98, 147, 162
Gregg, John Fee, 126–27, 177, 185
Grosvenor, Cyrus, 54, 59, 61, 63–64, 77, 78
Gudgeirsson, Meg, 194

Haiti, 52, 57, 88
Hale, John Parker, 45
Hampton University, 203
Hanson, John, 130, 177
Harlan, John Marshall, 204
Harlem Renaissance, 12–13
Harper's Ferry (VA), 77, 83, 116
Harris, Blanche (Brooks), 81–84, 86–87, 97, 102–4, 110
Harris, Francis, 103
Hartford (CT), 19
Harvard Medical School, 163
Harvard University, 74, 97, 192, 212, 240n69

Hathaway, James S., 178–81, 183 (fig. 6.3), 184–88, 190, 194–96
Haudenosaunee, 59
Haven, Eliza, 56
Hayden, Joseph, 66
Hazle, Ann, 84, 85 (fig. 3.3), 86
Heldman, Caroline, 85
Hewlett, Aaron Molyneaux, 240n69
High School for Young Colored Ladies and Little Misses, 2
Highgate, Edmonia, 100–102, 104
Hills, A. C., 60
Hillsdale College, 222–23n54
History of Oberlin, A (Smith), 35–36
Hofstadter, Richard, 7
Holley, Sallie, 46
Hooks, Benjamin, 246n94
Hooks School of Music, 246n94
Howard University, 73, 112, 143, 151, 187, 242n9
Hudson, 219
Hughes, J. W., 192, 194–95
Hughes, Langston, 12–13
Hunt, Ida Gibbs, 153
Hutchins, Robert Maynard, 212
Hutchins, William, 260n63

Illinois, 47, 194
Imes, Benjamin A., 160, 169
immigration, 191
imprisonment, 2
Indiana, 74, 222–23n54
Institute for Colored Youth (Philadelphia), 108
International Review, 148
interracial romantic relationships and marriage: at Berea College, 119–20, 123–32, 175, 178, 199; at New York Central College, 58, 66–69, 74; at Oberlin College, 10, 35–36, 46–48, 87–88, 101, 114, 151–52; social opposition, 4–5, 16, 25, 27–29, 119–20, 201
Iowa, 163
Iroquois Confederacy. *See* Haudenosaunee

Jackson, Fanny M. (Coppin), 48 (fig. 1.2), 49, 81–84, 86–90, 94–100, 104, 108, 110, 119, 147, 151, 155, 168, 211
Jackson, John Henry, 124, 177, 179, 181, 187–88
Jackson, Jordan C., Jr., 179, 203
Jamaica, 245n67
Jefferson County (IN), 74, 222–23n54
Jim Crow laws, 8, 10–11, 138, 154, 156, 169, 171, 173, 176, 178–80, 183–84, 202, 204, 207, 209, 258n128
Johnston, Adelia Field, 159
Jones, Elias T., 231n172
Jones, John C., 231n172
Jones, Joseph, 205
Journal of Blacks in Higher Education, 210

Kansas, 157
Kathie's Diary (Eggleston), 150–53
Keep, John, 3, 6, 29, 42, 44, 87, 92, 94, 160
Keep, Mary, 160
Kelley, Mary, 33
Kenny, Gail, 245n67
Kentucky, 6–7, 33, 112–13, 115, 119–22, 129, 173, 178, 184–89, 197, 200–204
Kentucky State Teacher's Association, 203
Kentucky State University. *See* State Normal School for Colored Persons
King, Henry Churchill, 206–8
King, Kenzia, 69
King, Martin Luther, Jr., 12
King, Mary, 66–68, 71, 74, 79
Kinson, Sarah Margru, 41, 84
Knox College, 222–23n54
Kornblith, Gary, 206
Ku Klux Klan, 117

Ladies' Board of Care, 120, 135
Ladies' Board of Managers, 84–85, 120
Ladies' Literary Society, 42, 45, 88, 142
Lane Seminary, 21–24, 27, 30–31, 37, 39, 52–53, 101, 115

Langston, Charles, ix, 1, 3, 5–6, 13, 34–37, 40
76, 83

Langston, Gideon, ix, 1, 3, 5–6, 34–36

Langston, John Mercer, 16, 17 (fig 1.1), 45–48,
70, 83, 88–93, 140–44, 151, 164, 166–69,
187, 205

Lasser, Carol, 84, 206

Lathrop, Sophia, 56

Leary, Lewis Sheridan, 83

Lewis, Diocletian, 105

Lewis, Mary Edmonia, 58, 75, 81–84, 87–94,
97, 104–8, 110, 123

Lexington (KY), 111, 118, 130, 184

Lexington Standard, 185–87, 194, 196

liberalism, 11, 14, 26, 89, 144, 146–49, 156,
158, 165, 168, 179–80, 193–94, 199, 205–6,
209, 212

Liberator, 23–24, 32, 63, 72, 74

Lillie, John, 136–37

Litts, Palmer, 103–4

Lincoln, Abraham, 78, 101

Lincoln Institute, 203–4

Lloyd, Penelope, 85

Lorain County News, 88, 92–93, 95

Lost Cause, 166

Louisville, 189, 203

Louisville Courier-Journal, 171

Louisville Times, 174

Lovejoy, Elijah, 36

Lyon, Rhoda, 127–29, 132, 244n65

Madison County (KY), 111, 115, 203

Madison County (NY), 123

Madison University, 52–53

Mahan, Asa, 23–26, 32, 39

Maine, 239n38

Manhattan (NY), 172

Manifest Destiny, 83–84

Mapps, Grace, 236n140

Martinsville, 47

Maryland, 57

Maryville College, 163, 201, 222–23n54,
252n124

Massachusetts, 66, 94, 107, 142, 240n69

May, Samuel J., 57, 68, 74

McGrawville, 54–55, 57–59, 64–69, 73–78

McGrawville Baptist Church, 54

Memphis (TN), 153, 246n94

Methodists, 62, 192–93

Michigan, 86

Middlebury College, 1

millenarianism, 28, 30, 59, 108–9

Miller, Fannie B., 177

Mingo, John H., 200

Mis-Education of the Negro, The (Woodson),
202

missions, 21, 27, 41, 140, 164–65, 245n67,
248n15. *See also* American Baptist Free
Mission Society; American Missionary
Association

Mississippi, 21, 102–4

Mitchell, Addie, 136–37

Mitchell, John G., 231n172

Mitchem, Georgina, 47, 120, 126

Money and Its Laws (Poor), 252n124

Moravians, 222n48

Morgan, Lewis Henry, 145

Morgan, John, 23–24, 32, 39

Monroe, James (congressman), 40

Morris, J. Brent, 32, 45, 224n64

Mott, James, 62

Mott, Lucretia, 62–65, 74, 78

Moulton, Amber, 4

Mount Pleasant Classical Institution, 219n3

Mount Sterling, 184

Natchez (MS), 102–4

National Anti-Slavery Standard, 147

National Association for the Advancement of
Colored People, 153, 207–8, 246n94

National Association of College Women,
207

National Association of Colored Women,
153, 207

National Center of Education Statistics,
201

National Colored Conventions, 76

National Convention of Free People of
Colour, 1

National Young Men's Literary Association,
86

Native Americans, 18, 20, 27, 58–59, 87, 91,
105, 210

Nature of Prejudice, The (Allport), 6

Nelson, Charmaine, 107

Nelson, David, 202

New England Freedmen's Aid Society, 107

New Hampshire, 2, 45, 219n3

New National Era, 95, 110, 124

New South, 168

New York, 2, 5, 18–19, 20–21, 25, 54–55, 57–59,
64–69, 73–78, 96, 153, 172, 219n3

New York Board of Regents, 75

New York Central College: alumni, 71, 74–75;
closing, 72–79, 87, 114, 209; curriculum, 50,
58; demographics, 50, 57–58, 65–66, 68–70,
112, 121; desegregation, ix, 6–9, 13–14, 34,
59–60, 77; enrollment, 50, 65–66, 68, 70,
75, 211; faculty, 55–57, 63–74, 79; founding,
52–57; finances, 50–51, 57, 64–65, 71–79,
211; property, 75–76; recruitment, 116; reopening, 75–79, 163; trustees, 50, 65–69,
76–78

New York City, 22, 28, 34, 57, 66, 75

New York State Lunatic Asylum, 77

New York Times, 171–72

Newman, William P., 36, 39

Newport (RI), 86

Norfolk (VA), 100, 102–3

Norris, Francis Josephine, 88

North Carolina, 84, 88, 104, 125, 151

Noyes Academy, 2, 219n3

Oberlin Band, 160

Oberlin (OH), 3, 41, 83, 86, 88, 92, 142–44,
151, 170, 212

Oberlin Anti-Slavery Society, 30–33, 94

Oberlin College: abolitionism, ix, 1, 3, 5–9,
12–14, 15–21, 30–37, 111, 212; admissions,
15–20, 24–30, 63, 116, 163, 170; alumni, 70,
81, 80–110, 115–16, 118, 123, 132–33, 147, 157,
166, 168–69, 173, 187, 206–8, 244n49; curriculum, 19–21, 38, 248n15; demographics,
50–51, 58, 87, 112, 121, 139–40, 150, 161–62,
182, 208–9; faculty, 25–29, 96–99, 131,
157–60, 162, 166, 170, 181, 187; finances, 16,
21, 25–26, 37, 118, 181; founding, 18–21, 119;
housing, 21, 88, 131, 139, 155–58, 206–7; racism at, 140–41, 145–46, 152–53, 155–61, 165–
66, 170; segregation, 138, 139–70, 206–9;
student memoirs, 150–156; trustees, 16, 21,
24–25, 26, 28–29, 33, 37–39, 42, 44–49, 163,
246n109

Oberlin Evangelist, 15, 39–40, 42–44

Oberlin Female Moral Reform Society, 84

Oberlin, Jean Frédéric, 18

Oberlin Liberty School, 143

Oberlin Lynching, 123

Oberlin Professorship Association, 25–26, 34

Oberlin Review, 139, 141–42, 144–49, 154, 157–
58, 160–61, 164–65, 167–70

Oberlin Temperance Alliance, 167

Oberlin-Wellington Rescue, 83

Ohio, ix, 3, 16, 18, 21–24, 29–36, 40–42, 45–
46, 47, 51, 86, 91–93, 100, 120, 139, 142–44,
151, 190, 193, 205–6, 219n3

Oliver Street Colored School, 200

Oneida County (NY), 2, 64

Oneida free love community, 123

Oneida Institute, 2, 20, 22, 34, 37, 51, 63, 123,
219n3

Onondaga tribe, 59

Oregon, 35

Ottawa tribe, 18

Otterbein University, 163

Panic of 1857, 75

Panic of 1893, 193

Parker, Theodore, 72

Patterson, Mary Jane, 86, 88, 96, 100, 231n172

Payne, Daniel Alexander, 219n3

Peabody, Elizabeth Palmer, 107

Pearce, Alexander, 122–25
Pearsons, Daniel K., 194–95
Peck, Alice E., 244n65, 245n66
Peck, Elisabeth, 121
Peck, Henry, 88–89, 92
Pendleton Civil Service Reform Act, 156
Pennsylvania, 37, 58, 61–62, 73, 76, 92–93, 108, 219n3
Pennsylvania Anti-Slavery Society, 4, 62
Perkins, Linda, 98
Phi Delta (Berea), 125–26, 135, 194, 200, 202
Phi Delta (Oberlin), 38, 142, 156, 169, 204–6
Phi Kappa Pi (Oberlin), 38, 142, 204
Phi Sigma (Oberlin), 204
Philadelphia (PA), 37, 58, 62, 92–93, 108
Philadelphia Female Anti-Slavery Society, 219n3
Phillips, Wendell, 63
Pierce, Anna, 61
Pittsburgh (PA), 37, 73, 76
Plessy v. Ferguson, 173, 200, 204
polygenesis, 83, 145
Poor, Henry V., 252n125
Port Royal, 222n48
Porter, John C., 65–66, 71
Pratt, Almon Bradley, 244n49
Pratt, Belle A., 244n49
Pratt, Hattie, 244n49, 244n65
Presbyterianism, 21, 181
Price, John, 83, 93
Purvis, Harriet Forten, 58
Purvis, Joseph, 61
Purvis, Robert, 58, 61

Quakers, 58, 104
Quran, 59, 69

racial egalitarianism, 4, 12, 44, 52, 64, 97, 102, 113, 123–24, 129, 133–34, 141, 156, 172, 174–75, 199, 209, 211
racial essentialism, 3–4, 15–16, 134, 146, 149, 169, 185, 195, 202
racial formation theory, 104

racial paternalism, 14, 18, 39, 43, 63, 110, 133, 185
Randolph, Benjamin F., 231n172
Ransom, Reverdy, 158–59
Rawlings, Cassius, 136–37
Reason, Charles, 50, 56–57, 62–63, 70, 75–76
Reconstruction, 7, 11–12, 14, 109–14, 132–34, 140, 150, 156, 160, 163, 169, 175–76, 191, 208–9, 222–23n54
Reporter (Berea), 195
Republican Party, 11, 77, 116, 143, 169, 184, 191
Revolutionary War. See American Revolutionary War
Rhode Island, 86–87
Rhode Island State Normal School, 86–87
Richardson, Joe, 134, 176
Ritchie, George, 52
Richmond (VA), 171, 181
Richmond Register, 174
Roberson, L. A., 160–61
Roberts, John D., 121
Robinson, John T., 121, 123, 133, 174–75, 177, 187, 192, 195–96, 199
Robinson, Mary, 126–27, 177
Rogers, John A. R., 116, 121, 123
Rome, 107
Roosevelt, Theodore, 191
Root, Azariah Smith, 205–6
Rosen, Hannah, 3, 132

Salem (MA), 240n69
Sampson, Benjamin, 231n172
Sandusky (OH), 46
Sayer, Lydia, 63
Sayers, Lena, 136
Scanado, Baptist, 59
Scarborough, William Sanders, 158, 187
Scripture. See Bible
Sears, Richard, 131
secession, 78
Second Great Awakening, 18, 52

segregation, 6, 15, 34–35, 80, 101, 108, 137–38, 139, 158–60, 173, 177–79, 184–85, 203–4, 206–7, 242n7. *See also* Jim Crow Laws

Separate Coach Bill (KY), 178–79, 184–85, 203

Seward Seminary, 80

Seward, Walter, 59

Shaler, Nathaniel, 192

Shanxi, 160

Shaw, Robert Gould, 105

Shaw University, 173

Shawnee tribe, 64, 115

Sheffield, 46

Sheffield Institute, 36

Sheldon, Mary, 43

Shipherd, John Jay, 18, 21, 24–25, 27–28, 163

Shurtleff, Giles Waldo, 166–68, 212

slavery. *See* abolitionism; emancipation

smallpox, 60–62

Smith, Azariah, 72–74

Smith, Christie, 6, 134, 170, 173, 191, 197

Smith, Delazon, 35

Smith, Edwin, 135–36

Smith, Gerrit, 37, 51, 55, 57, 62, 64, 71–78, 115, 117, 121

Smith, James McCune, 37, 75–78, 182

Smith, Judson, 74

Smith, Metcalf, 73–74

social evolutionism, 12, 14, 83, 145–46, 191–92, 195, 209

Sons of Temperance, 55

South Carolina, 30, 147, 222n48

Southard, Mary Ann, 239n38

Spaulding, Lewis, 74, 78

Spring, Erskine, 61

Stanford University, 212

Stanley, Sara (Woodward), 81–87, 97, 100–101, 104, 110

Stanton, Elizabeth Cady, 143

Stanton, Lucy, 41–46

Starbuck, Charles, 244n65

State Association of Colored Teachers, 179

State Normal School for Colored Persons, 187

Stewart, Philo, 18, 24–25

Stewart, William B., 181

Stickney, Angeline, 68, 71

Stone, Lucy, 40, 45, 63, 142–43, 164

Stowe, Harriet Beecher, 45

Strieby, Michael, 164–65, 176

suffrage. *See* voting rights

Sumner, Charles, 142–44

Supreme Court, 6, 41, 72, 165, 173, 203–4, 212

Syracuse (NY), 54

Talley, Thomas W., 201

Tappan, Arthur, 21–22, 24–26, 35, 37

Tappan, Lewis, 24–26, 31, 37

temperance, 22, 59, 92, 140, 144, 164, 167–68, 248n15

Taney, Roger B., 72

Tennessee, 153, 163, 201, 222–23n54, 246n94

Tenney, Angeline, 227n73

Terrell, Mary Church, 142, 143 (fig 5.1), 150, 153–56, 162, 187, 206–8

theology, 4, 21, 26, 45, 59, 62, 65, 67, 74, 86, 97–99, 101–2, 105, 109, 113, 116–18, 133–34, 145, 155, 179–81, 199. *See also* Bible; millenarianism

Thirteenth Amendment, 11, 141

Thomas, Amanda Ann, 151–52

Thome, James, 32–33, 38–39, 45

Thome, Mary, 33–34

Thompson, Charles H., 231n172

Tibbs, Lena, 179

Townsend, Tacie, 58, 60–61

transcendentalism, 72, 74

Troy (NY), 19

Tucker, Thomas D., 231n172

Tuskegee University, 203

Tylor, Edward Burnett, 145

Uncle Tom's Cabin (Stowe), 45, 67

Underground Railroad, 36, 57–58, 63

Union Church, 181

Union Literary Society, 38

Union Missionary Society, 41

University of Chicago, 212
University of Kansas, 223n55
University of South Carolina, 147, 163, 242n7
University of Wisconsin, 212
US Military Academy, 147

Vashon, George, 36–37, 39, 43, 45, 70–73, 75–76, 187, 205
Vermont, 61
veterans, 117, 132, 166–68, 177, 246n100
violence, 1–2, 5, 23, 30, 66–67, 78, 90–91, 96, 105, 113, 115, 117, 120, 130, 136–137, 146–47, 169, 176, 180, 192
Virginia, 5–6, 34, 64, 102, 171, 181
voting rights, 11, 52–53, 112, 114, 142–43, 151, 169–70

Waite, Cally, 248n15
Walker, Amasa, 39
Wall, Caroline, 47, 85
Wall, Isabel Irene, 151–55, 158
Ward, Lester Frank, 145
Wall, Orindatus Simon Bolivar, 151–52, 166–67
Wall, Stephen, 153
Ward, Samuel Ringgold, 55
Warner, Lucian, 204
Warren, Irene. See Wall, Isabel Irene
Warwick, William, 205
Washington, Booker T., 185, 191
Washington, DC, 57, 66, 86, 151, 153
Weierman, Karen Woods, 67
Weld, Angelina Grimké, 37
Weld, Theodore, 5, 8, 20, 22–23, 31–33, 35, 37
Wesleyan University, 163

West Point, 147–152, 154
West Virginia, 77, 83, 116
Western Reserve College, 18, 27, 219n3
Whatley, Richard, 38, 42
Wheaton College, 222–23n54
Whipple, George, 101–3
White, George H., 157, 162
Whitesboro (NY), 219n3
Whittaker, Johnson Chesnut, 147–50
Wilberforce University, 158, 187
Wilder, Craig Steven, 2
Willard, Emma, 19
Williams College, 163
Williams, Fannie Miller, 188
Williams, Frank, 188–89, 194–95, 200, 203
Williams, Henry, 205
Wilson, Julia, 157–58, 160
Wilson, Woodrow, 192
Winchester (KY), 200
Woman Suffrage Association, 143
Woman's Home Missionary Association, 157
Woman's Journal, 164
women's rights, 63, 142–43, 151, 154
Woodbury, William, 100–102
Woodson, Carter G., 78, 202
Woodson, Sarah Jane, 187
World War I, 209
Wright, Albert, 244n65
Wyandotte tribe, 18

YMCA, 204
Young Ladies' Anti-Slavery Society, 31, 227n73
Young Ladies' Domestic Seminary, 2, 34, 64
Young Ladies' Literary Society, 33
Young Men's Anti-Slavery Society, 45
Young Men's Lyceum, 38